Vesper Flights

ALSO BY HELEN MACDONALD

H is for Hawk
Falcon
Shaler's Fish

HELEN MACDONALD

Vesper Flights

New and Collected Essays

HAMISH HAMILTON
an imprint of Penguin Canada,
a division of Penguin Random House Canada Limited

Canada • USA • UK • Ireland • Australia • New Zealand •
India • South Africa • China

Published in Hamish Hamilton Hardcover by Penguin Canada, 2020
Simultaneously published in the United Kingdom by Jonathan Cape, an imprint of Penguin Random House UK, and in the United States by Grove

Some of these pieces have appeared in different form in the *New York Times Magazine*, *New Statesman* and elsewhere.

www.penguinrandomhouse.ca

LIBRARY AND ARCHIVES CANADA CATALOGUING IN PUBLICATION

Title: Vesper flights / Helen Macdonald.

Names: Macdonald, Helen, 1970- author.

Identifiers: Canadiana (print) 20190200979 | Canadiana (ebook) 20190200987 | ISBN 9780735235502 (hardcover) | ISBN 9780735235519 (HTML)

Classification: LCC PR6063.A1686 V47 2020 | DDC 824/.914—dc23

Cover illustration © Chris Wormell
Cover design © Suzanne Dean
Printed and bound in Canada

10 9 8 7 6 5 4 3 2 1

Contents

Introduction vii

Nests 1
Nothing Like a Pig 10
Inspector Calls 15
Field Guides 18
Tekels Park 23
High-Rise 32
The Human Flock 41
The Student's Tale 46
Ants 53
Symptomatic 56
Sex, Death, Mushrooms 65
Winter Woods 70
Eclipse 73
In Her Orbit 81
Hares 99
Lost, But Catching Up 103
Swan Upping 105
Nestboxes 116
Deer in the Headlights 120
The Falcon and the Tower 131
Vesper Flights 136

In Spight of Prisons 145
Sun Birds and Cashmere Spheres 148
The Observatory 155
Wicken 160
Storm 165
Murmurations 168
A Cuckoo in the House 175
The Arrow-Stork 184
Ashes 190
A Handful of Corn 195
Berries 200
Cherry Stones 204
Birds, Tabled 208
Hiding 216
Eulogy 221
Rescue 225
Goats 231
Dispatches from the Valleys 233
The Numinous Ordinary 245
What Animals Taught Me 253

Acknowledgements 259

Introduction

Back in the sixteenth century, a curious craze began to spread through the halls, palaces and houses of Europe. It was a type of collection kept often in ornate wooden cases, and it was known as a *Wunderkammer*, a Cabinet of Curiosities, although the direct translation from the German captures better its purpose: cabinet of wonders. It was expected that people should pick up and handle the objects in these cases; feel their textures, their weights, their particular strangenesses. Nothing was kept behind glass, as in a modern museum or gallery. More importantly, perhaps, neither were these collections organised according to the museological classifications of today. *Wunderkammern* held natural and artificial things together on shelves in close conjunction: pieces of coral; fossils; ethnographic artefacts; cloaks; miniature paintings; musical instruments; mirrors; preserved specimens of birds and fish; insects; rocks; feathers. The wonder these collections kindled came in part from the ways in which their disparate contents spoke to one another of their similarities and differences in form, their beauties and manifest obscurities. I hope that this book works a little like a *Wunderkammer*. It is full of strange things and it is concerned with the quality of wonder.

Someone once told me that every writer has a subject that underlies everything they write. It can be love or death, betrayal or belonging, home or hope or exile. I choose to think that my subject is love, and most specifically love for the glittering world of non-human life around us. Before I was a writer I was a historian of science, which was an eye-opening occupation. We tend to think of science as unalloyed, objective truth, but of course the questions it has asked of the world have quietly and often invisibly been inflected by history, culture and society. Working as a historian of science revealed to me how we have always unconsciously and inevitably viewed the natural world as a mirror of ourselves, reflecting our own world-view and our own needs, thoughts and hopes. Many of the essays here are exercises in interrogating such human ascriptions and assumptions. Most of all I hope my work is about a thing that seems to me of the deepest possible importance in our present-day historical moment: finding ways to recognise and love difference. The attempt to see through eyes that are not your own. To understand that your way of looking at the world is not the only one. To think what it might mean to love those that are not like you. To rejoice in the complexity of things.

Science encourages us to reflect upon the size of our lives in relation to the vastness of the universe or the bewildering multitudes of microbes that exist inside our bodies. And it reveals to us a planet that is beautifully and insistently not human. It was science that taught me how the flights of tens of millions of migrating birds across Europe and Africa, lines on the map drawn in lines of feather and starlight and bone, are stranger and more astonishing than I could ever have imagined, for these creatures navigate by visualising the Earth's magnetic field through detecting quantum entanglement taking place in the receptor cells of their eyes. What science does is what I would like more literature to do too: show us that we are living in an exquisitely complicated world that is not all about us. It does not belong to us alone. It never has done.

These are terrible times for the environment. Now more than ever before, we need to look long and hard at how we view and interact with the natural world. We're living through the world's sixth great extinction, one caused by us. The landscapes around us grow emptier and quieter each passing year. We need hard science to establish the rate and scale of these declines, to work out why it is occurring and what mitigation strategies can be brought into play. But we need literature, too; we need to communicate what the losses mean. I think of the wood warbler, a small citrus-coloured bird fast disappearing from British forests. It is one thing to show the statistical facts about this species' decline. It is another thing to communicate to people what wood warblers are, and what that loss means, when your experience of a wood that is made of light and leaves and song becomes something less complex, less magical, just *less*, once the warblers have gone. Literature can teach us the qualitative texture of the world. And we need it to. We need to communicate the value of things, so that more of us might fight to save them.

Nests

When I was small, I decided I wanted to be a naturalist. And so I slowly amassed a nature collection, and arranged it across my bedroom sills and shelves as a visible display of all the small expertises I'd gathered from the pages of books. There were galls, feathers, seeds, pine cones, loose single wings of small tortoiseshells or peacock butterflies picked from spiders' webs; the severed wings of dead birds, spread and pinned on to cardboard to dry; the skulls of small creatures; pellets – tawny owl, barn owl, kestrel – and old birds' nests. One was a chaffinch nest I could balance in the palm of my hand, a thing of horsehair and moss, pale scabs of lichen and moulted pigeon feathers; another was a song-thrush nest woven of straw and soft twigs with a flaking inner cup moulded from clay. But those nests never felt as if they fitted with the rest of my beloved collection. It wasn't that they conjured the passing of time, of birds flown, of life in death. Those intuitions are something you learn to feel much later in life. It was partly because they made me feel an emotion I couldn't name, and mostly because I felt I shouldn't possess them at all. Nests were all about eggs, and eggs were something I knew I shouldn't ever collect. Even when I came across a white half-shell picked free of twigs by a pigeon and dropped on a lawn, a moral imperative stilled my hand. I could never bring myself to take it home.

Naturalists in the nineteenth and early twentieth centuries routinely collected birds' eggs, and most children who grew up in semi-rural or rural surroundings in the 1940s and '50s have done it too. 'We only used to take one from each nest,' a woman friend told me, abashed. 'Everyone did it.' It's simply an accident of history that people two decades older than me have nature knowledges I do not possess. So many of them, having spent their childhoods bird's-nesting, still see a furze bush and think, *Linnet*, and can't help but assess the ability of last year's laid hedge to hold a chaffinch or robin's nest. They possess different wordless intuitions from me, ones relating to how one holds the landscape between head and eye and heart and hand. In my own history of the countryside, nests weren't things that were made to be found. They were carefully maintained blind spots, redacted lines in familiar texts. But even so, they had special salience when I was very young. For children, woods and fields and gardens are full of discrete, magical places: tunnels and dens and refuges in which you can hide and feel safe. I knew, when I was small, what nests were about. They were secrets.

I followed the flights of blackbirds and tits and thrushes and nuthatches through my garden. And every spring their nests changed how I felt about home. To have the presence of these birds shrunk down to that one point of attachment, the nest, made me anxious. It raised questions of vulnerability, made me worry about predatory crows and cats; made the garden a place of threat, not safety. Though I never searched for nests, I'd find them all the same. I'd be sitting at the kitchen window eating a bowl of Weetabix and I'd spot a dunnock flit into the forsythia, a mouse-sized bird, all streaks and spots and whispers. I knew I should look away, but I'd hold my breath at my transgression and track the almost imperceptible movement of leaves as the disappeared bird hopped up and across through twigs to its nest. Then I'd see the blur of wings as the bird slipped free of the hedge and was gone. And once I'd determined where it was, and saw that the adults were gone, I needed to know. Most of the nests I found were higher than my head, so I'd reach my hand up and curl my fingers until their tips touched what might be warm, glossy smoothness. Or the unbearable fragility of small flesh. I knew I was an intruder. Nests were like bruises: things I couldn't help but touch, even though I didn't want them to be there. They challenged everything that birds meant for me. I loved them most because they seemed free. Sensing danger, sensing a trap, sensing any kind of imposition, they could fly away. Watching birds, I felt I shared in their freedom. But nests and eggs tied birds down. They made them vulnerable.

The old books on birds that lined my childhood shelves described nests as 'bird homes'. This confused me. How could a nest be a home? Back then I thought of homes as fixed, eternal, dependable refuges. Nests were not like that: they were seasonal secrets to be used and abandoned. But then birds challenged my understanding of the nature of home in so many ways. Some spent the year at sea, or entirely in the air, and felt earth or rock beneath their feet only to make nests and lay eggs that tied them to land. This was all a deeper mystery. It was a story about the way lives should go that was somehow like – but not anything like – the one I'd been handed as a child. You grow up, you get married, you get a house, you have children. I didn't know where birds fitted into all this. I didn't know where I did. It was a narrative that even then gave me pause.

I think differently of home now: it's a place you carry within you, not simply a fixed location. Perhaps birds taught me that, or took me some of the way there. Some birds' nests are homes because they seem indivisible from the birds that make them. Rooks are rookeries – birds of feathers and bone that are also massed assemblages of twigs in February trees. House martins peering from the entrances of their nests under summer gables are beings of wings and mouths and eyes but also all the architecture of gathered mud. But some birds' nests seem so far from nests at all that the word itself drifts and almost loses purchase. The form of one such nest is: chips of old rock and bones and hardened guano, where the overhang supplies shade. The form of another is: a raft of weeds that rises and falls with the ebb and flow of water. Another: a dark space under roof tiles where you can crawl on your mouse feet and your wings drag like feathered blades the colour of carbon steel. Peregrine. Grebe. Swift.

Nests increasingly fascinate me. These days I wonder about how they seem to be one kind of entity when they contain eggs and a different kind of entity when they contain chicks. How nests and eggs are good things to think about when considering matters of individuality, and the concepts of same, and different, and series. How the form of a nest is part of the phenotype of a particular bird species, but how local conditions foster beautiful idiosyncrasies. How we humans are intrigued when birds make nests out of things that belong to us: house finches lining their nests with cigarette butts, nests of Bullock's orioles fashioned from twine, kites decorating their tree platforms with underwear stolen from washing lines. A friend of mine found a ferruginous hawk's nest wrought almost entirely from lengths of wire. It's satisfying to consider the incorporation of human detritus into the creations of birds, but it is troubling, too. What have they made out of what we have made of this world? Our world intersects with theirs and our habitations are strangely shared. We have long rejoiced at birds building nests in unusual places. We love the robin rearing chicks in an old teapot, a hen blackbird sitting tightly on a nest tucked above the stop bulb on a traffic light: these are nests that gesture towards hope, as birds use our things for their own ends, making our technologies redundant, slowed down, static, full of meaning that is no longer entirely our own.

But that is what nests are. Their meaning is always woven from things that are partly bird and partly human, and as the cup or wall of a nest is raised, it raises, too, questions about our own lives. Do birds plan like us, or think like us, or really know how to make knots, or slap beaks full of mud in series, or is this merely instinct? Does the structure they're making begin with some abstract form, a mental image, to which the bird plans, rather than thinking, step by step, *There, that is where that goes*? These are questions that pull on us. We make things according to plans, but all of us also have that sense of where things should go. We feel it when we arrange objects on mantelpieces, or furniture in rooms. Artists feel it when they construct collages, when they sculpt, when they bring pigment to bear on a surface, knowing that the dark smear of paint just here provides or provokes a sense of balance or conflict when viewed in relation to the other marks upon the scene. What is it in us? We are fascinated by the difference between skill and instinct, just as we police the differences between art and craft. If pigment is smeared on to a guillemot's eggshell as it rotates before being laid in drip-splashes that resemble in their exuberance and finesse the paintings of Abstract Expressionists, what is our delight in those patterns saying about us? I think of that need to collect that sometimes is billionaires hoarding de Koonings and Pollocks and sometimes tradesmen hiding plastic margarine tubs full of exquisitely marked red-backed shrike eggs beneath beds and floorboards.

We see our own notions of home and family in the creatures around us; we process and consider and judge, and prove the truth of our own assumptions back to us from a hall of twigs and mud and shells and feathered mirrors. In science, too, the questions we ask are commonly woven this way. I think of Niko Tinbergen's eminence in the field of ethology – and remember, too, his patient attention to the way ritualised gestures appeased aggression in colonies of nesting gulls, and how they related to his anxieties about the relationship between overcrowded cities and human violence. I think of the young Julian Huxley, full of all the sexual confusion of youth, spending one spring watching the courtship of great crested grebes, speculating on mutual sexual selection and ritualised behaviour. And I see interwar anxieties about marriage in Henry Eliot Howard's work on bird behaviour; he puzzles over the concept of territory, of nest building, of extra-pair copulations, and is desperately keen to understand the reasons behind the sexual attractiveness of particular females who lure males from their established mates. And, in literature, too, everywhere. Nesting birds naturalising the English class system in T. H. White's *The Once and Future King*, where seabird-nesting cliffs of auks and kittiwakes make 'an innumerable crowd of fish-wives on the largest grandstand in the world', exclaiming phrases like 'Is me hat on straight?' and 'Crikey, this isn't 'arf a do!' while White's skeins of aristocratic pink-footed geese pass high over the slum, singing Scandinavian goose-themed sagas as they fly north.

Friends of mine who grew up in marginal rural communities mostly have little truck with the mainstream rules of nature appreciation and the laws that enforce them. Most of them hunt with longdogs. Some of them are poachers. Some have collected eggs. Some of them probably still do, though I don't get to hear about that. Most have limited financial or social capital, and their claim on the landscape around them is through local field knowledge, rather than literal possession. Egg collecting in this tradition makes me wonder about the terms of ownership, investment and access to pleasure that economically deprived communities are allowed to have in the natural world. I think of Billy, the boy in Barry Hines' *A Kestrel for a Knave*, who refuses to play football, refuses to work down the mine, rejects all the models of masculinity he's given. What opportunities for tenderness does he have? He strokes the backs of baby thrushes in their nest. He keeps a kestrel that he loves. What kinds of beauties can be possessed? If you are a landowner, you get the whole compass of the watered-silk sky and the hedges and the livestock and everything in it. But if you're a factory worker? There's the rub. Egg collecting requires skill, bravery in the field, hard-won knowledge of the natural world. It can become an obsession for minds gripped with stilled beauty. It is a practice that halts time. The collectors grant themselves the power to withhold new lives and new generations. And egg collecting is also, at the same time, one in the eye for the elite and all their rules about what is and what is not an acceptable way to relate to nature.

Egg collecting was especially derided in the cultures of natural history operating during and after the Second World War. At that time, British birds were laden with new significance. They were what the nation was made of, what we were fighting for. In this milieu, species with a perilous foothold on British soil, such as avocets, little ringed plovers and ospreys, had their rarity bound up with imperilled nationhood. Thus, the theft of their eggs was seen as an act akin to treason. And protecting the birds from the depredations of collectors seemed analogous to military service. Again and again, in books and films of this period, injured servicemen who have proved their bravery on the field of battle now show their love for their country by protecting rare birds trying to raise families. 1949's *The Awl Birds* by J. K. Stanford, for example, where the threatened nest belongs to avocets, or Kenneth Allsop's *Adventure Lit Their Star*, published the same year, where it belongs to little ringed plovers. The historian of science Sophia Davis has written on how the villains of these books are egg collectors, routinely described as 'vermin' and 'a menace to England', and how the nests in their pages are guarded by heroes with the fate of the nation close to their heart. Indeed, gangs of egg protectors guarding the nests of rare birds were a true-life legacy of the war. After years in a German POW camp, the ornithologist George Waterston sat with his colleagues by the first Scottish osprey nest for fifty years and kept it under observation through the telescopic sights of rifles. And in the 1950s, J. K. Stanford wrote of his own experiences guarding avocets. 'Keyed up by the general air of secrecy,' he reminisced, 'we sat till long after dusk, prepared for anything, even an amphibious raid by armed oologists.' Egg collectors today tend to be seen as beings in the grip of hopeless addiction, simultaneously suffering from great moral failings. These characterisations were firmly codified in the cultures of post-war ornithology as threats to the body politic.

Eggs and war; possession and hope and home. In the 1990s, years after my natural historical collection was disassembled and my childhood home was gone, I worked at a falcon-breeding centre in Wales. In one room were banks of expensive incubators containing falcon eggs. Through the glass, their shells were the mottled browns of walnut, of tea-stains, of onion skins. This was before the advent of newer incubators that mimic the press of a brood patch through hot air-filled plastic pouches. These were forced-air incubators with eggs on wire racks. We weighed them each day, and as the embryo moved towards hatching, we'd candle them: place them on a light and scribe the outline of the shadow against the bright air-cell with a soft graphite pencil, so that as the days passed the eggshell was ringed with repeated lines that resembled tides or wide-grained wood. But I always left the incubation room feeling unaccountably upset, with a vague, disquieting sense of vertigo. It was a familiar emotion I couldn't quite name. I finally worked out what it was one rainy Sunday afternoon. Leafing through my parents' albums I found a photograph of me a few days after my birth, a frail and skinny thing, one arm ringed with a medical bracelet and bathed in stark electric light. I was in an incubator, for I was exceedingly premature. My twin brother did not survive his birth. And that early loss, followed by weeks of white light lying alone on a blanket in a Perspex box, had done something wrong to me that echoed with a room full of eggs in forced-air boxes, held in moist air and moved by wire. Now I could put a name to the upset I felt. It was loneliness.

That was when I recognised the particular power of eggs to raise questions of human hurt and harm. That was why, I realised, the nests in my childhood collection made me uncomfortable; they reached back to a time in my life when the world was nothing but surviving isolation. And then. And then there was a day. One day when, quite by surprise, I discovered that if I held a falcon egg close to my mouth and made soft clucking noises, a chick that was ready to hatch would call back. And there I stood, in the temperature-controlled room. I spoke through the shell to something that had not yet known light or air, but would soon take in the revealed coil and furl of a west-coast breeze and cloud of a hillside in one easy glide at sixty miles an hour, and spire up on sharp wings to soar high enough to see the distant, glittering Atlantic. I spoke through an egg and wept.

Nothing Like a Pig

I'm baffled. My boyfriend and I are standing up against a short barbed-wire fence shaded by sweet chestnut leaves. Woods are quiet in autumn: just the sifting hush of a small wind above and a robin making dripping-water noises from a holly bush.

I'm not quite sure what to expect because I'm not sure why I'm here. The boy said he'd show me something I'd never seen before in the woods, which made me raise an eyebrow. But here we are. He whistles and calls, whistles again. Nothing happens. Then it happens: a short, collapsing moment as sixty or seventy yards away something walks fast between trees, and then the boar. The boar. The boar.

When I saw *Jurassic Park* in the cinema something unexpected happened when the first dinosaur came on screen: I felt a huge, hopeful pressure in my chest and my eyes filled with tears. It was miraculous: a thing I'd seen representations of since I was a child had come alive. Something like that was happening now and it was just as affecting. I've seen pictures of boars all my life: razor-backed beasts on Greek pottery, sixteenth-century woodcuts, trophy photographs of twenty-first-century hunters kneeling over them with rifles, ink drawings of the Erymanthian boar in my book of Greek legends. There are animals that are mythological by virtue of being imaginary: basilisks, dragons, unicorns. There are animals that were once just as mythologically rich, but have had so much exposure to us now that their earlier meanings have become swamped with new ones: lions, tigers, cheetahs, leopards, bears. They've been given modern stories. For me, boars still exist inside those older stories, are still emblematic, still rich and passing strange. And now here one was, called into the real world.

This creature was not what I expected, despite its slap of familiarity. It had the forward-menacing shoulders of a baboon and the brute strength and black hide of a bear. But it was not really anything like a bear, and what surprised me most of all was that it was nothing like a pig. As the beast trotted up to us, a miracle of muscle and bristle and heft, I turned to the boy, and said, surprised, 'It's nothing like a pig!' With great satisfaction he grinned and said, 'No. They're really not.'

For the first time in centuries, free-roaming wild boars are thriving in British woods, descendants of animals bred for meat that escaped from captivity or were released on purpose. Adaptable and resilient, wild boars are also increasing in number across continental Europe and in places far from their natural range, which spans Eurasia from Britain to Japan. From the first introduction of boars to New Hampshire in the 1890s, boar-like wild pigs have now been reported in at least forty-five states in the United States. In Britain, they have strongholds in Sussex, Kent and the Forest of Dean in Gloucestershire, an ancient hunting preserve that stood in for an alien planet in the movie *The Force Awakens*. Sixty farm-reared animals were secretly and illegally dumped there in 2004; eleven years later, night-time thermal-imaging surveys suggested the population has grown to more than a thousand.

I lived near the forest some years ago and I went looking for them. My motives were more than just natural-historical curiosity: their presence made me feel I was stepping into something like the wildwood of ancient times. I never saw them, but I did come across signs of their presence: deep ruts and broken ground on woodland paths and grassy roadsides where they'd rooted for food. Boars are landscape engineers that alter the ecology of their woodlands. Wallowing holes fill with rainwater and become ponds for dragonfly larvae, seeds and burrs caught on their coats are spread wide, and their rooting on the forest floor shapes the diversity of woodland plant communities.

Knowing that boars lived in the forest I walked through also charged the English countryside with a new and unusual possibility: danger. Boars, particularly farrowing sows protecting their young, can be aggressive, and will charge and attack intruders. Since the boars' return to the Forest of Dean, there've been reports of walkers being chased, dogs gored, horses newly nervous upon familiar paths. As I walked, I found myself paying a different quality of attention to my surroundings than I ever had before, listening apprehensively for the faintest sounds and scanning for signs of movement in the undergrowth. It made the forest a wilder place but in a sense a far more normal one, for conflict between humans and dangerous wildlife is commonplace in much of the world, from elephants trampling crops in India and Africa to alligators in Florida dining on pet dogs. In Britain, wolves, bears, lynxes and boars were long ago hunted to extinction, and we have forgotten what this is like.

The boar I met up against the fence wasn't a threat. It was a captive boar, one of a few kept by a local gamekeeper and safely behind wire, but it provoked intense introspection about my place in the world. This creature was one of the semi-legendary beasts charging straight out of the medieval literature I'd read at university, the quarry hunted in *Sir Gawain and the Green Knight* and Malory's *Le Morte d'Arthur*, creatures renowned for their formidable ferocity and power. In medieval romances, boars were seen as a challenge to masculinity and hunting them a test of endurance and bravery. When we meet animals for the first time, we expect them to conform to the stories we've heard about them. But there is always, always a gap. The boar was still a surprise. Animals are.

We have a long history of territorial anxiety over wild animals intruding on our spaces. The seventeenth-century English garden writer William Lawson advised his readers of the tools they'd need to keep their properties free of marauding beasts: a 'fayre and swift greyhound, a stone-bowe, gunne, and if neede require, an apple with a hooke for a Deere'. Concerns about the danger of Gloucestershire boars have led to efforts by the Forestry Commission to reduce their population in the Forest of Dean: three hundred and sixty-one were shot in 2014 and 2015, despite anti-hunting activists attempting to get in the way of hunters to prevent the cull. The controversy over how to manage English wild-boar populations points to the contradictory ways that we understand animals and their social uses. Wolves can be depredators of livestock or icons of pristine wilderness; spotted owls can be intrinsically important inhabitants of old-growth forests or nuisances that inhibit logging and livelihoods. These creatures become stand-ins for our own battles over social and economic resources.

When animals become so rare that their impact on humans is negligible, their ability to generate new meanings lessens, and it is then that they come to stand for another human notion: our moral failings in our relationship to the natural world. The world has lost half its wildlife in my own lifetime. Climate change, habitat loss, pollution, pesticides and persecution have meant that vertebrate species are dying out over a hundred times as fast as they would in a world without humans. The single boar appearing from behind the trees felt like a token of hope; it made me wonder if our damage to the natural world might not be irreversible, that creatures that are endangered or locally extinct might one day reappear.

So many things were affecting about this encounter: not just the calling-forth of an animal icon into flesh, but the realisation that there is a particular form of intelligence in the world that is boar-intelligence, boar-sentience. And being considered by a mind that is not human forces you to reconsider the limits of your own. As the boar looked up at me, it was obvious that my knowledge of boars was limited, and only now, face to snout with a real one, its eyes fixed on mine, did I wonder what a boar really was and, oddly, what it thought of me. I had fitted the boar into my medievalist memories, but my friend, who was once a boxer, admired its physique. Talked of its cutlass-curved, razor-sharp tusks. Its small legs and hindquarters that work to steer the huge muscular bulk of the front end. Its manifest, frightening power.

As he spoke, the boar pressed itself up against the fence and sniffed loudly through its wet nostrils. Rashly, I moved my hand towards it. It looked up, flat-faced, with red boar eyes considering, and sniffed again. I drew my hand away. Then, after a while, I lowered it again. The boar stood. It allowed me to push my fingers gently into its arched black back. It felt like a hairbrush with too many bristles and backed with thick muscle, not wood. There was wool underneath the hair. 'He'll be getting his winter coat soon,' said the boy. 'Six-inch guard hairs.' I scratched the beast's broad hump and felt, as the seconds passed, that some tiny skein of aggression in his heart was starting to thrum. I have learned not to distrust intuitions like this. Suddenly we both decided that this was enough, my heart skipping, he grunting and feinting.

Wandering off, he sank on to his knees, nose to the ground, then, with infinite luxury, sat and rolled on to his side. Ripples ran down his hide. I was entranced. For all my interest in this creature, the boar had become bored with me and simply walked away.

Inspector Calls

I've a territorial, defensive soul. There's nothing like a visit from the landlord to put me on the back foot and then some. After most of the night cleaning the house I was spilling with contagious rage. I'd even considered burning the bastard building to the ground. It seemed a logical means of preventing any complaints about coffee rings on the Ercol dining table.

By eleven, things are calmer. I'm upstairs marking essays at my desk. The air is soothing, the window open upon cool grey. A red Ford draws up outside and a man and woman get out. The prospective tenants have an eight-year-old son, and he is autistic, my landlord told me. There's no sign of him. But these are parents; they're moving with the almost imperceptible restraint of manner born of care so he must be in the back of the car. Yes. And as he climbs out my heart folds and falls, not because he is wearing a stripy red and orange jumper but because he is grasping in each hand a model sea lion.

Downstairs the grown-ups are talking, and the boy is bouncing about in the semi-darkness of the hall. He is totally bored. I look down at his hands. Each of the sea lions has chips of missing paint about its nose where it has interacted with the other, or with something hard, and I ask him if he wants to see my parrot. His eyebrows rise and he waits. A brief, wordless OK from his parents, and we ascend the stairs. He counts each step out loud. And we stop in front of the cage. The bird and the boy stare at each other.

They love each other. The bird loves the boy because he is entirely full of joyous, manifest amazement. The boy just loves the bird. And the bird does that chops-fluffed-little-flirting twitch of the head, and the boy does it back. And soon the bird and the boy are both swaying sideways, backwards and forwards, dancing at each other, although the boy has to shift his grip on the plastic sea lions to cover both ears with his palms, because the bird is so delighted he's screeching at the top of his lungs.

'It is *loud*!' says the boy.

'That's because he is happy,' I say. 'He likes dancing with you.'

And then, after a few moments, I tell him that I like his sea lions very much.

He frowns as if he's assuming upon himself the responsibility of my being one of the elect.

'Lots of people think they are ...' he pauses contemptuously, '*seals*.'

'But of course they are sea lions!' I say.

'Yes,' he says.

We glory in the importance of accurate classification.

His parents come into the room. They have decided the house is too small for them and their son. So much for my week of cleaning purgatory.

His mother looks anxious. 'Come on, Antek! We are going now.'

There is, suddenly, one of the most beautiful moments of human–animal interaction I have ever seen. Antek nods his head gravely at the parrot, and the parrot makes a deep, courteous bow in return.

A minute later I hear the front door open, and just before they cross the threshold, I can hear clicking that I suspect might be the collision of sea lions' noses, and then Antek makes an announcement. 'I am going to sleep in the room with the parrot, when we live here,' he says. Such hard words to hear, uttered with such certainty, in the hall.

Field Guides

From a high lookout near a spectacular three-tiered waterfall in Australia's Blue Mountains National Park, the peaks in the far distance reflect sunshine scattered through a haze of aromatic eucalyptus terpenes; the light has turned them a bleached and dusty blue. At my feet the land falls away into a virgin forest of graceful, pale-barked trees that stretches as far as the eye can see. Further up the slope are leggy shrubs with flowers resembling bright plastic hair curlers: banksias, I think. When a small bird appears in the foliage below I fix it in my binoculars. White, black and acid yellow with eyes like tiny silver coins, it's wiping its down-curved beak on a branch of a shrub with strappy leaves. I don't know what the shrub is, and I'm not sure what the bird is, either. I think it's a honeyeater, but I don't know what anything is, not precisely. Not here. The air smells faintly of old paper and something a little like jet fuel. I feel lost and very far from home.

I grew up in a house full of natural-history field guides, everything from Locket and Millidge's 1951 two-volume guide to British spiders, with its hairy, many-eyed line drawings, to illustrated books on trees, fungi, orchids, fishes and snails. These books were the unquestioned authorities of my childhood. I marvelled at the names entomologists had given to moths – the figure of eighty, the dingy mocha, the dentated pug – and tried to match their descriptions to the drab living specimens I found on the walls of the porch on cool summer mornings. The process of working out what things were often felt like trying to solve a recalcitrant crossword puzzle, particularly when it involved learning technical terms like *scopulae* and *thalli*. The more animals and plants I learned, the larger, more complex and yet more familiar the world around me became.

It was a long time before I understood that even the simplest of field guides are far from transparent windows on to nature. You need to learn how to read them against the messiness of reality. Out in the field, birds and insects are so often seen briefly, at a distance, in low light or half-obscured by foliage; they do not resemble the tabular arrangements of paintings in guides, where similar species are brought together on a plain background on the same page, all facing one way and bathed in bright, shadowless light so they may be easily compared. To use field guides successfully, you must learn to ask the right questions of the living organism in front of you: assess its size and habitat, disassemble it into relevant details (tail length, leg length, particular patterns of wing cases or scales or plumage), check each against images of similar species, read the accompanying text, squint at tiny maps showing the animal's usual geographical range, then look back to the image again, refining your identification until you have fixed it to your satisfaction.

The process of identifying animals in this way has a fascinating history, for field guides have closely tracked changes in the ways we interact with nature. Until the early years of the twentieth century, bird guides, for example, mostly came in two kinds. Some were moralised, anthropomorphic life histories, like Florence Merriam's 1889 *Birds Through an Opera-Glass*, which described the bluebird as having a 'model temper' while the catbird possessed a 'lazy self-indulgence'. 'If he were a man,' she wrote of the latter, 'you feel confident that he would sit in shirt sleeves at home and go on the street without a collar.' The other kind of guide was the technical volume for ornithological collectors. In those days birds were often identified only after being shot, so such guides focused on fine details of plumage and soft parts. 'Web between bases of inner and middle toes,' runs the description of the semipalmated plover in Chapman's 1912 edition of his *Color Key to North American Birds*. But with the rise of recreational birdwatching following the First World War, when the morality of killing birds was increasingly questioned and the advent of inexpensive binoculars brought birds into visual range, such details were of limited use. A new way to identify birds was needed.

The first of the modern field guides was Roger Tory Peterson's 1934 *Field Guide to the Birds*. It was inspired partly by a chapter in the popular 1903 children's book *Two Little Savages*, written by Ernest Thompson Seton, first chief scout of the Boy Scouts of America. In it, a nature-minded boy despairs of learning the birds from books that require you to hold them dead in your hands. He decides instead to make 'far-sketches' of the ducks he sees in the distance and arrange them into a 'duck chart' that shows the characteristic 'blots and streaks that are their labels ... like the uniforms of soldiers'. Peterson's paintings, like Seton's charts, tabulated and simplified birds, and he went further, adding small black lines on the page that pointed to distinctive characteristics that were most easily visible: the black band on the end of a crested caracara's tail, the 'ink-dipped' wings of the flying kittiwake.

When he was a young man in the 1920s, Peterson was a member of the Bronx County Bird Club, a group of competitive, iconoclastic young naturalists. In the days before portable guides, field identification aids could take unusual forms: one club founder carried around an envelope containing coloured plates cut from a copy of E. H. Eaton's lavish but unwieldy ornithological guide *Birds of New York* that he had found in a trash can. The group was mentored by Ludlow Griscom, a stern, exacting teacher who became renowned for inventing the technique of identifying a bird instantly in the field, even when flying. 'All the thousands of fragments we know about birds – locality, season, habitat, voice, actions, field marks and likelihood of occurrence – flash across the mirrors of the mind and fall into place – and we have the name of the bird,' Peterson later explained of Griscom's method. This split-second, *gestalt* ability to recognise a species built from combining book knowledge with long field experience became the mark of ornithological expertise, and was at the heart of a growing culture of competitive bird-spotting that lives on today. For there's an immense intellectual pleasure involved in making identifications, and each time you learn to recognise a new species of animal or plant, the natural world becomes a more complicated and remarkable place, pulling intricate variety out of a background blur of nameless grey and green.

Today, electronic field guides are becoming increasingly popular, and photo-recognition apps like Leafsnap and Merlin Bird ID let you identify species without the skills required to use field guides. They can do what print guides cannot: play animal sounds and songs, for example. But they also make it harder to learn those things we unconsciously absorb from field guides: family resemblances among species, or their places in the taxonomic order. When I was growing up, the materiality of these guides, their weight and beauty, was part of their attraction. I spent hours staring at their coloured plates of butterflies and birds, distinguishing each from each and fixing the painted images in my mind. The first time I saw a silver-spotted skipper butterfly basking on bare chalk on high downland pasture, I instantly knew the name of this dusty-golden dart with pale, ragged patches on its wings. Field guides made possible the joy of encountering a thing I already knew but had never seen before.

Back in my hotel room, I pull two Australian field guides from the bottom of my suitcase, eager to find out what it was that I had seen. Flicking through the first, I find a page of honeyeaters: nine birds arranged on a pale green background. That striking pattern of white and yellow and black is found in two species, but those round silver eyes are distinctive. I check against the distribution maps and the short description on the facing page. What I saw was a New Holland honeyeater. And turning to the plant guide, which describes only a few hundred of the thirty thousand different plant species found in Australia, I decide, tentatively, that the shrub it sat on was probably a waratah, and the banksias I saw by the path were hairpin banksias, with their 'protruding, wiry, hooked styles'. These species are well known here, but for me they are small triumphs. Now I know three things. A few hours ago, I looked over a valley at sunset and knew nothing at all.

Tekels Park

I shouldn't do the thing I do, because motorway driving requires you to keep your eyes on the road. I shouldn't do it also because pulling at your heart on purpose is a compulsion as particular and disconcerting as pressing on a healing bruise. But I do it anyway, and it's safer to do it these days, because this stretch is being transformed into a smart motorway, so the long slope of the M3 as it falls towards Camberley is packed with speed cameras and 50 mph signs, and when I'm driving there on my way somewhere else I can slide my car into the outside lane to bring me closer and slower to the section of fence I'm searching for, running west and high under skies white as old ice.

Perhaps a hundred thousand vehicles pass this place each day. Back in the mid 1970s I could lie awake in the small hours and hear a single motorbike speeding west or east: a long, yawning *burr* that dopplered into memory and replayed itself in dreams. But like snow, traffic noise thickens with time. By the time I was ten I could stand by Europe's second largest waterfall, listen to it roar, and think, simply, *it sounds like the motorway when it's raining.*

I shouldn't look. I always look. My eyes catch on the place where the zoetrope flicker of pines behind the fence gives way to a patch of sky with the black peak of a redwood tree against it and the cradled mathematical branches of a monkey puzzle, and my head blooms with an apprehension of lost space, because I know *exactly* all the land around those trees, or at least what it was like thirty years ago. And then the place has passed, and I drive on, letting out the breath I'd been holding for the last thousand feet or so, as if by not breathing I could still everything – movement, time, all of the dust and feet that rise and fall in a life.

Here's an early memory. A ridiculous one, but true. I learned to speed-read by trying to decipher military warning signs that bordered the roadside on my way to primary school. KEEP OUT was simple, but DANGER – UNEXPLODED ORDNANCE took me months. I needed to read the words *all at once*, because my mother's car was moving and the signs were very close. Each weekday morning I'd stare out of the window as the army land approached and wait for the words to appear so I'd have another chance at them. And the feeling I had then, of wanting to apprehend something important that was passing by me very fast: that's the feeling I have now when I look for the place behind the motorway fence where I grew up.

I was five in my first summer in the Park. It was 1976. Cape daisies bloomed and died in the flowerbeds, and pine cones in the trees behind the house crackled and split through endless indigo afternoons. Standpipes, orange squash, dry lawns, and a conversation in which the matter of *drought* was explained to me. That's when I realised for the first time that not every year was the same, or perhaps that there were such things as years at all. My parents had bought this little white house in Camberley, Surrey, on a 50-acre walled estate owned by the Theosophical Society. They knew nothing about Theosophy but they liked the house, and they liked the estate too. There'd been a castle here once, or Squire Tekel's early nineteenth-century approximation of one, all faux-gothic battlements and arrow slits, peacocks and carriages. After it burned down the Theosophists bought the grounds in 1929 for £2,600 and set about turning it into a place for them to live and work. Residing here was a privilege, the residents were told. A privilege for service. Members built their own houses, bought tents for a campsite and a second-hand Nissen hut from the Army to put there too. They grew food in the walled kitchen garden; opened a vegetarian guesthouse. In the 1960s, after leaseholders were granted the right to purchase the freeholds of their properties, outsiders like us slowly began to populate the place.

Theosophy had been banned in Nazi Germany, so many of our neighbours were refugees from the war, and others were the black sheep of good families: elderly women, mostly, who had refused the roles society had reserved for them: the quiet Lolly Willowes of Surrey Heath. One wore ancient Egyptian jewellery she'd been given by Howard Carter; another kept a great auk egg in a drawer. Spies, scientists, concert pianists, members of the Esoteric Society, the Round Table, the Liberal Catholic Church, the Co-Masonic Order. One former resident sent his beard clippings back from Nepal to be burned on the estate bonfire. On discovering that I had gone to Cambridge, another, years later, inquired of me where I had stabled my horse – for he'd had dreadful trouble finding livery for his hunter while a student there in the 1930s. Everyone had lives and pasts of such luminous eccentricity that my notion of what was, and wasn't, normal took a battering from which it's never recovered. I am thankful for that, and for the women in particular, for giving me models for living a life.

But most of all I'm thankful for the other freedoms I had there. After school I'd make a sandwich, grab my Zeiss Jena 8x30 Jenoptem binoculars and strike out for my favourite places. There were ivy-covered walls and specimen trees, redwoods planted to commemorate the death of Lord Wellington – they called them Wellingtonias back then, of course they did – and creosoted summerhouses with fly-specked windows. 'Arthur Conan Doyle liked to sit here,' I was told, of the smallest summerhouse beneath the sparse shade of a balsam poplar, the one with original prints of the Cottingley Fairies hanging on its cream-washed walls. There was a round, shallow pond on the Italianate terraces that held an intermittently-broken fountain, smooth newts and great diving beetles, and from which vespertilionid bats dipped to drink at night; a 9-acre meadow with decaying stables on one side, acres and acres of Scots pine, and damp paths obscured by bracken, rhododendrons, swamp laurels with piped-icing flowerbuds, and there were roads that went nowhere, for when the motorway was built on land compulsorily purchased from the Theosophists in the 1950s, it cut the estate in two. I loved those roads. Bare feet on the rotting tarmac down by the straight avenue of sessile oaks that ended in drifts of leaves and a new desire path that curved right to trace the perimeter of the motorway fence. One dead-end lane at the back of the Park had 10-foot sandy banks I'd scramble up towards the vast grey beech carved with hearts and dates and initials, and I was awed by the notion that anyone had found this tree, because I'd never seen anyone near it, ever, and one afternoon I dug up a rotted leather drawstring bag from the humus beneath it that spilled threepenny bits into my hands. There had been glow-worms here, and snipe, and ponds, before the motorway came, I was told. Everything on the other side was already houses.

I was allowed to roam unchallenged because everyone here knew me – though they'd have quiet words with my parents after they'd yet again spotted me knee-deep in the middle of the pond looking for newts, or walking past the guesthouse with a big grass snake, two feet of supple khaki and gold twined about my arms. Reg the gardener took me for rides on his tractor-trailer, and we'd putter down the road singing music-hall songs he'd taught me:

It's the same the whole world over
It's the poor what gets the blame
It's the rich what gets the pleasure
Ain't it all a bloomin' shame?

And while Reg rolled a cigarette I'd race off to explore the bracken and scrub in the back woods, where rhododendrons had grown to near-trees with branches shaped by ancient prunings. They were *superb* to climb when I was small: frames of right-angled kinks and acute wooden curves I could hoist myself into and up, and sit inside a canopy of dark leaves that clicked and pattered with tiny rhododendron leaf hoppers that on closer inspection resembled the brightest of bestiary dragons. In the back woods too was the wood ants' nest, that glittering, shifting particulate mound which moved from year to year and reeked of formic acid. You could turn blue flowers pink if you tossed them on the top before the ants carried them away, and for a while I'd prepare skeletons of the dead birds I found by folding them carefully in little cages of wire mesh and lodging them on top of the nest. When I pulled them free weeks later they'd been reduced to clean white bone that never quite stopped smelling of ants.

Almost by accident I'd been granted this childhood of freedom and privilege, partly through a quirk of location, partly through my parents' trust in the safety of this place, and I lived in the familiar setting of so many of my children's books, from *The Secret Garden* to *Mistress Masham's Repose*, though I wasn't half as posh as their protagonists. I was a state-school kid running free in crumbling formal parkland that might have been written on paper as metaphor for the contracting Empire, or a wilder life, or social transgression, or any number of dreams of escape forged in the imagination of writers years before I was born.

I didn't know how unusual my freedom was, but I knew what it had given me. It had turned me into a naturalist. And for a new naturalist like me, the nine-acre meadow was the best place of all. So much of what was there must have arrived in hay brought for long-dead horses, as seeds from lowland meadows: scabious, knapweed, trefoil, harebell, lady's bedstraw, quaking grass, vetches, diverse other grasses and herbage. And butterflies, too, marooned in this small patch of the nineteenth century: common blues, small skippers, grizzled skippers, marbled whites, small coppers, and grasshoppers that sang all summer and pinged away from my feet. The other side of the meadow was different, and more what you'd expect on acidic soil: a low sea of sheep's sorrel, stars of heath bedstraw, white moths, small heaths, anthills and wavy hair grass brushed with fog by the sun. I knew that meadow intimately. It was richer, more interesting, had more stories to tell than any other environment in my life. I'd press my face in the grass to watch insects the size of the dot over an 'i' moving in the earthy tangle where the difference between stems and roots grew obscure. Or turn over and prospect for birds in the thick cumulus rubble of the sky.

So many of our stories about nature are about testing ourselves against it, setting ourselves against it, defining our humanity against it. But this was nothing like that at all. It was a child's way of looking at nature: one seeking intimacy and companionship. When I learned the names of these creatures from field guides it was because I needed to know them the same way I had to know the names of my classmates at school. Their diverse lives expanded what I considered as home way beyond the walls of my house. They made the natural world seem a place of complex and beautiful safety. They felt like family.

When you are small, the things you see around you promise you they'll continue as they are forever, and you measure life in days and weeks, not years. So when the mowers came one day in early August to cut the meadow as they had done every year since the meadow was made, and I saw what was happening, I burned with terrified outrage. There was no time to think about what I was doing. I ran. I stumbled. I sat in front of the mower to make it stop, then mutely, passively, held my ground in front of the bewildered driver, who came down to quite reasonably ask me what the hell I was doing, and I ran home crying. I didn't understand how hay meadows work. All I saw was destruction. How could I know that the mower's job was to hold history in suspension, keeping the meadow exactly where it was against the encroachment of heather and birch and time?

Every year the meadow grew back and thrived and was as rich as ever, right up until we left the Park in the 1990s. A decade later, I returned on a grey summer afternoon, nervous of what I would find. Driving up Tekels Avenue the passing scenery possessed the disconcerting, diffuse, off-scale and uncanny closeness of things in dreams. I was frightened by what I might see when the car crested the curve down to the field. But there the meadow was: impossible, miraculous, still crowded with life.

Then I went back in my forties, less scared now, more certain of myself and what I would find when I got there. But I was wrong. Someone who thought meadows should look like football pitches had treated it like a lawn and mowed it repeatedly for several years until the exuberant moving life I'd known and loved was gone. The meadow now looked how that man thought it should look: blank and neat and flat and easy to walk upon. I cried when I saw it: a woman weeping not for her childhood, not really, but for everything that had been erased from this place.

Losing the meadow is not like losing the other things that have gone from my childhood: Mac Fisheries, Vesta paella, spacehoppers, school lunches, *Magic Roundabout* toys, boiled sugar lollipops when I'd finished my meals in roadside café chains on holiday trunk roads. You can mourn the casualties of fast capitalism for your own generation, but you know they've merely been replaced with other programmes, other media, other things to see and buy. I can't do that with the meadow. I can't reduce it to nostalgia *simpliciter*. When habitats are destroyed what is lost are exquisite ecological complexities and all the lives that make them what they are. Their loss is not about us, even though when that meadow disappeared, part of me disappeared, too, or rather, passed from existence into a memory that even now batters inside my chest. *Look*, I can't say to anyone. *Look at the beauty here. Look at everything that is*. I can only write about what it was.

When Henry Green started writing his autobiography in the late 1930s it was because he expected to die in the oncoming war, and felt he did not have the luxury of time to write a novel. 'That is my excuse,' he wrote: 'that we who may not have time to write anything else must do what we now can.' He said more. He said, 'We should be taking stock.' I take stock. During this sixth extinction we who may not have time to do anything else must write what we now can, to take stock. When I sat on the verge that day and wept I told myself over and over again that he was a nice man, that perhaps he had simply not known what was there. Had not known what was there. And I thought something that I was talking about with a friend just the other day: that the world is full of people busily making things into how they think the world ought to be, and burning huge parts of it to the ground, utterly and accidentally destroying things in the process without even knowing they are doing so. And that any of us might be doing that without knowing it, any of us, all the time.

A few years ago the Park was sold to a property developer. Today when I drive past the fence the pull on my heart is partly a wrench of recognition when I see those trees, knowing they are the standing ghosts of my childhood. But it's also the knowledge that with care, attention, and a modicum of love and skill, the meadow could be incorporated into the site plan and turned into something very like it had been only a few years ago. The pull on my heart is also the pain of knowing that this is possible, but that it is very unlikely. Centuries of habitat loss and the slow attenuation of our lived, everyday knowledge of the natural world make it harder and harder to have faith that the way things are going can ever be reversed.

We so often think of the past as something like a nature reserve: a discrete, bounded place we can visit in our imaginations to make us feel better. I wonder how we could learn to recognise that the past is always working on us and through us, and that diversity in all its forms, human and natural, is strength. That messy stretches of species-rich vegetation with all their attendant invertebrate life are better, just *better*, than the eerie, impoverished silence of modern planting schemes and fields. I wonder how we might learn to align our aesthetic and moral landscapes to fit that intuition. I wonder. I think of the meadow. Those clouds of butterflies have met with local extinction, but held in that soil is a bank of seeds that will hang on. They will hang on for a very long time. And when I drive past the fence these days, staring out at 50 mph, I know that what I am looking for, beyond the fence, is a place that draws me because it exists neither wholly in the past, nor in the present, but is caught in a space in between, and that space is a place which gestures towards the future and whose little hurts are hope.

High-Rise

Dusk is falling over Midtown Manhattan on this chilly evening in early May. I've been googling the weather forecast all day, and pull out my phone to check it once again as I walk down Fifth Avenue. *North-north-easterly winds and clear skies.* Good.

At the Empire State Building the line snakes around the block, and because I'm the only person in it wearing a pair of binoculars around my neck, I feel a little self-conscious. I inch forward for the next hour, up escalators, through marble halls, past walls of soft gold wallpaper, before squeezing into a crowded elevator and emerging on the eighty-sixth floor. At over a thousand feet above the city, there's a strong breeze and a spectacular sea of lights spilling far below.

Behind the tourists pressed against the perimeter fence there's a man leaning back against the wall. Above him the Stars and Stripes flap languidly in the night air. I can't see his face in the gloom, but I know this is the man I've come to meet because he's holding a pair of binoculars that look far better than mine, and his face is upturned to sky. There's an urgency to the way he stands that reminds me of people I've seen at skeet shoots waiting for the trap to fire the next target. He's tense with anticipation.

This is Andrew Farnsworth, a soft-spoken researcher at the Cornell Laboratory of Ornithology, and I'm joining him here in hope of seeing a wildlife phenomenon that twice a year sweeps almost unseen above the city: the seasonal night flights of migrating birds. It's an absurdly incongruous place for a nature-viewing expedition. Apart from the familiar exceptions – pigeons, rats, mice, sparrows – we tend to think of wild creatures as living far from the city's margins, and nature as the city's polar opposite. It's easy to see why. The only natural things visible from this height are a faint scatter of stars above and the livid bruise of the Hudson running through the clutter of lights below. Everything else is us: the flash of aircraft, the tilt of bright smartphones, the illuminated grids of windows and streets.

Skyscrapers are at their most perfect at night, full-fledged dreams of modernity that erase nature and replace it with a new landscape wrought of artifice, a cartography of steel and glass and light. But people live in them for the same reason that they travel to wild places: to escape the city. The highest buildings raise you above the mess and chaos of life at street level; they also raise you into something else. The sky may seem like an empty place, just as we once thought the deep ocean to be a lifeless void. But like the ocean, this is a vast habitat full of life – bats and birds, flying insects, spiders, windblown seeds, microbes, drifting spores. The more I stare at the city across miles of dusty, uplit air, the more I begin to think of these super-tall buildings as machines that work like deep-sea submersibles, transporting us to inaccessible realms we cannot otherwise explore. Inside them, the air is calm and clean and temperate. Outside is a tumultuous world teeming with unexpected biological abundance, and we are standing in its midst.

Above us, LED bulbs around the base of the spire cast a soft halo of pale light up into the darkness. An incandescent blur of white skips across it. Through binoculars it resolves into a noctuid moth, wings flapping as it climbs vertically towards the tower. No one fully understands how moths like these orient themselves while migrating; there's speculation that they might navigate by sensing Earth's magnetic fields. This one is flying upward in search of the right airflow that will allow it to travel where it wants to go.

Wind-borne migration is an arthropod speciality, allowing creatures like aphids, wasps, lacewings, beetles, moths and tiny spiders hoisted on strands of electrostatically charged silk to travel distances ranging from tens to hundreds of miles. These drifting creatures are colonisers, pioneers looking for new places to live, and they'll make a home wherever they find one. Place a rose bush out on the arid environment of a top-floor balcony and soon wind-borne sap-sucking aphids will cluster on its stems, followed by the tiny wasps that parasitise them.

Insects travel above us in extraordinary numbers. In Britain, the research scientist Jason Chapman uses radar systems aimed into the atmosphere to study their high-altitude movements. Over seven and a half billion can pass over a square mile of English farmland in a single month – about 5,500 pounds of biomass. Chapman thinks the number passing over New York City may be even higher, because this is a gateway to a continent, not a small island surrounded by cold seas, and summers here are generally hotter. Once you get above six hundred and fifty feet, he says, you're lofted into a realm where the distinction between city and countryside has little or no meaning at all.

During the day, chimney swifts feast on these vast drifts of life; during the night, so do the city's resident and migrating bats, and nighthawks with white-flagged wings. On days with north-west winds in late summer and early fall, birds, bats and migrant dragonflies all feed on rich concentrations of insects caused by powerful downdraughts and eddies around the city's high-rise buildings, just as fish swarm to feed where currents congregate plankton in the ocean.

It's not just insects up there. The tallest buildings, like the Empire State, One World Trade Center and other new super-towers, project into airspace that birds have used for millennia. The city lies on the Atlantic Flyway, the route used by hundreds of millions of birds to fly north every spring to their breeding grounds and back again in the fall. Most small songbirds tend to travel between three and four thousand feet from the ground, but they vary their altitude depending on the weather. Larger birds fly higher, and some, like shorebirds, may well pass over the city at ten to twelve thousand feet. Up here we'll be able to see only a fraction of what is moving past us: even the tallest buildings dip into only the shallows of the sky.

Though you can see migrating raptors soaring at altitudes well over eight hundred feet above the city during the day, most species of diurnal birds migrate after nightfall. It's safer. Temperatures are cooler, and there are fewer predators around. Fewer, not none. Just before I arrived, Farnsworth saw a peregrine falcon drifting ominously around the building. Peregrines frequently hunt at night here. From high-rise lookout perches, they launch flights into the darkness to grab birds and bats. In more natural habitats, falcons cache the bodies of birds they've killed among crevices in cliffs. The ones here tuck their kills into ledges on high-rises, including the Empire State. For a falcon, a skyscraper is simply a cliff: it brings the same prospects, the same high winds, the same opportunities to stash a takeout meal.

We stare out into the dark, willing life into view. Minutes pass. Farnsworth points. 'There!' he says. High above us is a suspicion of movement, right at the edge of vision where the sky dissolves into dusty chaos. I swing my binoculars up to my eyes. Three pale pairs of beating wings, flying north-north-east in close formation. Black-crowned night herons. I've only ever seen them hunched on branches or crouched low by lakes and ponds, and it's astounding to see them wrenched so far from their familiar context. I wonder how high they are. 'Those are pretty large,' Farnsworth says.

'When you look up into the light, everything looks bigger than it is, and closer than it is.' He estimates that the herons are about three hundred feet above us, so they're about one and a half thousand feet from ground level. We watch them vanish into darkness.

I feel less like a naturalist here and more like an amateur astronomer waiting for a meteor shower, squinting expectantly into the darkness. I try a new tactic: focusing my binoculars on infinity and pointing them straight upwards. Through the lenses, birds invisible to the naked eye swim into view, and there are birds above them, and birds higher still. It strikes me that we are seeing a lot of birds. An awful lot of birds.

For every larger bird I see, thirty or more songbirds pass over. They are very small. Watching their passage is almost too moving to bear. They resemble stars, embers, slow tracer fire. Even through binoculars those at higher altitudes are tiny, ghostly points of light. I know that they have loose-clenched toes tucked to their chests, bright eyes, thin bones and a will to fly north that pulls them onward night after night. Most of them spent yesterday in central or southern New Jersey before ascending into darkness. Larger birds keep flying until dawn. The warblers tend to come earlier to earth, dropping like stones into patches of habitat further north to rest and feed over the following day. Some, like yellow-rumped warblers, began their long journeys in the south-eastern states. Others, like rose-breasted grosbeaks, have made their way up from Central America.

Something tugs at my heart. I'll never see any of these birds again. If I weren't this high, and the birds weren't briefly illuminated by this column of light cast by a building thrown up through the Depression years to celebrate earthly power and capital confidence, I'd never have seen them at all.

Farnsworth pulls out a smartphone. Unlike everyone else holding screens up here, he's looking at radar images from Fort Dix in New Jersey, part of a National Weather Service radar network that provides near-continuous coverage of airspace over the continental USA. 'It's definitely a heavy migration night tonight,' he says. 'When you see those kinds of patterns on radar, in particular, those greens,' he explains, 'you're talking about one thousand to two thousand birds per cubic mile potentially, which is almost as dense as it gets. So it's a big night.' After days of bad weather for birds wanting to fly north, with low cloud and winds in the wrong direction, a bottleneck of migrants built up, and now the sky is full of them. I watch the pixellation blossom on the animated radar map, a blue-and-green dendritic flower billowing out over the whole East Coast. 'This is biological stuff that's up in the atmosphere,' Farnsworth says, pointing one finger to the screen. 'It's all biology.'

Meteorologists have long known that you can detect animal life by radar. Just after the Second World War, British radar scientists and Royal Air Force technicians puzzled over mysterious plots and patterns that appeared on their screens. They knew they weren't aircraft and christened them 'angels' before finally concluding that they were flocks of moving birds. 'That was their contamination, right?' Farnsworth says of radar meteorologists. 'They wanted to filter all that stuff out. Now the biologists want to do the reverse.' Farnsworth is one pioneer of a new multidisciplinary science, fit for an era in which weather radar has become so sensitive it can detect a single bumblebee over thirty miles away. It's called aeroecology, and it uses sophisticated remote-sensing technologies like radar, acoustics and tracking devices to study ecological patterns and relationships in the skies. 'The whole notion of the aerosphere and airspace as habitat is not something that has come into the collective psyche until recently,' Farnsworth says. And this new science is helping us understand how climate change, skyscrapers, wind turbines, light pollution and aviation affect the creatures that live and move above us.

At ten o'clock, cirrus clouds slide overhead like oil poured on water. Ten minutes later, the sky is clear again, and the birds are still flying. We move to the east side of the observation deck. A saxophonist begins to play, and in concert with this unlikely soundtrack we begin to see birds far closer than before. One, in particular. Though it is overexposed in the light, we detect a smear of black at its chest and a distinctive pattern on its tail: a male yellow-rumped warbler. It flickers past and disappears around the corner of the building. A little while later, we see another flying the same way. Then another. It dawns on us that this is the same bird, circling. Another one joins it, both now drawn helplessly towards and around the light, reeling about the spire as if caught on invisible strings. Watching them dampens our exuberant mood. The spire is lit with pulsing rivulets of climbing colour like a candle tonight to mark the building's eighty-fifth anniversary. And these birds have been attracted to it, pulled off course, their exquisite navigational machinery overwhelmed by light, leaving them confused and in considerable danger. After being mesmerised in this way, some birds drag themselves free and continue their journey. Others don't.

New York is among the brightest cities in the world after Las Vegas, only one node in a flood of artificial illumination that runs from Boston down to Washington. We cherish our cities for their appearance at night, but it takes a terrible toll on migrating songbirds: you can find them dead or exhausted at the foot of high-rise buildings all over America. Disoriented by light and reflections on glass, they crash into obstacles, fly into windows, spiral down to the ground. More than a hundred thousand die each year in New York City alone. Thomas King, of the New York pest-control company M&M Environmental, has had calls from residents of high-rise buildings asking him to deal with the birds colliding with their windows during migration season. He tells them that there's no solution, but they can talk to their building manager about turning off the lights. It helps. Programmes like New York City Audubon's 'Lights Out New York' have encouraged many high-rise owners to do the same, saving both energy and avian lives.

Every year the 'Tribute in Light' shines twin blue beams into the Manhattan night as a memorial to the lives lost on September 11. They rise four miles into the air and are visible sixty miles from the city. On peak migration nights songbirds spiral down towards them, calling, pulled from the sky, so many circling in the light they look like glittering, whirling specks of paper caught in the wind. On one night last year, so many were caught in the beams that the few pixels representing the 'Tribute' site glowed super-bright on the radar maps. Farnsworth was there with the Audubon team that got the lights shut off intermittently to prevent casualties. They switched off the 'Tribute' eight times that night for about twenty minutes at a time, releasing the trapped birds to return to their journey. Each time the lights went back on, a new sweep of birds was drawn in – the twin towers made ghosts of light visited over and over by winged travellers intermittently freed into darkness before a crowd rushed in to take their place. Farnsworth is a lead scientist in BirdCast, a project that combines a variety of methods – weather data, flight calls, radar, observers on the ground – to predict the movements of migrating birds throughout the continental United States and forecast big nights like this that might require emergency lights-out action.

The flow of birds over the observation deck continues, but it's getting late. I make my farewell, take the elevator back down the building and wander uphill to my apartment. Though it's long past midnight, I'm wide awake. Part of what high-rise buildings are designed to do is change the way we see. To bring us different views of the world, views intimately linked with prospect and power – to make the invisible visible. The birds I saw were mostly unidentifiable streaks of light, like thin retinal scratches or splashes of luminous paint on a dark ground. As I look up from street level, the blank sky above seems a very different place, deep and coursing with life.

Two days later, I decide to walk in Central Park, and find it full of newer migrants that arrived here at night and stayed to rest and feed. A black-and-white warbler tacking along a slanted tree trunk deep in the Ramble, a yellow-rumped warbler sallying forth into the bright spring air to grab flies, a black-throated blue warbler so neat and spry he looks like a folded pocket handkerchief. These songbirds are familiar creatures with familiar meanings. It's hard to reconcile them with the remote lights I witnessed in the sky.

Living in a high-rise building bars you from certain ways of interacting with the natural world. You can't put out feeders to watch robins and chickadees in your garden. But you are set in another part of their habitual world, a nocturne of ice crystals and cloud and wind and darkness. High-rise buildings, symbols of mastery over nature, can work as bridges towards a more complete understanding of the natural world – stitching the sky to the ground, nature to the city. For days afterwards, my dreams are full of songbirds, the familiar ones from woods and backyards, but also points of moving light, little astronauts, travellers using the stars to navigate, having fallen to Earth for a little while before picking themselves up and moving on.

The Human Flock

Under heavy rain the lakes have turned to phosphorescent steel. Pygmy cormorants hunch on dead trees. Twelve of us stand on the shore. Some have set out spotting scopes on tripods on the grass, others carry binoculars. Silently we stand in wait for the Hungarian dusk. As the sun slips behind the expanse of water the air grows colder. We strain our ears until – there it is – we hear a faint noise like baying hounds or discordant bugles, at first hardly discernible through the wind rattling the reeds before it grows into an unearthly clamour. 'Here they come!' someone whispers. Overhead, a long, wavering chevron of beating wings is inked across the darkening sky. Behind it flow others, and there are others behind them, all passing overhead in ever-increasing waves, filling the air with a barrage of noise and beauty.

The birds above us are long-necked, graceful Eurasian cranes. Every autumn more than a hundred thousand of them stop off on their southward migration from Russia and Northern Europe to spend a few weeks in the Hortobágy region of north-eastern Hungary, feeding on maize left in the fields after harvest. Every night they fly to roost in huge numbers in the safety of shallow fish-farm lakes, attracting wildlife tourists who come here to witness the spectacle of their evening flights. Similarly impressive congregations can be seen in other places. In Nebraska, more than half a million sandhill cranes fatten up in cornfields before continuing their spring migration; in Quebec, watchers are awed by blizzards of snow geese blotting out the sky as they rise from the Saint-François River. In Britain, clouds of wintering starlings flying to their roosts draw crowds of all ages.

Standing close to vast masses of birds affects everyone differently: some people laugh, some cry, others shake their heads or utter profanities. Language fails in the face of immense flocks of beating wings. But our brains are built to wrest familiar meaning from the confusions of the world, and watching the cranes at dusk I see them first turn into strings of musical notation, then mathematical patterns. The snaking lines synchronise so that each bird raises its wings a fraction before the one behind it, each moving flock resolving itself into a filmstrip showing a single bird stretched through time. It is an astonishing illusion that makes me blink in surprise. But then, part of the allure of flocking birds is their ability to create bewildering optical effects. I remember my amazement as a child watching thousands of wading birds, knots, flying against a cool grey sky, vanish and reappear in an instant as the birds turned their counter-shaded bodies in the air. Perhaps the best-known example is the hosts of European starlings that assemble in the sky before they roost. We call them murmurations, but the Danish term, *sort sol*, is better: black sun. It captures their almost celestial strangeness. Standing on the Suffolk coast a few years ago, I saw a far-flung mist of starlings turn in a split second into an ominous sphere like a dark planet hanging over the marshes. Everyone around me gasped audibly before it exploded in a maelstrom of wings.

Though the rapid dynamism of flocking birds is a large part of their beauty, news sites and magazines often publish still photographs of murmurations that look like other things: sharks, mushrooms, dinosaurs. In 2015, an image of one flock over New York City shifting into the shape of Vladimir Putin's face went viral, though it may have been fake. It's not difficult, when presented with such a strange phenomenon, to believe in signs and wonders. The changing shape of starling flocks comes from each bird copying the motions of the six or seven others around it with extreme rapidity; their reaction time is less than a tenth of a second. Turns can propagate through a cloud of birds at speeds approaching ninety miles per hour, making murmurations look from a distance like a single pulsing, living organism. In a 1799 notebook entry, Samuel Taylor Coleridge wrote of a murmuration that shaped itself into various forms and moved 'like a body unindued with voluntary power'. Sometimes they seem uncannily like an alien, groping entity, living sand or smoke moving through a suite of topological changes. Murmurations are thrilling, but they can also provoke an emotion akin to fear.

And fear is in large part why many of these flocks exist. Cranes, for example, roost in shallow water because it is safer than sleeping on the ground; and the sheer profusion of beating wings makes it hard for predators to focus on any single starling in a murmuration. No starling wants to be on the edge of the flock, or among the first to land. Anne Goodenough, who runs the Royal Society of Biology and University of Gloucestershire international starling survey, speculates that murmurations may act as signposts to invite other starlings to join a specific roost and increase its size – in cold weather, large roosts keep birds warm. But in the air, fear is the factor shaping the flocks, pressing and contorting them as they fly. A dark, shivering wave running through a mass of starlings is often a response to a raptor diving into the flock in search of a meal.

It is nearly dark now at the Hortobágy fishponds, and my ears ring with the cacophony of calling cranes. There is boiling confusion over the lake as flocks come from all directions to join the mass on the water that now looks like stippled, particulate fog. White-fronted geese are pouring in, too, tumbling and sideslipping from the sky through swathes of other wings. Suddenly it is almost too much to bear. I feel uncomfortably disoriented. Big flocks of birds can do this. Birders have described the experience of watching flocks of rooks at nightfall as so confusing and noisy that it produces in the viewer something close to motion sickness.

In search of something solid, I peer through a spotting scope focused on the far side of the lake. In the circle of the viewfinder, the confusion resolves into individual birds. It's so dark that their colour has leached away. I am watching stately groups of cranes in greyscale, landing, drinking, shaking their loose feathers, greeting one another and getting on with the business of finding a place to sleep. The switch in recognition is eerie: I go from seeing rushing patterns in the sky to the realisation that they are made of thousands of beating hearts and eyes and fragile frames of feather and bone. I watch the cranes scratching their beaks with their toes and think of how the starling flocks that pour into reed beds like grain turn all of a sudden into birds perching on bowed stems, bright-eyed, their feathers spangled with white spots that glow like small stars. I marvel at how confusion can be resolved by focusing on the things from which it is made. The magic of the flocks is this simple switch between geometry and family.

As I stand there watching the cranes, my mind turns to human matters. The village we'd stayed in the previous night had felt so much like my home in the fens. It had the same damp, underwater air, chickens roaming around backyards, poplars, piles of winter firewood. Before I came here I'd asked a few British friends who'd spent time in Hungary what it was like, and several said that the strangest thing about it was how much it felt like home. It's painful to recall that now. It has been nagging away at me all the time I've been here, the razor-wire fence the government has erected more than a hundred miles south of here to stop Syrian refugees walking across the border from Serbia; the thought of crowds moving slowly north-east as the cranes move south-west. Watching the flock has brought home to me how easy it is to react to the idea of masses of refugees with the same visceral apprehension with which we greet a cloud of moving starlings or tumbling geese, to view it as a singular entity, strange and uncontrollable and chaotic. But the crowds coming over the border are people just like us. Perhaps too much like us. We do not want to imagine what it would be like to have our familiar places reduced to ruins. In the face of fear, we are all starlings, a group, a flock, made of a million souls seeking safety. I love the flock not simply for its biological exuberance, but for the way it has prompted me to pick similarity out of strangeness, for the way its chaos was transformed, on reflection, to individuals and small family groups wanting the simplest things: freedom from fear, food, a place to safely sleep.

The Student's Tale

There's a window and the rattle of a taxi and grapes on the table, black ones, sweet ones, and the taxi is also black and there's a woman inside it, a charity worker who befriended you when you were in detention, and she's leaning to pay the driver and through the dust and bloom of the glass I see you standing on the pavement next to the open taxi door and your back is turned towards me so all I can see are your shoulders hunched in a blue denim jacket. They're set in a line that speaks of concern, not for yourself, but for the woman who is paying the fare. I wave through the window and you turn and see me and smile hello.

This is a borrowed house that we're talking in. It's not my home.

We sit at the table and I don't know where to begin.

I don't know anything about you.

It is hard to ask questions.

You want me to ask questions, because you say it is easier to answer questions than tell your story. I don't want to ask you questions, because I think of all the questions you must have been asked before. But you want me to ask you questions, and so I begin with: when did you get here? And you write, in careful Persian numerals, *12, 2016*. December. And I ask more questions, and you answer them, and when the English words won't come, you translate using your phone, and this takes some time, and the sun slaps its flat gold light upon the table and the bowl of grapes and the teapot, all these quiet domestic things, as I wait to know what you might mean. Here are the words you look up while we talk: *Apostate. Bigoted. Depraved. Hide.*

You are a student of epidemiology. Epidemiologists study the mode of transmission of disease, the way it runs through populations from person to person. You tell me that back in your country you used to meet with your friends in your restaurant at night so you could talk of Christianity and read the Bible. There were Christian signs in your restaurant. You knew that you might be arrested for doing this. Secrecy is paramount, but faith is also faith.

This is what happens when you are denounced as an apostate. The authorities speak of you as if you were one of the agents of disease that you have studied. At prayers one Friday they denounce you, by name, in five regions, two cities and three villages. They said that a woman at your university had depraved you, by which they meant she had encouraged you to become a Christian. They said that you had changed your religion. And that now you possess this faith, you spread it to other men.

They see your belief as a contagious disease. They want to isolate it, contain it, and like all such malevolent metaphors that equate morality with health, the cure is always extinguishment. You know what happens to apostates, to those who have changed their religion, in your country. Even I know what happens. I am holding my breath just thinking of it.

When the intelligence services came looking for you at your grandmother's home she called you and told you that these men were your friends even though they spoke the wrong language for the region and they were wearing distinctive clothes that made it obvious, really, who they were, and why they were there, but she was old and you couldn't blame her for expecting friendship when what was offered was its scorched obverse. Your uncle knew better. He told you to flee. *Your life is in danger*, he said. Truth. So you fled. You left everything.

You drove from city to city and, in a city more distant, met two friends of your uncle. They told you they could take you to Europe with others by car. And once you were there, you wondered where you should go. Your uncle said, *The UK is good*, and he offered to pay the smuggling agents to get you here. The car unloaded you all in an unkempt garden and you had to hide there until the middle of the night when the truck came, and you got in.

Days in the darkness inside a lorry on its way north. A freezer truck. How many people were in there with you? I ask. And you laugh, and say, *Ten? I don't know. It was dark!* And I laugh too, a little ashamed, and wonder why I want to press you for these little details. None of us want to know what this is like. We don't want to know how it feels to not eat or drink or sleep for five days and nights, to be sustained in terror and darkness merely through the hope that there is light the other side. None of us wants to know what it feels like to be threatened with a knife, as you were threatened. To be held at gunpoint by people you have paid to bring you to safety.

You say, *It was the worst feeling*. Then you say it again. *The worst feeling*.

Several times, you tell me, *I see my death*.

Then you say it again. *I see my death*.

The hardest things, I realise, you are saying them all twice.

And what I am thinking, as you say *sorry* into the silence while you wait to be able to once again speak, is this. I think of how scientists have only just found out how our brains make memories. They used to think that we record a short-term memory, then archive it later, move it to a different part of the brain to store it long term. But now they've discovered that the brain always records two tracks at once. That it is always taping two stories in parallel. Short-term memories, long-term memories, two tracks of running recollection, memory doubled. Always doubled.

Which makes everything that ever happens to us happen twice.

Which makes us always beings split in two.

You are an epidemiologist. You are a refugee.

You were one of the best epidemiology students in the whole country.

You are also an asylum seeker who has seen detention-centre inmates cut themselves with razors, lash out in violence, numb themselves with Spice.

The government wants to send you back to the European country where you first arrived, but that would be dangerous because of people there who know who you are, who have threatened you, who have contacts with the authorities back home. So now you are in a hostel, with four hundred others. You have to sign in once in the morning and once again at night. You are a student, a brother, a son, who manages to speak to your family back home through Telegram, through WhatsApp, and you are also a man who asks the receptionist for help when violence or sickness breaks out in the hostel and watches the receptionist shrug dismissively and no help comes. All the things you see between refugees, you tell me, are *harmful for brain, for mind, for spirit*. You say, of the hostel, in the quietest, gentlest voice, that *there, nothing is good, really. Nothing is good. It is a very nasty place*. You tell me, twice, that *some people have not even any clothes*.

In December you'd called the police from the frozen dark inside the lorry. The police opened the doors and took you to a cell, questioned you, detained you for seventy-two hours. And when you requested asylum they moved you to an immigration detention centre. You were there for eighty days. I have heard a lot about the conditions there, this place that is known as a hellhole. So it is a mark of your kindly reticence that all you can say about it is, *The situation in detention was very bad.*

You are a refugee who sings in a talent competition in a detention centre where people are held indefinitely and you are also a man sitting at a sunny dining table laughing out loud at your mistake when you realise that you said your father is literature when what you meant to say was your father is illiterate. You are a man who can laugh at the ridiculousness of mistranslation, and you are also a man who has left a life behind, your father, your little brother, your ailing family members, and every corner of home, and that loss pours from you, silent through the laughter, like a cold current of air that sinks to the floor and fills the room beneath everything light that is spoken here.

You don't want to talk about yourself, except to give the facts. What you want to talk about are the problems facing the people around you. Your charity-worker friend tells me that after you saw an advert for WaterAid you asked her to donate what little funds you had to the children who were suffering, because the way the system works, you weren't allowed to do it yourself. She tells me, though she apologises for speaking because it is not her story, that you have been buying fruit and lentils for the children in the hostel because the food is so bad, it makes people sick, and you can see the children are malnourished.

You are a man whose eyes are bright with unspilled tears when you tell me of the horror of your journey here. But when you think of the people who have shown you kindness? That is when you break down and cry. You say, of the woman sitting with us, *I would maybe have suicide, without her*. When I ask you if the people in the city where you live are good to you, you say yes, because if you ask them an address, they will tell you where it is. They will tell you where it is.

I think about all the stories we tell about refugees and how they are always one story or another, never both at once. Tragic stories or threatening stories. Victims or aggressors. Never complicated, always simple, always with clean edges. Easy pigeonholes to fit people who have been forced to take wing.

But a hole is not just a pigeonhole. It's the space between two things. It's a hole that's the gap between a word in Urami, or in Farsi, or in English. It's the space between past and future, between old lives and new. Between years. When New Year came in March you went to the park in the city where the hostel is, and you sang songs welcoming the New Year by the water of the lake. What can a new year mean, when you are young and all you are able to do is wait?

I want to be useful, you say. *I don't want to spend my time in the hostel, waiting*. And then you rub your eyes with one hand and you say, *Please pray for me*. You say, *This issue is very distracted my brain, my mind. I want to quickly take a part in this society. And the culture. At the moment I haven't any certificate, because I am an asylum seeker. And I don't take a part in helping people because I don't have any money, I don't have any device for helping the people, and I think my living is very precious. Precious?* You try the word out as a question, as if the word is itself somehow wrong.

I don't like be spend it by the time, waiting, you say. *Because I am young.*

You are young. You are a student, an epidemiologist, a Christian, a refugee. You want to help people so much it hurts my heart. You are a man who I drive, after we have talked that afternoon, to the hospital so we can take a photograph of you standing outside the School for Clinical Medicine, because bound up in a sense of your future is this brightness, that you might one day be able to help, to work in medicine here. And you are also a man who tips back his head and laughs when we discover that the School has been closed for rebuilding, and the windows are boarded up and the palings mean we can't see the building at all. We take pictures anyway. Us in front of the barriers. You alone, you with your charity-worker companion, you with me. We are all, all of us, waiting while the world is rebuilt.

Ants

At first there's nothing notable about my drive back from the supermarket. I pass packs of schoolchildren on street corners, see a glossy SUV make a dickish manoeuvre at a roundabout, listen to someone complaining about something or other on the radio. Then my attention catches on something high and to the right of me. I tighten my hands on the wheel, pull into a roadside space a little further on, I lock the car and walk back, car keys loose in one hand, eyes turned up to the sky.

Some natural events track seasonal changes, and we treasure them for it. We wait expectantly for our spring swallows and swifts, the first summer butterflies; we listen for the mating calls of autumn foxes and deer. But in Britain we don't have many visibly spectacular, large-scale yearly events whose precise calendar timing is unpredictable, like the spring spawning of thousands and thousands of silver grunion fish on Californian beaches for a few nights after a high tide. Even so, everyone here knows one. It doesn't happen on the same day everywhere, but wherever you live, there'll be one still, humid, bright day that triggers it, and today it's happening right here.

Above me is a towering column of flying ants. I only know they are there because there's also a column of about a hundred herring gulls borne on lean grey black-tipped wings, some cruising at rooftop height, others circling hundreds of feet above. They aren't flying in the usual laconic manner, a lazy flap and glide from one place to another. They're feeding. I can't see the ants that they're eating. But I know exactly where individual ants are, because every few seconds a gull twitches itself to one side, beats its wings once, twice, and snaps at the air. And another, and another. Above me is as much a feeding frenzy as any bait ball in a tropical ocean, but featuring gulls and ants rather than anchovies and sharks.

What I'm witnessing is the nuptial flight of a species of ant called *Lasius niger*, the common black ant of our town streets and suburban gardens. For the last twenty-four hours worker ants all across town and county have been enlarging the entrance holes to their underground colonies to make them big enough for winged virgin queens to emerge. The male drones, also winged, are already massing on the ground, and as the queens take flight, trailing pheromones, the drones chase them aloft. The queens take their pursuers higher and higher, waiting for males strong enough to reach them. They'll mate, sometimes with a few different males from different colonies, in brief coincidences that herald the birth of tiny empires. On their return to earth, the drones die, while the queens rub off their wings and search for a place to start a new nest. Though these queens may live another thirty years, they will never mate again. Every fertilised egg they lay for the rest of their life will use sperm they store in their bodies from that one ascent on a summer afternoon.

I watch gulls from all points on the compass flying in to join the bonanza. The ants are caught up in a thermal of rising warm air, and as the incoming gulls meet its outside edge, the tip of one wing is tugged by the updraught; they straighten their wings, circle into it, and rise effortlessly. This tower of birds is an attraction visible for miles, an ephemeral landmark above a roadside church in a small country town. And these flocks of predators are one of the reasons why ants from a whole district all emerge at the same time; the more ants in the air, the more likely it is that some survive the onslaught of beaks. A red kite joins the flock, drifting and tilting through it on paper-cut wings stamped black against the sky.

We so often think of science as somehow subtracting mystery and beauty from the world. But it's things I've learned from scientific books and papers that are making what I'm watching almost unbearably moving. The hitching curves of the gulls in a vault of sky crossed with thousands of different flightlines, warm airspace tense with predatory intent and the tiny hopes of each rising ant. It isn't merely the wheeling flock of birds that transfixes me, or the magic of how the ants have carved out a discrete piece of unremarkable air and given it drama and meaning. It is that the motive power behind this grand spectacle is entirely invisible. This vast stretch of sky, the gulls, the imperceptible ants, is a working revelation of the interrelation of different scales of existence, and it is at once exhilarating and humbling. Humbling because this contemplation on scale and purpose can't help but remind me that I'm little more than an ant in the wider workings of the world, no more or less important than any of the creatures here. Mesmerised, I watch a party of swifts pile in to take their turn at the harvest, wings scything, pink gullets open wide to scoop ants from the air. Craning my neck, I follow them up until the flock banks between me and the sun, and the fierceness of the light erases them from sight. My eyes water, and I look down to the ground I'd forgotten, to tarmac covered with the glittering wings of drones and queens all readying themselves for their first, and final, flight.

Symptomatic

Migraines: something like rain, something like a bullet that's only chambered one morning days after the threat of violence. A slug that ratchets through and slots into your spine before the slow shot begins with an umbrella-towering nimbus of empty pressure that makes you as dizzy as if there really were a storm-cloud of rising air growing, billowing up and outwards until its edges feather and coincide with your skull. Then come two thumbs pressing on your sinus and moving over your jaw, and strange strips of fast pain like summer lightning when you lift a cup, pick up a pen, burying themselves in your shoulder, deep into places which don't exist until they hurt. And when the pain comes it is one-sided, sometimes on the left of your skull and sometimes on the right, although it is so intense it can't be kept in either place, and it ripples like a flag cracking in strong wind, or thrums deep like a heartbeat, and sometimes one of your eyes waters, the one on the same side as the pain, and there's what doctors call a post-nasal drip, which makes the world taste of scalding metal and brine. A few times, in the midst of my own migraines, I've had a strong and sudden intuition I'm made out of cobalt: partly it's that taste in my mouth, partly how heavy I feel, but mostly because the interference in my brain runs sometimes along the lines of those delicate scrawls of blue-flowered decorations on ancient Chinese porcelain. Shipwrecks, bones, pearls. So yes, migraines put me in mind of metaphors, and then more metaphors, and more, for they are always *too much* in a way that makes them unbearable, all filters gone.

Thirty per cent of migraineurs experience visual disturbances with their headaches. I've had them only once, on a stormy night at a literary festival. I was busily signing books when a spray of sparks, an array of livid and prickling phosphenes like shorting fairy lights, spread downwards from the upper right-hand corner of my vision until I could barely see through them. In textbooks the phenomenon is called *scintillating scotoma*. It scintillated. I freaked out. I kept signing, kept smiling, gripped the inside of my shoes tight with all ten toes, and worried that I was going to die until the pain came.

Although they hurt, make bright light a brutal intruder and force me to take to bed and swallow as many painkillers as I am allowed to without harming myself, my migraines seem useful. Their utility isn't in the pain. The pain is terrible. I hate it. I hate the time it takes from my life, my helplessness in the face of it, the tears soaking the pillows I'm curled around. But migraines remind me we're not built with the solidity so many of us blithely assume. That the World Health Organization's 1948 definition of health – *a state of complete physical, mental and social well-being and not merely the absence of disease or infirmity* – refers to precisely no one, is a sweetly turned phrase more ableist than utopian. That perfection cannot be intrinsic to us, built as we are of chemicals and networks and causal molecular pathways and shifting storms of electricity; none of us are ever in perfect health.

Migraines are an incredibly common – more than a billion people suffer from them – but highly mysterious neurological condition. We're not exactly sure what they are, though it's likely they're a tendency for the brain to lose control of its inputs, a sensory processing disorder that is partly inherited. We know that meningeal blood vessels around the brain dilate during the headache, and that migraines are associated with activity in the trigeminal ganglion, the base of the nerve network that governs the face and the muscles used in chewing. We know that migraines with auras involve waves of electrical activity across the brain called *spreading cortical depression*. In the midst of a migraine, not knowing is very much to the point. Pain wipes you free of knowledge, makes understanding utterly redundant. There's nothing to know or understand. Subjects, objects, fail. All you are is all that is and all of it hurts.

Some people get migraines most often around the time of their period (three times as many women as men are migraineurs; sex hormones appear to play a role) and the correlation is pertinent to me not only because I am one of those women, but because menstruation is migraine's closest cousin in my life. There's no mistaking their occurrence – I bleed, or I curl up in pain and weep – and both involve a suite of premonitory symptoms.

It took me nearly thirty years to understand the robustness of my premenstrual pattern, but these days I know the week before my period will always include a single day in which I fantasise about murdering strangers, most specifically slow drivers, and another in which everything can reduce me to sentimental tears: supermarket adverts, the polished corner of an oak table glowing in the sun, a pigeon taking off from a hawthorn branch into the wind. For much of that week the voice of my interior critic is as seductive and honeyed as warm baklava. It tells me I am a terrible person and the worst writer in the world, and I believe it. But after decades of bafflement, these states are now something like old friends, and I greet them with a deal of archness.

The premonitory symptoms of my migraines are exceedingly specific. Two or three days before my head begins to hurt, my fridge fills with bottles of banana milk. I yawn a lot, become unaccountably thirsty. My joints ache. I shop for dark chocolate and sweet pickled beetroot. There's dust-and-ashes tiredness, and a bad mood so remorseless that even the sweetest birdsong irritates. I can enumerate them now, yet when the headache arrives, it is always a surprise. I never see it coming. These symptoms are aspects of the migraine's earliest stages, occurring in its *prodrome*, that part of it which precedes the pain. It turns out that some of the most infamous migraine triggers are not triggers at all – a desire to eat chocolate is just as much part of a migraine as the full-blown headache that follows.

After the pain subsides, the migraine's *postdrome* begins, and it is a peculiar muse of mine. Though it makes me feel weak, muffled, slow and stupid, it's inside it that writing comes easiest. Whatever is going on inside my brain makes the words flow, the world sharper; it tips me into days that seem newly forged and prone to surprising beauties. I'm writing at my kitchen table right now in the midst of a postdrome, a heat pack draped across my neck and shoulders to unknot muscles locked after two days of hurt. Just after sunrise this morning, I looked out over the back fence of my garden across a field of oats into the valleys and hills around my house, the sky nacreous and the lower-lying ground obscured by luminous mist. For a migraineur in fear of bright sunlight, the slow slide into autumn's softer days and earlier nights is an enormous relief.

But something was off. I shook my head. Then I shook it again, and wondered if I were sicker than I thought, because I could hear a loud drone, a low-frequency roaring like the sound of an airliner overhead, but an airliner held somehow motionless mid-flight, for there was no dopplering, no shifting in the sound; the tone was as unmoving as the mist. It seemed to have no discernible source, was emanating from the ground, from the air itself – perhaps, I thought with a start, from *inside* me. Maybe this was some previously unknown annexe to my migraines, a novel auditory hallucination. The anxiety caught like brushfire and prickled in sharp, glittering waves along my skin until a woodpigeon started to sing in the tree above me, a low cooing sent out into the air at the same frequency as the noise all around, and with a slide of amazement running straight down the nape of my neck and rising in goosebumps along my arms I understood that the roar was pigeons, hundreds of them, gathered here to glean the spilled grains from harvest. They were calling from trees and hedges and fence-posts for miles around, all at once, and in such number that their individual songs dissolved into one. I was not imagining it. This was not a symptom. It was *out there*. And amid the roar of hundreds of other minds, I was overcome by delight. No matter how old I am, I thought, sometimes I'll encounter things that are new. And perhaps my wonky neurology was reading too much from this experience, but sometimes, I went on to think, when you berate yourself, it might be the case that you do so needlessly. Sometimes it is not you. Sometimes the world is to blame.

I once told a friend about my perennial inability to recognise I'm in the midst of a migraine prodrome. Other people understand what their symptoms mean while they're happening, I said. Most people. Not me. I said, 'It's weird. I wonder if I'm in denial on purpose, because I hate having migraines?' She fell quiet for a while. 'It *could* be that,' she said carefully. Then she said, 'There's another possibility. Have you ever considered that your failing to identify the symptoms of your migraines while you're having a migraine may itself be a symptom? Because some things are structured so that not seeing them, not comprehending them, is part of the experience of what they are.'

Migraineurs like me are experts in denial. We know how it feels, that fingertip pressure behind the eyes and heart, knowing it's there and at the same time believing it does not exist. Which is why I keep thinking of migraines whenever I hear the news, although we have a much clearer understanding of the science of climate change than we do the science of migraines. As I write, forest fires in Siberia are tearing through millions of acres of slow-growing pine. The Amazon is burning. Villages are falling into the sea. Methane craters blossom across melting permafrost. Dogs drag sleds through meltwater. The hottest summer. The hottest summer, again. And again. Hurricanes lining up across the Atlantic. One, two, three. And while it's easy to grieve over a photo of a starving polar bear, be terrified by the predictive pronouncements of scientists, feel the utmost grief and horror at the human cost of hurricanes or floods, it's even easier to disavow the knowledge of systemic breakdown. We can't connect the dots. We know we're in trouble, but we shift anxieties to conjure terrors that are palpable, thinkable. We fret about the existence of drifting drinking straws and shopping bags that mimic jellyfish and ctenophores in trash-polluted seas. Some of us anchor ourselves in an imagined notion of home while home burns or drowns around us. Others conjure enemies who threaten our homes and familiar ways. We cleave to narratives online that canalise our terror into notions of cabals and great replacements, conspiracies fluttering like millenarian pamphlets, old hand-printed broadsides newly rendered in digital ink. But we know we're in trouble.

One explanation for our incomprehension is something I've read so many times it's started to seem the kind of repetition born of desperation. We are unable to conceptualise the fact of climate emergency, the argument runs, simply because of the way our brains have evolved. It's our deep evolutionary past that makes us unable to respond. We're hard-wired to not be able to comprehend something so big and all-encompassing. And while it's a relief to be told that it's not our fault, that is not relieving. The reason I think of migraines when I read about the climate emergency is that I have come to suspect that our inaction might work the way my migraines do. What if it is not our evolutionary past that makes us unable to see? What if it has nothing to do with selective pressures in the lives of early humans? What if it's us, right now, experiencing a structural issue that makes it impossible to comprehend symptoms as premonitions? My migraine symptoms are a concatenation of unrelated things that seem to have nothing to do either with each other or with the pain that follows them: beetroot, banana milk, yawning, phonophobia, exhaustion. It's hard to imagine how those things relate, or how they could fit together into a whole. And it's just as hard for us to comprehend that things we have been taught are unrelated to each other, that seem only incidentally connected to the workings of the world – things like agricultural production, food distribution, international trade agreements, global corporate culture, among a thousand others – it's hard for us to comprehend that such things might be causal symptoms of the climate emergency. We've been conditioned by our times not to process some types of problems and solutions because they do not fit with how we've been taught to think about society. We've been led to believe we can make decisions that change the world in the supermarket; that only our individual decisions matter; that to bring about large-scale change we should concern ourselves with the smallest actions: changing light bulbs, eschewing diesel cars and plastic straws. But sometimes it is not you. Sometimes the world is to blame. Defiance and change in process are collective acts, not individual ones. Massive, concerted cultural action is what we need, and that is what we should be hastening to organise.

For many years, a great fatalism would overtake me when I felt the first twinges of an oncoming migraine. I knew that it was too late – whether I took to a darkened room, drank pints of soda water, listened to tapes of whale song, nothing would make any difference at all. All I could do was hunker down and wait for the pain to come that would take away the world. Then, quite recently, I tried taking a migraine drug that works by mimicking the effect of the natural chemical serotonin to selectively constrict migraine-inflamed cranial blood vessels. It can be dangerous to postmenopausal women and people with heart problems, among others, so while it can be bought over the counter here in the UK, you have to fill out a comprehensive questionnaire and discuss your health at length with a pharmacist before you are allowed to buy it.

For so many years I had assumed that my only option was to ride the migraine out, lash myself to the mast and wait for the storm to pass. And that is still an option: some migraines are terrible, but not world-ending, and I'll suffer them because I know that frequent use of the drug will render it less effective. But if the pain ratchets up to breaking point – and I know when that is, when it happens, with absolute certainty – I will swallow a pill and in just over an hour the pain will be gone. The light of the sky will soften again, my eyes will cease watering, the agony will disperse like clouds after a passing weather front. I'll feel foggy and strange for days. But the pain will be gone. The most striking thing about this is that every time I take a dose of the drug I believe it won't work. It seems an absolute impossibility. Yet every time it does. Its action is as close to a miracle as anything I've experienced in my life.

Of course what is happening to our planet is not like what happens to a migraineur's brain. When it's only your own body, you are justified in making your own decisions about how to handle things that impinge upon it. But there are aspects that chime. My migraine mantra was always *that's just how it is* until I realised it need not be. We're already in the early stages of planetary ecological breakdown, the prodrome of catastrophe. Our eschatological traditions tend to envision the apocalypse as happening very fast, with the dawning of one final, single, dreadful day. But the systems of the wider world do not operate according to the temporalities of our human lives; we are already inside the apocalypse, and forest fires and category five hurricanes are as much signs of it as the rising of the beast from the pit.

Apocalyptic thinking is a powerful antagonist to action. It makes us give up agency, feel that all we can do is suffer and wait for the end. That is not what we must be thinking now. For an apocalypse is not always a cataclysmic ending, and not always a disaster. In its earlier senses the word meant a revelation, a vision, an insight, an unveiling of things previously unknown, and I pray that the revelation our current apocalypse can bring is the knowledge that we have the power to intervene. Just as the structures of the migraine-stricken brain can be altered, even if we don't believe it to be true until it happens, so might the structures of a world locked into what feels like an inevitable reliance on fossil fuels and endless economic growth. There are actions we can take that seem impossible and pointless and yet they are entirely, and precisely, and absolutely required. We can exert pressure, we can speak up, we can march and cry and mourn and sing and hope and fight for the world, standing with others, even if we don't believe it. Even if change seems an impossibility. For even if we don't believe in miracles, they are there, and they are waiting for us to find them.

Sex, Death, Mushrooms

It's raining hard and the forest air is sweet and winy with decay. I'm walking with Nick, an old friend and former Ph.D. advisor, emeritus professor of the history of science and amateur mycologist. For the last fifteen years I've accompanied him on autumn mushroom hunts; today we've come to Thetford Forest in Suffolk. We're carrying trugs, traditional English wooden baskets of willow and sweet chestnut, to hold our prizes, perhaps tiny fungi with hair-fine stalks, lumpy shelves broken from the trunks of rotting trees, masses like discarded round pillows, or splayed red starfish arms emerging from the ground.

Hunting for mushrooms can feel surprisingly like hunting animals, particularly if you're looking for edible species. Searching for chanterelles, I've found myself unconsciously walking on tiptoe across mossy stumps as if they might hear me coming. It doesn't work well if you walk around and try to spot them directly. They have an uncanny ability to hide from the searching eye. Instead, you have to alter the way you regard the ground around you, concern yourself with the strange phenomenology of leaf litter and try to give equal attention to all the colours, shapes and angles on the messy forest floor. Once you've achieved this relaxed and faintly predatory gaze, brilliant wax-yellow chanterelles often pop out from behind leaves and twigs and moss, and now they look quite unlike the false chanterelles growing beside them. Nick says that with enough experience, 'you can reliably tell, at least for the commoner species, what the thing is, even if they are enormously variable, and you could not begin to explain how'. He has been an enthusiastic mycologist since his teens and has the names of at least several hundred species committed to memory.

Mushrooms are the fruiting bodies of fungi that live as networks called mycelia, made up of tiny branching threads. Some are parasitic, others feed on decaying matter and many are mycorrhizal, growing in and around plant roots and sharing nutrients with their host. Picking a mushroom doesn't kill the fungus; in a sense, you're merely plucking a flower from a hidden, thready tangle which may be vast and extraordinarily ancient: one honey fungus in Oregon covers almost four square miles and is thought to be nearly two and a half thousand years old.

Soon Nick and I come across scores of mushrooms set in ragged half-circles, their broad tops like cooling milky coffees inexplicably placed among dead leaves. They're cloud caps, a common species here, and considered to be rather toxic. We leave them and walk on. A little while later, Nick spots a yellowish gleam in the long grass. This one is more interesting. He crouches beside it and, frowning, pushes a thumb and index finger underneath the specimen and gently pulls it free of moss and grass. '*Tricholoma*,' he says, with satisfaction. '*Tricholoma sulphureum*.' Mycologists generally use scientific names to describe fungi, as their common names vary widely. The mushroom he holds is sometimes called the sulphur knight or the gas agaric. He offers it to me, gesturing that I should smell it, and an unpleasantly sulphurous tang makes me wrinkle my nose. He stows it in the basket.

I am not very good at identifying fungi, but I am better than I used to be. Over the years I have not only learned to identify a few species by looking at them or smelling them, or seeing the colour their cut surfaces turn, but I've become more and more intrigued by the curious place they occupy in our imaginations. We've been foraging and eating mushrooms for millennia, and they still have the power to disturb us, to conjure the deepest human mysteries of sex and death. Nineteenth-century sensibilities were especially horrified by the common stinkhorn, a fetid fly-attracting species that bursts out of a membranous egg into a shape well described by its scientific name, *Phallus impudicus*. In her later years, Charles Darwin's daughter Henrietta went into the woods to collect stinkhorns for the express purpose of bringing them back to be 'burned in the deepest secrecy of the drawing-room fire, with the door locked; because of the morals of the maids', according to a memoir by her niece. Our continuing pieties about sex are reflected in the way some modern field guides describe the distinctive odour of mushrooms like Inocybes as 'unmentionable' or 'disgusting' rather than the more accurate 'spermatic'.

The unpredictable flowering of beautiful alien forms from rotting wood, dung or leaf litter in a forest moving towards winter is a strong and strange conjuration of life-in-death – in Baltic mythology, mushrooms were thought to be the fingers of the god of the dead bursting through the ground to feed the poor. But mushrooms have a more direct relationship to mortality. Many of them, of course, are deadly. You might survive after eating a destroying angel or death cap, but to do so you'll probably need a liver transplant. What's more, the particular toxicity of fungi is as mysterious as the forms they take. A mushroom can contain more than one kind of toxin, and the toxicity can change according to whether it has been cooked, how it has been cooked, whether it has been eaten with alcohol or fermented before ingestion. Mycologists talk about poisonous fungi the same way herpetologists talk of 'hot' snakes: with more than a modicum of transgressive relish.

If you're collecting fungi to eat, your expertise in identification is all that keeps you from death or serious illness. There's a daredevil side to the activity, a sense of repeatedly staking your life against terrifying possibilities. Today's vogue for wild foods, spurred in part by famous foraging chefs and a nostalgic desire to reconnect with the natural world, has resulted in some popular guides that feature a selection of edible and poisonous species. Nick thinks many of these are irresponsible, even dangerous. 'They don't explain the full range of things you might be running into,' he warns. Many toxic fungi closely resemble edible ones, and differentiating each from each requires careful examination, dogged determination and often the inspection of spores stained and measured under a microscope slide.

Puzzling out tricky specimens is satisfying in itself: if you call on Nick the evening after a fungus expedition, you'll find him at a table spread with fungi, several frighteningly expensive volumes on mycological identification, a microscope and a magnifying lens, and he'll be wearing an expression of joyous, fierce concentration. 'For some species, the colours are unbelievably variable,' he enthuses about one group, the russulas, 'and they get washed out by rain, and then the exact distribution of the warts on their spores is an alternative. So you're doomed, as an ordinary citizen. Because the colours won't do it, and you haven't got a powerful enough microscope.' Fungi force us to consider the limits of our understanding: not everything fits easily into our systems of classification. The world might be, it turns out, too complicated for us to know.

After a couple of hours, the rain is beginning to ease. We're soaked but triumphant. Nick's trug is full of small, difficult and poisonous species. Mine is heaped with edibles, including several crab brittlegills whose shining caps are the colour of toffee apples. We start to make our way back to the car through a dense stand of pines. The air is damp and dark in here. Taut lines of spider silk are slung between their flaking trunks; I can feel them snapping across my chest. Fat garden spiders drop from my coat on to the thick carpet of pine needles below. I'm about to step back on to the path when something catches my eye under a tree a few yards away. I know instantly what it is, though I've only ever seen it in books. 'Cauliflower fungus!' I cry, and run up to it. It's a pale, translucent, fleshy protuberance the size of a soccer ball that seems to glow in the dripping shade, its complicated folds an unnerving cross between boiled tripe and a sea sponge. Looking at it, I remember its Latin name, *Sparassis crispa*, and that it is parasitic on conifers. And also that it is fragrant and delicious when torn and simmered in stock. I sit down on the wet ground to regard it more closely.

We are visual creatures. To us, forests are places made of trees and leaves and soil. But all around me now, invisible and ubiquitous, is a network of fungal life, millions of tiny threads growing and stretching among trees, clustering around piles of rabbit droppings, stitching together bush and path, dead leaves and living roots. We hardly know it is there until we see the fruiting bodies it throws up when conditions are right. But without fungi's ceaseless cycling of water, nutrients and minerals, the forest wouldn't work the way it does, and perhaps the greatest mystery of mushrooms for me is in how they are the visible manifestations of an essential yet unregarded world. I reach forward, break off half the brittle, furled mushroom and place it in the basket, eager to taste this souvenir from a place full of life hidden from our own.

Winter Woods

I try to walk in woods for a few hours before nightfall on every New Year's Day. I've walked them in low sun, deep snow, rain, and in dank mist that clings to the skin and seems more water than air. I've walked blocks of scruffy adolescent pines, ancient lowland forests, beechwoods, farm copses; I've made my way down muddy paths through stands of alder and birch. Sometimes I'm with family or friends. Most often I'm on my own. I'm not sure exactly when my New Year walks began, but over the years they've become as familiar a winter tradition as overcooking the turkey or spending too much money on a Christmas tree.

There's a special phenomenology to walking in woods in winter. On windless days there's a deep, soft hush that makes the sound of a stick breaking underfoot resemble a pistol shot. It's a quietness that fosters an acute sensitivity to small sounds that earlier in the year would be buried under a riot of birdsong. The rustle of a vole in dead bracken at my feet, the dry scratches of a blackbird turning over dead leaves in search of spiders. Now the trees are leafless, wildlife is more visible, but so am I. I'm often met by the alarm calls of jays, nuthatches, robins, grey squirrels, harsh noises designed to inform me that they know I am there. Being sworn at by woodland creatures is disquieting, but comforting too. Modern cultures of nature appreciation so often assume the natural world is something to watch and observe merely, as if through thick plate glass. These alarm calls remind me that we have consequential presence, that the animals we like to watch are creatures with their own needs, desires, emotions, lives.

A winter wood reveals the bones of the landscape it grows upon, the geographical contours of slopes, gullies and hollows. Its trees become exercises in pattern recognition, each species possessing its own texture of bark, its own angles and arrangements of branches and twigs. After the leaves have fallen, winter lets light and weather into the wood, and trunks newly exposed to sunlight turn green with algae as winter days lengthen towards spring.

Because life is less obvious in a winter wood, where it does subsist, as bright stars of moss, or fungal fruiting bodies enduring winter frosts with antifreeze-packed cells, it demands attention. One year a cloud of winter flies in a patch of weak sun in the middle of a woodland ride held me spellbound for long moments, intensely aware of their fragility, their momentary purchase on this world. And the lack of obvious life in winter reminds me of the limits of my own human perception. Most of the life here is too small for me to see or exists underground. Beneath my feet, an intricate network of mycorrhizal fungal threads links plant roots to each other and the soil. They not only grant trees access to crucial nutrients, but give them a means of communication.

It's easy for us to think of trees as immutable, venerable presences against which we can measure the span of our own lives, our own small histories. But trees grow, leaves fall, winters grip the ground. That woods are places of process and constant change was something that took a long time for me to understand. As a child I assumed that the woods near my home would stay the same for ever. Today, many of the paths I used to walk are blocked with thickets of birch trees, though my memories of those routes live on.

Summer forests give me little sense of time past, or times to come; they're rich with a buzzing, glittering, shifting profusion of life. Everything seems manifested; there's no obvious sense of potentiality. But forests in winter do the opposite: they evoke the passage of time. Winter days are always moving fast towards darkness, and when the wind is bitter it's not easy to walk without thinking of what it will be like to be back in the warmth of home. Above and around me are last year's birds' nests, built to hold broods long fledged, along with signs of life usually obscured by dense growths of summer vegetation: woodpecker nest-holes, deer-nibbled saplings, fox earths, tufts of badger hair on low thorns. And while my feet are treading on last year's leaves, those of next spring are already furled in buds on the tips of twigs around and above me.

After a light covering of snow, the prints of woodland mammals and birds can be read to rewind time. Pheasant tracks end with an imprint of wings, each indented primary feather furred with frost, recording the moment the bird took off from the ground the previous evening to fly to roost. In a Wiltshire wood that seemed utterly devoid of animal life, I once followed the prints of a brown hare right across the snow to a pool of dark water, saw the place where it drank, and, from the spacing of the prints of each padded foot, saw how fast or slow it had travelled on its way.

So often we think of mindfulness, of existing purely in the present moment, as a spiritual goal. But winter woods teach me something else: the importance of thinking about history. They are able to show you the last five hours, the last five days, the last five centuries, all at once. They're wood and soil and rotting leaves, the crystal fur of hoarfrost and the melting of overnight snow, but they are also places of different interpolated timeframes. In them, potentiality crackles in the winter air.

Eclipse

Long ago, when I first decided I wanted to see a total solar eclipse, I planned to do so in romantic solitude. I was in my early twenties, was inclined to think myself the centre of the universe, and imagined the eclipse to be an event in which the sun and moon – and me – would line up to provoke some deep and abiding revelation. The presence of other people would detract from the meaningfulness of it all, I thought, convinced that the best way to experience the natural world was to seek private communion with it. It's embarrassing to recall this conviction now, because as soon as I saw my first solar eclipse I knew that the last thing I needed was to be alone as it happened.

Witnessing a total eclipse wreaks havoc on your sense of self, on rational individuality. Nineteenth-century scientists on eclipse-viewing expeditions saw them as a test of self-control. They were beset by anxiety that they might fail to maintain their objectivity in the face of the overwhelming emotions totality would bring. In the event, as the historian Alex Soojung-Kim Pang has described, their hands shook so much that many could barely record their data, and one observer was so overwhelmed by the 1871 eclipse in India he was forced to retreat to his room and plunge his head into water. Charles Piazzi Smyth, the Edinburgh Astronomer Royal, wrote in surprise that during the eclipse of 1851 it was not just the 'volatile Frenchman' who was 'carried away in the impulses of the moment' but also the 'staid Englishman' and the 'stolid German'. National stereotypes aside, his concerns point to the exquisite contradiction of solar eclipses. While their paths and timings can be predicted with astonishing mathematical accuracy, their action is always to instill the very opposite of empirical description and objective science: they provoke a flood of primal awe.

Before my first eclipse I'd always been nervous of crowds. It's not just because I'm an introvert. Growing up watching television in Britain in the 1970s and '80s was a primer in their dangers. Political demonstrations, rock festivals, riots: all were to be feared for the same reason nineteenth-century scientists feared eclipses. That is, they made you forget yourself. Dissolving all individual rationality and restraint, coursing with uncontrollable instinct and emotion, this conception of crowds as irrational and contagiously violent entities was the legacy of European theorists like Gustave Le Bon, whose own views had been shaped by the political turmoil of late-nineteenth-century France. To him, crowds were barbarous agents of destruction. All this social history fed into the nervousness I already felt about being in groups of people. I used to spend a lot of time out on my own in woods and fields mostly because I wanted to watch wild animals, which are hard to sneak up on if you're part of a crowd. But there were more troubling reasons behind my desire to be alone. It's reassuring to view the world on your own. You can gaze at a landscape and see it peopled by things – trees, clouds, hills and valleys – which have no voice except the ones you give them in your imagination; none can challenge who you are. So often we see solitary contemplation as simply the correct way to engage with nature. But it is always a political act, bringing freedom from the pressures of other minds, other interpretations, other consciousnesses competing with your own.

There's another way of escaping social conflict, of course, and that is to make yourself part of a crowd that sees the world the same way that you do, values the same things as you. We're familiar with the notion that America is a land of rugged individualists, but it turns out that it has a long tradition of sociability when it comes to seeking out the sublime. As the historian David Nye has argued, groups of tourists who travelled to natural sites like the Grand Canyon or to witness awe-inspiring events like space-program launches were engaged in a distinctly American kind of pilgrimage. Their experience of the sublime supported the idea of American exceptionalism, with marvelling crowds newly assured of the singular grandeur and importance of their nation. But the millions of tourists who flocked to the total eclipse of 2017 didn't see something time had fashioned from American rock and earth, nor something wrought of American ingenuity, but a passing shadow cast across the nation from celestial bodies above. Even so, it's fitting that this total eclipse was dubbed The Great American Eclipse, for the event chimed with the country's contemporary struggles between matters of reason and unreason, individuality and crowd consciousness, belonging and difference. Of all crowds the most troubling are those whose cohesion is built from fear of and outrage against otherness and difference; they're entities defining themselves by virtue only of what they are against. The simple fact about an eclipse crowd is that it cannot work in this way, for confronting something like the absolute, all our differences are moot. When you stand and watch the death of the sun and see it reborn there can be no them, only us.

In 1999 my father and I walked on to a packed beach in Cornwall to witness the first total eclipse to cross the UK in over seventy years. We found ourselves standing between milling tour guides, eclipse-chasers, schoolchildren, camera crews, teenagers waving glowsticks, New Age travellers and folks in fancy dress. It was my first-ever eclipse. I was nervous of the people around me and still clinging to that sophomoric intuition that a revelation would only come if none of them were there. Depressingly, the sky was thick with clouds, and as the hours passed it became obvious that none of us would see anything other than darkness when totality came. But when the light dimmed, the atmosphere grew electric, and the crowd became a thing of overwhelming importance, a palpable presence in my mind. I felt a fleeting, urgent concern for the safety of everyone around me as the world rolled, and the moon too, and night slammed down on us. Though I could hardly see a hand held in front of my face, far out across the sea hung clouds tinted the eerie sunset shade of faded photographs of 1950s atomic tests, and beyond them clear blue day.

And then the revelation came. It wasn't what I'd expected. It wasn't focused up there in the sky, but down here with us all, as the crowds that lined the Atlantic shore raised cameras to commemorate totality, and as they flashed, a wave of particulate light crashed along the dark beach and flooded across to the other side of the bay, making the whole coast a glittering field of stars. Each fugitive point of light was a different person. I laughed out loud. I'd wanted a solitary revelation but had been given something else instead: an overwhelming sense of community, and of what it is made – a host of individual lights shining briefly against oncoming darkness.

The experience of viewing an eclipse in a cloudy sky is not anything like seeing one in the clear. Seven years after the Cornwall eclipse, that is what I witnessed, and it is an event that still lives in the part of me where everything is in the present tense, as if it is still happening, as if it will never stop happening.

I travel with friends to see it, to a ruined city called Side on the Turkish coast. On the allotted day we find a place to stand amid drifts of sand and bushes of flowering sweet bay, in the branches of which flit scores of plump warblers snatching leggy, winged insects from their leaves and sticky flowers. Spectacled bulbuls sing. There is life everywhere. And slowly, over the course of an hour, the moon will move in front of the sun and eventually cover its face.

There are four of us. Three men in sneakers and T-shirts who are experts in maths and coding, and a woman wearing a straw hat and carrying a pair of binoculars who can barely add up a list of simple figures without making an elementary error. That's me. As we pace about our small wilderness of wrecked stone and scrub I look left to where dunes have made inroads into the ruined city, heaped high upon half-buried walls. Behind them, the desert is running with sleek lizards and crested larks, pale sands crossed with myriad painted tortoise tracks. I watch the birds, idly, as we stand and wait, our little pack of people on a dune-top. Similar groups of people are everywhere, some focusing telescopes on to flat white paper to show first contact, the moment where a tiniest scoop of darkness eats into one side of the sun. It takes a long while between first and second contact – that is, when the sun is completely covered by the moon; it's a long, steady diminution in the amount of light reaching the world. For a long while my brain tricks me. It has a vested interest in reassurance: *Nothing is wrong*, it says. It tells me I must be wearing reactive sunglasses, which is why I'm seeing the world changing through tinted glass. Why everything, the luggage-strap leaves of dune grass under my toes, the broken walls, bay trees, the sea in front, the mountains behind, everything's still darkly fine. Then I remember I'm not wearing sunglasses, which hits me with the bad-dream force of an arm brought down hard across a piano keyboard, the psychological equivalent of that discordant crash as I have a fraught little struggle with my brain. Then I shiver. Surely it was absurdly hot here an hour ago? There's a horrible old chestnut about boiling a frog to death. Put a frog in a pan of cold water and put it on the stove, and apparently the blithe amphibian will fail to notice the incremental rise in temperature until it's dead. There's something of that story's creeping dread in what is now going on. I feel a strong need to warn people, to somehow jump out of the pan. Everything is changing, but our brains aren't equipped to notice things on this scale. My eyes dance over the landscape in an automatic, anxious search for familiarity. Lots of things are familiar. Groups of people. Bushes. Sea. Walls. But though their shapes are reassuring, the content isn't. For everything is the wrong colour, the wrong hue.

Remember those day-for-night filters they used to use filming old westerns? Watching afternoon matinees on television as a child, I assumed that night-time in America was different to night-time in England. Much later I realised it was always day, stopped down and filmed through a blue filter. So: imagine you're watching a night scene in a Technicolor western. Maybe Gary Cooper is hiding behind a crag, rifle in hand. Doesn't that night look strange? Now imagine the same footage with an orange, rather than a blue cast. Everything around me is washed heavy, damp and alien. The sand is dark orange, as it might be at sundown, but the sun is high in the sky. We're all mesmerised by the refracted point-source glitter from the sea in front of us. I don't have any grasp on the physics, but the white brilliance playing on the dark Mediterranean feels somehow far too sharp. And on the ground, right by our feet, even stranger things are happening. Where I expect to see sun-dappled shadow cast on the sand through branches – as confidently as I expect any other unacknowledged constant of the world – I am confounded: amid the shade are a perfect host of tiny crescents, hundreds of them, all moving against the sand as a wind that has come out of nowhere pushes at branches.

The backs of the swallows tracing their sinuous hunting flights over the ruins are no longer iridescent blue in the sun, but a deep indigo. They're calling in alarm. A sparrowhawk is flying over, slipping down the sky, losing height, stymied in its search for thermals to soar upon. They're all disappearing in the rapidly cooling air. The hawk shrugs its way north-west, falling all the while. I check the sun, again, through my eclipse glasses. All that is left of it now is a bare, fingernail curve of light. The landscape is insistently alien: short, midday shadows in a saturated world. The land is orange. The sea is purple. Venus has appeared in the sky, quite high, up to the right. And then, with a chorus of cheers and whistles and applause, I stare at the sky as the sun slides away, and the day does too, and impossibly, impossibly, above us is a stretch of black, soft black sky and a hole in the middle of it. A round hole, darker than anything you've ever seen, fringed with an intensely soft ring of white fire. Applause crackles and ripples across the dunes. My throat is stopped. My eyes fill with tears. Goodbye, intellectual apprehension. Hello, something else entirely. Totality is so incomprehensible for your mental machinery that your physical response becomes hugely apparent. Your intellect cannot grasp any of this. Not the dark, nor the sunset clouds on every horizon, nor the stars, just that extraordinary wrongness, up there, that pulls the eyes towards it. The exhilaration is barely contained terror. I'm tiny and huge all at once, as lonely and singular as I've ever felt, and as merged and part of a crowd as it is possible to be. It is a shared, intensely private experience. But there are no human words fit to express all this. Opposites? Yes! Let's conjure big binary oppositions and grand narratives, break everything and mend it at the same moment. Sun and moon. Darkness and light. Sea and land, breath and no breath, life, death. A total eclipse makes history laughable, makes you feel both precious and disposable, makes the inclinations of the world incomprehensible, like someone trying to engage a stone in discussions about the price of a celebrity magazine.

I'm dizzy. My skin crawls. Everything's fallen away. There's a hole in the sky where the sun should be. I sink to the ground and stare up at the hole in the sky and the dead world about me is a perfect vision – with its ruins and broken columns – of the underworld of my childhood imagination, straight out of *Tales of the Greek Heroes* by Roger Lancelyn Green. And then something else happens, a thing that still makes my heart rise in my chest and eyes blur, even in recollection. For it turns out there's something even more affecting than watching the sun disappear into a hole. Watching the sun climb out of it. Here I am, sitting on the beach in the underworld, with all of the standing dead. It is cold, and a loose wind blows through the darkness. But then, from the lower edge of the blank, black disc of the dead sun, bursts a perfect point of brilliance. It leaps and burns. It's unthinkably fierce, unbearably bright, something (I blush to say it, but here it comes) like a word. And thus begins the world again. Instantly. Joy, relief, gratitude; an avalanche of emotion. Is all made to rights, now? Is all remade? From a bay tree, struck into existence a moment ago, a spectacled bulbul calls a greeting to the new dawn.

In Her Orbit

Nathalie Cabrol was five years old when she watched the first moon landing on television. She pointed at Neil Armstrong in a snowy haze of transmission and lunar dust and told her mother that this, *this*, was what she wanted to do. Even before then she used to stare up at the stars in the night sky from her home in the Paris suburbs and knew questions were up there waiting for her.

Cabrol is an explorer, an astrobiologist and a planetary geologist specialising in Mars. She is the director of the Carl Sagan Center at the SETI Institute, the nonprofit organisation based in Mountain View, California, that seeks to explore, understand and explain the origin of life in the universe. Its work has the glamour of science fiction, but it involves rigorous research and, as Cabrol told me, 'people who are passionate enough that they can put themselves into dire straits'. That is what she does, travelling to some of the world's most extreme and dangerous environments in search of organisms that live in conditions analogous to those on Mars. Cabrol was the chief scientist on a team testing an experimental rover in the Atacama Desert in 2002 and was instrumental in choosing the landing site on Mars for Spirit, the rover that explored the planet from 2004 to 2010; she has dived in volcanic lakes at high altitudes to study the creatures within, and designed and installed an autonomous floating robot on an Andean lake standing in for lakes on Titan, one of Saturn's moons.

I met Cabrol on an October morning in Antofagasta, a port city of oxide-coloured high-rises and copper sculptures that sprawls between dry hills and the dark waters of the Pacific. I'd travelled to Chile to join her team for an expedition to high-altitude desert to test methods of detecting life on Mars. I'd flown from London to Madrid, and then to São Paolo, and then on to Antofagasta. I had brought a sleeping bag, altitude-sickness pills and a considerable amount of anxiety about the conditions we'd meet ahead.

Petite and slight, with short-cropped silver hair and a striking, finely carved handsomeness, Cabrol, who is fifty-four, resembles Isabella Rossellini with an otherworldly dash of David Bowie. Her eyes shine like grey-green polished granite, always emphatically outlined with eyeliner even when she is deep in the desert. She's charismatic, warm and extremely funny but possesses an indefinable, unpredictable wildness: talking to her sometimes disconcertingly reminded me of encounters I have had with forest animals uncertain whether to flee or defend themselves. That first bright morning in Antofagasta, watching her break into peals of smoky laughter as she held up a SETI Institute flag for the camera, I realised I liked her very much.

Over the past few decades the search for life beyond Earth has entered a new phase. Some models have suggested that perhaps a hundred million planets in the Milky Way might hold complex multicellular life. We have learned too that planets need not closely resemble Earth to potentially harbour life; subsurface oceans on distant moons like Saturn's Enceladus and Titan, for instance, could support microbial organisms. The universe, Cabrol told me, is probably full of such simple life, and the purpose of this expedition would be to refine methods of finding it – of detecting biosignatures. These are signs of life, or lives once lived: organisms, or the structures they have made, even the chemical compounds they have produced.

Over the next few weeks, we would visit five sites at varying altitudes. The higher we climbed, the further we'd go back in time – not on Earth, but on Mars. The high-altitude sites are water-rich, with a thin atmosphere and high levels of UV radiation. They resemble Mars at the beginning of the transition it underwent three and a half billion years ago, when solar winds began to strip away its atmosphere, allowing cosmic rays to reach its surface, and the water that once flowed there vanished into space or was locked deep underground or at the planet's poles. During this period, any life on the surface would have died or taken refuge in the same kinds of places in which life exists in inhospitable regions like the Atacama. The surface of Mars is exposed to harmful radiation; no life can survive on it today, Cabrol told me, but it might still be hiding underground. The salty, arid sites we visited first were terrestrial analogues for present-day Mars.

For Cabrol, there is much more in the search for life on Mars than answering the old question, 'Are we alone?' Billions of years ago, rocks thrown off by comets and asteroids colliding with Earth reached Mars, and vice versa. Perhaps some carried early life. Finding evidence of the transition from prebiotic chemistry to life here on Earth is impossible, because any such records were long ago destroyed by the Earth's rapid geological activity, by erosion and plate tectonics. But ancient rocks from the time Mars's crust cooled down are still present on that planet's surface; if we share our ancestry with Mars, traces of our own life might still be found there. 'Mars may hold that secret for us,' Cabrol says. 'This is why Mars is so special to us.'

It's October 2016, and Cabrol is in her second year of leading the SETI Institute team on a biosignature-detection expedition to Chile. A stiff Pacific breeze blows dead mimosa blossoms across the pavement as I climb inside a minibus to join them on the long drive to our first field site, where the team had scheduled three days of sampling and working on the problems of how best to find signs of life. Through the blue-tinted windows, the soft yellows and buff oxides of weathered rock and sand are turned a dusty, livid red. Fredrik Rehnmark, a mechanical engineer from Honeybee Robotics, is fizzing with delight. 'If they built a road on Mars, it would look like this!' he exclaims.

We drive north, passing pale rocks arranged into the patterns of names and initials on hillsides. Almost nothing moves in this desert. There are places here that haven't much changed in five million years. Those names written in stone are a kind of biosignature that will outlive not just the people who set them there but all of us and all we know.

Salt begins to spread along the edges of the sandy road as we turn inland. Time drifts. Everything outside the windows is so featureless it seems like a theatrical backdrop. At the site, we set up tents on the shores of Salar Grande, a nine-mile-long salt flat that was a lake millions of years ago. There are flats similar to this on Mars.

The salty air makes my face twitch and burn; I blink constantly. The hyper-arid core of the Atacama is far to the east; here, fog rolls in from the Pacific and has shaped the landscape around us. Close up, the salt flat is composed of broad polygonal plates whose edges are heaped with something that looks like half-melted lemon sorbet, or the dirty, refrozen snow that collects along the roadside in winter. Other salt nodules are heaped in piles like dry and dirty bones, and the ground behind our tents is littered with the detritus of long-abandoned salt-mining operations: boots, open sardine cans, scraps of newsprint, corroded lumps of metal.

Drills echo in the morning air. The engineers from Honeybee are excavating salt cores to test prototype tools for future rovers. A team from the University of Tennessee deploys a drone to map the terrain, a tiny dark star that sounds like a distant nest of wasps. The SETI Institute research scientist Pablo Sobron is analysing salt samples with a laser spectrometer; one will be a feature on future rovers. And students from the Catholic University of the North in Antofagasta are out collecting salt nodules for microbiological lab analysis with the SETI Institute and NASA scientists Kim Warren-Rhodes and Alfonso Davila.

Cabrol picks up a chunk of salt and holds it to the light. 'Look,' she says. Inside the nodule are two bright bands of colour: pink on top, green below. These are communities of halophilic – salt-loving – microbes that can survive this extreme environment only by living inside translucent nodules. The green bacteria photosynthesise nutrients from the light filtering through the pink colony above. The pink pigment works as a sunscreen, protecting both colonies from UV radiation that would otherwise damage their DNA.

I'm humbled. I've been walking on these nodules all day, and I hadn't seen the life beneath my feet. 'Habitability is not something very obvious,' Cabrol says to me. 'It can be hidden.' I look at her slight figure, the salt dusting her gloved fingertips, the faintly mischievous smile on her face, and then stare out at the vastness of the landscape around us. It's dizzying to think of the scales her work spans: millions of miles of space, billions of years of planetary evolution, the vastness of the universe, the canyons and valleys of Mars, the expanse of salt here, our small forms standing upon it, and these exquisitely tough, tiny, almost invisible signs of life held between finger and thumb.

An only child, Cabrol spent a lot of time alone in her family's small apartment while her parents worked, and in her solitude she created an imaginative, hermetic world of her own to live in, filling her hours with words and symbols and numbers, writing stories and tracing lines upon atlases. She told me that as a child she had a talent for connecting things that were not obvious to others. She believes that this is still one of her greatest strengths as a scientist. But even as she started to apprehend the vastness of space, her social world remained circumscribed. 'For a long time,' she said, 'I thought that I could do without interacting with others. I didn't have many friends at all, and I didn't look for them. I had enough. I was busy enough in my mind.' Her parents saved to buy her astronomy books and magazines. Her mother understood her passion. Her father was less certain. 'For him, that was a phase, you know?' she said wryly. 'That was a phase that lasted a long time!'

Cabrol's teenage years were troubled. Things were difficult at home, where her parents were fighting; she didn't fit in and was bullied at school. Some of her schoolteachers thought she lived in a fantasy world. Although she wanted to study planetary sciences, she studied the humanities, for until she taught it to herself later in her career, maths was not her forte.

Cabrol was taking earth sciences in her final year at Paris Nanterre University when her lab director suggested that she visit the historic Meudon Observatory south of Paris to meet Professor André Cailleux, a pioneer in planetary geology. Cailleux showed her maps of Mars and explained that his colleagues were working on the history of water on the planet. Would she be interested in joining them? 'All these years I thought I was going 180 degrees from where I needed to go, but the path was taking me exactly where I needed to be,' she told me. Stepping out from that first meeting, she gazed around at the observatory domes and felt them strangely familiar. 'All these domes I had been drawing as a little girl, always repeating the same landscape, the planetary landscape, of a planet that was completely desert. And with Saturn in the background, always a dark sky and domes.' At Meudon, she had finally found a way to get nearer to Mars.

During the day she worked on her master's degree on the evolution of water-carved valleys on Mars, but she spent her nights looking through Meudon's famous nineteenth-century telescope, the Grande Lunette, dragging a sleeping bag there to rest between hours of observing. Through the eyepiece, there was Mars. It was small, and at first she couldn't see much, but the more she looked, the more she saw on the dusky, changing face of the planet that would become a focus of her career, a planet whose gullies and dried lakes have become as familiar to her as the backs of her hands. And it was at Meudon too that she had a moment which left an indelible mark. Professor Audouin Dollfus, the eminent astronomer who had discovered Saturn's satellite Janus, asked her if she would like to see moon dust. 'Duh! Do I want to see lunar dust?!'

He produced a small container from a safe, and Cabrol looked at it and was disappointed. 'I had a feeling like: *So? That's it?*' she told me. Politely enthusiastic but secretly unmoved, she left the lab to go home, but when she looked up and saw the moon hanging bright over Paris, she was stricken with awe. 'All of a sudden this moon dust that looked like nothing looked like the most precious thing ever,' she said. 'Because it is not so much what it is but the journey it took to get here.' It was a revelation. 'I don't think that anything I saw through an eyepiece told me the same thing: the journey it took, the spirit of exploration, the danger of exploration, the things you have to accept, that there is a sacrifice, and the sacrifice might be your own life.'

Exploration lights her imagination. 'I breathe it, imagine it every day of my life, and I dream about it at night,' she wrote recently in a private manuscript. She told me of a childhood memory: her father carefully opening prickly sweet chestnut cases for her to uncover the glossy, marbled nuts inside. She was entranced. Early moments like this planted the desire for discovery inside her, an urge to find again the wonder of seeing hidden things brought to light.

While working on the question of how flowing water formed lakes on Mars for her Ph.D. at the Sorbonne, Cabrol met Edmond Grin, an eminent retired hydrogeologist who had gone back to earn a Ph.D. in astrophysics. 'This is his thing,' she told me. 'When he has nothing to do, he plays with Einstein's equations.' She was twenty-three and he was sixty-six when she first saw him talking to a professor before her class began. 'For some reason,' she said, 'I could not look in any other direction. I was stuck. I was looking at him, and at that time in my brain, that was like: *I know this man. I know this person. From where do I know him?*' He sat near her in the class, they looked at each other and: 'That was it – it took us, you know?' she said. 'I cannot explain, but I was waiting for him to show up.'

In the years that followed, Grin helped focus her work and her research methodology and was a transformative presence in deeper ways. 'He did a magical act on me,' she told me. 'From being an introvert writing those codes and symbols and novels and papers, it's like he took a glove and turned it inside out, and all of a sudden everything that was inside came out.'

When Cabrol travelled to NASA's Ames Research Center in Silicon Valley in 1994 to work on a landing-site study for a proposed mission to search for life on Mars, Grin went with her. All they took with them was one suitcase, and inside it was a map of the 100-mile-wide Gusev Crater on Mars, made of taped-together photocopied images from the Viking mission, the unmanned spacecraft that surveyed and landed on the planet in the 1970s. 'The two of us had to take a very big leap of faith,' she said. More than thirty years after their first meeting, they are still together, still inseparable, now married. In 2010, they edited *Lakes on Mars*, the first academic book on the subject. Cabrol calls him Merlin, after the magician. He has grown frail now, and this is the first time Cabrol has been to the Atacama without him. That he had to stay behind is a source of deepest sadness for her, something that I realise only later in the expedition, when she leaves the group at a lookout near San Pedro de Atacama to walk down an incline and gaze at the pyramidal, distant slopes of Licancabur, a volcano they once climbed together. She tilts her head to one side and doesn't move for a long time. She looks small and terribly alone.

We move south, up on to the Altiplano, the second-largest plateau on Earth, where the landscape has an astonishing luminosity; it glows like a scene painted on fine bone china. It's wetter, too; there are golden grasses on the hillsides. When Cabrol first came to this place and saw the snow-capped Andes, it was a shock. She felt, she told me, as if she were back somewhere she belonged. There was a connection, just as when she first saw the Atacama Desert through a live feed from an experimental rover, its arid landscape projected on to a screen in a science-operation room. Even with that distance, that robotic mediation, she said, 'the love story started', and 'there was something that I knew was drawing me to this place'.

She has a similar affinity with the Gusev Crater, into which water may once have poured from the immense canyon of Ma'adim Vallis. She and Grin studied it and chose it as a landing site for the Spirit rover. 'I had the same feeling when I first saw Gusev from the surface. I was the first person on the planet to see a new landscape. And you don't get over this. You cannot. I will die with these images. It's in me for ever.'

On one of our long expedition drives, Cabrol stares out of the window, shoulders tensed with what I realise is happy anticipation only when we crest a rise and see the first dark peaks of volcanoes before us. She turns to us all with a blazing smile and announces, 'I'm home.'

At first, Salar de Pajonales is a distant patch of white between dark volcanic slopes, but as we meet it and drive through its broad expanse of gypsum sands, sunlight flashes across thousands of crystalline flakes, ephemeral points of fierce white light. The salts here are chemically different from those at Salar Grande. Cabrol visited the site briefly five years ago and is thrilled to return and discover what it held. Underfoot, the ground crunches and tinkles; it's like treading on sugar mixed with broken glass. Huge bosses of gypsum are dotted around us, round structures like crumbling coral, the colour of milk chocolate. Fascinated, I pull out the sun-rotted blades closest to their surface with my hands, as if extracting teeth.

Life is less easy to locate here. Only when Bill Diamond, the SETI Institute's chief executive, kicks a rock do we find a broken chunk colonised by those familiar microbes in shades of pink and green. Her face half obscured by mirrored glasses and a scarf, Cabrol tenderly uncovers the fossilised imprints of ancient bacterial colonies called stromatolites. They look like pitted fragile cups, chalky fingerprint impressions. Samples are photographed, noted, bagged to be sent on to the lab. Overhead, the drone starts mapping this terrain, struggling in the wind.

That afternoon, I hop in a truck with a biologist and a biochemist from the Catholic University of the North who want to take bacterial samples from a nearby lake. Its turquoise waters are surrounded with pale gypsum blades like thickets of kitchen knives. It is too surreal; I return to the truck feeling unaccountably blinded, though I can see. It is as if a white light is shining behind my eyes. My nose runs; my sinuses ache. The things I write in my notebook have become increasingly bizarre. I scrawl *questions asked in glass* across a whole page, an uncanny aide-memoire for something I never remember. As we drive back to the main study site, I see Cabrol in the distance, a slight shadow moving slowly across the pale fire of sunbaked gypsum, something strangely like a mirage of a person.

That night we sleep in an abandoned mining camp. In the early hours, in the rat-dropping-dusted particleboard and corrugated-iron shack we are using in lieu of tents, I lie in increasingly irritated denial until I drag myself out of my sleeping bag to pee. It is minus 0.4 degrees outside. Above me, the Southern Hemisphere stars are all dust and terror and distance and slow fire in the night, and I stare up, frozen, and frozen in wonderment.

Then we climb higher still, to volcanic sites that resemble formations found on Mars, so high that there isn't enough oxygen for the engine of our minibus. It stalls halfway to our destination. We make a U-turn, return to Antofagasta and rent a new minibus. This also stalls. When we finally reach the geyser field of El Tatio, it is deserted. At about fourteen thousand feet, it is one of the highest active geothermal sites in the world. Tourists flock here at dawn, when the freezing air turns the locale into columns of roiling steam. Some geysers are low to the ground and hardly visible, just a faint shimmering of warm air above them; others look like tall berms of clay pouring out thick gouts of steam. This kind of volcanic, fumarolic environment would have been present four billion years ago on Mars, and old hydrothermal environments like it are one of the most likely habitats to hold life, or the remains of former life, on the planet.

Cabrol dons her red-and-black rucksack, black fleece hat and mirrored glasses, picks up a geologic hammer and starts hacking at an inactive geyser. The surface looks devoid of life, but soon she is delighted to discover bright emerald colonies of chasmoliths – microbes that live in cracks and fissures – thriving on the underside of lumps of geyserite. The hot springs here are full of algal mats and organisms which have evolved to live in water that is almost boiling; they glow purple and dark pink in the sun, their colours protection against UV rays.

Cabrol has always been drawn to both volcanoes and lakes, to fire and water. They're completely opposite, she says, 'but if they work synergistically together, they create steam, which is a source of energy. And then you can produce power. And you create things with that. But if the water goes on the fire, then you have destruction. And my entire life is just trying to find this balance between creation and destruction. For the things that I create and the things that are eating me inside. And it's a very fine balance.' There is a pattern in her life, she tells me, where the highest of highs are swiftly followed by the lowest of lows. She speaks to me of the deaths of her mentors, friends and family members, of times she came close to death, of times when she struggled with inner darkness. 'What people see in me is the successful woman, the leader, but all of this is built on sweat and work and temper, you know? It's losses, tragedy, death and tears. I guess you cannot be strong if you never have been hurt and learn how to survive that.' As she tells me this, she looks bone-tired. It is the third week of our expedition, and she is sleeping badly, two or so hours a night, she says. And the altitude medicine she is taking is making her sick.

Cabrol's search for life in extreme conditions began in the Atacama but took a turn in 2000, after she watched a French television documentary that showed the crater lake atop Licancabur on the Bolivian Altiplano. There it was, onscreen, the perfect place to search for extremophile life adapted to the punishing conditions of high-altitude lakes. She wrote a research proposal and three years later donned a black wetsuit with a weighted belt and free-dived into the lake at an altitude of nearly twenty thousand feet, discovering zooplankton species new to science.

'Water is my thing,' Cabrol tells me. 'I feel comfortable. I feel at peace.' On a family vacation when she was two years old, she wore water wings to float on the surface of Lake Garda in Italy. She clambered onshore, took off the wings and went back to the water. 'I am thinking to myself that if I go underwater, I cannot sink,' she laughs. Submerged, she swam instinctively in a new world of shining pebbles and vivid colours. She learned to free-dive as a teenager in Cap d'Agde in the South of France. 'It was always beautiful and peaceful; there was no stress,' she says. 'There was this sense of being responsible for myself, of being in charge and seeing beautiful things, and exploration and discovery.' We are talking in her tent, and the silence between her words is filled with the crack and ripple of nylon stock, the sides of the tent inhaling and exhaling in the wind, the floor billowing up around our planted feet.

'When I entered that lake,' she went on, 'I was thinking I was entering the past, actually entering a time machine that was telling me what Mars was like four billion years ago. It's really a place where time and space get warped.' Diving in these high lakes provokes emotional states, she says, that are intensely beautiful and spiritual. There was one time, in 2006, when she was suspended in the middle of the volcanic lake, caught midway between earth and sky, the water arctic blue and each ray of sunlight diffracting around her, so that she felt surrounded by diamonds. 'And on top of that,' she says, 'copepods, little zooplankton, tiny shrimps, and they are so red. It's a symphony of colour. I'm suspended like that, and time stands still. And for one fraction of a second, everything is perfect. I don't need to have to explain anything. For that very moment, you understand everything. And there is nothing to understand.' Then she remembered she was on a not-so-dormant volcano. 'I thought, *I have a suit and forty-five minutes of oxygen*,' she says and shakes her head. 'My last thought would have been so serene and so peaceful.'

As we take the trucks in a convoy up to our final site, I look back on the Atacama and think of the Apollo astronauts. Far behind and below us is a haze-softened blue expanse streaked with clouds, making this climb feel like a journey away from Earth. We are among volcanoes now, vast blisters on the plateau. Cabrol points out Simba, which the group plans to climb to sample the bacteria in its crater lake. Cabrol has a history with Simba. She was climbing it with her team in 2007 when the Tocopilla earthquake hit. They avoided the avalanches, but when Lascar, the volcano sharing a slope with Simba, began to emit poisonous gases, Cabrol fell into what she called a 'surgically cold' mindset, concerned only with logic, practicality, survival. During their descent, a large tumbling rock just missed her. 'And this,' she said, 'was when I got mad.' She stood up in the middle of the gully and started yelling at the volcano. '"Is it going to be all today?! Is there anything yet you can?!" I was shouting! I was outraged!' She got everyone down safely and then nearly passed out in the truck back to base camp – partly from an adrenalin crash, partly from the knowledge that everyone might have died.

We camp under an extinct volcano in an abandoned military barracks that the team calls Chilifornia. The cinder-block rectangle has no roof, but the walls shelter our tents from the wind. Cabrol gathers us together and warns us not to go wandering. In the 1970s, this territory was disputed with neighbouring Bolivia, and there are still landmines here. It's a worry. I grow even more anxious when I overhear Cabrol and Cristian Tambley, who is handling logistics for the expedition, talking about installing UV-monitoring systems in this region. Strong UV radiation damages DNA, and the World Health Organization warns against being outside when the UV index is over eleven. In 2003 and 2004, Cabrol observed unexplained UV storms here of extraordinary intensity, though they lasted only a few hours. On Licancabur, she detected UV spikes of over forty-three. That night I dream of wearing a spacesuit.

It takes an hour to drive to Laguna Lejía the next morning, a copper-coloured lake shivering in the hard light of the sun. Cabrol is visibly shocked as we arrive. 'It's substantially reduced in size compared with when I last saw it, in 2009,' she says. 'Our planet is actually changing in front of our eyes,' she tells me later, 'at a speed that is extremely scary.' We are heading along what was once a drove route for cattle from Argentina into Chile, and I can't look away from the bones littering this place. The skulls left behind are so old that the keratin layers of their horns have peeled apart to make them things like delicate pine cones or the brittle pages of old books left in the sun.

Cabrol has worked closely with robotics engineers for many years, and her 2011 Planetary Lake Lander project set an autonomous floating robot in Laguna Negra in the Andes. Ever since, Cabrol has made it her mission to push the two things together: climate change on Mars and climate change on Earth. The Planetary Lake Lander wasn't just preparation for future missions to lakes and seas beyond Earth, or simply an analogue for climate change on Mars, but a way of investigating climate change here and now. The region near Laguna Negra is suffering from rapid deglaciation, and we see that change too. We move to another lake, surrounded by creeks and frozen grass. The wind is brutal, the sky the darkest blue. Cabrol crouches at a site where she found freshwater springs seven years earlier. Fascinated and forlorn, she tells us that this is like Mars three billion years ago. The surface water has receded, but there is some water underneath. She is shocked by how fast the climate is changing here. 'Seven years ago, this was a beautiful spring, a pond with zooplankton, but now you can't tell the difference between this and the rest of the desert.' She scrapes gently at frozen mud with the point of her geologic hammer. Later, she points out that the Earth itself is in no danger whatsoever. 'It will survive whatever we throw at it. What is in danger is the environment that made us possible. We are pretty much cutting the branch we are sitting on. So either we understand that very quickly or life will go on – but a different one.' She thinks it will not be a slow disappearance. 'It's going to be sudden and frightening,' she says.

At night in my sleeping bag, I woozily speculate on the meaning of life and death, the fate of Earth, the end of things. I ask Mario, one of the expedition doctors, if déjà vu is a recognised symptom of altitude. 'Absolutely,' he says. I am relieved. It keeps happening. It is starting to scare me. The day before, a llama sheltering from the wind behind an outcrop stepped down with leisurely, measured grace across talc-dusted slabs of rock. I knew I'd seen it before. More than twice, certainly. Perhaps five times, six. I knew I hadn't, of course, but these miraged recollections were instantly telescoped and pleated together like a pack of cards all of the same suit flicked through with a thumb. There is a sense that reality is unreliable here, as if I could put a hand to the air and it could slip right through to another universe if I weren't paying sufficient attention, or paying a little too much. As if I could free another reality by rubbing corners of air together like trying to open a recalcitrant plastic bag. And the wind pours on us as we drive, making dust devils spin over the distances, everything outside seemingly inimical to breath.

These high places, Cabrol says, were sacred to the Inca people, who would climb the mountains to make ritual offerings to the gods. Crouching behind a rock to keep us out of the sharp mountain wind, she explains how up here the scientific search for life beyond Earth and the spiritual search for meaning cannot help but run in parallel. 'The Incas would come here to the mountains to ask questions of God – and so, in a way, are we,' she says. 'That's the same question. Who we are, where we are coming from, what's out there? We are trying to connect to our own origins. So we are doing this scientifically; they were doing it in a more intuitive way.'

Cabrol has a deep respect for the cultural histories of the landscapes she works in. Her Quechua guide Macario made offerings to Pachamama, an Incan goddess, before he and Cabrol's team climbed volcanoes, and Cabrol always makes offerings, usually crystal spheres, to the high crater lakes she dives in on mountains. She had planned to climb to Simba's crater lake at the expedition's end, but she hadn't brought an offering to give its blood-coloured waters. Tentatively, she asks me if I have anything that might work as a replacement. I hand her a piece of lapis lazuli polished into the shape of an egg that I bought in San Pedro de Atacama. The exchange seems an entirely rational act. Both halves of Cabrol, scientific and spiritual, are perfectly conjoined in her work, in her insistent, careful reaching for the deepest of questions: why are we here?

Cabrol has stopped working. She's staring at plumes of vapour rising from the volcano on the near horizon. Bright white at their bases, they soften rapidly into haze that climbs up and up, before losing coherence and resolution against the sky. The steam is ascending vertically, even in this vicious wind, so there is serious force behind it. The volcano is Lascar, the one that shares a slope with Simba. And the team has people on Simba right now, local guides preparing our ascent.

Cabrol calls everyone in. We stand in a line before her, waiting for orders. She pushes her mirrored glasses up on to her hat and speaks to us with terse authority. As soon as the guides are down from Simba, she says, we'll go back to camp. She'll get out the satellite phone and speak to Bill Diamond, who is now back at the SETI Institute, and call the United States Geological Survey and the University of Chile to find out more about the situation here. And then we will need to decide not only if the team should cancel the planned ascent of Simba but also whether any of us should stay in camp at all.

The phone call brings no immediate bad news, so we stay. Cabrol will keep an eye on Lascar's activity and let us know if it worsens. She instructs us to sleep in our clothes and keep our passports at hand, ready to leave in the middle of the night if need be. All of this gives me a strange kind of dread. It has a lazy, slow, opiated quality. It's been a long time since I've had none of the tools I need to judge a situation. We find out that very recently there'd been a 5.5-magnitude earthquake in Calama, only an hour and a half away. That isn't optimal: if water makes its way into the magma chamber beneath the volcano, the volcano might explode. This is not comforting. I withdraw to my little orange tent, sit on my cot and scroll through photos of home on my phone. Outside, the light is dying on the old volcano. I can hear people packing and the generator buzzing behind the cinder-block wall. Tambley is assembling a weather station and playing Pink Floyd's 'Shine On You Crazy Diamond', the saddest of songs, on his laptop. Zips, whispers, laughter, the sounds of Pelican cases being hauled over rough ground.

I stare at my hands. They look like ancient lizard skin, each crease outlined in pale dust. All my clothes are white with it. My hair feels like greased fur. There is a moth in my tent, but I am too numb to move it. Blankly, I watch this scrap of life bump about the orange walls. The tent flap is open; all it needs to do is turn around and fly the other way. It does not. I lose sight of it for long minutes, then jump at its touch. It has bumbled its way on to my hand and rests there, quivering. I put it outside. We leave the next day.

Hares

I'd left the snow behind for a work trip to California, for hot blue air and palm trees and bougainvillea and a mockingbird that serenaded my first sleepless night with an exquisite repertoire of stolen phrases. Numbing cold at home, searing heat in Santa Barbara brought a confusion that was more than jetlag; I'd lost any sense of the season I was in. Driving back from Heathrow a week later the snow had gone but my seasonal disorientation was worse than ever, disquiet lying dully inside. But as I passed a field of winter wheat beside the A505, somewhere between Royston and Newmarket, I glimpsed something that made everything right itself, slam me back into what I knew must be spring. Brown hares, five of them, circling, running, hopping, turning to stand on their hind legs to box at each other, kicking mud around under wide and wet silver skies.

I first saw boxing hares out on a misty field near Winchester when I was a teenager, convinced that what I was witnessing were buck hares competing with each other for does. So perfectly did this reading of their behaviour correspond with our societal mores, it had the force of absolute truth. The hares circling the fights, I thought, were does, carefully assessing the pugilists' prowess, and I assumed the victor would take all. I was wrong. Most boxing hares are does unwilling to mate with bucks making sexual advances on them. They rise up and fight them off, an animal analogue to a form of violence just as much a feature of our society, though only in recent years have we begun openly to speak of it.

Talk to people of hares and you'll hear the word 'magical' again and again. Books about hares are rich with lore and legend. Of the hare Boudicca kept under her cloak to release before a battle, the direction of its flight a prediction of the outcome. Of shapeshifting hares. Of hares with an affinity to the moon. Hares as a sign of Easter, of resurrection, of renewal, of spring. Most of us think of hares as magical and mysterious because lore and legend tells us they are so. But these old stories were based on the behaviour of real hares, which are indeed mysterious. They might not be able to change sex at will, as early modern writers assumed, but female hares can become pregnant again before they give birth to their young – leverets that enter the world fully furred with open eyes and rapid independence. Hares eat their own droppings, can run at forty miles an hour – they're our fastest land animal – and they feed mainly at dusk and dawn, dim presences in the gloom. Solitary animals, they'll gather in numbers to feed when pickings are rich. Two years ago I was standing in a Norfolk field of beet at sundown when down the tractor lines loped a crowd of hares, astonishingly slow and eerie, their ears glowing red in the dying light and their fur sabled by shadow.

Humans brought hares from the Continent and released them into our landscape around the time of the Romans, or perhaps earlier, and these creatures from elsewhere quickly turned to natives with a talent for invisibility. Hares don't burrow. They live always under the sky, making a series of depressions called forms across their territories. These are body-shaped spaces into which they'll crouch, close to the ground, turning themselves into a low curve of russet you are sure must be a rock sunk in winter cereal before you notice two black-tipped ears laid to its back. A form is the space a hare makes to see everything and be invisible. Tread too close to one and the hare will spring up at your feet, tearing herbage with its hind claws, white tail flashing, and your heart thumping in surprise as it races into the distance. Hares are things of eyes and speed and fear; they have an astonishing capacity to outrun, jump and dodge things that pursue them – foxes, dogs, eagles.

Predators aren't the reason hares are declining in Britain; it's agricultural intensification that has hit them hard. Leverets crouching in silage fields are mown down by harvesters and modern monocultures leave adults short of food. I don't see hares often these days. I encounter them mostly in photos, in paintings, or in shop windows displaying boxing hare figurines – stylised, long-eared forms wrought into shapes of graceful confrontation. But you don't need to have ever seen a real hare to know what it is supposed to mean. They're magical harbingers of spring.

Spring has of late become thin to me. It's starting to mean supermarket daffodil bunches and Easter promotions, rather than its richly textured changes, the scent of new herbage, algae greening on the trunks of oaks, the echoing drum of woodpeckers, rising skies and the return of that indefinable light to hollow out winter. All these are things I've missed after a few years of mostly working inside. And just as the meanings we have given hares are nowhere near as rich and complex as the living, breathing creatures hares are, so our firm ideas about spring belie what is happening to it. Climate change has made our seasons creep; now catkins appear in winter, cuckoos are rarely heard, and rather than a slow progression, springs are increasingly a short flash of sudden warmth before summer, hardly a season at all. Those boxing hares were a glorious sight, but behind their sparring forms flickered a shadow of disquiet, a glimpse of how the meanings we have given things like hares and seasons persist so strongly once their models have gone that it's hard to see, sometimes, the precipitous alteration in things we've long assumed eternal.

Lost, But Catching Up

Fate saw fit to make me allergic to horses, dogs and foxes. I discovered my dog allergy early: we had a dog. I discovered my horse allergy during riding lessons, and my fox allergy while skinning a road-killed fox to turn into a rug. Which, I realised, I couldn't have in my house.

Allergies never fail to make life new. A few days ago I discovered I was allergic to reindeer. Indeed, the longer life goes on, the more I realise that most quadrupeds make me ill. Though I can ride, I can't ride for long. Twenty minutes on a horse, and my eyes are closed, my hands mottled with nettle rash and I've lost the ability to concentrate on anything other than fighting for breath.

So – quite apart from my moral qualms – it's unsurprising that I've never ridden to hounds. And I've never really understood foxhunting. I've never been part of that particular rural crowd, and even though the Hunt met often outside my parents' house, by the grain dryer at the top of the hill, ready to take in miles of good country, I never really understood what it was all about. I only ever saw the pink coats and the horses and the hounds clustering and the fence-menders and the police and the saboteurs. That didn't seem very interesting to me. And I also felt very sorry for the fox.

It was a Saturday, and I was at my mother's house. It was a day of heavy rain and wind, and I was tired, and sad, and distracted, for it had been a year that week since my father died. And while lots of times, talking to Mum or my brother helped share the pain, sometimes the words wouldn't come, and the loneliness stoppered me up, and I couldn't talk at all. So much pressure was building up inside me that day that by mid-afternoon I had to hide. I left the house to have a cigarette out on the porch. And standing in the murky light by the drive, I heard the music of hounds.

Even with my sporting ignorance, it seemed clear that the Hunt was drawing the covert at Ham Farm, a thick copse of coppiced hazel, sweet chestnut and bluebells just across the road and away. I pulled up the collar of my coat and walked out into the near-sleet. Sure enough, a succession of muddied, battered 4x4s passed where I stood at the edge of the drive, windows steamed on the inside. They all turned left down the track to Wadgett's Copse.

After they'd gone, a long silence but for the hounds in the distance. A giddy, wet, rainy echo of a cry. My hair was soaked and my cigarette damped to extinction. The asphalt at my toes was running with water, and shallow pools were slowly being born in the waterlogged paddock across the road.

And I heard a light pattering of footfalls growing louder; a pattering of nails and pads through water to tarmac. Coming along the road towards me on his way to the covert, his head high, his body smeared all breast-deep in clay that stained the lower half of him copper-ochre, came a foxhound. A pale hound. He was alone, which was wrong. But being alone made him the type of all hounds that ever existed. He was running as if he'd been running all day, and he was running as if he would never stop, tongue out and eyes fixed. He was running to be with the rest of the hounds, and the sound was drawing him along the rainy roads as if he were underwater and swimming up to the light to breathe. I was transfixed. I'd never seen a hound be a hound before. He was doing exactly what he needed to be doing, and he was tired but joyful. He was late, but getting there. Lost, but catching up.

Swan Upping

In the days after the Brexit vote, I became obsessed with an oil painting called *Swan Upping at Cookham*, which portrays a scene from an ancient and colourful English tradition. Swan upping refers to the annual summer voyage of a flotilla of wooden skiffs that sets off from the town of Sunbury-on-Thames on a five-day journey to catch all the swans on the upper reaches of the River Thames. The crews check the parentage of young birds and place a mark on them to claim their ownership: some belong to the Queen, others to the Worshipful Company of Vintners and the Worshipful Company of Dyers, two ancient trade guilds based in the City of London. The painting depicts a traditional stop on the uppers' trip. Here is the river and the Ferry Inn, wooden punts, moody clouds, women carrying cushions, a fretted iron bridge and a swan bound and hoisted in coils of rope and canvas, white neck craning from a man's shoulder.

Swan Upping at Cookham was painted by the mystical, eccentric English artist Stanley Spencer, who left it half-finished in his bedroom in Cookham when he went off to war in 1915, and the knowledge that it was there sustained him over the next three years. He longed to explain to his military superiors that he couldn't take part in attacks because he had a painting to finish at home. On his return, he picked it up. 'Well there we were looking at each other,' he wrote in his diary. 'It seemed unbelievable but it was a fact. Then I wondered if what I had just come from was fact & caught sight of the yellow of the Lyddite or whatever the Bulgars used in their shells on my fingers & finger nails.'

He finished his painting. But the war is caught up in it. Years before he had laid complex, sunlit ripples on the river below the bridge, but the lower post-war parts of the picture are lifeless, muddy and dark. Boats are painted odd colours and have the wrong shapes, his familiar childhood landscape coursing with new and ominous strangeness. And in the days after the referendum, as the purple 'Take Back Control' pro-Brexit posters on telephone poles near my house faded to violet in the sun, and as I read of a 42 per cent upturn in hate crimes since the result came in, I realised two things: first, that Spencer's painting had unwittingly recorded a schism in national history, and second, that it was haunting me because I felt I no longer recognised my country, that everything around me had become ominous – muddy and dark.

The past was always conjured in Brexiteers' dreams of the future, as it was in Donald Trump's stump speeches across the Atlantic. The winning power of the Brexit campaign slogan used by the UKIP leader Nigel Farage, 'We want our country back', lay partly in its vagueness, which let it appeal to all manner of disaffected constituencies, but also in its double meaning. 'Take it back' in the sense of saving the nation from things perceived to threaten it – seen variously as immigrants, faceless European Union bureaucrats, globalisation, the 'Westminster elite' of Britain's political establishment – and 'take it back' also in the sense of back in time, to some ill-defined golden age. Preserving a continuous national heritage and tradition was an explicit part of the 'Leave' campaign. For years I had read in tabloid articles that the EU was destroying much-loved English traditions – baseless claims that its bureaucrats were going to ban everything from English breakfasts for truck drivers to the

Queen's favourite dog breed, even barristers' wigs. The quaintness of these conjured shibboleths was no accident: Brexit rhetoric was all about a battle to save English values and an English way of life beleaguered by waves of immigration and European interference. It had weaponised history and tradition.

In its antiquity, its pageantry and its evocation of deep English history, the subject of Spencer's painting exemplified these themes, and I wondered if seeing swan upping first-hand could help me understand a little more about the state I was in. In a few weeks, the uppers would set out on their journey. I decided to go with them for part of the way. I could have chosen to witness any number of English customs, from Morris dancing to village cricket matches, but swan upping drew me, partly because of the painting but also because I'm fascinated by the relationship between natural history and national history. Symbolically, swans have long been entwined with nationhood and identity. Politics is bound up with them.

The swans on the Thames are mute swans, a native species with a curious history in Britain. In past centuries, when they were commonly served roasted at feasts, fewer free-flying wild ones existed here, and even today they seem to me more like feathered livestock than birds: huge, faintly menacing inhabitants of local parks and rivers, neither fully wild nor fully tame. Swans' royal ownership dates at least to the twelfth century, and certain flocks – known traditionally as games of swans – were granted by royal charter to hundreds of favoured dignitaries and institutions. All the young swans in the country were once upped each summer, the last joint of one wing cut away to render them flightless, and patterns incised in their bills or webbed feet to establish ownership. Exquisitely inked manuscript records of these marks still exist: lines and crosses scribed across diagrammatic beaks. As geese and turkeys became popular eating – less territorial than swans, they were much easier to keep – ownership of swan flocks reverted to the Crown in all but a few locations, like the Thames.

In Britain, killing a swan still generates unexamined outrage: it is wounding the body politic, a thing akin to treason. The symbolism of swans is so commonly understood in Britain – emblems of the monarchy, and by extension the nation – that these birds have long been counters in the game of what is us and what is not. Perceived threats to swans closely track the imagined enemies of British society. All the swans on the Thames, or so one story goes, were killed by Cromwell's soldiers during the Civil War, and the river was restocked only with the restoration of the monarchy. Mournful Victorian obituaries for Old Jack, the swan who lived at the seat of the monarch at Old Buckingham House, relate how his decades-long reign over his pond was brought to an untimely end by a gang of warlike Polish geese. A nineteenth-century magazine article claimed that swans in the royal parks were killed and skinned and their remains tied to trees by Jewish feather traders.

It's easy to read these fables of nationhood as curios from another age. But they are not. In the early 2000s, the *Sun* tabloid accused asylum seekers of stealing the Queen's birds for barbecues. Later it transpired that the basis of the story was a telephone call to a swan sanctuary to report that someone had been seen pushing a swan in a shopping trolley.

'Undoubtedly people do eat swans,' Chris Perrins, a swan expert and retired Oxford ornithology professor, told me. Perrins accompanies the uppers every year as the Queen's swan warden. He thinks the culprits are as likely to be British as they are to be immigrants. Many swans are killed by young men with air rifles, bricks and bottles, but these crimes receive far less attention from the news media.

***

On 19 July, nearly a month after the Brexit vote, I stood expectantly inside the view that Spencer had painted. It was the hottest day of the year, the air heavy and luminous. Moored in slack green water in the shade of a sycamore was a collection of skiffs flying flags embroidered with swans and crowns. Waiting for the uppers to emerge from the Ferry Inn, I chatted with an older woman named Siân Rider sitting alone at a table. She wore a straw hat festooned with daisies and a gold-starred blue tabard that she had sewn herself from an EU flag. She loathed the engineers of Brexit and was dismayed by the number of people who had revealed their racist colours to her since the vote. She was following the swan uppers partly because walking the river was good exercise, but also because it offered a reassuring continuity to set against political upset. 'It would be a shame to lose our old customs,' Rider said. 'Especially what's been happening this past year all over the world, where we all seem to be going to hell in a handbasket. It is just nice to have something that ... What's the word? Sustains?' She shook her head at the tide of recent history and offered me a mint.

'It's just a slice of English tradition and pageantry,' Casey Fleming told me. Fleming is a trim, cheerful man with silver hair who works as a sustainability manager in Qatar. Friends with one of the Queen's uppers, he had come with his young son, Reilly, to watch from the press boat in which I, too, had been granted a seat. Fleming was careful to stress that upping is a quintessentially English, rather than British, phenomenon. 'By nature,' he mused, 'I think the English are traditionalists. Conservative. And we like to hang an anchor to the past. And this sort of event gives us that. It's culture. Lineage. And without that, without celebrating past events or keeping traditions alive, what defines you as a country or as a race?' People in Britain have been too ready to sneer at events like this, he told me, but they are beginning to realise that they should be celebrated. 'To be proud of being English, ten years ago, was to be thought of as being small-minded, racist – you know, had negative connotations. But I think now it's different. And I think Brexit has helped that.' The meanings of traditions can change over time, their social functions can shift. Swan-upping data is now used to monitor the health of the Thames' swan population, and before they set out each morning the uppers meet with local schoolchildren to teach them about swans and river conservation.

David Barber, the Queen's swan marker, who oversees the upping, emerged from the Ferry Inn, resplendent in a red jacket detailed with gold braid, a swan feather tucked into his captain's hat. He was followed by Perrins and the crews of the Queen's boats and the boats of the Vintners and Dyers, skilled watermen from the lower reaches of the Thames clad in white cotton caps and coloured shirts. Here, too, was Wendy Hermon from Swan Support, a charity that rehabilitates sick and injured wild swans. I clambered into the press boat, an elegant wooden umpire launch, and we set off upstream searching for swans.

It didn't take long. Two feathered white bergs and a lone cygnet drifted serenely past the riverside mansions of Bourne End. '*Allll up!*' cried the crews, manoeuvring their skiffs to box the swans into a shrinking patch of water. Confusion. Raised oars, shoulders, shouts. The male swan raised his wings heraldically, defensively, and was grabbed by the neck. 'There's a catch!' Then things went awry: the female and the cygnet ducked under a gangplank and escaped downstream. The boats raced after them, heading them off, and tried again. 'That worked well,' Barber shouted across the water. 'That's how it should be done.'

Soon the female and the cygnet were in the bottom of a skiff, their black webbed feet tied above their tails with strings of the soft braided cotton the uppers kept looped into the belts of their white cotton trousers, and the adult bird's wings tied, too. I couldn't see the swans clearly from the press boat – just one distant curved white neck like the spout of an elegant porcelain coffee pot. As we drew closer, I noticed the uppers' strangely courteous conduct now that there were swans on the boat, quite at odds with the decisive force it had taken to grab them. 'My swan hook's broke,' a waterman said to me, sadly holding a long pole like a shepherd's crook. He thought it might have been a hundred, maybe a hundred and fifty, years old. He pulled a wry face. 'You just can't get good swan hooks these days.'

Hauled up from the skiffs, the swans were set down reverently upon the lawn of a riverside house. Close up, the adult swan had a snaky neck, glittering black eyes and a waxy orange bill that opened to make nasal, squeaking grunts like an unoiled gate. The bird was a strange coincidence of solidity and air. Sleek contour feathers over thick down, pearls of water running over white feathers thick and curled as paper sculpture. The 18-week-old cygnet resembled a huge, skinny plush toy. Hermon knelt next to it and opened her box of rings. Swan uppers haven't clipped swans' wings for decades; these days the birds are marked with stainless-steel leg rings, not knives.

After the ownership of the cygnet's mother was ascertained – she was one of the Queen's birds – and the correct ring was selected and fitted to the cygnet, Barber, his face tanned dark, the feather in his cap glowing with steely light, explained to Reilly what they were doing. 'You have to check them over to make sure everything is OK,' he said, gently picking up the cygnet. 'Here.' Reilly took a deep breath and extended both hands in front of him, and the swan was deposited into his outstretched palms, his shoulders bowing slightly to take its weight. I asked him later what it was like.

'Like it had a silk wrapping on it,' he said, and the smile he gave me then was shy and full of astonishment. 'How did it make you feel?' I asked. He told me it would stick in his mind for the rest of his life. 'Hopefully it will come back to me and inspire me,' he said. 'Hopefully it will inspire me to be somebody.'

The sun dipping westward, we set off once more upriver. Pulled by motorised tugs for this section of the Thames, the watermen lay back in the skiffs checking their phones. We were passing by some of the most expensive real estate in Britain, architecture inspired by feverish dreams of lost golden ages: vast mock-Tudor mansions, fake castles with crenellated concrete battlements. There were willow trees, summerhouses, immaculate sun-drenched lawns, water-meadows where cattle stood hock-deep in the river, dazed by the heat. A crowd of teenagers smoking weed by a disposable barbecue. A woman sitting with her shopping bags on a wooden bench by a car park, tossing fragments of supermarket sandwiches to ducks on the water below. She waved at us. So did the teenagers. Everyone did. They waved and smiled, and I waved and smiled back.

I had expected to be cynical about this voyage. But as we progressed upstream, I began to feel a luxuriant, drunken joy. Under the boat, constellations of tiny fry darted through sunlit weeds. The river surface was thick with craft following us: large passenger boats with bars serving beer and decks crammed with sightseers, a near-naked man sunk so deeply in a tiny rubber dinghy that it crowded into his shoulders as he paddled, grinning, along the middle of the river. We passed rowing boats, catamarans, sleek pleasure craft resembling 1920s Daimlers. A common tern clipped overhead, translucent supple wing beats over a river crowded with traffic, and something about its flight made me think that it was flying under clouds, but there were no clouds, there were no clouds anywhere and had not been all day, and the sky was the stretched, varnished perfection of linseed-thinned oils.

I had got lost inside a hallucinatory English dreamscape. And no wonder. So many of the books I had read as a child were written about this place, like *The Wind in the Willows* and *Three Men in a Boat*. This was where Noël Coward had set his elegant comedies of manners, where Enid Blyton and Edgar Wallace had lived. It was where the stories were written that taught me what it was to be English. And so I listened agog when the affable press coordinator, Paul Wilmott, pointed out one of the Little Ships, part of a seven-hundred-strong fleet of private boats that rescued British and French servicemen from Dunkirk during the Second World War. And I laughed out loud at his story of the Spitfire pilot flying under the bridge at Marlow to impress his girlfriend, only to be hauled over the coals by an air commodore who witnessed the feat. These were stories designed to foster a reassuring sense of national pride, one in which the war is stripped of horror and political complexity and turned into a patriotic tale of plucky English derring-do.

Swan upping is a progress in the old-fashioned sense, a journey upriver that claims the right not only to own swans but to own their meanings, the meanings of the river, the meanings of Englishness. You move through a landscape thick with narratives handed to you by others, and what you read from the banks as you pass is part of what you choose to believe about your nation and who you are. You might see only Dunkirk boats and lines in the air carved by ghostly Spitfires. You might see leisurely eighteenth-century landscapes in the loose herd of cattle standing in the river. But you might see there, too, the ghosts of forgotten farmworkers, or feel fellowship with a woman eating sandwiches from a plastic packet on a bench or with a gaggle of youngsters smoking pot around a barbecue. Lying in the boat as we hastened towards a new group of swans, I thought of how we choose to see only the things that speak to us of the way we are told the world should be, and then felt a small burst of shame and the breaking of my fever-dream.

Staggering off the boat at Marlow at the end of the day, I thought of Reilly's rapt face as he held the swan, the genial conviviality of the uppers, the sun-splashed slipway at Cookham and then Stanley Spencer again. Not the painting this time, but the story of a trip he made to Beijing in 1954 as part of a cultural delegation. Towards the end of the tour, Zhou Enlai, the Chinese premier, gave a long speech about how much Chinese people loved China and then asked for a response. It was a politically perilous moment. No one knew what to say. 'There was a silence,' the cultural historian Patrick Wright, who wrote a book on the subject, *Passport to Peking*, told me. 'And then Spencer got up, much to everyone's absolute horror, and said: "The Chinese are a home-loving people, well, so are the English. Have you heard about, have you ever heard of Cookham? Have you ever been to Cookham?"'

It was a stunningly successful gambit and sparked an animated conversation with Zhou. Spencer told him that the people of Cookham are the same as people everywhere: they want to get on with their lives, get on with their neighbours and, as Wright put it, not be bombed. 'I feel at home in China,' Spencer said, 'because I feel that Cookham is somewhere near.' He is often mocked for his parochialism, his attendance to small things, but, as Wright maintains, his vision was ultimately one in which 'through the small, through the located, you enter a more universal domain of human experience'.

Heritage traditions like swan upping have clear conceptual value for nationalists; they promote a sense of seamless historical continuity that works to erase differences between past and present, burnishing an illusion of unchanging Englishness. But remembering the story of Spencer in China made me wonder if swan upping could offer us something other than these exclusionist dreams of a sacrosanct Englishness deep-rooted in an imagined past. For besides the pageantry, what I had watched that day was a beautiful display of expert animal handling and river knowledge. Skiffs crewed by men who know how to row, how to navigate complicated waters, how to catch swans, how to corral them, how to deal with a bird the size of a dog with a flexible neck and wings that can break ribs.

These are craft knowledges, ones learned by apprenticeship, not from books, and universal in the very nature of their specificity. Like Spencer's Cookham villagers in China, they are global by virtue of being local and cannot easily be fitted to simple stories of race and nationality, of us and them. Later that evening, watching a full moon rise through air thick with the scent of lime blossom, I thought of how there are always counter-narratives, hidden voices, lost lives, other ways of being, and how it is possible to see a different, more inclusive England in the most recondite of traditions. And I cherished the thought that grand historical and political narratives might falter, just slightly, in the face of skilful interactions with things that are not us. Small things. Swans, rivers, boats, currents, knotted loops of braided cotton string.

Nestboxes

I ordered them on the internet; they arrived in two cardboard boxes packed with brown paper. Four rough brown bowls with truncated backs and tops fitted tight against right-angled plywood boards. Made from a mixture of concrete and wood fibre, each has a scoop cut out of the front. When they're fitted under the eaves of my new house, I'm hoping those scoops will be the point of entry for pairs of house martins, those delicate, orca-coloured migrant birds whose arrival is one of the milestones of north Palaearctic springs. They can build their own nests, of course, made of a thousand or so beakfuls of mud collected from local puddles and pond-edges and carefully pushed together, one by one, to dry. Last year's drought made their nest building difficult, and with catastrophic declines in their flying-insect food, their populations have been nosediving year on year. I bought these nestboxes to help birds in trouble. But only partly.

In India a few years ago I stayed in a hotel room that also held a pair of nesting laughing doves. The hotel was fine about it: the housekeeper put fresh newspaper on the floor each morning to catch the mess. They'd squeeze inside through a gap above the AC unit and fly to their nest with pattering wingbeats, and at night I'd watch their eyes blink closed as they fell asleep. It would have been less delightful if I'd been fearful or allergic to birds, but there seemed a grace and generosity to that quiet sharing of space which swelled my heart out of all proportion to the presence of birds in the room. It brought home to me how fiercely in Britain we are ridding our human spaces of everything that isn't us. None of us wants rats and cockroaches, but what of swifts? They need holes in eaves and under roof tiles to nest, and we're increasingly blocking them up. Sparrows like ivy-covered walls and thickets of bushes, but they're messy and no longer fashionable in gardens. And while it's illegal to destroy active birds' nests, developers have started netting trees and hedges to stop them from nesting at all. The recent furore about netted trees is testament that for now, at least, we still balk at extending our zone of control outside of our gardens to things so obviously not ours.

On the web, you'll find martin nestboxes in the category of 'specialist' boxes, along with those for treecreepers, owls, swifts, dippers, grey wagtails and ducks. The kinds you can buy in any garden centre or hardware shop are far simpler: boxes with a round hole in the front for great tits and blue tits, and those with a half-open front for robins. These were the kind we put up in my childhood garden. We did it for the pleasure of having familiar birds raise a family in a home we'd supplied. I remember the curious thrill of seeing a prospecting great tit drop into the darkness of the box hung on the side of my house. It was a little flush of pride dangerously near possession. One spring my father built a backless nestbox and mounted it against the single glass window of our garden shed. Inside, a blackout curtain kept the nest dark. After school, my brother and I would creep inside, shut the door, lift the curtain and press our noses to the glass. What we saw was all secret: three inches of moss and feathers and, pressed deep into it, the back of an incubating blue tit, so close we could see the rising and falling of its breathing, the tiny feathers around its beak lit with the light falling through the hole above. The nest fledged successfully and later that spring we'd sit on the lawn hearing the begging calls of blue tit fledglings and think, *They're ours*. These days, nestboxes in gardens faintly remind me of the provision of workers' cottages on landed estates. Indeed, one nestbox pioneer was the eccentric nineteenth-century naturalist Charles Waterton, who installed sand martin nest pipes and other avian households at Walton Hall, his Yorkshire estate now famed as being perhaps Britain's first nature reserve.

In Britain, the class system inflects nestboxes as it does everything else. You can buy boxes that resemble scale models of pubs or churches, ones with poems or flowers painted on the front, or with tiny glued-on gates and picket fences. These are frowned upon by the gatekeepers of British nature appreciation, who recommend plain wooden ones. The Royal Society for the Protection of Birds explicitly warn against using decorative boxes in case their bright colours attract predators, even though they've admitted there's no real evidence for this. Yes, metal boxes are a bad idea because they can overheat nestlings, but a handwritten 'Home Sweet Home' isn't much of an issue when robins can and will nest happily in discarded teapots.

Like garden gnomes, decorative nestboxes fail to conform to the aesthetics of middle-class garden design. Making them cute and homely raises the spectre of anthropomorphism, something still anathema to bird protection organisations who in their earliest days battled for cultural capital by denying accusations of sentimentality and cleaving instead to hard ornithological science. Nestboxes are supposed to be for the birds, not us, in this view. There's a kind of performative largesse about the utilitarian ugliness of plain nestboxes in gardens, whereas decorative ones bespeak delight for people too. The birds don't care, of course. They really don't. And while my house martin nests aren't colourful, I am all about the personal enjoyment I hope they will bring me.

I bought them because I want those birds here. I want their submarine chirrups to fall through the open windows while the late-spring evenings lengthen, want to watch their hawking flights to scoop flies from the burnished air. I want the mess, the drifting feathers, the small faces of youngsters peering down at me as I walk up to our own front door.

Deer in the Headlights

The deer drift in and out of the trees like breathing. They appear unexpectedly delicate and cold, as if chill air is pouring from them to the ground to pool into the mist that half obscures their legs and turning flanks. They aren't tame: I can't get closer than a hundred yards before they slip into the gloom. I've been told these particular beasts are fallow deer of the menil variety, which means their usual darker tones have been leached by genetics to soft cuttlefish and ivory, and they're the descendants of a herd brought here in the sixteenth century as beasts of venery, creatures to be pursued and caught and cooked. The look of the estate hasn't changed much since then. It's still an extensive patchwork of pasture and forest – except now the M25 runs through it, six lanes of fast-moving traffic behind chain-link fence threaded with stripling trees. The mist thickens, the light falls, the deer appear and disappear, and the deep roar of the motorway burns inside my chest as I walk on to the bridge that spans it. This bridge is grassed along its length, and at dusk and dawn, I've been told, the deer use it as a thoroughfare from one side of the estate to the other. I know my presence will dissuade them from crossing so I don't want to stay too long, but I linger a little while to watch the torrent of lights beneath me. For a while the road doesn't seem real. Then it does, almost violently so, and at that moment the bridge and the woods behind me do not. I can't hold both in the same world at once. Deer and forest, mist, speed, a drift of wet leaves, white noise, scrap-metal trucks, a convoy of eighteen-wheelers, beads of water on the toes of my boots and the scald of my hands on the cold metal rail.

Deer occupy a unique place in my personal pantheon of animals. There are many creatures I know very little about, but the difference with deer is that I've never had any desire to find out more. They're like a distant country I've never wanted to visit. I know the names of different deer species, and can identify the commonest ones by sight, but I've always resisted the almost negligible effort it would take to discover when they give birth, how they grow and shed their antlers, what they eat, where and how they live. Standing on the bridge I'm wondering why that is.

Perhaps my feelings about deer might partly be down to their place in British culture. About five years ago, their images started appearing on soft furnishings and homeware. Deer candles, deer drinking glasses, stag's-head wallpaper, prints of antlers on curtains and cushions, mock trophy heads stitched out of patchwork tartan. I was used to reindeer motifs all over Christmas, but this cervine proliferation was new. At the time, one design spokesman ascribed it to the British public's love of cosy country hotels and log fires in winter. But I suspect there was more to it than a yen for seasonal hotel atmospherics. The years following the financial crash of 2008 were marked by a growing glorification of myths of Englishness, ranging from a flourishing of books on the countryside and rural life to 'Keep Calm and Carry On' Second World War posters and chintz-printed aprons – and a strong shift towards political populism. When a country is hurting it so often grasps for ideas of itself in a longed-for past, and a simple motif like a stag's head can function like an upholstery button to pleat together a whole slew of useful meanings.

Deer tend to signify a conservative view of the world. I learned that in my twenties, at a time when I was spending a lot of time with hunters, mostly men, many of whom expressed a sneaking admiration for the antics of powerful stags who battled each other to take possession of harems of docile hinds. And it was around that time that I spent a rainy afternoon wandering around an exhibition of paintings by Edwin Landseer in a London gallery. The walls were hung with sad dogs, gleaming horses, various British game animals being torn to pieces, and numerous portraits of red deer stags that seemed the very type of elite Victorian manhood. These stags were grand and harried and very good at striking poses, Monarchs of the Glen whose fragile rule was perpetually threatened by upstarts, whose crowned heads were always lit perfectly by mountain sunlight, paragons of strength bound entire into unshakeable courses of action by virtue of being what they were.

The wash of traffic noise subsides as I leave the bridge to regain the path. It's too dark now to see the deer but I can hear the hollow thump of hooves trotting on sward and when I look behind me the motorway casts the palest, faintest glow behind the trees. Something about this place, I think, will solve the puzzle of my attitude to deer, and I'm beginning to understand that this puzzle isn't just about a type of mammal. It's about animals more generally, and what it might mean to not want to know more about them: a much bigger why.

I trudge back to the car, wondering whether motorists passing this place sometimes glance up and see a procession of antlers against the sky, a slow parade of ancient beasts walking across modern infrastructure. The thought brings to mind much older notions of deer, like the white stags that were Celtic emissaries from the underworld, or creatures in medieval romances whose appearances portended the beginning of a quest or great adventure. In this tradition they're slippery, spooky beings in possession of the deepest spiritual significance and their visitations are always a surprise. I think of one quiet, cold afternoon nearly twenty years ago when I was glumly traipsing through a small wood near my parents' house musing on the shape of my life and finding it sorely wanting. As I approached a tangle of briars growing over a fallen tree I saw a small, slow curl of smoke rising from behind it, glowing palely on its ascent through rays of winter sunlight. It was exceptionally unsettling. I moved closer and was treated to more incomprehensibility; a sweeping arc of something like upraised bone, something skeletal behind the leaves, and then the resting fallow buck whose rising breath I had been watching leapt up and crashed away into the trees. My heart kicked and raced and for a long while afterwards the wood seemed made anew, fretted with rich possibility, and for a long while after that my life also.

Not knowing very much about deer has made my encounters with them less like encounters with real animals and more like tableaux of happenstance, symbolism and emotion. My ignorance, I think, has been purposive. It has been me saying: *I wish there was more magic in the world*. And then the deer have appeared to say, *Here it is*. This is what deer are for me. They stand for the natural world's capacity to surprise and derail my expectations. And I have wanted them to do that more than I have wanted them to be anything else.

Driving home in the dark I know I've reached this understanding because of the geography of the place I've just visited, its conjunction of asphalt and trucks and deer. For the capacity of deer to surprise, to hijack the quotidian, is not merely a matter of legend or of remote and ethereal speculation. It is a blunt fact, bloody and frequently deadly, and it happens so often there's an acronym for it: DVC, which stands for deer–vehicle collision. Thankfully, it has only ever been an almost, for me.

A few years ago, driving a downhill curve at night, I saw a deer in the road in front of me, stark and tense with shock, and then the deer lofted itself into the air, bright and somehow motionless, like the etiolated horses with outstretched legs in eighteenth-century hunting prints. A blooming scald spread under my skin and the car felt as light as if it were sliding on water, even before I braked. What I remember most about that endless moment apart from the blind heat of it was the angular neatness of hind hocks and ankles, and the deer's hard landing against the hedge, the way it shoved itself into that cross-hatched, thorny difficulty before disappearing. And all the rest of that journey I saw nothing but deer crossing the road where there were no deer at all.

Deer are dangerous animals. In America around two hundred people die every year after their vehicles collide with them, and while official figures put the number of DVCs at about one and a half million, it's likely much higher, for many go unrecorded. The correct advice for drivers encountering a deer in the road is never to swerve, for most human deaths occur when people wrench the wheel away, hit trees, rocks, fences, other cars. But how can you not? There it is, right in front of you, cut out of black and surrounded by a suffused halo of reflected light, a beating heart the size of a fist in a hundred, a hundred and fifty pounds of pearl and terror. It's coming towards you at fifty, sixty miles an hour. How can you do anything else?

If you live in places prone to DVCs you can buy deer alerts: small whistles for the exterior of your vehicle that are supposed to warn deer of your impending arrival. Some drivers swear by them, but it might just be that knowing the alert is there makes you drive differently, perhaps a little more slowly, a little more defensively, a little readier to expect a deer to appear in your path, because I've read that there's no statistical proof that they have any effect and deer may not be able to hear them at all. They're tech solutions that work like nazar, those dangling blue and white glass charms against the curse of the evil eye.

It happened to my friend Isabella. She is an artist, and a truly excellent one. When I first met her she was gilding pieces of fresh fruit to make art of their slow collapse over the coming months into corrugated, shining nuggets. I asked her, 'You hit a deer. What was that like?' She drew her eyebrows together, just a little. 'It was like a collision with the divine,' she said. 'You've read Euripides, right?' I said, 'Yes. I have.' She said, again, 'Well. It was a collision with the divine.' Turning on to a fast road at night, lights shone in her eyes from a car in the wrong place. That car had already hit a red deer she couldn't see. It was lying right across the carriageway. 'I drove over it,' she said, shivering with the recollection of the rise and sink of the car's traverse, feeling the give of flesh and the cracking architecture of ribs. The deer may already have been dead, or perhaps was only stunned, but it was opened up by the weight of her car, which sent a wave of blood across the wet road. Her headlights shone on it. 'There was so much blood,' she said. She leaned forward when she told me this, her eyes on mine. 'So. Much. Blood.' She told me she could smell the terror of her daughter sitting in the seat next to her. The air around the car that night was foggy, yellow with sodium street-lamps, and there was, there was this sheet of blood running in front of the car for what seemed for ever.

'Was it like *The Shining*?' I asked.

She looked at me levelly, as if I'd not heard a word she'd told me.

'It was much worse.'

Roads belong to us. We don't expect things that aren't us to interact with them, to cross from their territory into our own, and with such brute physicality. Even if you escape unscathed, the effect of a DVC can be life-changing. You can see something of that in the way they are handled in the movies, where they're scripted narrative shocks, horror-movie jumps, choice *dei ex machina* that derail narratives as they total cars. Sometimes the deer breaks through the windscreen. There'll be blood, antlers that fill the car like candelabras, and the dying stag will have its eyes fixed on the character to whom this event has the deepest significance. Sometimes, in movies, the deer lies on the road in the aftermath of the DVC. If the deer is on the road, and the deer is not dead – and it is not very often dead in Hollywood – there's the matter of how to deal with this. Often it will be making noises that dying deer don't make. It will be an animatronic deer, for there are companies in Hollywood who will take a dead deer, skin it, flense it of fat, cure it, lay it over a form that contains a mechanism that, once covered with skin, will mimic the slow in and out of breath. DVCs on screen cast a fierce, traumatic light on the innermost hearts of the characters with the bad luck to experience them. And that is often what they do in reality, too.

All of us know at heart that driving is always challenging fate. We are just very good at pretending it isn't. A deer in the road is part of the wager we all make and do our best to forget when we drive, as we make our way through life. DVC survivors often maintain that everything changed after the accident, that their life felt recast into something more precious and precarious than before. The deepest ramifications of the DVC are tied intimately to their sense of who they are; they speak of the collision as an event that does not admit the secular, the random, the rational. Often they will not speak of it at all. 'The car was destroyed,' they'll say, or, 'The windscreen was smashed', as if mentioning the other participant in the collision was taboo. And that one line, over and over again: 'It came out of nowhere.' Fate comes up out of nowhere in the headlights glowing like a goddamned unicorn, and whatever meaning drivers choose to take from the collision falls upon them as inescapably as any medieval allegory. *Look at yourself*, says the DVC, cutting through all that is quotidian, cutting it all away. *Look at yourself. Here you really are*. The old dramatists called that moment of self-understanding anagnorisis.

Most DVCs occur between nightfall and midnight, and again in the small hours before dawn. That's when deer are moving, but also when we are most prone to oneiric states of mind. Driving in dusk and darkness is a perfect dream of solipsism. Headlights unspool into rises and curves and bulks of fences and passing houses; you call these things into momentary existence, smear them with light and mass before they are gone. And because everything you see is ceaselessly pulled towards and under you, it's easy to fall prey to the illusion that you are stationary and the world is flowing into you. The fractional somatic forces the terrain exerts, the ghostly burr of the road surface, the small forces of corners and hills are things you feel in your physical frame and the liquids of your ears. And this all means that if a deer appears in front of you, it can feel more than a surprise; it can seem as if some part of you called it into existence, as if it were fashioned by your subconscious mind.

Since returning from the deer forest, my own subconscious mind is full of DVCs. I have tightened my hands on the wheel in anxious anticipation of disaster as I drive through rural woods. At night I've dreamed of roads, of mist, of slicks of oil printed with hoofmarks, windscreens crazed by impacts, herds of running deer. I mention this strange new preoccupation to a friend in an email. 'Are you OK?' they reply. 'Is something bad happening in your life?' I write back and say, 'I'm fine; I think I want to write about deer collisions, is all.' They have a suggestion: 'Have you checked YouTube? You know there are *actual supercuts*?' Of course there are. I don't want to watch them, just as I don't want to watch videos of other traumatic events that are clickable currency on the internet, things far worse than the accidental coincidence of a deer with an offside fender. But I sit down, find one of the videos and press play.

The video is made of dashcam footage from many different vehicles edited into a long montage of DVCs. The first thing it makes me think of is first-person shooter video gameplay, with deer bursting into view so unexpectedly they seem ghostly artefacts on the screen – until they hit metal. It happens again. Another hit. Another cut. Now dusk, the lights of a gas station, the murmur of talk radio. A roe deer colliding with the car, turning over and over in the air before it lands deadweight on the grassy verge. The car slows and halts. A woman gets out. She wears a blue fringed top and a woollen shrug pulled over her shoulders. She walks to where the deer lies, looks down, looks back at the driver, raises both hands, palms up, in a gesture of helplessness. The driver gets out, shoulders set, ignores the deer and leans down to examine the front of his car. Another vehicle, another overheard conversation, another collision, another dashcam dislodged from the dashboard to point upwards at stricken faces. I pause the video, get up, pace about the kitchen. I sit back down, watch some more, stop again. It's getting harder to continue. Sometimes the deer leaps high over the hood of the car and escapes all harm; most often it does not, and it will fall lengthways onto the bonnet and slide down, or smash the windscreen, or spin balletically away in parabolae of antlers and flesh and bone. I see the puff of fur as a fender makes contact, hear the click of hooves hitting steel. What most surprises me as I watch this repeated, terrible carnage is how high the deer are thrown in the air. Ten, twelve, twenty feet, tumbling end over end, limp and pathetic. Towards the end of the video I start reading the comments beneath it. I expect them to be grim and they are. 'Cool ragdoll physics,' says one. Another suggests that deer have very low IQs. Another thinks deer are suicidal. 'Am I the only one who thinks it's funny when they B O U N C E off of the cars?' The answer is no. 'Oh man,' writes another, 'I haven't laughed this hard at a compilation in a long time, great job seriously.'

I don't laugh. I sit very still. It takes me a long while to work out how upset I am. My pet parrot understands what I'm feeling faster than I do; he jumps from his perch on the back of a chair, runs along the tabletop and snuggles against my forearm, extending his soft feathery neck to nibble gently at the back of my hand.

I've witnessed a series of extremely violent deaths, and the bodies of deer are sufficiently large that they can't help but remind us of our own. But I don't think that's the reason for my upset, not entirely. The tone of the comments is perturbing, but pretty much par for the course on the internet. Besides, inappropriate laughter is not an unusual response to emotional difficulty. No, my upset is more about how the commentators view the deer as obstacles to progress like the random antagonists in videogames; things that have consequential presence but no meaningful existence in and of themselves. And that's when I realise that most of my upset is directed at myself.

I've valued deer for their capacity to surprise and delight me, which is why I've resisted learning more about them. The more you know about something, the less it can surprise you. But it's hard to feel sympathy with a thing whose reality you have chosen to ignore, which makes my attitude not so very different from those who would write approvingly of the physics of a dying deer, or how the best thing about a deer collision is how funny it can be. Deer–vehicle collisions have gripped me so tightly because they are my own attitude to deer writ large and covered in blood and tattered fur and broken glass: everything about them is made of deer being surprising, deer derailing our expectations of the world. I sit at the table and think of deer that die because they have no conception of the nature of roads. Deer that die because they are creatures with their own lives, their own haunts and paths and thoughts and needs. I don't think I could ever laugh at the sight of a deer being hit by a car. But I have not been innocent. I close the YouTube window, go to a website that sells second-hand natural history books. I buy a book called *Understanding Deer*.

The Falcon and the Tower

I'm standing on cracked asphalt by a high-security fence at the eastern edge of Ireland. The sky is cold pewter, the salt wind bitter. Though I've come all the way here to watch wildlife I've just turned my back on the only birds I can see. The miles of sand behind me have been washed by the Irish Sea into a perfect blankness, pearled with gulls and flocks of migrant waders. It's beautiful. But my friends Hilary and Eamonn have told me to look instead at Dublin's Poolbeg Power Station, a giant's playset of brutal turbine halls facing the shining sands. Set amid sewage works, derelict redbrick buildings, wharves, cranes and shipping containers, this is a bizarre spot for a wildlife pilgrimage. Two decommissioned cooling chimneys tower above us, marked with vertical washes of rust and horizontal bands of red and white. Rising from the horizon, they are your first sight of Ireland if you arrive from the east by sea and the last when you leave. Visible throughout the city, they have come to mean home for a whole generation of Dubliners – and for the peregrine falcons that have nested on them for years.

For a while, not much happens. We watch flocks of pigeons clattering about the roofline in shadowless winter light. My face grows numb with cold. Then, below the chimneys, a pigeon cartwheels like a thrown firework through a broken window into the darkness beyond. There is something horrible about its descent. Had it been shot? Had some kind of fit? It takes me a little while to work out that the pigeon was trying to get inside as fast as possible, and it's then I know that the falcons have come.

A narrow black anchor appears, falling fast towards the west chimney as if on an invisible zip wire. Seeing something alive descending to earth at such speed brings a hitch to my throat. A faint, echoing call drifts towards us, the unlikely *ee-chip, ee-chip* of a swinging, unoiled door. It is the male, the tiercel. He swerves, spreads his wings wide to brake and alights upon the rail by a nestbox that has been fixed to a metal walkway a hundred feet above. He shakes his feathers into place and sits looking towards the estuary, flat-headed, an inverted bullet shape black against the sky.

'Do you want to see?' Eamonn says, gesturing to his telescope. Through the device, the falcon is oddly two-dimensional, rippling in the bright circle as if seen through water, and my eyes ache as I try to focus on small points of sharpness: the barred feathers of his chest, his black hood, a faint chromatic fringe ghosting him with suggestions of dust and rainbows. He's exquisite, the colour of smoke, paper and wet ash. He starts preening his feathers, puffs out his belly, half closes his eyes, angles his head back to zip single scapulars through his neat, curved beak. Gusts of wind rising up the chimney face blow his feathers the wrong way. His talons are curled around rusting steel. The wind has ice in it. He looks utterly at home.

This perch gives him vantage on miles of hunting territory: estuary, docks, city streets, parks and golf courses. The divisions between those things are of little consequence to him. But they are to us. What we are watching is a small, feathered rebuke to our commonplace notion that nature exists only in places other than our own, an assumption that seems always one step towards turning our back on the natural world, abandoning it as something disappearing or already lost.

For much of the twentieth century, falcons were celebrated as romantic icons of threatened wilderness. The mountains and waterfall gorges where they chose to nest were sublime sites where visitors could contemplate nature and meditate on the brevity of human existence. But there's a romanticism to industrial ruins too. The rusting chimneys and broken windows of the Poolbeg site have their own troubling beauty, that of things that have outlasted their use. Falcons haunt landscapes that speak to us of mortality: mountains, by virtue of their eternity; industrial ruins, by virtue of their reminding us that this, too, in time will be gone, and that we should protect what is here and now.

Perhaps the peregrine is becoming the imagined essence of landscapes like these. When Eamonn was a child, he went with his father to search for peregrines in the Wicklow Mountains because books told him they nested on cliffs and crags. He saw none at all. His first wild peregrine was sitting high on a Dublin gasometer. Falcons have nested on tall buildings for centuries, but the rise of urban peregrines is a relatively recent phenomenon. In the 1950s and '60s, the pesticide DDT sent peregrine populations into free fall across Europe and North America, before it was gradually banned. As their numbers recovered, peregrines moved into cities, lured by flocks of feral pigeons. In the eastern United States, no wild falcons remained, so Cornell University's Peregrine Fund released captive-bred birds from artificial nests on towers and tall buildings to repopulate their former range. Traditional nest sites on cliffs were deemed too dangerous: lacking parents to protect them, inexperienced youngsters fell prey to great horned owls. When grown, these falcons gravitated to buildings and bridges, searching for nest sites that resembled their own. Additional release programmes followed.

Today peregrines have become a familiar sight in cities. New York has about twenty breeding pairs, London around twenty-five. Nesting on high-rises, coursing pigeons through city streets, they have developed novel behaviours in response to their surroundings. Some have learned to hunt at night, ascending into darkness to grab birds lit from beneath by streetlights. Urban environments are not without risk: the sheer sides, reflective glass and unexpected gusts of wind around tall buildings can result in crash-landings when young birds take their first flights, and dedicated locals who follow the lives of particular pairs through binoculars, telescopes or webcams sometimes intervene to rescue grounded birds from traffic. Even so, peregrine populations are growing in cities. Perched high on corporate headquarters, scanning the sky and streets below, the falcons can readily be viewed as reflections of our own fascination with vision, surveillance and power. But falcons are not merely handy symbols for human anxieties. Their greatest magic is that they're not human at all.

Eamonn comes to this site in Dublin nearly every day and has been doing so for years. He started watching the Poolbeg peregrines after a personal bereavement because it 'was … *away*', he told me. I understood what he meant. At times of difficulty, watching birds ushers you into a different world, where no words need be spoken. And if you're watching urban falcons, this is not a distant world, but one alongside you, a place of transient and graceful refuge. These days, working in Dublin, Eamonn keeps one eye on the sky, scanning churches and city towers. Up there, he sees falcons looking down on the streets below. 'Bits of eternity,' he calls them. Sometimes he sees one speeding overhead, a black silhouette over Temple Bar or the Olympia Theatre. In an instant, his city is transformed. Buildings become cliffs, streets canyons.

Time passes. The tiercel has gone. Now the female appears on the edge of the nestbox. She is larger and paler than her mate. For a minute or two, she sits undecided, looking about.

Then she opens her wings, wheels and glides down towards the other chimney. I raise my binoculars, wincing at the difficulty of focusing them with frozen hands. I see her wings flex and her primaries flare. She turns slowly in mid-air. There is a change in the quality of her flight. I'm not sure what it is. Then with a skip of the heart, I see an incautious pigeon flying low towards her, flapping in a leisurely manner. It can't have seen her. But she has seen it. The world shrinks to the space between the two birds. I hear an intake of breath from my companions as she sideslips and falls towards it with the finality of a rock flung from a bridge. The stricken pigeon dodges, closes its wings and drops to last-minute safety in the buildings below. The falcon circles, climbs and disappears inland.

We take the binoculars from our eyes and look at one another. We have all been reminded that a day can be cut in two by three seconds of a hunting peregrine and leave you stilled into silence and the memory of each curve of its flight. I'd swear, if I were of a more mystical persuasion, that a hunting peregrine changes the quality of the atmosphere it flies through, makes it heavier. Like thunder. Like slowed-down film in which the grain shows through. The Poolbeg site is about as far as you can get from a thriving natural ecosystem, but the act of watching a falcon chase its prey above the scarred and broken ground below feels like quiet resistance against despair. Matters of life and death and a sense of our place in the world tied fast together in a shiver of wings across a scrap of winter sky.

Vesper Flights

I found a dead swift once, a husk of a bird under a bridge over the River Thames, where sunlight from the water cast bright scribbles on the arches above. I picked it up, held it in my palm, saw the dust in its feathers, its wings crossed like dull blades, its eyes tight closed, and realised that I didn't know what to do. This was a surprise. Encouraged by books, I'd always been the type of Gothic amateur naturalist who preserved interesting bits of the dead. I cleaned and polished fox skulls; disarticulated, dried and kept the wings of road-killed birds. But I knew, looking at the swift, that I could not do anything like that to it. The bird was suffused with a kind of seriousness very akin to holiness. I didn't want to leave it there, so I took it home, swaddled it in a towel and tucked it in the freezer. It was in early May the following year, as soon as I saw the first returning swifts flowing down from the clouds, that I knew what I had to do. I went to the freezer, took out the swift, and buried it in the garden one hand's-width deep in earth newly warmed by the sun.

Swifts are magical in the manner of all things that exist just a little beyond understanding. Once they were called 'devil birds', perhaps because those screaming flocks of black crosses around churches seemed pulled from darkness, not light. But to me they are creatures of the upper air, and of their nature unintelligible, which makes them more akin to angels. Unlike all other birds they never descend to the ground. As a bird-obsessed child, I was frustrated that there was no way for me to know them better. They were so fast it was impossible to focus on their facial expressions or watch them preen through binoculars. They were only ever flickering silhouettes at twenty, thirty, forty miles an hour, a shoal of birds, a pouring sheaf of identical black grains against bright clouds. There was no way to tell one bird from another, nor to watch them do anything other than move from place to place, although sometimes, if the swifts were flying low over rooftops, I'd see one open its mouth, and that was truly uncanny, because the gape was huge, turning the bird into something uncomfortably like a miniature basking shark. Even so, watching them with the naked eye was rewarding in how it revealed the dynamism of what before was merely blankness. Swifts weigh about forty grams, and their surfing and tacking against the pressures of oncoming air make visible the movings of the atmosphere.

They still seem to me the closest things to aliens on Earth. I've seen them up close now, held a live grounded adult in my hands before letting it fall back into the sky. You know those deep-sea fish dragged by nets from fathoms of blackness, how obvious it is that they aren't supposed to exist where we are? The adult swift was like that in reverse. Its frame was tough and spare and its feathers bleached by the sun. Its eyes seemed unable to focus on me, as if it were an entity from an alternate universe whose senses couldn't quite map on to our phenomenal world. Time ran differently for this creature. If you record swifts' high-pitched, insistent screaming and slow it down to human speed you can hear what their voices sound like as they speak to one another: a wild, bubbling, rising and falling call, something like the song of northern loons.

Often, during stressful times when I was small – while changing schools, when bullied, or after my parents had argued – I'd lie in bed before I fell asleep and count in my head all the different layers between me and the centre of the Earth: crust, upper mantle, lower mantle, outer core, inner core. Then I'd think upwards in expanding rings of thinning air: troposphere, stratosphere, mesosphere, thermosphere, exosphere. A few miles beneath me was molten rock, a few miles above limitless dust and vacancy, and there I'd lie with the warm blanket of the troposphere over me and a red cotton duvet cover too, and the smell of tonight's dinner lingering upstairs, and downstairs the sound of my mother busy at her typewriter.

This evening ritual wasn't a test of how much I could keep in my mind at once, or of how far I could send my imagination. It had something of the power of incantation, but it did not seem a compulsion, and it was not a prayer. No matter how tightly the day's bad things had gripped me, there was so much up there above me, so much below, so many places and states that were implacable, unreachable, entirely uninterested in human affairs. Listing them one by one built imaginative sanctuary between walls of unknowing knowns. It helped in other ways, too. Sleeping was like losing time, somehow like not being alive, and drifting into it at night there sometimes came a panic that I might not find my way back from wherever I had gone. My own private vespers felt a little like counting the steps up a flight of steep stairs. I needed to know where I was. It was a way of bringing me home.

Swifts nest in obscure places, in dark and cramped spaces: hollows beneath roof tiles, behind the intakes for ventilation shafts, in the towers of churches. To reach them they fly straight at the entrance holes and enter at full tilt. Their nests are made of things snatched from the air: strands of dried grass pulled aloft by thermals; moulted pigeon-breast feathers; flower petals, leaves, scraps of paper, even butterflies.

During the war, swifts in Denmark and Italy grabbed chaff, reflective scraps of tinfoil dropped from aircraft to confuse enemy radar, flashing and twirling as it fell. They mate on the wing. And while young martins and swallows return to their nests after their first flights, young swifts do not. As soon as they tip themselves free of the nest hole, they start flying, and they will not stop flying for two or three years, bathing in rain, feeding on airborne insects, winnowing fast and low to scoop fat mouthfuls of water from lakes and rivers. European swifts spend only a few months on their breeding grounds, another few months in winter over the forests and fields of the Congo, and the rest of the time they're moving, making a mockery of borders. To avoid heavy rain, which makes it impossible for them to feed, swifts with nests in English roofs will fly clockwise around low-pressure systems, travelling across Europe and back again. They love to assemble in the complicated, unstable air behind weather depressions to feast upon the abundance of insects there. They depart us quietly. In the second week of August the skies around my home are suddenly empty, after which I'll see the occasional single straggler and think, *That's it. That's the last one*, and hungrily watch it rise and glide through turbulent summer air.

On warm summer evenings swifts that aren't sitting on eggs or tending their chicks fly low and fast, screaming in speeding packs around rooftops and spires. Later, they gather higher in the sky, their calls now so attenuated by air and distance that to the ear they corrode into something that seems less than sound, to suspicions of dust and glass. And then, all at once, as if summoned by a call or a bell, they rise higher and higher until they disappear from view. These ascents are called vespers flights, or vesper flights, after the Latin *vesper* for evening. Vespers are evening devotional prayers, the last and most solemn of the day, and I have always thought 'vesper flights' the most beautiful phrase, an ever-falling blue. For years I've tried to see them do it. But always the dark got too deep, or the birds skated too wide and far across the sky for me to follow.

For years we thought vesper flights were simply swifts flying higher up to sleep on the wind. Like other birds, they can close one eye and put half of their brain to sleep, with the other half awake and the other eye open for flight. But it's likely that swifts properly sleep up there too, drift into REM states where both eyes are closed and flying is automatic, at least for short periods. During the First World War, a French aviator on special night operations cut his engine at ten thousand feet and glided down in silent, close circles over enemy lines, a light wind against him, the full moon overhead. 'We suddenly found ourselves,' he wrote, 'among a strange flight of birds which seemed to be motionless, or at least showed no noticeable reaction. They were widely scattered and only a few yards below the aircraft, showing up against a white sea of cloud underneath.'

He had flown into a small party of swifts in deep sleep, miniature black stars illuminated by the reflected light of the moon. He managed to catch two – I know this is impossible, but I like to imagine that he or his navigator simply stretched out a hand and picked them gently from the air – and one swift was pulled dead from the engine after the flight returned to earth. The remote air, the coldness, the stillness, and the high birds over white cloud suspended in sleep. It's an image that drifts in and out of my dreams.

No longer do I conjure the stratifications of earth and air as I go to sleep. Instead, I play an audiobook on my phone, set it on my bedside table and let the whisper and catch of the narrator's voice turn to white noise as I drift away. Hearing the same words spoken by the same voices over and over again is a habit that began after my father died, when letting my attention wander as I dozed took me to places I didn't want to go, towards matters of whys and wheres and hows and what-ifs. Listening to mystery novels was a perfect distraction, and to begin with I'd be caught up in their plots. But after a few weeks of repeats, what I learned to love most of all was the soft predictability of each oncoming line, the comfort of knowing the words about to be spoken. I started this night-time ritual over a decade ago, and I'm finding it hard to shake the habit.

In the summer of 1979 an aviator, ecologist and expert in the science of aircraft bird-strikes called Luit Buurma began making radar observations in the Netherlands for flight safety purposes. His plots showed vast flocks of birds over the wide waters of the IJsselmeer that turned out to be swifts from Amsterdam and the surrounding region. Every evening in June and July they flew towards the lake, and between nine and ten o'clock they hawked low over the water to feed upon swarms of freshwater midges. Just after ten they began to rise, until fifteen minutes later all were more than six hundred feet high, gathered together in dense, wheeling flocks. Then the ascent began: five minutes later they were out of sight, and their vesper flights took them to heights of up to eight thousand feet. Using a special data processor linked to a large military air-defence radar in the north of Friesland to more closely study their movements, Buurma discovered that swifts weren't staying up there to sleep. In the hours after midnight they came down once again to feed over the water. It turns out that swifts, beloved *genii locorum* of bright summer streets, are just as much nocturnal creatures of thick summer darkness.

But he made another discovery: swifts weren't just making vesper flights in the evenings. They made them again just before dawn. Twice a day, when light levels exactly mirror each other, swifts rise and reach the apex of their flights at nautical twilight.

Since Buurma's observations, other scientists have studied these ascents and speculated on their purpose. Adriaan Dokter, an ecologist with a background in physics, has used Doppler weather radar to find out more about this phenomenon. He and his co-workers have written that swifts might be profiling the air as they rise through it, gathering information on air temperature and the speed and direction of the wind. Their vesper flights take them to the top of what is called the *convective boundary layer*. The CBL is the humid, hazy part of the atmosphere where the ground's heating by the sun produces rising and falling convective currents, blossoming thermals of hot air; it's the zone of fair-weather cumulus clouds and everyday life for swifts. Once swifts crest the top of this layer, they are exposed to a flow of wind that's unaffected by the landscape below but is determined instead by the movements of large-scale weather systems. By flying to these heights, swifts cannot only see the distant clouds of oncoming frontal systems on the twilit horizon, but use the wind itself to assess the possible future courses of these systems. What they are doing is forecasting the weather.

And they are doing more. As Dokter writes, migratory birds orient themselves through a complex of interacting compass mechanisms. During vesper flights, swifts have access to them all. At this panoptic height they can see the scattered patterns of the stars overhead, and at the same time they can calibrate their magnetic compasses, getting their bearings according to the light polarisation patterns that are strongest and clearest in twilit skies. Stars, wind, polarised light, magnetic cues, the distant rubble of clouds a hundred miles out, clear cold air, and below them the hush of a world tilting towards sleep or waking towards dawn. What they are doing is flying so high they can work out exactly where they are, to know what they should do next. They're quietly, perfectly, orienting themselves.

Cecilia Nilsson of the Cornell Laboratory of Ornithology and her team have discovered that swifts don't make these flights alone. They ascend as flocks every evening before singly drifting down, while in the morning they fly up alone and return to earth together. To orient themselves correctly, to make the right decisions, they need to pay attention not only to the cues of the world around them, but also to each other. Nilsson writes that it's likely that swifts on their vesper flights are working according to what is called the *many-wrongs principle*. That is, they're averaging all their individual assessments in order to reach the best navigational decision. If you're in a flock, decisions about what to do next are improved if you exchange information with those around you. We can speak to each other. Swifts have no voices, but what they can do is pay attention to what other swifts are doing. And in the end it can be as simple as this: they follow each other.

The realm of my own life is the quotidian, the everyday. It's where I sleep and eat and work and think. It's a space of rising and falling hopes and worries, costs and benefits, plans and distractions, and it can batter and divert me, just as high winds and rainfall send swifts off course. Sometimes it's a hard place to be, but it's home.

Thinking about swifts has made me think more carefully about the ways in which I've dealt with difficulty. When I was small I comforted myself with thoughts of layers of rising air; later I hid myself among the whispers of recorded works of fiction. We all have our defences. Some of them are self-defeating, but others are occasions for joy: the absorption of a hobby, the writing of a poem, speeding on a Harley, the slow assembly of a collection of records or seaside shells. 'The best thing for being sad,' said T. H. White's Merlin, 'is to learn something.' All of us have to live our lives most of the time inside the protective structures that we have built;

none of us can bear too much reality. We need our books, our craft projects, our dogs and knitting, our movies, gardens and gigs. It's who we are. We're held together by our lives, our interests, and all our chosen comforts. But we can't have *only* those things, because then we can't work out where we should be headed.

Swifts aren't always cresting the atmospheric boundary layer at dizzying heights; most of the time they are living below it in thick and complicated air. That's where they feed and mate and bathe and drink and *are*. But to find out about the important things that will affect their lives, they must go higher to survey the wider scene, and there communicate with others about the larger forces impinging on their realm. So I'm starting to think of swifts differently now, not as angels or aliens, but as perfectly instructive creatures. Not all of us need to make that climb, just as many swifts eschew their vesper flights because they are occupied with eggs and young – but as a community, surely some of us are required, by dint of flourishing life and the well-being of us all, to look clearly at the things that are so easily obscured by the everyday. The things we need to set our courses towards or against. The things we need to think about to know what we should do next. Swifts are my fable of community, teaching us about how to make right decisions in the face of oncoming bad weather, in the face of clouds that sit like dark rubble on our own horizon.

In Spight of Prisons

There's a species of summer magic I chase every year. It's small, fierce and insistently beautiful, and my best chance of seeing it is on hot nights in June and July. Tonight I'm searching for it in a disused chalk quarry on the outskirts of my university town, an eerie, lunar landscape of towering white cliffs and patches of bare ground resembling snowfields strewn with bones. This is a nature reserve – one of only three UK sites where moon carrots grow – and it is crowded with life. Green longhorn moths the colour of stained gold velvet decorate pale scabious flowers; rabbits graze in drifts of trefoil, kidney vetch and thyme. The evening air is full of huge wood-coloured beetles with handlebar antennae, hooked feet and wildly erratic flights: cockchafers. I feel small, insistent tugs as they get entangled in my hair and impatiently comb them free with my fingers. I've not come here for them; I'm waiting for something else, and it's nearly time. With a little thrill of anticipation I see that light is fading fast. By ten o'clock the last snowy glow has faded from the cliffs, replaced by thin starlight and a soft, mothy blackness. And then the magic begins.

Twenty feet away a point of intense light winks into existence. Over there, another. And another: tiny motes of cold fire mapping a sparse starfield over the ground. I walk up to one, kneel and peer carefully at the otherworldly brilliance. It comes from the tail end of a small, elongated, wingless beetle, clutching hold of a stem of grass and waving its abdomen in the air. It, and the lights around me, are glow-worms, *Lampyris noctiluca*, things both sublime and ridiculous: half intimations of remote stellar distance and half waggling beetle bums.

Only female glow-worms shine like this. They can't eat, drink or fly, but spend their days burrowed deep in stems and under debris, emerging after twilight, when the light drops to around 0.1 lux, to clamber up plant stems and glow to attract the smaller, winged males. Once mated, the females extinguish their light, lay fifty to a hundred and fifty small, spherical, faintly luminous eggs, and die. Their adult lives are short and made of light – but in their two years as larvae they are creatures of macabre darkness, using their proboscises to inject snails with paralysing, dissolving neurotoxins before sucking them up like soup.

Kneeling by this glow-worm and transfixed by its light, this encounter in the summer night feels more like the workings of magic than chemistry, though I know that the light is the result of a reaction when the enzyme luciferase acts upon a compound called luciferin in the presence of oxygen, ATP and magnesium. The precise mechanism of their cold luminescence long puzzled natural philosophers. In the seventeenth century Robert Boyle found that the glow was extinguished if they were kept in a vacuum – and went on to muse that the light of his experimental glow-worms, trapped behind glass, was akin to 'certain truths' that shine freely 'in spight of prisons'. In the early nineteenth century, John Murray conducted laborious experiments on Shropshire glow-worms, placing their luminous parts in water heated to various temperatures, or in acid, naphtha, oil or spirits. His accounts of these faintly gruesome experiments are almost as magical as his subjects. One specimen glowed for several nights when suspended in olive oil. 'Viewed at a distance of about 10 feet, it twinkled like a fixed star,' he recounted, while 'the eye steadily and tranquilly observed the beautiful phenomenon'. It is hard to write about glow-worms without recourse to metaphors of stars and lamps; their singular light populates myriad works of literature. These are the creatures of an 'ineffectual fire' in *Hamlet* and the 'living lamps' of Marvell's *Mower to the Glow-Worms*, courteous beasts who guide wanderers home to safety.

Glow-worms prefer chalky, limestone habitats and you can find them on old railway lines and embankments, in cemeteries, hedgerows and gardens. But no one knows how many there are in Britain; they often go unnoticed because their light is easily obscured by headlights and torches. Certainly they are threatened by habitat degradation and urban development – males are attracted to streetlights and brightly lit windows, and this particular colony survives partly because the sodium glow of the surrounding town is blocked by quarry walls. Because the females do not fly, colonies are often venerable in age and easily rendered extinct: it is hard for them to move. But where they are known, colonies are often guarded passionately, and glow-worm tours and walks have become a much-loved summer's-night tradition in many parts of the country: local experts guiding visitors around the natural light show, often with drinks and snacks laid on.

We live in a world of distracting, endless glowing screens, but even so these shining, tiny beacons retain an allure that draws people out in droves to stand and wonder. It is hard in these days of ecological ruination to find ways to reconnect people to a natural world more commonly encountered on television and video than in its living reality. The greatest magic of these shining beacons that draw people out in hordes to stand and wonder is that it cannot be meaningfully captured on film. Glow-worms are part of our hidden countryside; like Marvell's living lamps, they are still able to guide distracted wanderers.

Sun Birds and Cashmere Spheres

I only saw them once. I didn't know I'd never see them again. I assumed they'd be eternal, like Pan Am, and the Soviet Union, and so many other things in the world that existed when I was born. I went out early that morning, sun glowing faintly through stratus, and drove north-west until shapes rose syrup-slow on the far horizon. They looked like buildings, like aircraft hangars or warehouses, but they were stands of poplars planted in the 1950s by Bryant & May, the safety match manufacturers. Disposable plastic lighters and cheaper wood imports turned the trees into economic relics. But these plantations were beloved of birders because they were the only place in the country you could see breeding golden orioles. They were legendary birds. I'd read about them for years. They're dazzlingly pretty – the males buttercup yellow with shiny black wings and a strawberry-red beak, the females soft olive green – but much of their glamour came from their rarity. If you live somewhere other than Britain, you might see orioles all the time. There are many in the Americas, and golden orioles are common garden birds in countries across the Palaearctic. But in Britain we only had this one tiny outpost.

I'd arranged to meet my guide by the entry gate. I'd never met him before, but there wasn't much doubt that he was the man in a woollen hat waving at me with a pair of binoculars. Peter was a friend of a friend, an expert on these orioles, and he had, it turned out, been sleeping in his car all night on site waiting for daylight. He told me I'd missed the bitterns booming in the reed beds at dawn, that it was the strangest of sounds, like someone blowing across the top of a deep and wide-necked bottle. But, he continued, the orioles were still singing. And as we walked down the dew-soaked track towards the wood, I heard them, fluting, rich, melodic phrases that cut across distance and the rattle of leaves and the loud chatter of singing reed warblers as if they were drifting in from an impossibly remote place. That place, I realised, might be the past, the birds speaking of history. Chaucer wrote of a bird called *Wodewale*, which has been variously identified by experts as a woodpecker, a woodlark or an oriole. I'm convinced it's the latter, for the word is such a beautiful phonetic approximation of an oriole's song: *Wo-de-wal-e, wo-de-wal-e*, a phrase like the curl of the cut ends of a gilded banner furling over the page of an illuminated manuscript.

It was easy to hear orioles. Seeing them was a different matter. The poplar plantation resembled, somehow, a scaled-up tabletop cardboard theatre set, and peering into it pulled me into all manner of perspectival tricks and traps. Rows of equally sized grey, columnar trunks marched back to vanishing points in the dim distance, and because poplar branches begin high up, the arches where the leaves met between the rows of trees seemed part proscenium, part cathedral buttress. It was *noisy*, too, with a near-continuous rattle and clatter. Poplar's heart-shaped leaves are arranged in little fists of long, flexible petioles that make them twist and flap, flag-like, in the least breath of wind. The whole forest looked as if it were made of torn paper, and somewhere in its leaves were orioles. They called, moved. Sang, then called again, moved unseen to a distant tree, called again, made a different call, a sharp cat-call *hzzzt*!, moved, called, sang, and then moved once more. They stuck to the very tops of the tree canopy, and after a while I began to wonder if they could throw their voices. We stood there for a very long while, binoculars raised, necks getting cricked, and we saw no orioles at all. Driving home, I held the memory of their song with me like a pebble in the palm of one hand. I hadn't been disappointed by my morning in the poplars. Even so, I knew I needed to come back and try again.

This was thirteen years ago, in 2006, and our little population was about to blink into nonexistence. At that point the outpost was only about forty years old: its first colonisers had come here from the Netherlands in the 1960s, where they nested in trees in the Polders just like these. They must have crossed the North Sea and found themselves somewhere that felt like home. They quietly thrived. By the 1980s there were about thirty pairs, but there was already concern for their future, for many of the most expansive poplar stands in the area were scheduled to be felled. People clubbed together to form a group to study, survey and help protect the birds, and some new poplar belts were planted in hope of future colonisation. But the largest block of trees was hewn down all the same, and their numbers plummeted. This coincided with the beginning of a wider decline in oriole populations across their northern range in the Netherlands, Denmark, Finland. It might have been the effect of environmental changes in the Congo, where orioles spend their winters, or perhaps because increasingly early springs in Europe have led to a mismatch in timing between the emergence of the insects that orioles feed upon and when they are most needed to feed their young. In Britain the end came fast. Three years after my visit, only one nest remained, after which there were no more British-bred orioles. They had been a visitation, living in a little snippet of economic history, settling gold on the papery branches, making the fens obliquely glorious with their song. We never thought of these birds as immigrants;

this was no Lost Colony. We thought of them as returning natives, and cherished their foothold in our time.

I returned a week later in hot, thundery darkness just before sunrise. The site had been turned into a bird reserve a few years previously, and the carrot fields around the poplar plantations had been flooded and planted with *phragmites* reeds. My walk to meet Peter ran through these reeds, passing patches of unreflective water, flat pools with surfaces matte with milky pollen-dust, tiny froglets scrambling away from my feet, the grass running with scores of miniature, urgent amphibians. Though beautiful, reed beds are unsettling places. Unlike deserts and open water, they're not inimical to supporting human life except in a very literal sense. You can walk across deserts, foot by foot. You can't walk on water at all. With reed beds, who knows? Their stalks are spiky and soft at once, and reed beds do, in some places, become islands, as in the Danube delta, and sail off in matted arks of rot and life. They're delicate, different and faintly dangerous places. Let no one underestimate the strange effect on human psychology of not knowing whether the ground underfoot is ground at all. Unless you have special, local knowledge, reed beds can be as forbidding and as lethal as mountains.

As I looked over the reeds I heard a pinging sound, then four or five small, long-tailed birds flew in little musical slurs across the water and landed to catch like little spherical burrs in the reeds right in front of me. They were bearded reedlings, birds utterly reliant on stands of *phragmites* like these. The adults raise a couple of families a year, and this was a brood of adolescents let loose upon the reeds. Adult male bearded reedlings are legendarily glamorous, possessing grey cowls and long black moustaches. But these youngsters weren't in grown-up dress; they were sleek and fawn-coloured, as if they were made of very expensive cashmere, and somehow wearing long, black velvet evening gloves. Their tiny waxen beaks resembled the heads of all-weather matches, and set in a thumb-smear of sooty kohl were strange, pale eyes that caught the light oddly as they clambered among the reeds. Their movements were bewitching. They're birds built for a world of verticals. Their legs are long, black and glint like obsidian, and they have huge, cartoon bird feet. Orioles forgotten, I stood and watched these little cashmere balls bouncing up and down in the reeds, and was delighted to see that quite often a bird hopped from one reed stem on to two, grabbing one stalk in each foot before sitting there happily doing the splits to pick reed seeds from the nearest overhanging frond.

This time Peter had brought the technology; he had set up a telescope on the bank and already trained it on the nest. The nest adhered to the tree the way that papery burnet moth cocoons adhere to stems of grass. It was shaped something like a half coconut woven carefully from a hammock of thin grass and slung between two whippy branches sixty feet up in the air, and it was like no nest I'd seen before, although for a long while I couldn't see it at all. Through the telescope there was barely enough ambient light for depth and modelling to appear, but as the sun rose higher, what I saw became something like looking into a Magic Eye picture. Here was a circle, and in it a thousand angles of stalk and leaf and scraps of shade at various distances, and every straight stalk or branch was alternately obscured and revealed as the wind blew. I began to feel a little seasick watching this chaos, but then, as magically as a stereogram suddenly reveals a not-very-accurate 3D dinosaur, the muddy patch just off centre resolved itself into the nest.

As soon as it happened I tensed with the effort of not losing it again. The telescope's focus was slightly out for my shortsighted eyes, so it required physical effort to keep what I saw from derealising back into nonsense. I wanted so much to see an adult oriole leaping on to the nest to make it real, the gaping mouths of begging chicks emerging from inside it, the flapping of newly grown feathers. But nothing happened.

If there were birds inside that nest, at this time of year they'd be close to fledging and leaving it, I thought, so why couldn't I see anything in it move? They'd be restless, surely, at this hour? I surrendered the telescope to Peter along with my misgivings, spread my coat on the grass and sat down. Our mood grew sombre as we came to suspect, then believe, then finally know that there was nothing in this nest at all. It had been exceptionally windy the previous day, so we wondered if the young had fallen from the nest. After thinking this, there was no question but that we needed to go into the wood and look for the chicks that might be underneath the tree.

I shrugged my coat back on. The wood was at least five feet deep in stinging nettles. I'd done a lot of birding, and walking, and hawking, in nettles, and knew that the correct way to treat banks of big nettles is to wear reasonably thick clothes and not give a cuss for them. Wade through and be damned. It's like the Red Sea miracle – with faith, they'll part harmlessly in front of you. But what I wasn't used to dealing with was nettles emerging from a swamp. We stepped through rushes growing etiolated through wet black mud, and across places where the ground was so saturated there was no vegetation at all but something akin to quickpeat. Mostly we walked in nettles, their stems so densely packed that neither of us had much idea of what was beneath them as we struggled through. The poplar branches here were low, permitting us only a tiny tunnel of clearance between the top of the stinging nettles and the thatch of twigs and leaves. It felt like river caving, tilting our chins upward to the foot and a half of air between water and rock. It was claustrophobic, intense, the greens rich and dark, and it felt very far away from England. Like Louisiana, perhaps. Mosquitoes descended on us, swarms of big *Anopheles* whose delicate stripes and long noses drifted purposively towards our faces. We halted at the nest tree, kicked carefully about. There was nothing beneath it but nettles. I slapped away one mosquito after another, noticed there was blood all over my hands.

Then we heard an oriole. It wasn't the oriole's otherworldly song, but a series of short, rasping calls. Then, very softly from the foggy, papery green, a soft *hoot hoot hoot* was sent back to it – the contact call of a chick. Then came the glorious swirling flute of one of the parents as he swept in from nowhere to feed. And that's when I saw him. Finally, I saw my oriole. A bright, golden male. It was a complex joy, because I saw him only in stamped-out sections, small jigsaw pieces of a bird, but moving ones, animated mutoscope views. A flick of wings, a scrap of tail, then another glimpse – this time, just his head alone – through a screen of leaves. I was transfixed. I had not expected the joyous, extravagant way this oriole leapt into the air between feeds, the enormously decisive movements, always, and the little dots like stars that flared along the edge of his spread-wide tail. It's hard to comprehend that in all these views through my binoculars, he was never more than the size of a fingernail at arm's length. But then a fingernail at arm's length is, I guess, exactly the size of the visible sun.

The Observatory

I never cared much for swans until the day a swan told me I was wrong. It was a cloudy winter morning and I was suffering from a recently broken heart. I sat myself down on a concrete step by Jesus Lock and was staring at the river, feeling the world was just as cold and grey, when a female mute swan hoist herself out from the water and stumped towards me on leathery, in-turned webbed feet and sturdy black legs. I assumed she wanted food. *Swans can break an arm with one blow of their wing*, I remembered, one of those warnings from childhood that get annealed into adult fight-or-flight responses. Part of me wanted to get up and move further away, but most of me was just too tired.

I watched her, her snaky neck, black eye, her blank hauteur. I expected her to stop, but she did not. She walked right up to where I sat on the step, her head towering over mine. Then she turned around to face the river, shifted left, and plonked herself down, her body parallel with my own, so close her wing-feathers were pressed against my thighs. Let no one ever speak of swans as being airy, insubstantial things. I was sitting with something the size of a large dog. And now I was too astonished to be nervous. I didn't know what to do: I grasped, bewildered, for the correct interspecies social etiquette. She looked at me incuriously, then tucked her head sideways and backwards into her raised coverts, neck curved, and fell fast asleep.

We sat there together for ten minutes, until a family came past and a toddler made a beeline for her. She slipped back into the water and ploughed upstream. As I watched her leave something shifted inside me and I began to weep with an emotion I recognised as gratitude. That day was when swans turned into real creatures for me, and it has spurred me since to seek out others.

My favourite place to see swans in winter is the Welney Wildfowl and Wetlands Trust reserve. It's on the Ouse Washes, part of the highly engineered wetland landscape of the East Anglian Fens. The observatory here is far from the usual ramshackle wooden hide. It's heated and carpeted and even has a glass case of taxidermied swans inside. Age has rendered them nicotine-yellow so they resemble the live birds outside the way smoked kippers resemble live herring.

Just as unusual are the crowds sharing the observatory with me. There are a few wolfish-looking men with spectacular telescopes of a species common to nature reserves. But there are also impressively bouffanted ladies of a certain age peering through binoculars so elderly they resemble opera glasses. There's a woman in a wheelchair who sings joyously all the way down the bumpy slope to the door. There are teen Goths and toddlers and couples in their twenties and sixties and eighties and a baby in pink tights and a glittery top. All of us – apart from the baby, who is transfixed by the Goths – are looking out of the panoramic plate-glass windows across a mile of water broken by tiny islands and dotted lines that are the stalks of drowned grasses and huddles of sleeping black-tailed godwits. There are no shadows anywhere out there except in the moving lines between ripples that chase themselves across miles of shallow water. As the light diminishes, distant structures become unmoored and float on the horizon: trees, pylons, wind turbines. Closer, willows are frozen like ice on glass. The lake is mercury-bright and patterned with thousands of birds as far as the eye can see: moving dots of mallard, wigeon, pochard – and miniature bergs that are swans.

A lake the size of Loch Lomond appears here every winter and drains to wet pasture in spring. Famed for wildfowling and winter skating, it's become a traditional wintering site for thousands of swans that come to feast on potatoes left in the ground after harvest, on sugar beet, on winter wheat. These aren't the familiar mute swans of town parks and lakes, not the species that came up to me and made its presence known. They're whooper swans and Bewick's swans, birds that breed in arctic Iceland and Siberia, and they are very different beasts.

Whoopers cross the North Atlantic non-stop to get here, flying for twelve hours at around twenty thousand feet through icy and oxygen-poor air. They're huge and impressive creatures. But it's the smaller species here, Bewick's swans, that are the favourite of WWT warden Shaun, who has come into the observatory to talk with us before the evening feed. Shaun is a stockman, of sorts. In summer he looks after cattle that graze on the Washes. When it is flooded, he looks after the swans. 'The yellow from their beaks continues up and around their eyes,' he says reverently of his Bewick's. 'Like yellow eyeliner. They're such pretty little birds.'

Near the case of swans in this observatory there's a bronze bust of the WWT's founder, Sir Peter Scott. He loved them too. Fifty years ago he noticed that every swan had a different pattern of yellow and black on its bill. Fascinated, he started to name them and paint tiny swan reference mugshots of each bird. This developed into a 'face book', a visual catalogue of individual swans that is continued today. Even now, WWT researchers memorise birds by sight, and Scott's initial tracing of swans and their family trees has become one of the longest-running wildlife studies in the world. In conjunction with radio-tracking and ringing studies, the data it produces is crucial for conservation. While whooper populations are healthy, Bewick's are not: climate and habitat change seem likely factors in their rapid decline.

When I was small, Bewick's swans were strange and glamorous because they migrated here from the Soviet Union, crossing the Iron Curtain with absolute unconcern. I've often wondered what lay behind Peter Scott's fascination with them. To an ex-naval officer, explorer's son and champion glider pilot, the heroic North Sea flights of whoopers would certainly appeal. But it's tempting to imagine that a particular strand of English conservatism influenced his desire to individuate Bewick's swans, to turn them into families rather than flocks, trace their family trees and give them names like Casino, Croupier, Lancelot, Jane Eyre and Victoria, before they returned to the Soviet Union each spring. Politics are so easily caught up in science, the Cold War unwittingly pleated into swans' rushing, beating wings.

Now the floodlights are switched on and the water shivers. There's a hush of anticipation as Shaun leaves the observatory and reappears pushing a wheelbarrow along the shoreline, casting great scoopfuls of corn into the lake. We crowd to the window. A raft of winter wildfowl is feeding busily beneath us: conker-headed pochards, mallards, scores of whoopers and Bewick's with cloudy pinions and snowy necks. These birds are entirely wild, yet here they are, tame as farmyard ducks, feeding on a wet stage lit up like a West End theatre. The experience is joyous, but messes with your everyday notions of what a wild animal is, what wildness is at all.

But something is missing. I'm chasing something like the feeling the Cambridge swan had given me, and it isn't here, though I have an intimation of where I might find it. Leaving the observatory I head for the old wooden hides next door, raise a narrow window and let in the soundscape outside. What do thousands of arctic swans sound like? A vast amateur brass band tuning up in an aircraft hangar. My heart soars. Every few seconds comes a carillon of new voices. The swans are coming home to roost in little family groups, silhouettes that rise over the observatory and plane down to the black water. They are calling to each other in the night, these beautiful migrants, some of their faces stained yellow, some dark with potato-mud, their broad webbed feet splayed to brake as they descend. They land, call, flap their wings, squabble, dip their heads under the water, preen, drink thirstily. This is why I came. It's impossible to regard the natural world without seeing something of our own caught up in it. Back on that wintry riverside, a swan had come towards me and offered me strange companionship at a time when I thought loneliness was all I could feel. And what comforts me now, watching these arctic swans in our era of rising political nativism, is how clearly they are at home.

Wicken

On a foggy morning a long while ago, I took my brother and very young niece for a walk around one of Britain's oldest nature reserves. Wicken Fen is a tiny fragment of the lost marshland ecosystem that once covered around two and a half thousand square miles of eastern England. We spent a couple of hours in its mosaic of grassland and sedge, strolling in wet fields cut with scrub-shadow and water. It was spring, and everywhere was bursting with life: singing nightingales, snipe winnowing and bleating through the upper air, cuckoos tilting from the tips of willows and water rails squealing and grunting in reeds. As we crossed one of the fen's ancient waterways, a barn owl floated past us, mothy wings shining through particulate mist; at our feet a drinker moth caterpillar inched furrily across the path like a cautiously mobile moustache. We knelt to watch its progress. Then my niece turned to me and asked, curiously: 'Auntie Helen, when they made this place, where did they bring the animals from?'

I didn't understand at first.

'What do you mean?'

'There are so many animals here. Did they come from a zoo?'

That was when I realised her intuition was a perfectly rational one, for the countryside that my niece knew was mostly green desert.

'They always lived here,' I said gently. 'All the countryside used to be like this. Little bits like this are all that is left.' And her frown made my heart break.

I have been coming to Wicken for many years, bewitched by its strangeness and beauty. And today I'm back again, walking its paths under drifts of pallid cloud, still haunted by my niece's reasonable inability to understand that the life that is here was once everywhere. But that was, after all, why we had come. Nature reserves are places in which we can experience the past – the British environmentalist Max Nicholson once described them as outdoor living museums. Fen landscapes are unstable places where familiar categories of water and land are disconcertingly confused, and they feel temporally unstable, too, rich with a sense of their layered ages. Walking in them is an act of virtual time travel.

I think of the natural wealth of the eleventh-century fens, where fish and wildfowl existed in such astonishing plenitude that local debts were settled with payments of eels – known as fish-silver – and Saxon warlords hid in the swamps from Norman invaders. I think of seventeenth-century villagers who were at home here, who cut sedge and reed for thatching and dug peat for domestic fuel. In the nineteenth century naturalists flocked to Wicken in search of insects. So many people brought lamps to attract moths at night that there were complaints that the fen looked lit by streetlights. Charles Darwin collected rare beetles from Wicken-cut reeds sent to Cambridge in boats to light university fires, and sugar-smeared poles stuck in the ground by amateur entomologists specifically to draw moths to their sweetness took root and grew into today's vast willows. I pass one of these trees at the corner of the path, lately fallen, its split trunk spilling with old bee honeycomb. It had been planted by a visitor to the fen whose relationship to nature was very different from that of my niece. To him it was something to collect, fix and catalogue. To her, it is a thing separate from us, something to revere and observe from a remove.

It is pleasurable to imagine that you can commune with the past in a place like this. But there are consequences to feeling that kind of pleasure. If you start to see ecologically rich habitats as temporally separated from us, then the lack of wildlife in modern landscapes seems unremarkable. Why bother reducing pesticide use on farms, or preventing housing development at the edge of a city, when a reserve exists a few miles away? Living museums may be comforting to visit, but the problem is that they cannot ever be really insulated from the present. Dam construction outside the McCloud River Preserve in California, for example, rendered the river's native bull trout extinct. In the Charcoal Tank Nature Reserve in New South Wales, Australia, many species have been lost through habitat degradation and predation by foxes and cats. Once they are gone, these species cannot recolonise, because the small reserve is now an isolated island in a sea of impoverished habitat.

The wildlife and vegetation around me here are not frozen remnants of another time but things with their own histories, moving and shifting ceaselessly in response to local conditions, and able to return to places where we thought them gone. Humans have shaped this fen for centuries, halted its natural processes of ecological succession and maintained its delicate and complicated life. During the past two decades, the custodians of Wicken Fen have undertaken an ambitious century-long rewilding project to enlarge the reserve by slowly returning about thirteen thousand acres to its former wetland state. The project is already winding time backwards: in the years I've come here I've seen farm fields turn back into wetlands and meadows. But it's also turning time forward. Herds of Highland cattle and Polish konik ponies now live on the fen, their grazing shaping its vegetation as part of a management regime designed to let the land develop over time. It is impossible to predict in detail how the course of this rewilding will run, but our separation from it is intrinsic to the plan. There will be no return of the intensive local human interventions that once shaped the fen. This rewilded landscape will be a place for humans to visit, not to live and work.

At Sedge Fen, the path narrows between walls of high reeds, its surface steeped in tea-coloured water that reflects the sky piecemeal from my feet, and the ground rocks with every step. When one boot sinks calf-deep in black mud, I'm forced to turn back. Places like this resist modern assumptions that everything is visible and accessible. When I first came here years ago, I found it frustrating and sometimes even boring. The reed beds were flat expanses of impenetrable vegetation, undulating in the breeze like the sea. Like the sea, I couldn't see into them. I couldn't walk in them. And like the sea they teemed with invisible life: warblers, bitterns, spotted crakes, otters, water voles and marshland insects like reed leopard moths.

At first I used to watch the ditches and droves that cut through the reeds like streets between skyscrapers, waiting for animals to appear. Then I saw my mistake. I learned to stop needing to see. I learned to listen, to tune in to noises and let them guide my eyes. I'd hear the faintest creak or splash or call, and fix on that spot. I might sit there for minutes and see nothing. But sometimes things would appear. Most often I caught only the briefest glimpses. A brown flash in the stems that could have been a reed warbler, a sedge warbler, a Cetti's warbler. That tiny squelching noise that might be a teal feeding in a pool obscured by reeds. An almost imperceptible disturbance moving slowly across the reed bed that could be an otter, a bittern or a snake.

Wicken Fen has taught me not only that I won't always see the animals that I know live there, but that sometimes knowing where an animal is but not knowing *what* it is can be better than seeing it. I've learned how to identify birds in pieces, through scraps of colour and shape glimpsed through undergrowth: an eyebrow stripe, a wing-bar, an up-cocked tail. I've come to know the inhabitants of this place through a long series of brief, partial encounters in which the animal in question becomes more and more distinctive over time, and never once resembles the flat portraits in field guides.

Wicken does let me visit the past, but it's not the past of a Saxon warlord, a Victorian naturalist or an imagined unsullied wilderness. It is an older way of observing animals, distinct from the way they are usually viewed today, through binoculars, from behind hides and blinds, or in close-up footage on television screens. It's nothing like visiting a living museum or a zoo. This way of watching wildlife is full of difficulty and mystery, and it makes the landscape seem intrinsic to what its creatures are: things in the present moment – bewitching, complicated and always new.

Storm

Driving on the M25 on a summer evening I found myself headed for a wide column of storm-lit rainbow above Heathrow. The sky was congested and bruised, and even at seventy miles an hour, the pull of wind towards the storm tugged at my car, rushing across the elevated motorway section to fill the vacancy left by air pulled up thousands of feet to the cloud's blossoming apex. I couldn't see its white top stroked windward, but I could see the small crosses that were transatlantic jets steering their courses around the storm's perimeter. Half-feared for them. There were clips of lightning through this atmospheric carnage, and small turquoise pools of clear sky. And across one of these I saw a flock of parakeets flying straight and fast, with clipped wingbeats and streaming tails straight out behind them. It was a moment cut from a few seconds of moving history that will hang bright in my mind forever.

Most summer weather seems to me merely a backdrop to half-remembered scenes: a sun-baked lawn, misty mornings by the sea, city streets in the rain. All my clearest summer memories are of storms. The afternoon in the early 1980s on the Kennet and Avon Canal when I heard my first nightingale singing into charged grey air, accompanied by distant thunder that swung closer and seemed a voice answering the bird. Or that hot week in Gloucestershire in the 1990s when thunderstorms came every evening so the air turned sepia at six and before the first drops of storm rain sent pollen-dust up in puffs from the skylight I'd open the windows and wait for thunder while little owls called through the thick air, and in the morning tiny white dots of storm-blown blossom covered the house with wet French lace. I've measured all my summers by their storms.

There are people in America who climb into cars to chase thunderclouds across the Great Plains. But part of the thrill of British summer storms is not that one seeks them out, but that when the conditions are right, they come to you. For all the anxiety that spreads within you as you hear the crackling static of lightning breaking through voices on the radio, or smell the petrichor of newly soaked ground borne in on a rising wind, the predictability of the life-cycle of a thunderstorm is strangely reassuring. Stand far enough away and you can watch a summer cumulus, a thing born of sun-warmed air and water, grow into an entity the size of a mountain, unleash hail and brilliant hell, then disappear. A thundercloud takes perhaps an hour or so to cycle through its life, first stretching and pushing upwards until its top hits the troposphere and is pushed sideways and brushed into ice. As water droplets are pulled up into the cloud they freeze, eventually growing too heavy to ascend further, and so they fall, bumping into smaller fragments on their way up. Each collision transfers electrons, so that the lower parts of the cloud collect a negative charge while the upper parts collect a positive charge. Eventually lightning leaps across these differentials between the cloud's top, its base and the ground, casting out shockwaves of superheated air that make the sound of thunder. The destructive power of storms forces you to recall the vulnerabilities of your human frame, and all the limits, safeties and certainties of your everyday world. *Unplug your television and telephone. Get out of the bath. Do not shower. Stand away from windows.*

But storms are made of more than stuff. They're also things of metaphors and memory. Storms distressed my grandmother; to her, thunder recalled the terror of the Blitz. But to me thunder still carries that glowing moment as my father explained to small me how storms are born from sunlight and hot earth, moving air and water, and how you can count the seconds it takes between lightning and thunder – *one Mississippi, two Mississippi* – to work out how far away the storm is. Five seconds is a mile. You can calculate its progress towards you. And even now when I count those seconds, I feel a slow wonder that is as much connected to the passage of years as it is to that of a cloud over rain-soaked ground.

Summer storms conjure distance and time but conjure, too, all the things that come towards us over which we have no control. Such storms have their place in literature; the heavy air and mood of suppressed emotion as the storm brews so often standing for an inevitable catastrophe. A murder in Agatha Christie's *The Mysterious Affair at Styles* or Leo's revelation in Hartley's *The Go-Between*. No weather so perfectly conjures a sense of foreboding, of anticipation and waiting, as the eerie stillness that often occurs before the first fat drops of rain, when storm light makes luminous all roofs and fields and strands black silhouettes of trees on the horizon. This is the storm as expectation. As solution about to be offered. Or all hell about to break loose. And as the weeks of this summer draw on, I can't help but think that this is the weather we are all now made of. All of us waiting. Waiting for news. Waiting for Brexit to hit us. Waiting for the next revelation about the Trump administration. Waiting for hope, stranded in that strange light that stills our hearts before the storm of history.

Murmurations

Words to accompany Sarah Wood's 2015 film *Murmuration x 10*

I lost my passport. Blind panic. I needed one fast. So one morning I drove up the A14 north past the sex shops and service stations half-buried in fog and the convoys of container trucks *Maersk Sealand Hanjin* with an envelope containing two photographs of myself, one signed by an accountant, and my details in capitals in black biro on three pages of orange paper. And at 9.15 a.m. somewhere near Wisbech a flock of plovers flew low in front of the windscreen and hung there before vanishing into nowhere. Seamless fog. No visible land or sky. And I thought of the blank air-age globes they sold in the 1930s that had no geography on them at all, that were perfectly white except for the printed names of airports because we were all to look skyward back then, for history had brought us wings and borders would fade into obsolescence. Hope was a thing with feathers.

At the passport office thirty tight-lipped people file singly through X-rays. We turn off our phones and computers. Our bags are searched for sharp objects and compressed gas canisters. And we sit waiting to be processed, feet on grey carpet. Soft murmurs. Flatscreens. We watch BBC news in spooling text and clips, riots and far wars and a seaside political party conference.

That party conference was in Brighton. I was there one winter. I stood on the pier at dusk and watched the starlings coming in to roost, blobs of running oil over the ocean rising in packs to settle in the ironwork under the planked wooden floor, and as they settled in the dark beneath the arcade lights they began to sing and their songs mimicked the fairground music from the sideshows above, the same notes in new avian order, tapes spliced and doubled and whistling, a thousand shortwave radios tuning between circus stations out east, across the Baltic from whence they came. And I stood there hearing mimicked human music under the floor and the sea beneath us was slick and pointed with tiny lights and

> *Nay,*
> *I'll have a starling shall be taught to speak*
> *Nothing but 'Mortimer,' and give it him*
> *To keep his anger still in motion.*

I look at the security guards at the passport office and they look at me and I remember a British officer called Peter Conder who spent the Second World War in prison camps in Germany. He survived by watching birds. Goldfinches. Wrynecks. Migrating crows picking through the waste spread on the frozen fields. Hours and days and years on end. When he came home he didn't talk. He stayed with his sister and stared out of the window at London starlings roosting in long lines on ledges of Portland stone. With war-worn eyes he perceived that they spaced themselves equally, just far enough apart to reach the next bird, so they could deliver a blow or a rebuke. Bunks and camps spooled out again in post-war ornithology. He christened it the *principle of pecking distance*.

And before that, after the First World War had made caustic maps of Flanders fields and woods, built no man's land, built fields of mines and wire and ingraved trenches of men and filthy water, a man called Henry Eliot Howard decided that birds held territories too. He told us that they did not sing for love. Told us that males sang to other males, and there was warning in every note. Each curl of song was staking a bird's small claim to a patch of English ground. And the birds' bright colours weren't to attract a mate. The plumages they wore were badges of threat: little warring uniforms.

I think of Julian Huxley on the wireless back in 1942, explaining that if you don't know your birds you can't fully know your country. He said the yellowhammer's song was the essence of hot country roads in July. The crooning of the turtle dove of English midsummer afternoons. Birds were 'the heritage we are fighting for'. When war broke out and the Navy sent Peter Scott to sea he looked back from the deck of his destroyer and knew he was fighting to protect the mallards and teal that reared their ducklings in the reed beds of Slapton Ley. Somehow they were England.

I clutch my numbered ticket and wait to be processed. I think of the new nature writing. Of *Springwatch*, migrant watch, leaflets through our doors. It has happened before, when things collapse, when ideas fail, when economies slide, when newsprint is crisp with fears of invasion and the loss of who we are. We mark ourselves on our maps to consider our territory. We police. We turn inward. Seek ourselves in the mirror of the countryside. See nature as refuge. As ours. As us. In the winter of 1934 Norfolk farmers learned the skylarks in their fields were migrants from the Continent. They shot them for raiding their spring wheat. 'No protection for the Skylark' ran the headlines in the local press: 'Skylarks that sing to Nazis will get no mercy here'.

A woman in a blue coat is sitting three chairs away, her eyes closed, her knuckles white against the envelope of application forms. Is she asleep? Can you sleep and hold something so very tightly? I close my eyes too. Perfect forms, held steady. Forms of sympathy.

When I was a child I had a book called *Garden Bird Study* that told me to draw a map of the land around my house. To mark upon it the singing positions of its resident birds. If you watched very carefully you could work out where one territory ended and another began. I did what the book told me to do. I drew lines on my map. I marked nests. I kept lists of birds, resident, summering, wintering, overflying. Every smudge of pencil tied myself closer to the birds and the garden. But it untied me too. It unfolded layers of other eyes, other lives, other visions of what the world might be. When we left that house, years later, I mourned the memory of all my childhood rooms. But I mourned, too, the lines, the lists, the little crosses for the pigeon's nest, the blackbird's nest, the robins outside the door. They had become part of the nature of home.

1933 saw the formation of the British Trust for Ornithology. This new organisation didn't protect birds. It studied them, and it recruited the British public for its large-scale investigations. Birds were no longer to be watched. They were to be *observed* by a volunteer army made of sharp-eyed citizen-scientists. Trained observers on bicycles who followed the movements of swifts. They filled in cards and reports and questionnaires. They had their orders: to buy 'a 1-inch ordnance map of the whole district, a 6-inch map of local surroundings, and a 25-inch map of the immediate neighbourhood' upon which they could mark the distribution of birds. 'Use these,' they were told, 'and do not be afraid to mark them.' Thousands of new observers, tied to the idea of a nation through acts of looking, acts of walking, acts of counting, tallying, recording what was there. What they were doing was war work.

Auguries, perhaps. No one knew. Strange phenomena in the days of fear of invasion. Birds entering houses. Sparrows stripping wallpaper. Blue tits stealing cream from cardboard-topped milk bottles. Have you read Daphne du Maurier's *The Birds*? Not the film, the story. An English story, a fable of some great change that turned birds into foes, massing on the fields and sea before flying inland to attack humanity. *What he thought were the white caps of the waves, were gulls. Hundreds, thousands, tens of thousands ... They rose and fell in the trough of the seas, heads to the wind, like a mighty fleet at anchor, waiting on the tide. Someone should know of this. Someone should be told.*

But there could be no signs and wonders for Britain's mid-century birdwatchers. Irrationalism and superstition were things of the past. Sentimentality was to be replaced by science; poetic vagueness by conscious control, by constructive, critical thought. Even so, something more than science made itself out of little England and all its delicate cliffs. White chalk. Coastal early-warning radar stations called Chain Home. Everyone was observing. Everything watched. The Royal Observer Corps sent reports of aircraft movements while other observers sent reports of birds. James Fisher grew ever more obsessed with fulmars, ghostly onyx-eyed seabirds that were spreading their range along British shores. *From Lundy to Land's End and Tintagel; from Land's End to Scilly and Lizard; from Lizard to Start Point; from Start Point to Swanage; from Swanage to the Seven Sisters; from the Seven Sisters to Hastings ... fulmars have been seen, recently, flying by the cliffs of Broadstairs and Margate*, he wrote. *I do not know where it will stop*. He recruited Coastal Command stations to watch for fulmars as well as enemy aircraft. He arranged RAF reconnaissance flights to photograph fulmar breeding sites. Confusions of wings and eyes. All the world at war.

***

There are bird observatories at prime migration points all around the British coast. Bardsey. The Calf of Man. Cape Clear. Dungeness. Flamborough. Gibraltar Point. Portland Bill. The Isle of May. Their great flowering came after the war. Imagine: you are a prisoner in Germany. You have an Army number, you have a POW number. When you are freed you come home. But you are not entirely free because you have to do it again, and again, and again. Some part of you is fixed in the past courses of troop movements and maps and borders and escape and hope and home. If you are George Waterston, you start a bird observatory. You establish it in ex-military buildings on the far-flung edge of Britain, on remote Fair Isle. And there you and your colleagues trap lost and migrating birds in nets and cages and give them numbered rings before you release them again. You hope that someone will find them, so you can draw maps that show the invisible movements of birds across the globe. You let them go, but part of you goes with them. Your birds are feathered proxies, transcending human borders. You envy them.

In the booth the passport officer holds my photograph up to the screen and narrows his eyes. There is no shadow anywhere in the booth; there is an entirely even distribution of light. *Yes, it is you*, he says. I am relieved. He turns to my forms on his desk and scribbles a string of figures on them. In the bright and glassy calm I think, *What do they mean?* Doubts wheel and swarm. Facts insubstantial.

There was a man called David Lack. He worked during the war on the early-warning chain of coast-watching radar stations. When the wavelength of their transmitted radar waves shortened to ten centimetres the operators started reporting echoes out at sea. They were not ships or aircraft. They were ghosts. They moved at thirty knots. Air-raid warnings resulted. Planes were scrambled. Nothing was ever there.

Lack and his colleagues established that they were the radar reflections of seabirds. But there was more. When higher-power radar was invented, more ghosts appeared. Operators called them angels. They were commonest in spring and autumn. They didn't drift with the wind. They disturbed those who saw them. In Marconi's research laboratory, scientists wrote of lines of angels moving along the coast. *Scintillating discrete angels broke away from the line during its strongest period*, they said. *And a well-marked stream of persistent angel echoes could be seen moving up the Thames estuary*. The angels were starlings rising from their roosts in pulsing circles, lapwings moving north along weather fronts, pushed by heavy snow. The whole sky etched livid with aircraft and the reflections of moving wings. This was a new thing. Science turned to romanticism. The particulate beauty of unimagined hordes of lives that aren't our own, tracked minute by minute across the sky and rising out of mystery. This is a music made comprehensible by war, but the songs the birds sing are hymns of slowly moving light.

I leave the building with the promise of a passport and so does the woman in the blue coat and the man with the shopping bag and the elderly couple off to meet their grandson in Australia for the first time and the teenage boy going to Ibiza with his mates and I'm walking to my car thinking of when a bird-bander told me what happens if you mist-net long-tailed tits. Because they forage in family flocks, these mouse-sized birds get trapped in mist-nets all at once. Freed one by one from the mesh they're hung in individual bags from hooks in the ringing shed, ready to be weighed and measured and ringed. And in that awful solitude they call to one another, ceaselessly, urgently, reassuring each other that they are still together, all one thing. And once the rings are closed about their legs, they're released, all together, to resume their lives, carrying their tiny numbers with them as they fly.

A Cuckoo in the House

It's a strange, sharp-winged grey bird with button-yellow eyes, a down-curved beak and an expression of perpetual surprise, and its song is one of the best-known and best-loved in Britain. But most people have never seen a cuckoo, and it is getting harder for anyone to do so. Over the past quarter of a century, England has lost more than 60 per cent of its cuckoos and no one knows exactly why. Habitat loss, the effects of climate change, or the myriad perils cuckoos encounter on migration are the likeliest culprits, and of all those the latter is the hardest to research.

We've only ever had the vaguest idea of where British cuckoos spend the winter, and no idea of the routes they take there and back. But we are starting to understand. Since 2011, the British Trust for Ornithology has fitted satellite tags to British-trapped cuckoos and tracked their migration routes to Africa and back. The project's 'band of feathered brothers', as the national press has christened them, have attracted huge media attention. And they are uncovering all manner of ornithological secrets.

The BTO project is important. But it carries with it more than science. When I read that BTO cuckoos are 'missing in action', I think of wars overseas. When I look at the project's migration route maps, I wonder how satellite-tagged 'sentinel animals' such as these cuckoos fit into our surveillance-hungry world, and into the digitised dreams of network-centric war. I remember, too, several international incidents in the past few years in which tagged and banded birds have been taken as spies – as feathered, living drones. And I start to wonder how notions of nationhood, defence, secrecy and surveillance are caught up in how we think about cuckoos.

When I was small, I read a book by a man called Maxwell Knight. It was the story of how he had reared a baby cuckoo. Back then I thought *A Cuckoo in the House* was just another animal book from the 1950s, and that Knight was just an ordinary man. But the BTO project spurred me to read it again, this time knowing more about Knight. On rereading, I found it a very different book – a troubling fable about the meanings we give to animals, and a book that unwittingly revealed all sorts of strange collisions and collusions between natural history and national history in post-war Britain.

This, then, is the story of Maxwell Knight – the man called M – and a cuckoo called Goo. Knight was a tall, patrician British intelligence officer in charge of MI5 departments dealing with counter-subversion on home ground. And yes, as 'M' he was the inspiration for James Bond's controller. From the 1930s to the end of the Second World War, Knight placed agents in organisations such as the British Union of Fascists and the Communist Party of Great Britain. He was an extraordinary character: secretly gay, a writer of appalling thrillers, a keen jazz trumpeter, a disciple of the dark magic of Aleister Crowley, and an inveterate keeper of animals – crows, parrots, foxes and finches all shared space with agents in Knight's safe house in the Home Counties.

After the war ended, Knight began a second career as a BBC radio naturalist. This new and much-loved Knight was an avuncular, tweed-clad expert, a regular fixture on programmes such as *Country Questions*, *The Naturalist* and *Nature Parliament*. On air he described the habits of British wildlife, and told young naturalists how to rear tadpoles and how to hone their observational skills by playing 'Kim's Game', tellingly named after the hero of Rudyard Kipling's novel about a boy training to be a spy. From a clandestine career to an audience of millions, agent-runner to family naturalist, Knight appeared to have had a spectacular change of identity. But that Kim's Game reference is a giveaway: the worlds of naturalist and spy were closer than one might think.

There are many similarities between the observational practices of field naturalists and spies. 'Birdwatcher' is old British intelligence slang for a spy, and if you read Robert Baden-Powell's *Scouting for Boys*, you'll see how long natural-history fieldcraft has been seen as a preparation game for war. In his MI5 communications, Knight had once recommended that agents should be taught 'when, where and how to take notes, memory training and accurate description'. And on the radio he gave exactly the same advice to young naturalists.

But it is Knight's animals, and their relation to his secret life, that are most relevant to this story. He shared his London flat with a bear cub, a baboon, vipers, lizards, monkeys, exotic birds and rats. And they were not confined to his home. 'He always had something live in his pocket,' recalled John Bingham, an MI5 colleague best known as inspiring John le Carré's character George Smiley. Writers on Knight are fascinated by his animal-keeping, but the animals themselves are always treated as ciphers: we are never given an inkling of his motives for keeping them, apart from the animals being, perhaps, a kind of camouflage or misdirection. In the words of the literary critic Patricia Craig, they 'helped to gain him a reputation for eccentricity, certainly an asset in the devious world of MI5, where a lot depends on your ability to keep things dark, to impress your associates, and to spring surprises'. But Knight's animals were no simple camouflage.

Despite his own exotic pets, Knight championed the keeping of British wildlife. In his 1959 book *Taming and Handling*

Animals, he described them as 'infinitely more instructive than creatures from far-away climes'. This sentiment is much in keeping with the sensibilities of the period, for during the war, British wildlife had become firmly embedded in myths of national identity. As invasion anxiety and spy-fever swept the nation, concerns about allegiance and patriotic identity rapidly colonised both popular and scientific understandings of wildlife. National and natural histories blurred. In a series of wartime radio talks, the evolutionary biologist Julian Huxley, brother of the writer Aldous, explained that birds had special importance because they were the means through which you oriented yourself to your country.

Knight's radio persona was built on such patriotic understandings: his *Letters to a Young Naturalist* from 1955 – a fictional correspondence between a nature-minded boy and his naturalist uncle – opens with the following: 'My Dear Peter. So you want to be a naturalist! You could not have chosen a better hobby, nor a better way of getting round me to help you. Apart from you becoming an England cricketer in the future I can't think of anything I could have wished you to do more.'

Ordinary pets held little interest for Knight. He was interested in wild animals: the ones you had to tame. In his books, he defined the term with care. First, he explained, animals might pass as tame, but not be; they might turn. And domesticated animals might appear to be tame, but they are liable to turn spiteful and difficult. Starving animals could also appear to be tame, but aren't; hunger has merely deadened their fear. These animals are not trustworthy. To trust an animal, he wrote in *Taming and Handling Animals*, one must tame it oneself, make it 'gentle and tractable':

> The accent is on the word 'make' because to tame a wild creature means that we have to gain its confidence, remove its natural fears, and in many cases even inspire affection, so

> that the animal concerned will feed readily and regularly; will look well; will refrain from biting and other forms of attack and will accept us as well disposed towards it – or possibly as one of its own kind.

One of its own kind. There's a world of counter-subversion right there, a ghosting of the topologies of his secret life. In his books, Knight wrote of the correct relationship between animal and handler in almost exactly the same terms he'd used to describe the correct relationship between agent-runner and agents – one in which the officer must 'at all costs make a friend of his agents' and the 'agents must trust the officer'. Most important of all, in both animal-taming and agent-recruiting, 'a basis of firm confidence must be built up'.

Our model of animal-keeping today commonly rests on an empathetic understanding between handler and wild creature. Knight's does not. For him, the lines between animal and human were sharply drawn. His animals were mirrors only so far as they reflected their keeper's expertise, and their tameness and trust were to be valued as evidence of the character and abilities of their owner. 'A fool of a person,' he said, 'will never own an intelligent pet; a nervous person will never succeed in winning the confidence of any wild creature.' And apart from demonstrating how skilful you were at gaining trust, animals had other uses: they were epistemological puzzles to solve. They allowed you to 'observe such things as the comparative intelligence of different species', or 'their readiness to adapt themselves to conditions of captivity'.

The boundaries between Knight and his animals were firmly policed, just as they were with his agents. In both cases, the aim was a familiar, expert, yet distanced, knowledge. Joan Miller, one of Knight's agents and his long-term companion, acerbically commented that 'M was always curious about animals, not fond of them; though ours, of course, were always loved sincerely by me'.

Knight's distanced model of animal-keeping ran into trouble when he decided to raise a cuckoo. It was a species for which Knight had a special regard. It's not difficult to see why. Cuckoos doubled as symbols not only of deep and abiding Englishness (their spring arrivals noted each year in the letters page of *The Times*), but also of suspicion, mystery and deceit. They laid their eggs in other birds' nests and their newly hatched chicks, after ejecting the eggs and chicks of their hosts, were raised by foster-parents that seemed quite unaware of the deception played upon them.

Parasitic, scientifically baffling, the cuckoo's ambiguous moral status revolved around concepts of cuckoldry, duplicity, sexual confusion and even species boundaries themselves: in books and in heated correspondence in the *Spectator*, the redoubtable Bernard Acworth, doyen of the Creation Science Movement, repeatedly claimed that cuckoos were, in fact, hybrids between male cuckoos and the female birds of host species.

The cuckoo also starred in a spectacular piece of popular science of the period. Using new techniques of flash photography, Eric Hosking and Stuart Smith's *Birds Fighting* (1955) made overt the place of the cuckoo in fables of nationalism, aggression and defence. Smith begins by quoting Pliny's description of the cuckoo as a 'common object of hostility among all birds' because 'it practises deception'. The book is a sort of ornithological death-match, a series of staged fights, photographed in blow-by-blow detail, of well-known, well-loved British songbirds tearing apart stuffed cuckoos in a frenzy of defensive aggression and 'extreme fury'. This was total war in the ecological realm: birds defending their families against an infiltrating enemy. The cuckoo – standing in for an invasion of the body politic – incited extreme violence in birds that were icons of rural Englishness.

Hosking and Smith wanted to find out what triggered this furious response. How does a bird recognise the enemy? What signifies 'cuckoo' to a wrathful nightingale? They made sectional cuckoo models, painted cardboard cutouts, and stuck stuffed cuckoo heads on sticks, then conducted a series of experiments born of cultural anxieties reflected on to a post-war nationalised avifauna. What they discovered was that British birds were reassuringly adept at uncovering dissimulation: a nightingale will still recognise and attack a stuffed cuckoo even if it has been draped in a spotted handkerchief.

This was the post-war cuckoo: a clandestine bird of deception and quiet murder. The enemy within. Knight, naturalist and counter-subversion specialist, was, of course, desperate to own one.

In *A Cuckoo in the House* (1955), Knight tells the story of how this came to pass. His networks of secret watchers and agents had been replaced by a vast team of natural-history informants recruited through the radio. When one wrote to him of a cuckoo chick in a back garden, Knight jumped at the chance to 'rescue it' from cats. He'd wanted to hand-rear a cuckoo for years. Why? Because they are interesting, he explained, and because they are familiar, but not well known. Though everyone knows the cuckoo's call, he continued, the bird itself was 'not thoroughly understood'. It is 'mysterious', he explained, with evident relish.

And indeed, the cuckoo's life beautifully mirrored the concerns of Knight's own. First, its sex life was mysterious and secretive. So was Knight's: for years, according to Joan Miller, he'd maintained a hearty heterosexual façade while picking up rough trade in local cinemas and employing motorcycle mechanics for reasons other than repairing motorcycles. Second, cuckoos were the avian equivalents of the officer-controller of penetration agents; they 'insinuated' their 'chameleon eggs' into the nests of their 'dupes'. A single cuckoo might lay eggs in as many as twelve nests, Knight explained, finding them by perching on a 'convenient look-out post from which she spies out the land with a sharp and particular eye'. Cuckoos were also 'competent and ruthless', and their secret identity was never compromised. Knight didn't share Smith and Hosking's conclusion that birds had an 'innate concept of "cuckoo"'. Far from it. He maintained that birds never knew they were cuckoos at all. Cuckoos lived their cover. Knight's view was that other birds attacked them because they resembled, or 'passed', as hawks.

As Knight reared Goo, his cuckoo, the careful boundaries he'd drawn between the worlds of animals and man, between agent and handler, began to crumble. He was delighted to observe the fledgling's initial aggression turning to absolute tameness and trust. Goo also had a 'very remarkable' discriminatory ability, and was easily able 'to sort out its regular friends from newcomers'. The words Knight used to describe Goo's behaviour were highly charged: friends, newcomers, handlers – all categories from his secret life. And not just his career in the intelligence services, but his love life, too: Knight's 'friendly advances' to the cuckoo were 'reciprocated in full'. 'Plumage, voice, and soft peckings showed quite plainly that he was pleased and satisfied, and strokings and murmured soft words were much appreciated too.' Reading Knight's book you sense his delight that this mysterious cuckoo has been turned, but also his disconcerted half-knowledge that what it has turned into is a strange, feathered proxy for Knight himself. For the first time, Knight admits, troubled, he is not sure that the 'gulf which exists between humans and other animals … is quite as wide as some people think'.

A Cuckoo in the House ends, of course, with the defection of Knight's avian agent. Young cuckoos migrate to Africa. Flying free in Knight's garden, Goo returned to his handler less and less frequently. Knight attached a numbered ring to the bird's leg to identify it, should it return the following spring, and when Goo left to fly south, Knight mourned his loss. The cuckoo, he said, was 'the most fascinating bird pet' he had ever owned. Of course it was: he identified with it hugely, saw it mostly as himself.

The story of the cuckoo and the spymaster tells us that our understanding of animals is deeply influenced by the cultures in which we live. But it shows, too, that we can – and do – use animals as our proxies; we use them to speak for us, to say things that we cannot otherwise articulate. It also reveals that the meanings we give animals can be strangely robust. Just as Knight's cuckoo was never just a bird, the cuckoos trapped and tagged as part of the British Trust for Ornithology's current project are never solely data points on a map. No matter how precisely they are tracked on their long migrations, they are still birds of mystery, things much greater than small bundles of bones and muscle and grey feathers. They tell us things about ourselves, about the way we see our world; and they carry their strange human histories with them on their way.

The Arrow-Stork

Displayed on a small plinth in a university museum in the German city of Rostock is a famously gruesome exhibit: a stuffed white stork whose sinuous neck is pierced by an iron-tipped wooden spear from Central Africa. This unlucky bird survived the attack and flew back to Germany, only to be shot by a hunter in the spring of 1822. Newspaper reports revealed the spear's distant origin, and the newly christened *pfeilstorch*, or arrow-stork, became celebrated for solving the puzzle of where German storks spent their winters.

In the eighteenth century, many experts still held Aristotle's view that birds hibernated during the cold months and believed fishermen's claims that clumps of live swallows could be pulled from beneath the ice of winter ponds. It wasn't until later in the nineteenth century that European naturalists began sustained research into bird migration, fitting the legs of birds with numbered metal bands and carefully plotting the locations where they were later recovered. The Rostock *pfeilstorch* is an early, macabre example of the workings of wildlife-migration science. From unintentionally carried spears to GPS and satellite tags, tracing animal movements requires augmenting the animals with human technology.

Many thousands of animals and birds carry tags today. They're attached to sea-turtle shells with marine epoxy glue and fired from boats into the blubber of passing whales.

Swans and bears wear tags on collars, and smaller birds are fitted with harnesses that mount solar-powered transmitters high on their backs. Each tag communicates with a network of satellites to fix the location of the animal.

By discovering the routes animals take during migration, scientists can assess the threats they face, like regions affected by habitat loss or the activities of hunters. But the movements of tagged creatures are no longer followed solely by the eyes of experts. For the rest of us, the increasing availability of visualisations of their journeys makes the world a more complicated and wondrous place. I'm able to sit at my computer and watch how great white sharks tagged in Californian coastal waters migrate over a thousand miles to spend their winters in a remote part of the Pacific Ocean now known as the White Shark Café, read of how Amur falcons might survive on their journey over the ocean between India and Africa by following swarms of dragonflies making the same trip and feasting on them in flight.

There are many websites on which the public can name, sponsor and follow tagged animals. I regularly visit one run by the British Trust for Ornithology, which tracks the annual journeys of individual cuckoos between Britain and Africa as part of a larger project investigating the species' rapid population decline in Britain: more than half have been lost since the 1980s for reasons that are still unclear. Today the internet informed me that a cuckoo called David has reached his home in Wales, though it's hard to know what home means to a cuckoo, for the project has shown that some spend only 15 per cent of their lives in their countries of origin. I click on David's photograph, and then those of sixteen other tagged cuckoos, nervous, golden-eyed bundles of grey feathers held in scientists' hands, so different from the fast-flying, sharp-winged silhouettes that flicker between trees near my house in spring. Each cuckoo's current position is represented on screen by a clickable icon on a Google Earth map. Coloured lines trace their flights from England across Europe and North Africa, over the Sahara and into the humid forest zone where they spend their winters. The default satellite view on the website has no overlays indicating cities or countries. It encourages me to see the world as an animal does: a place without politics or borders, without humans at all, merely a series of habitats marching climatically from cool northern mountains to the thick rainforests of Angola and Congo.

Projects like this give us imaginative access to the lives of wild creatures, but they cannot capture the real animals' complex, halting paths. Instead they let us watch virtual animals moving across a world of eternal daylight built of a patchwork of layered satellite and aerial imagery, a flattened, static landscape free of happenstance. There are no icy winds over high mountain passes here, no heavy rains, soaring hawks, ripening crops or recent droughts. Despite these simplifications, following a tagged animal on a map is an addictive pursuit. It's hard not to become invested in its fate. The bird might die, the tag might fail. You do not know where it will travel next. The bird is unaware of the eyes that watch its progress, and you veer from a sense of power at your ability to surveil at a distance to the knowledge that you are powerless to influence what happens next.

The more you watch, the more you feel that you are somehow also taking the cuckoo's journey, are engaged on a virtual exploration of the globe. The fantasy of a borderless world is quickly replaced by visions of heroic exploration. You take up the part of a lone traveller engaged on an arduous quest to cross countries and conquer unknown spaces on the map. Because satellite tracking is expensive, we can follow the progress of only a few named animals. You become attached to them as they make their astonishing journeys. You watch young cuckoos find their way to Africa with no parental help, see loggerhead turtles swim seven and a half thousand miles from feeding grounds off Mexico to the beaches of Japan; discover bar-headed geese migrating over the Himalayas, in doing so enduring extreme and sudden changes in elevation that would disable or kill a human. You can marvel at the bar-tailed godwits that make a nine-day, eleven-thousand-kilometre nonstop flight from Alaska to New Zealand across the Pacific Ocean. To us, these appear remarkable feats of physical endurance. We cannot help measuring the capacities of animals against our own.

Our unconscious desire to see ourselves in the lives of animals is shared by the scientists engaged in these projects, who often think of the tagged animals as colleagues and collaborators. Tom Maechtle, a biologist and environmental consultant who has worked on raptor migration at the University of Maryland, has spoken of how satellite tracking 'turns the animal into a partner with the researcher' and suggested that you can think of tagged falcons as biologists who have been 'sent out to find and sample other birds'.

Increasingly, animals are seen not only as proxies for scientific researchers but also as scientific-research equipment functioning like sensors or probes. In one project studying climate change in West Antarctica, for example, elephant seals with tags glued to their foreheads collect and transmit data on ocean conductivity, temperature and depth that is used for weather forecasting and climate research. This notion of autonomous biological-sampling devices confuses the distinctions between technology and living organisms, quietly erasing the animal's agency.

Tagged animals carry more than human technology; they carry human ways of visualising the world. Hybrid beasts, they perfectly fit our modern conception of the planet as an environment under constant watch, where eyes in the sky track animals moving from one country to another and plot them on a map just as they do moving ships and aircraft; a world where Defense Department researchers in the US are working on autonomous flying robots that mimic the flight of hawks and insects, where scientists fit electronic backpacks on giant flower beetles that enable them to be flown and steered by remote control.

Early pioneers in the remote tracking of animals sought military funding for their efforts and suggested that bird-migration studies could be used to improve navigation and missile-guidance systems, and the development of technology suitable for animal surveillance came from a microelectronics industry with strong early links to the military. In our age of drone warfare, it is hard not to see each animal being tracked across the map as symbolically extending the virtues of technological dominance and global surveillance.

If the stuffed *pfeilstorch* in the German museum is the iconic bird of early animal-migration science, I think today's equivalent is another stork, a young bird called Ménes that was satellite-tagged in Hungary in 2013 as part of an avian-migration tracking project sponsored by a European cross-border cooperation programme. After leaving his nest, Ménes travelled south across Romania, Bulgaria, Greece, Turkey, Syria, Jordan and Israel, landed in the Nile Valley in Egypt, and was there captured by a fisherman and taken into police custody. The stork, carrying a 'suspicious electronic device', was suspected of being a spy.

I've spent a long time looking at photographs of Ménes behind bars, half in shadow, beak lowered and toes spread upon concrete, a mournful casualty of a country in the grip of the deepest political tensions. Security experts cleared the stork of espionage, and he was released, only to be later found dead on an island near Aswan, a draggled corpse of a stork that had become a poignant avatar for human fears and conflicts. Media reports of his plight cast his story as one of almost comical paranoia. But although the stork was innocent – an unwitting player in a geopolitical game of surveillance and intelligence – the hybrid being made of the stork and device was far less clearly so.

Ashes

On a dank January day in the mid-1970s, I stood on an English hillside with my mother and watched men with chainsaws cutting up wrecks of trees and tossing brushwood on to fires. I was five years old, amazed by the roaring blades and drifting smoke, and troubled too.

'Why are they burning them?' I asked her.

'It's Dutch elm disease,' she said, pulling at the knot of her headscarf. 'All the elm trees are dying of it now.'

Her words confused me. I'd assumed until then that the countryside was an eternally unchanging place. At that time, Dutch elm disease was spreading across continents, blight had killed four billion American chestnuts, and catastrophic new tree diseases were to follow. Last week that cold hillside of my childhood came to mind as I drove through rural Suffolk, past painted farmhouses and arable fields sloping under a haze of summer clouds. The ash trees on this stretch of road were obviously dying. Their once-luxuriant crowns had thinned to an eerie transparency; instead of a shifting canopy of pinnate leaves, bare twigs showed stark against the sky.

It was my first sight of ash dieback disease, a new and virulent fungal infection that has spread westward across Europe and will likely kill nearly all the ashes in Britain. In America, the effects of the invasive emerald ash borer beetle have been just as devastating. Globalisation is the culprit. While there have always been outbreaks of tree disease, about as many have appeared since the 1970s as in all recorded history. The accelerating scale and speed of international trade has brought numerous pathogens and pests to species with no natural resistance to them. If you are a tree, death comes hidden in wood veneer, in packing material, in shipping containers, nursery plants, cut flowers, the roots of imported saplings.

Later that night, I compulsively searched for images of elms on the internet, seeking their buoyant, ragged silhouettes in snapshots of village fields or half-hidden behind actors in 1960s films. I saw trees like frozen cumulonimbus clouds towering over cricket matches at English public schools; postcards and photographs of elm avenues in Massachusetts and coastal Maine, lofty branches shading summer streets and suburban Oldsmobiles. These trees were the ghosts of half-remembered landscapes, and looking at them I realised that living trees could haunt you, too. That drive in Suffolk had changed the meaning of ash trees for me. From now on, each one I saw would mean death, no matter how healthy it might be.

But should they contract a mortal disease, trees cope better than we do. Many can regenerate. The vast Appalachian chestnut forests crowned with white flowers have all but disappeared, but fallen trees still sprout new shoots from their roots. As soon as they reach a certain height they again become susceptible to blight and die. Chestnuts and elms living in this endlessly youthful state are less fruitful than mature trees, and they trouble us because they are not what we think trees should be. We use trees to measure our own lives, to anchor our notions of time. To most of us, they represent constancy and continuity, living giants that persist through many human generations. We want them to achieve maturity; we want them to tower above us.

The spectral elms on the internet were images of a different kind of extinction from that of the passenger pigeon or dodo: the extinction of a landscape. For days afterwards, I found myself looking out at the blank brows of local hills, imagining there the billowing shapes of elms. I was preparing myself to think about what it would look like here when all the ash trees were gone. It was painful to force myself into a kind of anticipatory *solastalgia*, a term coined by the Australian environmental philosopher Glenn Albrecht to refer to people's emotional distress when their home landscapes become unrecognisable through environmental change. He was speaking of the effects of drought and strip mining in New South Wales, but solastalgia can arise in landscapes as varied as melting tundra and south-western states stricken by wildfire. Like droughts, tree diseases bring economic loss and ecological impoverishment while at the same time stripping familiar meaning from the places we live in. Writing about the slow death of American forests from a hundred years of tree diseases in his book *Nature Out of Place*, the writer Jason Van Driesche found himself almost mute: 'This is my home. How can you put something like this into words?'

But there are trees that can offer solace. I looked for photographs of them on the internet, too: the last few big American chestnuts, some of which have been given names. The Adair County Chestnut, found in 1999 in Kentucky, for instance. Rounded in form, it does not much resemble the gigantic, spiralling cathedral-columns of ancient Appalachian trees, but it is beautiful, spreading dark limbs and long, serrated leaves towards the sun. Around five hundred are left: the Hebron Chestnut in Maine; an unnamed chestnut in Ohio. People seek out these singular chestnut trees that have cheated death; some even steal leaves and pieces of bark from them as mementoes. The precise location of these trees must often be kept secret – encountering one, it is said, is an experience akin to finding Bigfoot.

Dedicated scientists, volunteers and nursery workers have spent many decades trying to restore the American chestnut with the aim of recreating the landscapes we have lost. Some organisations, like the American Chestnut Foundation, are backcrossing American trees with resistant Chinese varieties to produce seedlings that resemble American chestnuts but have sufficient Chinese qualities to survive the effects of blight. Others, like a team at the State University of New York College of Environmental Science and Forestry, insert genes from wheat and other plants into chestnut embryos to change their chemistry and make them more resilient to attack. Despite the increasing success of projects like these, some commentators regard them as a diversion, believing instead that it would be better to put resources into preventing new diseases than attempting to cure old ones. Their position makes sense if you think our reasons for wanting to restore the trees are merely ecological. Of course, they are not. They shape the landscapes of our lives and are a matter bound up with our sense of identity.

Increasingly, knowing your surroundings, recognising the species of animals and plants around you, means opening yourself to constant grief. Virulent tree diseases hit the headlines, but smaller, less visible disappearances happen all the time. The flycatchers that nested in my neighbourhood a decade ago have vanished; meadows in my hometown that were full of all kinds of life have become housing developments full of nothing but our own. People of a certain age tend to look back elegiacally at the things that have gone: the shop you used as a kid that closed, the room that became a memory. But those small, personal disappearances, however poignant, are not the same as losing biodiversity. Changes to city skylines are not the same as acres of beetle-blasted trees: though they are caught up in stories about ourselves, trees are not ever just about us. They support complex and interdependent communities of life, and as forests slowly become less diverse, the world loses more than simply trees. It has been suggested that the rise of Lyme disease in many parts of North America and Europe is in part because less diverse forests favour the ticks that carry it.

I am old enough to remember elms and the landscapes they made; people only a few years younger than me do not, and to them the elm-free fields are reassuringly normal. Are we now becoming inured to a new narrative of nature, in which ecosystem-level change in accelerated timescales is part of the background of everyday life? Children who are growing up watching glaciers retreat and sea ice vanishing, villages sinking, tundra wildfires raging and once-common trees disappearing – will they learn to regard constant disappearance as the ordinary way of the world? I hope it is not so. But perhaps when all the ash trees are gone and the landscape has become flatter and simpler and smaller, someone not yet born will tap on a screen, call up images and wonder at the lost glory of these exquisite, feathered trees.

A Handful of Corn

White-haired, soft-featured, and in possession of a faintly aristocratic glamour, Mrs Leslie-Smith lived alone in a wooden bungalow full of books and glossy houseplants a few doors from my childhood home. On a warm autumn evening more than thirty years ago, she invited my mother and me to watch her nightly ritual. She ushered us to chairs set before glass doors into her garden, picked up a biscuit tin, prised open the lid, then went outside to scatter handfuls of broken biscuits on the flagstones of her patio, where they glittered dustily under the light of an outside lamp. Back in the darkened room we sat and waited. We didn't talk; the event had all the hush and ceremony of theatre. From the edge of the illuminated lawn, a striped black-and-white face appeared and then retreated into darkness. Soon afterwards, two badgers trundled across the grass out of the night to crunch up the cookies, so close to us we could see the curves of their ivory teeth and the patterned skin of their noses. They weren't tame – if we had turned on the light, they would have bolted – but they were so close I had an urge to press my hands to the glass to make them understand I was there. The space between us in the house and these wild creatures in the garden was filled with unalloyed magic.

We didn't feed badgers in our childhood garden, but we fed the birds. So do a fifth to a third of all households in Australia, Europe and the United States. Americans spend over three billion dollars each year on food for them, ranging from peanuts to specialised seed mixes, suet cakes, hummingbird nectar and freeze-dried mealworms. We still don't clearly understand how supplementary feeding affects bird populations, but there's evidence that its enormous increase in popularity over the last century has changed the behaviour and range of some species. Many German blackcaps, for example, soft grey migratory warblers, now fly north-west to spend the winter in food-rich, increasingly temperate British gardens rather than flying south-west to the Mediterranean, as their ancestors had done, and feeding may be behind the northward spread of northern cardinals and American goldfinches.

Putting out food for birds in your back garden can attract predators, and virulent diseases like trichonomosis and avian pox can be spread through contaminated feeders. But even if its impact is not always positive for wildlife, it is for us. We give food to wild creatures out of a desire to help them, spreading cut apples on snowy lawns for blackbirds, hanging up feeders for finches. The writer Mark Cocker maintains that the 'simple, Franciscan act of giving to birds makes us feel good about life, and redeems us in some fundamental way'. That sense of redemption is intimately tied with the history of bird-feeding, for the practice grew out of the humanitarian movement of the nineteenth century, which saw compassion towards those in need as a mark of the enlightened individual.

In 1895, the popular Scottish naturalist and writer Eliza Brightwen gave instructions on how to feed and tame wild red squirrels to become 'household pets of their own free will'. In Britain, garden feeding was popularised by the formation of the Dicky Bird Society, a late-nineteenth-century children's organisation that required its members to take a pledge to be kind to all living things and to feed the birds in wintertime. The society was highly influential, even receiving letters from workhouse children explaining how they carefully saved crumbs from their own meals to feed the birds outside.

In the United States, one of the most significant figures in the new movement was the Prussian aristocrat Baron Hans von Berlepsch. A book detailing his ingenious bird-feeding methods, *How to Attract and Protect Wild Birds*, described how you could pour melted fat mixed with seeds, ants' eggs, dried meat and bread over conifer branches for birds to feed from in winter. 'Kindhearted people,' he wrote, 'have always taken pity on our feathered winter guests.' During the First World War, feeding American birds became something of a patriotic duty, for it helped them survive the winter so they could go on to eat insects that threatened agricultural production. By 1919, the nation's garden birds were to be considered, according to the ornithologist Frank Chapman, 'not only our welcome guests but our personal friends'.

Today, the opposite is true: close and intimate contact with animals is increasingly rare. We permit only a few types of animals to enter our homes as pets; interactions with wild animals tend to be restricted to experts like biologists or park rangers. But gardens and backyards are special trading zones that span the imaginary boundaries between nature and culture, domestic and public space. They are shared territory, places that both humans and wildlife consider home. Even so, when we feed animals, we want it to be on our terms, not theirs. We expect them to respect their place in an unspoken social order. When a wary squirrel or bird trusts you sufficiently to take food from your hand, it's gratifying and special, a reaching across the border between us and them, wild and tame. But if a squirrel runs unbidden up your arm demanding food or a seagull snatches a sandwich from your hands, it often generates an emotion close to outrage. Back in the early days, proponents of bird-feeding had to fight against the conviction that animals would become 'spoiled' by artificial feeding and would 'no longer do their work in nature's household'. Even today, it's hard to read articles giving advice on wildlife feeding without suspecting that they might be about something else entirely. We're told to feed foxes sporadically, so as not to cause dependence, for example, and we're warned that feeding them can make animals lose their 'natural respect' for us.

There are acceptable animals and unacceptable animals, as there have been deserving and undeserving poor, and the lines of respectability are drawn in familiar ways, through appealing to fears and threats of invasion, foreignness, violence and disease. As usual, animals reflect back at us our own assumptions about the natural structure of the world. 'Feeding foxes is one of those things you don't talk to people about,' one blogger confessed online, worried that her neighbours would find out her secret. To purposely feed the wrong animals – sparrows, pigeons, rats, raccoons, foxes – is an act of social transgression that's liable to get you reported to officials by whistleblowers who are concerned with mess, or health, or noise, or are powered by sheer indignation. Of course, with sufficient social capital, you can get away with whatever you like. Actress Joanna Lumley not only feeds tame wild foxes in her London garden but lets them into her house; newspapers have printed photographs of one fast asleep upon the cushions of her living-room sofa.

Feeding animals can be a deep solace to those who, for reasons of social or personal circumstance, find contact with others difficult or impossible. People who feed urban pigeons tend to be isolated and socially marginalised: older people, lonely people, homeless people. Sociologist Colin Jerolmack has memorably described such encounters with pigeons as ephemerally dissolving people's solitude, and some of the saddest wildlife reports in the media are those about individuals who have been fined or jailed because they refuse to stop feeding birds in their gardens. 'They are my whole life, because all my relatives are gone,' explained Cecil Pitts, a sixty-five-year-old fined five hundred dollars for repeatedly feeding large flocks of pigeons at his home in Ozone Park, Queens, in 2008. He is one of many people who have come to identify with the unloved denizens of their neighbourhoods, creatures that are ignored or despised, living behind the visible workings of the modern city.

Growing up with bird tables outside my window taught me a lot about animal behaviour – context gave meaning to the aggressive flicking of a squirrel's tail, the precise posture of a courting robin – but it taught me, too, that curious blend of familiarity and otherness that we see in wild creatures. Animals are not human, but they are enough like us to grant us a strange and strong sense of kinship. Mrs Leslie-Smith's badgers brought her the company of many guests keen to see these rare creatures at close quarters, but the company, too, of wild animals that chose to spend time at her house. This morning, as I filled the feeders in my garden, a flock of small passerines hopped about in the hedges while three jackdaws perched expectantly on the eaves above. One looked down at me, shook its dusky feathers and yawned, and I found myself yawning, too, in a moment of contagious fellowship. The birds that choose to come to my garden make my house a less lonely place. And that is why many of us feed animals – not merely because it's satisfying to feel we have helped them, but because it surrounds us with creatures that know us, are able to forge bonds with us, have come to regard us as part of their world.

Berries

On the first of December, I dragged my old artificial Christmas tree down from the attic and plugged it in. Instantly it glowed with light. On went my collection of odd Christmas baubles: a bescarfed tweed sausage dog, a golden stegosaurus, a crystal stag, a small ceramic robot and a handful of glass spheres dusted with glitter. The whole thing took less than five minutes, which left me feeling obscurely cheated by the ease of my seasonal effort. So later that afternoon, the light dying and the air outside thick with woodsmoke, I went out with a pair of secateurs to collect greenery from the big holly tree near my front door. It's tall, wreathed in ivy, and this year heavy with fruit. I shook each cut branch to rid it of wintering insects, dragged the whole lot inside and started laying down boughs on sills and mantels. The gloss of lamplight on the leaves and the gemlike clusters of berries made the house look spectacularly festive, but I felt a pang of guilt at bringing the outside in: those berries were meant for birds, not for me.

Berries grow to be eaten, not used for interior decoration. Most, packed with fats and carbohydrates around the seeds at their hearts, have evolved as vegetable offerings to birds; some even contain alkaloid compounds toxic to mammals. Passing through avian digestive systems, the seeds are carried far and wide before being deposited in droppings to take root and flourish. The little lights of haws, the fat dusty globes of sloes amongst blackthorn needles; hips like miniature lamps, the tiny-apple handfuls of rowans and whitebeams; and then the weirder berries like the pale, gelid orbs of mistletoe or spindleberries, the last looking as if Pucci decided to make tiny popcorn ornaments out of pink and orange wax. Blackcaps, plump little warblers, adore mistletoe berries. They pick away at their sticky flesh until their beaks are covered in goo then clean them on branches, where the seeds adhere and grow. In recent years German blackcaps that have started spending winters here rather than in Africa may be directly responsible for spreading mistletoe to new areas of the British Isles.

In early winter, mistle thrushes turn full Smaug: they'll claim possession of particularly fine yew trees, hollies, mistletoe clumps or bushes full of berries and defend them against intruders, chasing them away with strident, football-rattle calls of fury: the better they defend their hoard, the earlier and more successful their breeding attempts tend to be the following spring. But not all birds are so territorial. At this time of year our local blackbirds are joined by small flocks from Scandinavia and other parts of Northern Europe, and they'll feast on berries together. In the presence of such bounty they'll tolerate, if not entirely welcome, each other's presence.

With exceptions like dogroses and brambles, most shrubs and trees flower and fruit on that year's new growth, so the traditional yearly trim of hedgerows in autumn will deprive a whole community of valuable winter foodstuffs. But increasingly, as hedgerows become valued for wildlife rather than simply as stock barriers, they are cut on two- or three-year rotation, which ensures a supply of berries through the coldest months. Some berries are more palatable than others. Autumn blackberries disappear fast; by winter they've gone except for furry, frost-dried knots. Hawthorn and blackthorn, too. By late winter, few berries are left. Wood pigeons feast on the black fruits of ivy, clambering awkwardly on thin twigs and later depositing bright purple droppings under their roosts. As winter progresses, some berries ferment and become alcoholic, and it's not uncommon to see faintly disoriented birds wandering around beneath affected shrubs.

Among the last berries to be eaten in winter are those on ornamental shrubs and trees, either because they are relatively unpalatable or because they're coloured so unusually that many native birds do not recognise them as edible. It's these berries that become the targets of the unpredictable visitations of a bird that more than any other means winter's wonder to me. The last time I saw them was five years ago in a small pedestrian precinct in Alton, Hampshire. It was a bitter February day, everyone hooded and hatted, heads down, trudging stoically between shops. I was asking my mother where she'd like to meet for coffee after our errands were done when I heard an unearthly trilling noise, like a carillon of silver bells, and like a gravity-stricken whirlwind a pack of fat birds swirled down from the blank sky on to a slim twelve-foot sorbus tree right above us. They were waxwings, irregular visitors from the far north. They're neither pink nor grey nor brown but something in between that's no colour the way winter skies are no colour. They glommed on to the tree and began stuffing their maws with white berries, every so often rising en masse to the sky before resettling on the branches in a slightly different arrangement. They had elegant crests, bandit-black masks and flashes of russet, their black tails and wings patterned with daffodil yellow; and on their wing coverts, rows of the bizarre ornaments for which they're named, small waxy red protuberances that look exactly like the heads of matches. They're both highly classy and fantastically trashy to look at; no Christmas decoration could ever approach their absurd, animate beauty. Their magic isn't simply in the surprise of their comings and goings – some years they appear, often they don't – but where they're most often seen. They are particularly drawn to the fruits of tree cultivars beloved of town planners, so every winter there'll be reports of waxwing flocks on the internet that read something like: *Twenty birds, Aldi car park*, or *small flock behind PC Warehouse!*

My mother and I stood entranced. No one else noticed them, even though the nearest bird was two feet from our faces – they're so unconcerned by people they will even feed from apples held out in one's hands if they're hungry enough – and a few seconds later the winter vision swirled upwards again like leaves and was gone, leaving a bare tree and faint trills over the shopping-centre roofs.

Cherry Stones

Autumn 2017 has seen an unprecedented invasion from Europe. It's been reported all over the British press and set internet message boards on fire. People have left their homes expressly to search for the immigrants and some have set up microphones to detect their calls at night. Between mid-October and mid-November, fifty passed through Greenwich Park in London and more than a hundred and fifty were seen at one location in East Sussex. They've made their way to Britain because of food shortages in their countries of origin, and there's a general hope among those who look for them that they'll find what they need here, settle in and stay.

The immigrants are hawfinches, starling-sized finches on steroids dressed in tones of salmon pink, black, white, russet and grey. Their enormous, cherry-stone-cracking beak resembles a pair of side-cutting steel pliers and is quite capable of severing a human finger. With coppery eyes set in an ink-black bib and mask, overall their appearance always reminds me of an exquisitely dressed pugilist. They're rare and declining in Britain – around eight hundred pairs breed here. The first time I ever saw one was on a winter's evening in the late 1990s while driving through the Forest of Dean in a rainstorm at dusk. As I rounded a corner, a single bird flew up from the verge. Caught in my headlights, its pied wings strobed through bright lines of falling water before it disappeared back into the dark. The encounter was every bit as ghostly and strange as the species' reputation among British birdwatchers, for hawfinches are legendarily mysterious, secretive and difficult to see. Local populations frequently disappear completely for a number of years before reappearing in their old haunts for no obvious reason. They're most often detected by their call alone: a short, metallic, emphatic *szick*! They're easier to locate after the leaves have fallen, but are so skittish that most of my sightings have been tiny silhouettes set on the topmost branches of distant winter trees.

But things are very different in mainland Europe. Walking through Berlin's Volkspark Friedrichshain on a cold spring day some years ago with a friend who lived in the city, I stopped in frank astonishment under a cock hawfinch singing on a lime twig a few feet above my head. *It's a hawfinch!* I breathed. 'Yes, there's loads of them here, all over the place,' she said, casually, and shrugged. I waved my hands in frustration as the bird continued to sing. Faced with this absurdly tame creature, as much at home in the city as a feral pigeon, there was no way I could explain to her how enigmatic hawfinches were supposed to be.

The recent influx to Britain is likely to have been spurred by a failure of the hornbeam crop across Eastern Europe, though some blame it on unusual weather. One British Trust for Ornithology spokesman suggested that warm air pulled north-west by one of this year's biggest storms, Ophelia, has brought the hawfinches here. Whatever the cause, this unprecedented irruption of avian refugees fascinates me partly because it speaks so obviously of current issues – it's a truism that birds know no political borders – but also because it reminds me of how closely human concerns inform our understanding of nature. Today, our small population of resident hawfinches lives mostly in ancient woodlands or as small colonies in the forests and parklands of stately homes, to such an extent that I once heard a birder call them National Trust finches, after the heritage conservation charity that administers so many of Britain's most magnificent historic estates. So closely are hawfinches tied to these symbolic British landscapes that for years I assumed they were the last remnants of a native, much decreased ancient population whose present-day rarity was a function of modernity. My mind was blown when I found out that Britain had no breeding hawfinches until the mid-nineteenth century, when a number of prospecting pairs from mainland Europe started a nesting colony in Epping Forest. They spread from there until fifty years later there were birds in almost every English county taking advantage of apple orchards and leafy deciduous woodlands full of their favourite food sources: hornbeam, beech, maple, elm, yew, hawthorn and cherry. British hawfinch populations reached their peak in the 1950s, after which they went into precipitous decline.

The history of hawfinches in Britain reminds us how seamlessly we confuse natural and national history, how readily we assume nativity in things that are familiar to us, and how lamentably easy it is to forget how we are all from somewhere else. The loss of suitable habitat is one important factor in the decline of British hawfinches, but another is nest predation by grey squirrels, commonly seen as unwanted foreign invaders. Ironically, they appeared in the British landscape at about the same time as hawfinches.

Perhaps the immigrant finches will stay and raise young here. That's what a lot of people are hoping. I certainly am. But for now, what is most joyous to me about this once-in-a-lifetime influx is that birds renowned for their attachments to ancient woods and country estates are turning up in unexpectedly everyday places. They're clambering about yew branches in local churchyards and foraging in the leaf litter of suburban parks. In late November, eight were spotted at Mill Hill Sports Centre in London. 'At last!' wrote Ms Sue

Barnecutt Smith in a comment to one newspaper article about the invasion. 'I couldn't work out the identity of a bird my son spotted at my allotment last week (near Putney Bridge, west London). Now we know.' These spectacular refugees have eschewed the venerable treetops of stately homes to spend their time instead with sparrows, feeding happily upon sunflower hearts and peanuts scattered on garden bird tables.

Birds, Tabled

The strangest thing about the Bird Fair, Britain's premier birding event, is that there are no birds there. 'Yes there are!' hissed the man in the entry line behind us, though I'd been speaking only to my mother. 'There are *ospreys*.' It's true that wild ospreys live on the lakes at Rutland Water, the site where the Bird Fair is held, but there are no birds at the Bird Fair. What there are instead: thousands of people, the sweet scent of trampled summer grass, shaded marquees inside which are tables and touts for bird tours to every part of the Earth. Binoculars and spotting scopes. Books. A refreshment tent. An art tent. Tents for lectures. Every time I go to the Bird Fair I see people I know and love. But no birds.

A few years ago I drove to the West Midlands with my boyfriend, a birdkeeper, to visit a different kind of bird fair: a bird show. We parked in a Staffordshire field beside two hangar-like halls. The men walking past us looked nothing like the men at the Bird Fair, who tend to be pale and urgent of face and dressed in hiking boots and technical trousers. These men were laughing as they lugged boxes and cages and the tops of trestle tables. They wore rugby shirts, lumberjack shirts, hooded tracksuits, fishing waistcoats. There were tattoos and many baseball hats. There were no binoculars at all.

But there were a lot of birds. The halls were full of show cages. Far smaller than the cages and aviaries these birds lived in at home, they were designed to display the beauty of the creatures within. There were hooped wire ones like tabletop Victorian aviaries inside which hopped stout canaries; vertical stacks of wooden boxes fronted with the tiniest gauge wire for minute owl-finches and waxbills; bigger cages for pigeons and chickens and quail. A few tables of huge-headed, feather-perfect show budgerigars with spotted gorgets, birds that looked far more artificial than the plastic feed trays in their cages. I watched in awe as a man walked past holding a tight-feathered white pigeon the size of a baby. He told me it was a Hungarian Giant House Pigeon, and instantly my own house seemed the poorer for not having one.

An industrial propane heater roared in a corner and the halls echoed with Tannoy announcements instructing exhibitors to ensure that water and feed bowls were filled and their birds weren't too hot, or too cold, and showed no signs of distress. Wandering about from table to table I sneaked photos on my phone using all the tactical guile my father taught me from his years as a photojournalist. Keeping the phone low at my hip, maintaining eye contact and smiling with stallholders, I took a series of blurred and tilted shots using one thumb. Birdkeepers are wary creatures. I didn't want them to know what I was doing, for if the culture of watching wild birds has all the social acceptability of drinking wine, birdkeeping feels more like legalised cannabis use. Both involve a deep love of birds and displays of natural-historical connoisseurship, but birdkeeping is considered by many to be morally dubious and, at its fringes, prone to lawlessness.

Thankfully, all the birds at this fair were domestically bred. Legislation in the 1980s made the keeping of wild-trapped British birds illegal, and the international trade in wild birds has declined by 90 per cent since the European Union banned imports in 2005. That was a trade made entirely of heartbreak – I will never forget looking up at the window of a warehouse in West London's Cromwell Road as a child and seeing the flurried wingbeats of scores of distressed, disoriented, recently arrived cockatoos.

One section of this bird show was dedicated to what birdkeepers call *British*: native species, the same kinds as those that sing in our woods and gardens and forests and fields. Insectivorous and fruit-eating birds like blackbirds and thrushes were displayed in cages painted white inside, often with embellishments that hinted at their natural habitat, such as rocks for wheatears or a sheet of forest bark for redstarts. The show cages of British finches had glossy black exteriors and were painted inside with Brolac Georgian green, a mossy tone particularly favoured by interior designers in the eighteenth century. Inside them were goldfinches, linnets, redpolls, siskins, bullfinches, hawfinches.

One of these cages was attracting considerable attention. Inside it was a pied goldfinch, its plumage broken with freakish patches of white. Unusual colour mutations like these are highly prized among British bird aficionados – goldfinches with a white spot under their chin are called peathroats; those with an entirely white throat, cheverals. A group of Irish Travellers clustered around this cage, engaged in animated discussion about the merits of the bird while a pile of twenty-pound notes was counted out upon the table. *Seven-colour linnets*, they call goldfinches; it's a very old name, hardly ever used by birdwatchers. This one was likely destined to breed mules, a kind of bird beloved by Romani and Traveller birdkeepers. The offspring of a wild finch (usually a male goldfinch or linnet) mated with a domesticated canary, they're known as mules because like the offspring of a horse and a donkey, they're sterile. They're treasured for their intensely beautiful songs, which combine sweet, wide-ranging canary trills with the varied, sharp, metallic notes of their wild fathers.

A few years ago I spoke to a man who confessed to me that he used to trap wild goldfinches when he was younger, despite knowing it was illegal. 'I didn't keep them – I was catching hormone-addled males for muling,' he said. 'I'd pop them in a cage with a female canary, long enough for them to mate, then let them go. They'd be in the trap, in my hand, in the cage, for only a few minutes. Where was the harm in that? The problem is,' he said darkly, 'they don't like us keeping British at all.'

His use of the term *they* helps us understand one aspect of the difference between the Bird Fair and the Bird Show: that our attitudes towards nature are shaped by history and class and power. These two events mirror a longstanding division in the ways we relate to the natural world. One view is that nature is something pristine out there that should only be observed or recorded; the other sees it as something that can be brought into interior spaces and closely interacted with. It runs along the same lines as the division between field scientists and lab scientists, or between hunters and farmers. Such divisions are freighted with social meaning. Like so many battles about nature, at heart they're about who has the right to define what a creature is, who has the right to interact with it, and how.

Birding, along with similar forms of observational nature-appreciation, has near-universal cultural acceptability in the present day – there's considerable media coverage of the Bird Fair, for example – but the keeping of small native birds does not. It has long been a hobby associated with working-class and minority communities, like miners, immigrants, East End Londoners, Romani and Irish Travellers. The last long conversation I had about birdkeeping was with a Romanian taxi driver on the way to an airport very early on a Sunday morning. In the darkness the screen of his iPhone glowed with a photograph of a bird with a black cap, a pugnacious beak and a chest the colour of young red wine. I told him I thought it was a beautiful bullfinch, and he was beside himself with delight: *You know what it is! This is my bird!* And we talked about his birds for the rest of the journey. He'd got into it late, he said. When he was a young man he had no idea how perfect birds were: like precious stones, but alive. And their songs! He explained that his birds are his life, and they are like children in two ways: because he loves them and because he cannot remember the person he was before them.

The great anti-cagebird campaigns of my childhood were in part the crusade of bird lovers like Peter Conder, then Director of the Royal Society for the Protection of Birds, who had spent years behind wire in German prisoner of war camps. But that's not the only reason we don't like to see birds in small cages. Those cages radically attenuate the possibilities of a bird's life. I can't look at birds in them without my heart aching fit to burst, even if those birds look otherwise healthy and happy and well-adjusted. But we limit the lives of captive animals in myriad ways, and don't always judge their impacts according to the needs of the creatures involved. The high-density broiler operations of chickens kept in locked sheds, for example – birds bred to gain weight so fast that after only a few weeks many find it difficult to walk – are something hardly any of us see, and are thus easy to ignore. Moreover, we often fail to see many of the other cruelties we visit on animals because we don't consider what an animal's world ought to contain – the lives of single rabbits kept in cramped garden hutches have always broken my heart, no matter how beloved those animals might be.

Nearly every year I read news reports of the arrests of working-class men who have been keeping illegally trapped British finches. Their depredations must have a negligible impact compared to the ravages of habitat loss and agricultural chemicals on bird populations, but that's not the point. What they have done is not simply illegal, but considered highly immoral. Species perceived as animate elements of the British countryside have been deprived of their freedom and confined to cages for the delight of the working classes, for whom these birds possess very different meanings. There's a tender domesticity attendant to birdkeeping that cuts through familiar stories about working-class masculinity. Cages are cleaned, babies are tended, droppings are scraped, food is weighed, and birds are held quietly in the hand to be minutely and lovingly examined, activities that mirror the cleaning and housekeeping, cooking and child-keeping roles more familiarly ascribed to women. It's always struck me that people who keep and breed goldfinches, for example, have a far more detailed knowledge of their habits, their intraspecific variations, their breeding behaviour and songs than that of most birdwatchers, to whom goldfinches tend to be birds clinging to feeders in suburban gardens, or flocks that rise from stands of seeding thistles. I grew up watching birds, not keeping them. To me, redpolls have always been delicate and distant entities, small dots flitting around the tops of alder trees. I would never have known that redpolls are a thousand times more charismatic and full of personality than goldfinches had I not had the experience of seeing both kinds of birds close up in aviaries and cages.

It's not birdkeeping per se that is the problem. Some forms of it have almost entirely escaped censure because they have traditionally been the province of those of high social status. You can keep a singing goldfinch in the smallest of caravans, but you need money and land to keep lakes of swans and diving ducks. Waterfowl luminaries have included the aristocrat Lord Lilford; the artist-conservationist Sir Peter Scott; and the eponymous founder of British department store John Lewis, who maintained an enormous collection of ducks and geese on his Hampshire estate. It's still legal in Britain to ask a vet to pinion a young duck or goose or swan, to cut off the last joint of one wing so that forever afterwards it can walk and swim but never fly, a literal amputation to the nature of a migratory species whose wild cousins fly thousands of miles over tundra and ocean every autumn and spring. I have always wondered if a pinioned goose on the lake of a stately home might be experiencing hardships of the same order as that of a goldfinch confined to a cage.

Unlike finches inside houses, the waterfowl in such collections are not treated as an intimate part of the household, but as part of a wider demesne, as landscape-scale additions to an estate. Captive ducks swimming on a lake look pleasingly wild, even if they have had the end of one wing cut away to stop them escaping. An enormous amount of work is involved in creating this elite version of nature, which, as in the eighteenth-century landscape-garden tradition, is designed specifically to look untouched, eternal, natural and unaffected by human artifice, even though that is exactly how it has been made.

Conversely, as journalist Henry Mayhew wrote in the mid-nineteenth century, 'The buyers of singing-birds are eminently the working people.' He went on to describe the species that various classes of tradesmen and artisans preferred to keep – blackbirds and thrushes, for example, were favoured by grooms and coachmen. 'The fondness of a whole body of artificers for any particular bird, animal, or flower, is remarkable,' he concluded. It's the term *artificer* that sings, here, and of a matter that is at the heart of the class system: taste. Keepers of small birds love them not only as individuals but as possibilities and potentialities; over the years they design complex strategies of pairing and selecting to breed birds of particular shapes and patterns and colours and songs. Birdkeeping gestures towards the future as much as it does to those moments in the present when a goldfinch mule raises its head, puffs out its throat and pours forth song. It is, in ways that are not trivial, a deeply creative art. Obvious artifice is the issue: unlike the carefully constructed apparent naturalness of waterfowl kept on country estates, working-class birdkeepers delight in artificiality, creating hybrid finches and thrushes whose beauty is judged in how richly and elaborately it deviates from naturalness.

'Mine!' says the birdkeeper, of the goldfinch. 'Mine!' says the birder, of the same. 'Mine!' says the estate owner, of his flock of pinioned European geese. Outside the bird show, I hear a goldfinch singing from the top of a sapling behind me. While my boyfriend walks on to the car, I stop and listen for a while to a bird that is calling a claim to the whole of its life. It sings of seeds and thistledown, of mates and flights and the fragility of eggs in a moss-and-cobweb nest, and of territorial battles and parasites and sparrowhawks and scarcity and stress.

Hiding

A wildlife hide: a building whose purpose is to make one disappear. This one is a rustic wooden box with bench seats and narrow slits along one side. Walking up to it, it looks almost exactly like a small, weather-beaten garden shed.

I've made myself disappear in hides for as long as I can remember; structures like it are found in nature reserves all over the world, and they seem as natural a part of these places as trees and open water. Even so, a familiar, nervous apprehension flares up as I reach for the door, so I pause for a few seconds before opening it. Inside the air is hot and dark and smells of dust and creosote.

There's no one else here. I swing my legs over the bench-seat and lower the wooden window blind to create a bright rectangle in the darkness; as my eyes adjust, the space before me resolves into a shallow lagoon under streets of cumulus clouds. Almost automatically, I scan the scene with binoculars, ticking off species – three shoveler ducks, two little egrets, a common tern – but my mind is elsewhere, puzzling over that odd sense of apprehension, trying to work out what causes it.

Wildlife hides are not innocent of history. They evolved from photographic blinds, which in turn were based on structures designed to put people closer to animals in order to kill them: duck blinds, deer stands, tree platforms for shooting big cats. Hunting has shaped modern nature appreciation in myriad unacknowledged ways, including the tactics used to bring animals into view. As hunters bait deer and decoy ducks, so preserve managers create shallow feeding pools that concentrate wading birds near hides, or set up feeding stations for wary nocturnal mammals. In the Highlands of Scotland, one celebrated hide gives visitors a 95 per cent chance of seeing rare pine martens – lithe arboreal predators – munching on piles of peanuts.

What you see from hides is supposed to be true reality: that is, wild animals behaving perfectly naturally because they do not know they are being observed. But the side-effect of turning yourself into a pair of eyes in a darkened box is to distance you from the all-encompassing landscape around the hide, in so doing reinforcing a divide between human and natural worlds, encouraging us to feel that animals and plants should be looked at, never touched. Sometimes the window in front of me resembles nothing so much as a television screen.

You don't need to be invisible to see wild animals behaving entirely naturally. As scientists studying creatures like meerkats, chimps and the small brown birds called Arabian babblers have long known, with time you can habituate them to your presence. But hiding is a habit that is hard to break. There is a dubious satisfaction in the subterfuge of watching things that cannot see you, and it's deeply embedded in our culture. When wild animals unexpectedly appear close by and seem unbothered by our presence, we can feel as flustered and unsure about how to behave as teenagers at a dance.

A few years ago, I was walking with my friend Christina through a park in a small English town when characters I've only ever seen in bird hides began to appear: camouflage-clad photographers with 300-millimetre lenses and expressions of urgent concentration. We looked where the cameras were pointed. Three yards away, two of Britain's most elusive mammals were swimming in the shallow river running through the park. Otters! They didn't seem to see us; they certainly didn't care. Their wet flanks gleamed like tar as they rolled in the water. They broke the surface to crunch fish with sharp white teeth, showering droplets from stiff whiskers, then slipped back beneath the surface to swim down the river, the photographers chasing them like paparazzi and intermittently running backwards because the lenses they'd brought were the wrong ones for such close views. It was thrilling. We followed the otters downstream and stopped by a woman with a toddler and a baby in a pushchair, who were watching them, too. She told me she loved the otters. They were part of her town. Part of her local community. They'd eaten all the koi carp from the fishpond in the big house, she said, amused. 'Drove them bonkers, the people that lived there. Those fish were really expensive!' Then she tilted her head at the photographers. 'Aren't they weird?' she asked. Outside a hide, they did look ridiculous; so accustomed to their binoculars, camouflage and high-zoom lenses, they were compelled to use them even when they were entirely unnecessary.

While hides are places designed for watching wildlife, they are equally rewarding places to watch people who watch wildlife and to witness their strange social behaviour. One of the reasons I hesitated before entering the little hide is that I was worried there would be other people in it. Walking into a crowded hide is rather like arriving late at a live theatrical performance and trying to find your seat. There are unspoken rules in hides. As in a theatre or a library, you are required to be silent, or to speak in a low murmur. Some rules are ostensibly in operation to prevent animals detecting your presence – there's a general prohibition on telephone calls, slamming the door too hard, extending your hands out of the window. But others are more curious and they stem from a particular problem: your job in a hide is to pretend you are not there, so when there is more than one person in the hide, the sense of disembodiment the trick relies on is threatened. Regular visitors to hides often solve this conundrum spatially. When she started visiting hides for the first time, Christina – who is from Melbourne – wondered why people chose to sit at the far edges, leaving the seats with the best view unoccupied. 'I thought it was self-sacrificing English etiquette,' she said, 'before I realised that people sat at the far sides of the hide because they wanted to be as far from everyone else as possible.'

There's a constant monitoring of others' expertise in the hide as its inhabitants listen to one another's hushed conversations about the things they can see outside. It's an agony when people get things wrong. I remember the chill in the air one spring day in Suffolk after a man confidently told his companion that what he was watching was a water vole. Everyone else in the hide knew this lumbering creature with a long tail was a large brown rat. No one said anything. One man coughed. Another snorted. The tension was unbearable. With impeccable British reserve, no one felt they could correct his mistake and lessen him in the eyes of his friend. A few people couldn't bear the atmosphere and left the hide.

The uses of hides are as various as their inhabitants. You can sit with a camera hoping for the perfect shot of a passing harrier or owl. You can sit with a proficient naturalist and hear whispered identification tips, or use it as a place to sit down midway through a long walk. Most people sit and scan the view with binoculars for a few minutes before deciding there is nothing of sufficient interest or rarity to keep them there. But there is another kind of hide watching that I am increasingly learning to love. It is when you embrace the possibility that you will see little or nothing of interest. You literally wait and see. Sitting in the dark for an hour or two and looking at the world through a hole in a wall requires a meditative patience. You have given yourself time to watch clouds drift from one side of the sky to the other and cast moving shadows across ninety minutes of open water. A sleeping snipe, its long bill tucked into pale-tipped scapular feathers and its body pressed against rushes striped with patterns of light and shade, wakes, raises its wings and stretches. A heron as motionless as a marble statue for minutes on end makes a cobra-strike to catch a fish. The longer you sit there, the more you become abstracted from this place, and yet fixed to it. The sudden appearance of a deer at the lake's shore, or a flight of ducks tipping and whiffling down to splash on sunlit water, becomes treasure, through the simple fact of the passing of time.

Eulogy

By nine the sun has set behind the King's Forest. The sky is a soft Tiffany blue, darker above us, and there's not a breath of wind. Judith knows the place well, leads us through deep woodland to a few acres of open land, a block of head-height young pines growing through grass and brambles, surrounded by walls of mature trees.

We're waiting for something that won't happen until the light is nearly gone, so we amble for a while along the sandy paths. As night falls, our senses stretch to meet it. A roebuck barks in the distance, small mammals rustle in the grass. The faintest tick of insects. The scratchy, resinous fragrance of heathland grows stronger, more insistent. As we pass clumps of viper's bugloss we watch the oncoming night turn their leaves blacker, their purple petals bluer and more intense until they seem to glow. The paths become luminous trails through darkness. White moths spiral up from the ground, and a cockchafer zips past us, elytra raised, wings buzzing.

Soon all colour will be gone. The thought is a hard one. Over the last few weeks I've spent much of my time visiting Stu in a local hospice. He and his partner Mandy are among my dearest, closest friends. I first met him in the 1990s on a raw December morning at a falconry field meet in the East Anglian Fens. He was a giant of a man with curly hair and a huge old goshawk and he was formidable and faintly scary. But as I watched him handle his hawk and his dogs, I saw there an extraordinary gentleness and care. So many of my memories of Stu are of this gentleness; the way he'd look at his family, the expression on his upturned face as he followed his falcons' flight, the tender way he'd clean their hooked beaks between finger and thumb. He was a strong man, a strong-willed man, who carved his own, inimitable path through life, and he had an astonishing capacity to reassure, to teach, to inspire.

Stu was so ready to see magic in the world. He told me once, shaking his head in wonderment, that he'd watched a white stag stepping across the road at midnight like something out of a medieval legend. About the time he caught a bat in his motorcycle leathers while biking at top speed, and how he was so amazed and delighted he put it in his pocket and brought it home to show everyone before letting it go. And how, after he had been diagnosed with the illness that he knew would take him, he'd been walking with his pointer dog Cody across fields when she'd found two just-born leverets, twin baby hares, tucked in the grass. Stuart was the strongest of men, but he told me about them with tears in his eyes. They were so small. So new.

Now, watching the slow diminishment of sense and detail around me, I'm thinking of Stu and what is happening to him, thinking of his family, of what we face at the end of our lives' long summers when the world parts from us, of how we all, one day, will walk into darkness. Then the sound begins. It spools out from the trees behind the sapling pines, and I catch the flash of a smile on Judith's face in the gloom. The noise resembles a sewing machine running at top speed, or an unspooling fishing reel, but such mechanical analogies fail to capture its rich musicality. It's a deep and beautiful *churring* that lasts for four or five seconds before the creature that's making it breathes in, briefly lowering the pitch, and then starts up again. Judith cups a hand behind each ear and turns her head to pinpoint the source. She gestures out in front of us, a little to our left. Somewhere in that direction, sitting lengthways on a branch, his throat puffed out to raise this strange song to the night, is a nightjar.

Imagine a slim bird as long as your hand from wrist to fingertip, and with huge, black-ink anime eyes. Imagine its plumage is patterned with all woodland things rolled together: bark, rotting wood, the tips of dry fern fronds, cobwebs, the bright ends of broken twigs, dappled shadows, dead leaves. Nightjars are cryptic beasts for whom subtlety is safety; during daylight hours they rest and nest upon ground that so perfectly matches their feathers they are almost impossible to detect, even from a few feet away. Their neat beaks look ordinary enough until they open their mouths into a huge, froglike pink gape surrounded by bristly feathers that help them catch their flying prey: moths, beetles, other insects. The bird we're hearing spent his winter in Africa, has come here to mate and rear young in this chequerboard landscape of coniferous forest and heath before he heads back south in late August or September. Another *churr* begins, then another. Five birds, six? It's hard to tell, but they're calling all around us. It's exquisite music, but I'm hoping we get something more.

We do. There's a soft call, a different call, the one they make in flight. I whistle something like it back into the darkness. The call comes again, closer now, and as I strain my eyes into the noisy black I see the barest suggestion of a bird flying towards me, wings as thin, wavering lines appearing and disappearing over the distance between the noise and my upturned face. And then, sailing out just above our heads, dark against the sky, is a nightjar. It's remarkably odd, the shape of a skinny falcon, but somehow the quality of its flight makes it look like a paper aeroplane. It's so light in the air it seems to have no weight at all, and there's something mothlike about it too. I can just make out the barring of the underside of its wings, the lack of white near their tips – it's a female – and we watch as she hunches herself in mid-air, curls down to the left and hovers, briefly. A male joins her, white wing-patches blurring; they circle for a few seconds before breaking apart and disappearing into darkness. We hear a quick, flat clapping noise as the male slaps the top of his wings together in flight, a display that sounds like quiet applause, and then they are gone, slipping back into the nothing around us.

For years, on and off, I have woken in the dark, shouting out loud, stricken with horror at the impossible fact of death. It has been my most abiding and paralysing terror but it was Stu who banished it from me. At the hospice he looked me in the eye, very seriously, very quietly, and said, of what was happening to him, *It's OK. It's OK.* I knew it was not, that what he was doing was reassuring me, and it was an act of such generosity that for a while I couldn't find anything strong enough inside me to reply. *It's OK*, he said. *It's not hard.* Those are the words I am remembering as we walk onward, as the minutes pass, until night thickens completely and there is starlight and dust and the feel of sand underfoot. It's so dark now I cannot see myself. But the song continues, and the air around us is full of invisible wings.

Rescue

My friend Judith cuts the head off a dead cricket with a pair of nail scissors and discards its leggy, thorny thorax before dropping the abdomen into a small china bowl on the kitchen table, the kind of bowl that you'd use for olives or pretzels. The cricket's insides are as white and creamy as soft cheese. Outside, sparrows squabble in the garden, and their chirruping calls back the crunching scythe of blades through chitin and the wet patter of insect parts dropped one by one into the pile. Next to the bowl is a plastic washing-up tub. When I lean over to look inside it, dark eyes stare up at me from a huddle of pale-fringed faces.

The tub is full of baby swifts. Adults might be renowned for their aerial grace, but the baby ones in front of me resemble a cross between subway mice and a pile of unexpectedly animate kindling. Their clawed feet are so tiny that they cannot walk, only shuffle, and their impossibly long wings stick out at a variety of unlikely angles. Judith, a gentle and deliberate woman with silver hair cut in a practical bob, lifts up one of the nestlings and sets it upon a tissue-covered towel. Plucking a lump from the bowl, she touches it to the tip of its tiny beak, which opens into a huge pink maw that swallows the tip of her finger. The cricket vanishes down the bird's throat. Another follows.

Frowning with concentration, Judith feeds her birds with the calm assurance gained from long experience. Seventeen years ago she spotted what she thought was a pile of feathers by the side of the road while walking her dog. It was a swift chick. She picked it up and brought it home. Numerous experts told her that it would be too difficult to raise and would die. 'Of course it didn't,' she said. 'It survived. But it was a steep learning curve.'

She's now so renowned for her swift-rearing skills that orphans are brought to her from all over eastern England. Some arrive from vets, others from members of the public who have found her name on the internet having come across birds that have fallen from their nests. She's had around thirty in her care this year, and has raised them all on a diet of crickets and wax-moth caterpillars dusted with powdered vitamins. While some don't make it – usually because they've been given unsuitable food by their initial rescuers – most are successfully returned to the wild, triumphing over death. And the chance to observe that particular triumph is why I'm sitting in her small bungalow in a village near the American air base in Suffolk where she used to work in communications and public affairs. If the wind drops later this morning, we'll set some of her young birds free. 'It can be very tiring,' she says. 'The early mornings! But when you let one go, it's just sheer magic. And sometimes I'm in the garden in the evening, and I might see twenty, thirty, forty swifts in the air, and I think, *I know they're not, but they could be all mine*.'

We tend to physically touch wild animals only when they're hunted, studied or in serious trouble, and the latter is usually our fault. We dislodge nests, soak seabirds in oil, hit hares and foxes with cars, pick up casualties from beneath glass windows and power lines. When I was twelve I reared a brood of baby bullfinches brought to me by a neighbour who had felled their nest tree. When those chicks flew free, there was a strong sense of having righted a wrong that humans had perpetrated on the world.

Against a backdrop of environmental destruction and precipitous species decline, our social anxieties about the impact we have on the natural world are often tied to tragedies suffered by individual animals. Tending injured and orphaned creatures until they are fit to be returned to the wild can feel like an act of resistance, redress, even redemption. Rearing a single nest of finches in the 1980s didn't halt the decline of British songbird populations. But my simple sense of the justice of saving them was magnified by coming to see things about them I'd never otherwise have known: how they slept, how they communicated with each other, their myriad bewitching idiosyncrasies.

'We feel responsible,' says Norma Bishop, executive director of Lindsay Wildlife Experience in Walnut Creek, California, which operates America's oldest wildlife rehabilitation centre, founded in 1970. 'It's a little like the story of Noah rescuing the animals.' Rehabbers stress that their animals are never pets, and that their role is to return them to the wild as fast as possible, but inevitably they forge emotional bonds with their charges. British regulations allow individuals to tend to animal casualties themselves provided they adhere to established welfare guidelines. In America, wildlife rehabilitation is confined to licensed experts, often working for charitable institutions. But whatever the rehabber's position, the dedication involved is immense: keepers of orphaned elephants in Kenya, for example, sleep next to the animals every night, but they take turns with others because too great an attachment to any one keeper risks the baby elephant being overcome by grief when he or she takes the night off.

Why do people rescue wildlife? The eminent veterinarian John Cooper thinks 'there's something inside humans when they're faced with a helpless creature. We have an imperative. A duty.' Bishop agrees: 'I believe most people, especially children, simply cannot see an animal suffer.' The Lindsay rehab centre receives everything from bobcats to snakes, ducklings to songbirds, brought in by concerned members of the public who may have driven many miles to deliver them. Los Angeles-based hummingbird rehabber Terry Masear thinks that rescuing animals draws out 'raw emotions that unleash our deepest insecurities about our humanity, mortality and place in the natural world'. These insecurities often lead to mistaken attempts at rescue: most 'lost' fledgling birds in trees or sleeping fawns in long grass are not lost at all, but are still being fed by their parents.

Rehabbers are often criticised for being too sentimental, their work dismissed as acts of compassion for individual animals with little or no conservation benefit. It's a reasonable view, but one that misses the point. It's hard to feel a meaningful connection with creatures whose lives in the wild hardly coincide with our own. Bats are things of unnerving mystery to most of us, flickering aerial presences briefly and surprisingly appearing out of the night. But holding a little brown bat, staring into its bleary eyes from a few inches away, seeing its uptilted snout and delicate, mouse-like ears – that turns it into something much easier to love. The way rehabbers talk about what they do evokes in me precisely the feelings I've had about rescue animals in my own life: an intoxicating process of coming to know something quite unlike you, to understand it well enough not only to keep it alive but also to put it back, like a puzzle piece, into the gap in the world it left behind.

Judith has no truck with accusations of sentimentality when it comes to swifts, whose numbers in Britain have fallen by more than 35 per cent over the last twenty years. Each bird she saves, she tells me, may truly be precious to the species' fortunes. Increasingly, people are blocking up holes in the eaves of old buildings where swifts nest, and modern buildings often have nowhere for swifts to nest at all. Similar problems face chimney swifts in North America as defunct and crumbling chimneys are removed. Many renovators do not know about the swifts' reliance on our buildings, do not know they are destroying their homes, because they simply don't know they are there. Seeing a rescued swift can change all that. 'Once people have seen a swift in the hand, they're in awe of them,' Judith says. Her kitchen is full of cards from well-wishers and people who have brought her swifts, and rescuers drop by to see how their chicks are faring. Some of them have been motivated to build and fit swift nestboxes under their roofs, welcoming these birds into their homes.

The wind has dropped, and the sky above the house is a widening pool of blue. Judith has put seven swifts into a paper-towel-lined pet carrier, where they clump together in a feathery mass. One has reached across to gently preen the mantle feathers of a nest-mate. Watching them I realise I've never seen baby birds so desperate to snuggle. It's as if they've been magnetised to press themselves against each other, wing upon wing.

It's a short drive to Judith's favourite release site, the village cricket field. We arrive just as a local match is beginning, but after brief, good-natured negotiations, the cricketers stop playing and watch. Judith takes a swift from the box, plants a quick good-luck kiss on its feathery crown and hands it to me. People often presume that the way to release swifts is to throw them high in the air, but this can result in serious injury if the bird isn't ready to go. The right method is to hold the bird on your raised and outstretched palm, turn so it faces into the wind, and wait. In the bright air the swift looks a weird, unearthly creature, a delicate construction of scalloped feathers and ungainly wings. Hunched into itself, its miniature claws grip my fingers, its deep eyes like reflective astronaut visors. I wonder what it can see: lines of magnetic force, perhaps, rising air and flying insects and the suspicion of summer storms. The flat green beneath it has nothing to do with it at all. I lift my hand higher. All I can do now is wait.

It stares into the wind for a while, then starts shivering. Anticipation. I think. Functional explanations: this bird is warming up its pectoral muscles ready for flight. Emotional explanations: anticipation, wonder, joy, terror. The sensitive filoplumes growing between the feathers of its wings and sleek sides are being brushed by the breeze, feeling their element for the first time.

Nothing has visibly changed, but something is happening, like an aircraft avionics system coming online as it powers up. Blinking lights, engine check. *Check*. That doesn't work, though, not quite, as an analogy, because what I am watching is a new thing making itself out of something else. There is no doubt in my mind that this is as much a transformation as a dragonfly larva crawling from water and tearing itself out into a thing with wings. On my open palm a creature whose home has been paper towels and plastic boxes is turning into a different creature whose home is thousands of miles of air.

Then the swift decides. It tilts the pug-sharp tiny tip of its beak upwards, arches its back, and drops from my flattened palm, making an aching series of stiff and creaky wingbeats. For five or six seconds everything feels wrong. The bird is a mere foot above the grass, and my heart is beating fast. 'Up! Up! Up!' calls Judith. Nothing is broken. We are just watching a bird learning to fly. Hitching as if pulling into gear, the swift starts to ascend, flickering up and up into a sky streaked with evening cirrus. It describes one careful circle above our heads, then lifts even higher and straight-lines it to the south. The cricketers applaud. I look down at my palm. There's a little scratch on the meat of my thumb where its claws had gripped tight before letting me go, gripped tight to the hand that was the last solid thing the bird would touch for years.

Goats

As a child I discovered a simple game that's good to play with goats. You lay your hand flat on a billy goat's forehead and push, just a little. You push, and it pushes back, and you push harder, and it does too, and it's a little like arm-wrestling, but much more fun, and the goat always wins.

I told Dad about my love of pushing goats once, just as an aside while we were talking about something else. He must have filed this information away, because about a year later, he came home very crossly, and he was cross with *me*, and that was a very rare thing. In his capacity as a press photographer, he'd spent the day at London Zoo taking photographs for their Annual Animal Census, and at one point he happened to be standing with the rest of the press pack in the petting zoo.

And there he sees a goat.

And he says to everyone, *Watch this*.

I hadn't explained the activity very well. Because he puts his hand against the goat's forehead, with everyone watching. Then he pushes.

He pushes really hard.

And the goat falls over.

There's a long silence broken only by the sound of photographers and journalists saying, '*Jesus*, Mac!' and, 'What the *fuck?!*'

The goat gets up, stares at him and runs away. And the press pack never let him forget the time he pushed a goat over in front of all of them and it was all my fault.

Dispatches from the Valleys

There was a TV reality show a decade or so ago called *Victorian Farm*. I used to watch it with nostalgia and remember what life was like in the winter of 1997. Those were the days. I'd walk up the hill to the house at lunchtime, check the sheep, bring them hay, feed the hens, break the ice on the water troughs and drinkers, fill the scuttle in the outhouse, trudge inside to load the Rayburn range with coal, and then walk back down to the office along a country lane rutted with refrozen snow.

It was the age of *The X-Files* and *Friends*, Beck and The Prodigy, Dolly the Sheep and the death of Diana. I'd just graduated from university and had quite enough of libraries and the half-light of college refectories and university bars full of would-be poets. I was young, self-important, extremely self-absorbed. I wanted to *live*, wanted a real job in the real world, working with real and sensible people. So when I was hired by a falcon conservation-breeding farm in rural Wales, I was convinced I had found my perfect career.

I don't think of those times often. But they always come to mind if I'm watching a sci-fi movie in which an ill-matched crew with personality issues is stuck on a ship in deep space with nowhere to go. That's what it was like, although sometimes we all got in a car and went shopping in Swansea. We worked seven days a week, which was not good for our mental health, but at least we were doing what we loved, I'd tell myself, sometimes out loud in incantation, like after I heard the local builder muttering, 'They should tear this house down, it's a wreck,' outside our kitchen door.

The property belonged to our boss and his wife. A pebble-dashed box streaked with green algae, it had a pine-panelled kitchen and a low-ceilinged sitting room with the Rayburn, a brown vinyl sofa and eye-bending 1970s carpets that did bad things to you when you were drunk. I liked the house because it was home, even though towards the end of my stay bead-curtains of water pattered on to the carpet from the ceiling when it rained, and once I stood nonplussed as a rat ran out of the oven when someone opened the door. It could be idyllic in the summer, when swallows chattered and preened on the telephone wire outside my bedroom window, but it was often cold enough in winter that I'd need to train a hairdryer into the cave of my duvet to make it sufficiently warm inside that I could sleep. It was not a dry house. I wasn't allowed to bring falcons back home, the boss told me, because it was unlikely their delicate respiratory systems could cope with the atmosphere the staff lived in.

The house stood in rough pasture at the top of a steep mudstone valley. Behind us were dark woods and tussocky fields where the boss ran a small herd of mixed-breed steers that grew increasingly wild as the months went by. We lost them sometimes. Lost them in that they literally wandered off through gaps in the hedges. None of us were farmers, but we tried our best. In the evenings we'd make the long trek out to the pub for beer and pool and walk back in the small hours until the landlord barred us, as he'd barred everyone else that ever went there, and the pub closed down. At least, I think that's what happened. A lot of what happened back then has the quality of a fairy tale.

Hawk-obsessed volunteers flocked to us every summer of the four years I worked there. Among them were an aristocratic Mexican veterinary student, a kickboxing champion from the Kyrgyz Republic, and a lad who spent so much time jerking off in the bathroom we used to hammer on the door and yell at him to stop. All of them were men. And apart from a biologist who left a few months after I arrived, so were the permanent staff. In the office with me was a lanky dark-haired northerner studying for his part-time Ph.D. who ended up in a relationship with me. Everyone else was outside with the birds. There was the enthusiastic Geordie who explained to me that the correct mindset for running out on to a rugby pitch was, *Let's break arms!*; the wiry ex-Marine who managed the breeding programme and while expert at the complexities of falcon artificial insemination and incubation was repeatedly dismayed by his inability to cook rice without it sticking together; and a skinny lad who'd grown up on a caravan site and spent his days jet-washing shit-splattered aviaries with resigned good humour – he told me once that if he ever won the National Lottery, he'd buy himself a brand-new Ford Fiesta. There was the ebullient son of a white Zimbabwean tobacco farmer who stomped around in wellingtons and shorts and opined that accepting homosexuals was the symptom of a decadent and doomed society, and a quiet South African who'd make us *bobotie* and liked Hungarian folk music. He rebuilt the stone walls, cared for a kit of roller pigeons, and eventually acclimatised to our spartan life, though he spent his first night literally hugging the Rayburn to keep warm. This was the real world; these were the sensible people I'd left academia for.

Once, when it got really cold – the snow heaped high against the hedges and the fields littered with weak, emaciated arctic thrushes – I snapped with whatever the equivalent of the red mist is when you're just too frozen to deal. I filled the range as full as I could, eventually cramming lumps of coal in with my hands, opened up all the air vents as wide as they'd go and went back to work. A part of me knew this was not wise, and it was not. When I got home from work the house was full of smoke from the wallpaper burning away around the flue. But the Rayburn was our friend. It heated our water to Venusian temperatures, and saved us when the electricity went out, which it did from time to time, and we cooked chickens in it, often our own, young, poorly plucked, gristly cockerels bristling with filoplumes, which we chewed stoically by candlelight.

The office had a couple of hulking grey PCs and an internet connection so attenuated it took three days to download a sound file. The work we did there was fascinating and sobering. The recent collapse of the Soviet Union had opened up the breeding range of saker falcons to organised trapping and smuggling gangs, and falcon populations were in free fall. We ran field teams across their range to monitor their decline, ran sustainability education programmes, and sought to undercut the traditional market for wild-caught falconry birds in the Gulf States by sending out hundreds of home-bred falcons every autumn. I travelled out with them. I remember sitting in the night-illuminated cockpit of a 747 with a pilot who handed me a pink rose while explaining to me that aircraft greet each other in the darkness by flashing their lights. He let me throw the switches to do this, my heart lifting thousands of feet at the distant, impossible reply. Abu Dhabi itself was pale and dusty and in the midst of its mutation from coastal desert town to sci-fi high-rise metropolis, and my rooms on the Corniche looked out over one of the oldest buildings in town, the low concrete bulk of the 1972 British Embassy.

I treasure the times I spent in the UAE talking hawks and heritage with Emirati falconers. But the opportunity to spend time in the Gulf States wasn't what kept me at the farm. The birds did. They kept all of us there. As racehorse trainers know, young people will put up with almost anything to work with the objects of their passion. Every year we'd hand-rear a few falcons and raise them in the office. I'd find fledglings fast asleep on my keyboard, squeaking irritably and sending feather dust into the air when I gently nudged them awake and asked them to move so I could type. Sometimes I'd roll scrunched-up paper balls to them across the laminate floor and they'd run, stumpily, unsteadily, wings half-open, grabbing at their rolling targets with feet that weren't yet entirely coordinated, chittering with high excitement. Their presence made the office a much better place. But the breeding season was brutal for the bird staff. They slept in shifts to feed hatchlings through the night, and as the weeks went by became so exhausted they'd fall asleep in the middle of eating lunch, heads on folded arms, or pass out on the sofa and drool silently into the cushions. All spring they lived on pints of instant coffee and junk food and their lives were spent mincing frozen quail, changing paper towels, checking brooder temperatures, filling small falcon mouths begging for food again and again and again.

I learned a lot on the farm. Raptor biology, falcon breeding, for sure. But also how to work in a tight crew and love it; how to enjoy watching Premiership football matches on pub televisions, including the precise nature of the offside rule. I learned that counting sheep is harder than it appears, and that some sheep really are better looking than others. That the wet grass at the bottom of the field opposite the house was where the snipe were, and in deep winter, woodcock sifted down into the valley woods, their backs patterned like thumbprints and bracken fronds. I knew I'd leave the farm one day, but for a long time it was as vague and unexamined a notion as that of getting married or having children. What brought that intimation into focus was not my growing sense of dissatisfaction with this life, but the dreadful incident with the ostrich.

For there were ostriches. The wet valleys of West Wales were an unlikely place to find them, but the boss and his wife had repurposed a portion of their grazing land as an ostrich farm. It was the time of the Great British Ostrich Bubble, when ostrich steaks were heralded as the health food of the future and fertilised eggs were selling for £100 each. Soon this breeders' market would saturate and prices collapse along with most of the farms. Disaster was already in the air: I shiver at the memory of the Welsh ostrich farmers' social event we attended one night, where tables of former sheep farmers chewed sadly at ostrich steaks and took heart pills while a man in a lounge suit played show tunes on a Casio organ.

Ostriches are unlike falcons in that they're genuinely dangerous, so the high wire fence surrounding their fields had a gap at the bottom that you could roll through if they chased you. I had as little to do with the ostriches as possible, but occasionally I was asked to check the fences along their field boundaries – I blush to admit that I used to pretend I was walking the electrified dinosaur containments in *Jurassic Park* to make the job more interesting – and I was in the company of the boss's wife one morning doing just this when it happened. We saw a lump on the ground further up the hill that resolved, as we grew closer, into a female ostrich lying in a circle of trampled, blood-soaked mud. The poor bird had stuck a foot through the wire sometime the previous night, panicked, and had broken her leg trying to get free. She was still alive, somehow keeping her head off the ground though most of her neck lay flat in the dirt. The compound tibiotarsal fracture was so obscene, a chaos of torn red muscle and splintered white bone, that I went straight into full-on emergency mode. I searched my pockets and pulled out a miniature penknife branded with the logo of a local photographic shop. I unfolded it, picked up a big rock, hit the ostrich over the head to render it unconscious, then knelt down and cut its throat to put it out of its misery. Key-chain novelty penknives are not sharp. It took a while. You do such things when there's no other thing that can be done. I got up, watching the bird's one good leg kick until it stilled, the blankness of sheer necessity receding then to leave a wash of simple, overwhelming sadness in its wake. This was so senseless. This bird shouldn't have been able to break her leg. She shouldn't have suffered like this all night. She shouldn't have been here at all. I watched my hands wipe streaks of bloody mud down the front of my jeans, then looked up and saw the stricken face of my boss's wife. I had forgotten she was there.

Oh, I thought.

The chain of command had fallen away. A bright, fierce sense of personal agency flared up, newborn of the grimmest necessity. My head pulled from the sand. We walked back in silence. I never felt the same about the farm after that morning; always a part of my heart flickered and beat and thrummed with the need to escape, a bird trapped in a locked barn. I handed in my notice a few months later. The date of my departure may have been hastened by my boss telling me he wanted to enroll me on a secretarial course at the local college, but what finally made me leave were the cattle on the hill.

It was a blank summer evening. Everyone else had gone drinking in town. I hadn't wanted to go but I didn't want to sit at home either, so I set off for a walk in the woods at the back of the farmhouse. I was bored with my life. I was so bored I didn't know I was bored. I needed to do *something*. Then I saw the herd of bullocks on the lee side of a slope in the far distance. They had been left alone so long they were now almost entirely wild, and that was when the plan gripped me. I made some mental calculations. The valley was dark. The shoulders of the hill were bright with rays of low sun. The wind was in my face. There wasn't so much cover that I couldn't do it. Was I going to do it? I was.

I slipped deeper into the birch thicket and began stealthing my way towards them. A little later I grabbed some bracken fronds, tore and twisted them until they came free and tucked them into my T-shirt so my head was half-obscured, my hands gritty with fern juice, and then I took a handful of mud and rouged my face with it. I went full-on Captain Willard from *Apocalypse Now*.

It was an epic stalk. Cover, concealment, camouflage. No sudden movements, everything slowed into certainty. When I was within three hundred yards of my target, I got on my hands and knees and crawled. When I was even closer, I got on my belly. I spent a lot of time utterly motionless, because keeping still for long periods was a crucial part of the manoeuvre. I had expected this stalk to be absorbing. I did not expect it to be a truly mind-altering experience. Every time I stopped moving the world dipped and swung and held itself in suspension around me. I felt myself then loosely scattered, hardly a singular being, just a thing of leaves and dirt and stones. I suppose I was incredibly uncomfortable, though I didn't feel it, because later I found there was blood down one arm from a laceration, cause unknown, and my right knee hurt for weeks. But I persevered. I got right up to the herd. I got almost *into* the herd. They were sitting amid the thistly grass, flipping their tails on to the dried mud of their flanks, chewing the cud, flicking their ears. There was the rich smell of cow – I had crawled through God knows how many cowpats en route – and I was close enough to see flies and eyelashes.

And then I did it. I leaped up from the ground, waving my arms, and *yelled*. Under a low Welsh sky, to a herd of surprised cattle, I was a home-made ghillie-suited, dancing, mud-smeared monstrous apparition out of nowhere. The herd scrambled to its feet, lowing in entirely understandable terror, and stampeded. The earth trembled under their serried hooves. It was *perfect.* I yelled and yelled at the beasts as they flung themselves pell-mell hell-for-leather up and over the hill until they were all gone, and I knew the entire time that this was, hand to God, the most satisfying thing I had ever done in my whole life, and I limped back to the farm, with my mouth hurting from grinning, buzzing with thistle-prickles and adrenalin, and got myself in the bath, and lay there soaking away the mud, and as the adrenalin subsided, I realised I had absolutely no idea why I had done it.

Over the years I've told a few people that once I covered myself in mud and leaves and stalked a herd of cows on a hill. It makes me sound a little unbalanced, but then balance has never been my forte, and I had certainly been feeling the insulating blankness that accompanies certain forms of long-term depression. I almost never tell the story about the ostrich. A friend once told me it made me sound like a psychopath. 'No,' I countered, stung, 'the point of the story is the opposite: it shows how none of us are used to seeing death any more, let alone having to … Well, that's not really the point, the point is that no matter who we are, we can all do things that we don't think we can do, really hard things, if we have to.'

Their eyebrows rose. 'Like kill an ostrich with a rock and a novelty penknife?'

I tried to explain that when all options have narrowed to *must*, there comes a point where you can't even think about alternatives. 'Yeah,' they said slowly, 'but that just makes you sound even worse.'

It's true that most of us these days haven't ever killed an animal much larger than a fly, though humans kill more animals today than ever before – sixty-five billion chickens each year, for example. And it's also true that all of us have the capacity to do things we think unimaginable until the moment they are not. But that's not the point of the story either.

The point is that I would never have fled the farm without the ostrich and the cattle.

On my travels I've talked to many strangers about grief, and birds, and love, and death. And many have been generous enough to share with me a meaningful encounter they have had with an animal. With ravens or owls or hawks or bears; herons or cats, foxes, even butterflies. Each encounter has heralded a subtle but tectonic shift in the way the person related to the world, and so often they have involved animals appearing at a time of great hardship for the witnesser, and in places they should not be. A woman told me that after the death of a beloved parent in a city hospital she heard a lone wild goose frantically calling for the rest of its flock in the small courtyard outside before it took off and disappeared over the urban roofline. A man told of a magpie that flew down to the coffin in the midst of a funeral, where it sat for a long while staring directly at the mourners. A veteran helicopter pilot denied their flight licence began to be visited daily by a wild black hawk.

For the longest time I assumed these meaningful encounters were examples of confirmation bias. That when something deeply affecting has happened, you'll find yourself searching for meaning in the things around you, and it's then you'll see animals that had always been there but you had never before noticed. But the more stories I heard, the more I began to feel restless with that explanation, and knew I should think more carefully about what animals can mean. I'm sure that the barn owl that turned its face to stare at a grieving son was merely momentarily surprised before flying on. But even so there was more to that exchange than an animal and a person looking at each other.

We have corralled the meanings of animals so tightly these days, have shuttled them into separate epistemologies that are not supposed to touch. You can consider the Eurasian wolf as a social canid, or see it as an archetype with deep spiritual significance, but scientists aren't supposed to speak of magic, and New Agers tend not to bother with sustained research into animal physiology or behaviour. Of course we need science to comprehend the complexity of the moving world, and to help decide how best to conserve what there is still left. But there is always more. Perhaps one aspect of the sixteenth century is worthy of thinking about: the last great flowering of a form of emblematic natural history in which we could think of animals as more than mere creatures, each living species at the centre of a rich fabric of associations linking everything that was known about it with everything it meant to humans: matters allegorical, scriptural, proverbial, personal.

The ostrich and the cattle were living animals with their own life-worlds and deserving of their own stories. But they were also emblems to me, signs read by my subconscious mind to hasten me out of the quotidian incomprehension fostered by dismal circumstances. They were encounters with animals that resolved themselves into personal truths. And the nature of those truths were particular. They weren't hard-won through therapeutic dialogue. Nor were they revelations of divine intent. They were the kind of truths most akin, I think, to those offered by Tarot cards.

Like the I Ching, Tarot has a very peculiar sociocultural position. I've met many eminent people – scientists, writers, lawyers – who regularly turn to it, but they tend to keep this quiet because reading the cards is too *woo woo* to discuss in polite company. I've used Tarot too. Not often, but sufficient to know how little use the cards are in divining the future – and to see how unerringly the cards reflect my deepest states of being, emotions I'd not let myself feel at the time. I have no idea of the mechanism through which this could be possible, but even so I find myself inclined to trust that the Tarot can speak to us in ways to which we should pay the most careful attention.

Encounters with creatures are always with a real creature. But they are also built out of all the stories and associations we've learned about them throughout our lives. They are always already emblematic. And while we should honour their lived reality, and trust the science, I wonder if we might also be readier to accept what animals' emblematic selves are trying to tell us.

Sometimes the answers are simple. I understood what the ostrich had taught me almost instantly. But what the cows meant took me years. I was overtaking an animal transport truck on a motorway one afternoon when I glimpsed the wet pink nose of a cow pushed through its side. I felt pity, guilt, responsibility, sadness. I thought about the remorselessness of the system in which this creature had been caught up. And then I thought of the day I stalked the steers on the hill and it resolved into perfect clarity. For I had seen myself as one of those steers, one of a feral and uncared-for herd enjoying life in the middle of nowhere, not thinking about what would happen in the future, and not much worried about it, but knowing deep down that one day I was headed for the abattoir. There would be no escaping the deep sea for the shore. And my stalking and shouting was not mindless. It had been an inchoate attempt to knock them out of their contented composure. It had been a warning to make them run the *hell out of there*, because the valley we were all in was dark and deep and could have no good end.

The Numinous Ordinary

The 1960s radio in my childhood home had a mahogany wood case, milled metal dials and a glass face printed with bands and frequencies. To find stations you moved the indicator through a gamut of squeals and static by turning a dial, which always felt a little as if I were a burglar unlocking a safe: *click, click*, hair-fine attention, feedback between the printed whorls of my fingertips and the slow beat of the sound-sensing hairs deep in my ears making me just a shorting arc between them, so that it was easy to feel that the voices were waiting for me alone to find them. LUXEMBOURG, BREMEN, STRASSBURG, it said on the screen in fat capitals, BUDAPEST. BBC LIGHT. Polkas, waltzes, voices in unknown languages. That radio made Europe into an idea for me, and I loved it. But as I grew older my fascination with the 1960s radio ebbed and died and I spent far less time playing with it. It ended up on my bedroom bookcase tuned almost perpetually to BBC Radio 4.

But then, on occasional evenings in the early 1980s, I began noticing the strangest thing. Whatever the radio was playing – the news, perhaps, a discussion programme, a mystery drama – a melody would drift in behind the voices, fugitive as ash. Usually it was only barely discernible before burying itself again beneath the programme. But sometimes the music would come clear. Ten bell-like notes, rich with mystery, so plangent and eerie that I took to turning on the radio just in case they appeared. Decades later, after spending some time on radio enthusiast message boards on the internet, I worked out that in my small English bedroom I had been hearing the interval tuning signal of the All-Union Soviet station Radio Mayak. *Mayak*: Russian for lighthouse, beacon. The melody was from the famous Russian song 'Moscow Nights'. 'Речка движется и не движется,' runs the lyric. *River moving and not moving*. And ever since those days, certain unpredictable things will remind me of that ten-note melody – a photograph of thousands of bird skins laid out in open museum drawers, the dusty smear of the Milky Way, the details of spatter-coated samples in scanning electron micrographs, or the thin trails of summer meteor showers. I thought of it again yesterday while lounging on the sofa watching *Raiders of the Lost Ark*, hearing the amoral archaeologist René Belloq explain to Indiana Jones the nature of the Ark of the Covenant. 'It's a transmitter,' he says. 'It's a radio for speaking to God.' Somehow, the interval signal melody that slipped into the evenings of my everyday teenage life has become to me the music of the divine.

I was not raised in any faith. I was the child always surprised by grace before mealtimes at the houses of friends. The great authorities of my childhood were *National Geographic* and *New Scientist* magazines, though I wasn't ignorant of the Bible. My grandmother, a tall and striking woman with raven curls and stylish crimplene blouses, had given me *The Children's Bible* for Christmas before I could read. It was illustrated with scenes painted according to the aesthetic conventions of 1950s Technicolor Hollywood epics. The scenery mostly resembled southern Californian hillsides. There were scenes of hail raining upon dying cattle, men sweeping up frogs, an angel giving a shirtless Gideon the eye, and – my favourite because it was a bird I'd not yet seen – Elijah being fed lumps of meat by a raven. The Book of

Revelation posed certain issues for the artists, who, faced with matters traumatically eschatological, opted for blue-toned abstraction.

Growing up living on an estate owned by the Theosophical Society didn't bring me to faith, but it widened my understanding of what it could be. Our neighbours believed in reincarnation, occultism, in mysteries at the heart of all the world's religious texts, and when I'd walk past the open door of the Liberal Catholic Church on my way to watch birds in the woods I'd sometimes stop to take deep breaths of sweet incense, though I don't remember ever venturing inside.

During my teenage years I didn't think much about religion except that I didn't have it, didn't need it and that people who did were sad, an unexamined contempt that was perhaps misdirected envy at the thought that some people could so easily feel unconditional love. But it was around then that I had a dream about God. It happened precisely once, and there was no question of what I was dreaming. *It* – for this was no He – was tall, roughly the shape of a human, lacking eyes and any kind of facial feature, and Its surface perfectly reflected everything around It. A slowly moving, purposive mirror that spoke things that weren't words that I could feel in my bones, deep subsonics. It burned unbearably hot and unbearably cold at the same time. I don't recall that It had any regard for me in particular, nor why It should have been in my dream, but then, I suppose, I was not supposed to, and that was perhaps the point. The dream didn't make me believe. Nor has anything since. But recently I've been thinking about religion again.

What has led me to it is largely a matter of craft. When I was writing my book about the death of my father and dealing with the matter of grief by training a hawk, I kept trying to find the right words to describe certain experiences and failing. My secular lexicon didn't capture what they were like. You've probably had such experiences yourself – times in which the world stutters, turns and fills with unexpected meaning. When rapturousness claims a moment and transfigures it. The deep hush before an oncoming storm; the clapping of wings as a flock of doves rises to wheel against low sun; a briar stem in the sun glittering with blades of hoarfrost. Love, beauty, mystery. Epiphanies, I suppose. Occasions of grace.

For a long while I tried to write about such things by borrowing from the extensive literature on the philosophical concept of the sublime. It got me some of the way there, but never far enough. Only recently have I found the language I need – in writings about forms of religious experience. Books written by people like William James and Rudolf Otto, books that investigate the nature of our intuitions of the sacred. The experience of the numinous, in Otto's account, is of a mystery outside the self that is both terrible and fascinating, in the divine presence of which 'the soul, held speechless, trembles inwardly to the furthest fibre of its being'. These are texts you're probably handed on your first day of studying theology, but all of them are new to me. Trying to think and write after reading them feels a little as if I'm trying to learn glass-blowing on my own. Their concepts are hot, supple, incandescent, feel slightly dangerous, and I've not been taught anything about their tolerances, or what to do with them, and the things I will make of them will surely provoke pity and amusement from experts in this field. I'm a writer and historian, not a theologian or metaphysician. But even so I'm drawn to think about this stuff, to try to shape it, with all its burn and glow and texture.

The natural world is not, to me, a fabric of stuff that gleams with revelation of a singular creator god. Those moments in nature that provoke in me a sense of the divine are those in which my attention has unaccountably snagged on something small and transitory – the pattern of hailstones by my feet upon dark earth; a certain cast of light across a hillside through a break in the clouds; the face of a long-eared owl peering out at me from a hawthorn bush – things whose fugitive instances give me an overwhelming sense of how unlikely it is that in the days of my brief life I should be in the right place at the right time and possess sufficient quality of attention to see them at all. When they occur, and they do not occur often, these moments open up a giddying glimpse into the inhuman systems of the world that operate on scales too small and too large and too complex for us to apprehend. What I feel is certainly the mysterious terror and awe of Otto's *numinous consciousness*, the sense of something wholly other that renders me breathless and shaking – and something else, captured in four lines from William Blake's *Milton*:

> *There is a Moment in each Day that Satan cannot find*
> *Nor can his Watch Fiends find it, but the Industrious find*
> *This Moment & it multiply, & when it once is found*
> *It Renovates every Moment of the Day if rightly placed.*

I am far from an industrious soul, except in my capacity, perhaps, to pay close attention to things. But these words speak exactly of how those moments seem to me. Not only do they renovate each moment of the day, but multiply into everything there is and will be. They break time itself.

Part of the numinousness in these experiences of nature is how unpredictable they are. There is no point in searching for them. In my experience if you go out hoping for revelation you will merely get rained upon. But as the music of Radio Mayak showed me, I've found it easier, over the years, to encounter numinousness in a different way – in those moments where mystery arises from the meeting of human art and unpredictable natural phenomena. The gift of the

Radio Mayak interval melody was in how that melody reached me. It was carried to my ear on radio waves reflected from the ionosphere through a process called skip-propagation. From Moscow the signal rose high into the atmosphere, where it hit a layer of charged particles and was bounced back down towards me. I could never predict when the melody would ring clear and true because the ionosphere is always in flux, its conditions shifting according to the time of day, the season, even the stage of the eleven-year sunspot cycle, every alteration affecting the strength of the signal reflection. The sense of numinousness that interval signal gave me arose from the interaction of innumerable events – some chance, some law-bound. When I think of that melody now it contains the nature of space weather, regularities and irregularities in the shape of the world, the laws of electromagnetics, and the hope of unknown broadcasters in a distant Soviet radio station for listeners, for human minds that might attend to what they had sent into the air.

The most numinous ordinary object I own is a Sony BHF90 ferric-oxide cassette tape. Its black plastic casing is dented, its green label scuffed with age. It grinds and rattles when it plays. I've had it for nearly thirty years. It came into my possession mysteriously when I was a literature student spending a lot of time with friends in a college house in Cambridge. One of them was a tall man who possessed a kind of brooding softness, like a voice pitched *sotto* that makes you lean in and find yourself unexpectedly close. His best friend in the house had recently abdicated from manhood – not because he felt it failed to match his gender identity, but more that he had just worked out that the actions of men were mostly dreadful. He had a thing for Virginia Woolf, smoked roll-ups, wore his thick hair in a ponytail. Together they read Pasternak, and rejoiced in bizarre acts of motiveless violence against the house; they smashed chairs to the sound of Bartók string quartets, stuck cutlery into the plaster ceiling of the kitchen and left it there for its pleasing creepiness. Even so their company felt a safe harbour to me. Not many things did. I'd dropped out of college for a little while because I'd fallen in love with a married college professor, the kind of married college professor who much later told people I'd entirely made up our affair. It was a foggy summer, all late traces and contrails, grasshoppers singing in the thick grasses along the paths through the town commons where I'd walk for hours with no particular destination. I was very lost when the tape appeared.

There's only one track on it. It is a recording of Leonard Bernstein conducting Sibelius's Seventh Symphony. From the announcer's introduction, I think it was recorded from a radio programme in Japan. After it came into my possession I listened to it, rewound the tape and listened to it again. I listened to it hundreds of times. It wasn't soothing. The music was torqued at precisely the angle of the pain in my heart and it always felt too fast in places and far too slow in others and somehow the way that it flowed from one to the other felt like the way the human mind deals with the foreknowledge of death. The music coursed with every emotion I'd ever pushed away and pretended I didn't feel. But that was only a part of the recording's power. It wasn't a high-quality tape; the signal-to-noise ratio was poor. It stood even then for all the ways that age and distance corrode. Cosmic rays burying themselves in vaults of water. Rust on the tips of your fingers.

But these things alone didn't make the recording numinous. That was born of chance: it had been recorded from the radio during an electrical storm. The skies the signal had travelled through to reach the radio had been hot with potentiality, intermittent frequency overloads crackling and spitting and annihilating the broadcast with bursts of white noise. The lightning strikes were occasional at the beginning of the symphony, but towards the end they came so often it was hard to hear music at all, just scorching crepitation rampaging on and on, with faint strings behind it like cross-currents on a sea. When the lightning obliterated the music, the noise was so loud it was like silence. It felt as if God had put thumbprints on the tape.

I knew it to be an unrepeatable event, fixed, for ever, on tape, so that it could be played again and again, and there was something so transgressive about this that listening to it felt like heresy. I'm still not sure how much of my need for this tape was refuge and how much a desire for obliteration. I think of the son of one of my mother's friends who became pathologically obsessed with C. S. Lewis's *The Voyage of the Dawn Treader* when he was a child and no one knew why, and it turned out that he had found out about a great family secret, one that could never be spoken out loud, so he cleaved to this book about the end of the world, about a boy whose sins could be cut from him like skin. Maybe the tape was something like that. Something impossibly heavy that held me in thrall, a scrap of the divine not good for my soul, a thing that should never have been fixed in place on tape to be repeatedly overheard, a thing that stood between me and the telling of secrets. It went on for months until I decided, quite suddenly one morning, that I didn't want to listen to it any more. These days that tape is somewhere in my house in a box, still hot with what it meant back then, and I have picked it up a few times and held it, surprised by its lightness, and how difficult it is even now to hold. It is a relic of a particular hour, of a long-past time, of the person I once was, and its power now is precisely in the knowing that I will never play it again.

What Animals Taught Me

A long time ago, when I was nine or ten, I wrote a school essay on what I wanted to be when I grew up. I'll be an artist, and I will have a pet otter, I announced, before adding, *as long as the otter is happy*. When I got my exercise book back my teacher had commented, 'But how can you tell if an otter is happy?' and I boiled with indignation. Surely, I thought, otters would be happy if they could play, had a soft place to sleep, go exploring, had a friend (that would be me) and swim around in rivers catching fish. The fish were my only concession to the notion that an otter's needs might not match my own. It never occurred to me that I might not understand the things an otter might want, or understand much of what an otter might be. I thought animals were just like me.

I was an odd, solitary child with an early and all-consuming compulsion to seek out wild creatures. Perhaps this was part of the unfinished business of losing my twin at birth: a small girl searching for her missing half, not knowing what she was looking for. I upended rocks for centipedes and ants, followed butterflies between flowers, spent a lot of time chasing and catching things and not thinking much about how that made them feel. I was a child kneeling to extract a grasshopper from the closed cage of one hand, solemn with the necessity of gentleness, frowning as I took in the details of its netted wings, heraldically marked thorax, abdomen as glossy and engineered as jewellery. I wasn't just finding out what animals looked like, doing this, but testing my capacity to navigate that perilous space between harm and care that was partly about understanding how much power over things I might have, and partly how much power I had over myself. At home I kept insects and amphibians in a growing collection of glass aquaria and vivaria arranged on bedroom shelves and windowsills. Later they were joined by an orphaned crow, an injured jackdaw, a badger cub, and a nest of baby bullfinches rendered homeless by a neighbour's garden pruning. Looking after this menagerie taught me a lot about animal husbandry, but in retrospect my motives were selfish. Rescuing animals made me feel good about myself; surrounded by them I felt less alone.

My parents were wonderfully accepting of these eccentricities, putting up with seeds scattered on kitchen countertops and bird droppings in the hall with great good grace. But things weren't so easy at school. To use a term from developmental psychology, social cognition wasn't my forte. One morning I wandered off the court in the middle of a netball match to identify some nearby birdcalls, and was bewildered by the rage this induced in my team. Things like this kept happening. I wasn't good at teams. Or rules. Or any of the in-jokes and complicated allegiances of my peer group. Unsurprisingly, I was bullied. To salve this growing, biting sense of difference from my peers, I began to use animals to make myself disappear. If I looked hard enough at insects, or held my binoculars up to my eyes to bring wild birds close, I found that by concentrating on the creature, I could make myself go away. This method of finding refuge from difficulty was an abiding feature of my childhood. I thought I'd grown out of it. But decades later it returned with overwhelming force after my father's death.

By then I was in my thirties and had been a falconer for many years. Falconry was a surprising education in emotional intelligence. It taught me to think clearly about the consequences of my actions, to understand the importance of positive reinforcement and gentleness in negotiating trust. To know exactly when the hawk had had enough, when it would rather be alone. And most of all, to understand that the other party in a relationship might see a situation differently or disagree with me for its own good reasons. These were lessons about respect, agency and other minds that, I am embarrassed to confess, I was rather late in applying to people. I learned them first from birds. But after my father's death, they were all forgotten. I wanted to be something as fierce and inhuman as a goshawk. So I lived with one. Watching her soar and hunt over hillsides near my home, I identified with the qualities I saw in her so closely that I forgot my grief. But I also forgot how to be a person, and fell into a deep depression. A hawk turned out to be a terrible model for living a human life. When I was a child I'd assumed animals were just like me. Later I thought I could escape myself by pretending I was an animal. Both were founded on the same mistake. For the deepest lesson animals have taught me is how easily and unconsciously we see other lives as mirrors of our own.

Animals don't exist in order to teach us things, but that is what they have always done, and most of what they teach us is what we think we know about ourselves. The purpose of animals in medieval bestiaries, for example, was to give us lessons in how to live. I don't know anyone who now thinks of pelicans as models of Christian self-sacrifice, or the imagined couplings of vipers and lampreys an allegorical exhortation for wives to put up with unpleasant husbands. But our minds still work like bestiaries. We thrill at the notion we could be as wild as a hawk or weasel, possessing the inner ferocity to go after the things we want; we laugh at animal videos that make us yearn to experience life as joyfully as a bounding lamb. A photograph of the last passenger pigeon makes palpable the grief and fear of our own unimaginable extinction. We use animals as ideas to amplify and enlarge aspects of ourselves, turning them into simple, safe harbours for things we feel and often cannot express.

None of us sees animals clearly. They're too full of the stories we've given them. Encountering them is an encounter with everything you've ever learned about them from previous sightings, from books, images, conversations. Even rigorous scientific studies have asked questions of animals in ways that reflect our human concerns. In the late 1930s, for example, when the Dutch and German ethologists Niko Tinbergen and Konrad Lorenz towed models resembling flying hawks above turkey chicks and saw them freeze in terror, they were trying to prove that these birds hatched with something like the image of a flying hawk already in their minds. Later research, however, suggested that it's likely young turkeys learn what to fear from other turkeys – and to me these 1930s experiments seem shaped by the anxieties of a Europe threatened for the first time by large-scale aerial warfare, when pronouncements were made that no matter how tight national defence, 'the bomber will always get through'.

Simply knowing that fragment of history and knowing that domesticated turkey chicks freeze when a hawk-like shape flies overhead makes them more complicated creatures in my mind than farmyard poultry or oven-ready carcasses. For the more time spent researching, watching and interacting with animals, the more the stories they're made of change, turning into richer stories with the power to alter not only what you think of the animal, but who you are. It has broadened my notion of home to think of what that concept might mean to a nurse shark or a migratory barn swallow; altered my notion of family after I learned of the breeding systems of acorn woodpeckers, where several males and females together raise a nest of young. It's not that creatures work as models for human lives – no one I know thinks that humans should spawn like wave-borne fish or subsist entirely on flies – but the more I've learned about animals the more I've come to think there might not be only one right way to express care, to feel allegiance, a love for place, a way of moving through the world.

Trying to imagine what life is like for an animal is doomed to failure. You cannot know what it is like to be a bat by screwing your eyes tight, imagining membranous wings, finding your way through darkness by talking to it in tones that reply to you with the shape of the world. As the philosopher Thomas Nagel explained, the only way to know what it is like to be a bat is to be a bat. But the imagining? The attempt? That is a good and important thing. It forces you to think about what you don't know about the creature: what it eats, where it lives, how it communicates with others. The effort generates questions that are really about how different the world might be for a bat, not just how being a bat is different. For what an animal needs or values in a place is not always what we need, value or even notice. Muntjac deer have eaten the undergrowth where nightingales once nested in the forests near my home, and now those birds have gone. What to my human eye is a place of natural beauty is, for a nightingale, something like a desert. Perhaps this is why I am impatient with the argument that we should value natural places for their therapeutic benefits. It's true that time walking in a forest can be beneficial to our mental health. But valuing a forest for that purpose traduces what forests are: they are not there for us alone.

For some weeks I've been worried about the health of family and friends. Today I've stared at a computer screen for hours. My eyes hurt. My heart, too. Feeling the need for air, I sit on my back doorstep and see a rook, a sociable species of European crow, flying low towards my house through greying evening air. Straight away I use the trick I learned as a child, and all my difficult emotions lessen as I imagine how the press of cooling air might feel against its wings. But my deepest relief doesn't come from imagining I can feel what the rook feels, know what the rook knows – instead, it's slow delight in knowing I cannot. These days I take emotional solace from knowing that animals are not like me, that their lives are not about us at all. The house it's flying over has meaning for both of us. To me it is home; to the rook? A waypoint on a journey, a collection of tiles and slopes, useful as a perch, or a thing to drop walnuts on in autumn to make them shatter and let it winkle out the flesh inside.

But there is something else. As it passes overhead, the rook tilts its head to regard me briefly before flying on. And with that glance I feel a prickling in my skin that runs down my spine, my sense of place shifts, and the world is enlarged. The rook and I have shared no purpose. We noticed each other, is all. When I looked at the rook and the rook looked at me, I became a feature of its world as much as it became a feature of mine. Our separate lives coincided, and all my self-absorbed anxiety vanished in that one fugitive moment, when a bird in the sky on its way somewhere else sent a glance across the divide and stitched me back into a world where both of us have equal billing.

Acknowledgements

Vast thanks to my agent Bill Clegg, for his astonishing critical acumen, warmth, support, inspiration and wisdom. From our very first meeting I felt I'd known him for ever. I'm so happy to have found a home with the Clegg Agency. Thank you to all the staff there, who have been, and are, marvellous: Marion Duvert, David Kambhu and Simon Toop deserve particular gratitude, not least for putting up with my appallingly slow email replies.

Dan Franklin at Jonathan Cape is not only a legend in publishing but among the finest people the world has ever made, and I am honoured to count him not only as my editor but as a friend. Thank you, Dan, for everything. Huge thanks also to Bea Hemming, Rachel Cugnoni, Aidan O'Neill, Alison Tulett, Sarah-Jane Forder, Suzanne Dean, Chris Wormell, and all the other people who have worked to make this book a real live thing. It is a delight and an honour to work with you all.

Elisabeth Schmitz at Grove Atlantic is a marvel in so many ways it would take an encomium the size of a book to enumerate them all. I am so thrilled to work with her, and owe her so very much. Undying and very special thanks to you, Elisabeth. And enormous thanks also to all those I've been lucky enough to work with at Grove: Morgan Entrekin, of course; Deb Seager, John Mark Boling, Judy Hottenson, and so many more. Your offices in New York always feel like home.

To the booksellers, festival and event organisers and volunteers, and the readers, interlocutors and audiences I have met with over the last few years, thank you all. The conversations I have had with you over this time have enriched my life and thought beyond all measure. Special thanks to the refugee who met and spoke to me as part of Refugee Tales, an outreach project of the charity Gatwick Detainees Welfare Group, and the volunteer who accompanied him to our meeting. Neither can be named here, but I hope that the words that came from that meeting communicate the injustice of the hardships that the structures and strictures of the world visit upon those who do not deserve anything other than happiness.

Some of these pieces were written for friends, for the joy of exploring a subject, for piecing together a story or investigating something that troubled or fascinated me. Many began life as assignments for the *New York Times Magazine*, where I have had the joy of working with the truly brilliant editor Sasha Weiss. She has taught me so much about forging and fashioning pieces like these. I will never stop being grateful to her and her colleagues. Thank you, Sasha! Many of the other essays included here began life as meditations on seasonality for the *New Statesman*: thank you, Tom Gatti, for commissioning them and for putting up with my habitual last-minutery with such patience and good humour. Others were written for inclusion in anthologies (thank you, Tim Dee, Andy Holden, Anna Pincus and David Herd), for the online magazine *Aeon* (thank you, Marina Benjamin), or, in the case of 'Murmuration', to accompany the work of the wonderful artist Sarah Wood.

Deep love and thanks to my family: Barbara, Mo, James, Cheryl, Aimee, Beatrice, Alexandrina and Arthur, and my much-missed dad Alisdair – wherever he is, he's probably still cross about my telling him how to push goats. Deep love and thanks also to my BFF Christina McLeish, who has a brain the size of Jupiter and a heart of about the same size, and more than any other person has helped shape and test my thoughts about things. She is the only person who has ever video-called me to show me a bright green newly emerged cicada wandering around her open palm. That is how excellent she is.

This book was born of the inspiration, friendship, assistance and support of many, many people. My thanks to Thomas Adès, Christine Anders, Sin Blaché, Nathan Budd, Nathalie Cabrol, Casey Cep, Jason Chapman, Garry and Jon Chapman, Marcus Coates, Alan Cumming, Sam Davis, Bill Diamond, Sarah Dollard, Ewan Dryburgh, Abigail Elek Schor, Amanda and Stuart Fall, Andrew Farnsworth, Melissa Febos, Tony Fitzpatrick, Marina Frasca-Spada, Stephen Grosz, Meg and Larry Kasdan, Nick Jardine, Olivia Laing, Michael Langley, Hermione Lister-Kaye, Sir John Lister-Kaye, Toby Mayhew, Andrew Metcalf, Paraic O'Donnell, Fil OK, Stacey Reedman, Eamonn Ryan, Jan Schafer, Grant Shaffer, Kathryn Schulz, Pablo Sobron, Isabella Streffen, Cristian Tambley, Béla Tokody, Mukund Unavane, Judith Wakelam, Hilary White, Lydia Wilson, Jeanette Winterson, Jessica Woollard. I am a lamentably disorganised person and very likely to have omitted some people from this list by accident. It's likely that I will, over the next few months, be waking in the small hours in a total panic as I remember them, one by one. My apologies to them in advance.

And while he cannot read, and is likely to shred this page into fragments should he get his beak to it in the future, I want to thank my parrot Birdoole for his feathery companionship and his ability to make long hours of writing less lonely. I love him very much, even when he sits on my keyboard and bites my fingers as I'm working to urgent deadlines.

C0-ATO-523

LAST RESORTS

Emergency Assistance and
Special Needs Programs in Public Welfare

This is a volume in the

Institute for Research on Poverty Monograph Series

A complete list of titles in this series appears at the end of this volume.

LAST RESORTS

Emergency Assistance and Special Needs Programs in Public Welfare

JOEL F. HANDLER

University of Wisconsin Law School
and Institute for Research on Poverty
University of Wisconsin–Madison
Madison, Wisconsin

MICHAEL SOSIN

Department of Social Work
and Institute for Research on Poverty
University of Wisconsin–Madison
Madison, Wisconsin

ACADEMIC PRESS

A Subsidiary of Harcourt Brace Jovanovich, Publishers
New York London
Paris San Diego San Francisco São Paulo Sydney Tokyo Toronto

This book is one of a series sponsored by the Institute for Research on Poverty of the University of Wisconsin pursuant to the provisions of the Economic Opportunity Act of 1964.

ACADEMIC PRESS, INC.
111 Fifth Avenue, New York, New York 10003

United Kingdom Edition published by
ACADEMIC PRESS, INC. (LONDON) LTD.
24/28 Oval Road, London NW1 7DX

Library of Congress Cataloging in Publication Data

Handler, Joel F.
Last resorts.

(Institute for Research on Poverty monograph series)
1. Public welfare--Government policy--United States. 2. Supplemental security income program --United States. 3. Assistance in emergencies-- United States. I. Sosin, Michael. II. Title.
III. Series.
HV95.H258 1983 361.6 83-6034
ISBN 0-12-322950-2

PRINTED IN THE UNITED STATES OF AMERICA

83 84 85 86 9 8 7 6 5 4 3 2 1

To Stephen, Adam, and Frances Handler
J. H.

To my parents
M. S.

The Institute for Research on Poverty is a national center for research established at the University of Wisconsin in 1966 by a grant from the Office of Economic Opportunity. Its primary objective is to foster basic, multidisciplinary research into the nature and causes of poverty and means to combat it.

In addition to increasing the basic knowledge from which policies aimed at the elimination of poverty can be shaped, the Institute strives to carry analysis beyond the formulation and testing of fundamental generalizations to the development and assessment of relevant policy alternatives.

The Institute endeavors to bring together scholars of the highest caliber whose primary research efforts are focused on the problem of poverty, the distribution of income, and the analysis and evaluation of social policy, offering staff members wide opportunities for interchange of ideas, maximum freedom for research into basic questions about poverty and social policy, and dissemination of their findings.

Contents

LIST OF TABLES *XIII*
FOREWORD *XVII*
ACKNOWLEDGMENTS *XIX*

1
Standardized Systems and Individual Needs 1

From Discretion to Standardization 2
The Countertrend: Emergency and Special Needs Programs 8
Factors Shaping the Balance 12
The Character of Specialized Aid 16
Methods of Study 17

2
The Impact of Standardization on Basic Welfare Programs 23

How the Major Consolidated Programs Deal with Emergencies and Special Needs 23
The Political Context of the Consolidated Grant 45

3
Reactions to Standardization: Attempts to Fill the Gap 59

Range of Programs Dealing with Emergency Assistance and Special Needs 59
Coverage in Emergency Assistance and Special Needs Programs 62
The Hodgepodge of State and County Programs 93

4
The Influence of State Public Welfare Policies on Specialized Programs 97

Conflicting Commitments and Pressures 97
Sorting Out the Influences: Measures of Welfare Commitments 100
The Relationship between Characteristics of the AFDC System and Specialized Assistance 103
The Relationship between the Goals of the System and Specialized Assistance 106
The Relationship between Community Pressures and Specialized Assistance 110
Regression Analyses 113
Three Types of States 115

5
Rules, Procedures, and Delegation in State Programs 117

State Rules and Procedures in Specialized Programs 119
Relating Rules and Procedures to Costs and Caseloads 132
Administrative Purposes of Rules and Procedures 137
Appendix: Rules and the Welfare Policy Context 138

6
County Administration of Specialized Programs 147

County Rules and Procedures in Specialized Programs 149
State and County Differences: Methodology or Substance? 157
County Administrative Characteristics and Program Size 159
Discrepancies between State and County Variables Predicting Program Size 164
The Administrative Relationship between States and Counties 167

7
Administrators' Perceptions of How Well the Specialized Programs Work 169

Character of Program Administration 170
Adequacy of the Specialized Programs 176
Administrative Response to Increased Pressure 183
The Toughest Problems 185
The Dilemma of the Administrators 189

8
Private Charity and Other Community Programs 191

Responses to Inadequate Public Programs 191
Availability of Community Resources and Private Charity 194
How Community Resources and Private Charity Work: Case-Study Data 195
The Mission of Private Charity 212

9
A Comparative Note: Meeting Individualized Need in the British Supplementary Benefits Scheme 215

The British Welfare System 215
The Operation of the Supplementary Benefits Scheme 218
Reform Proposals 226
The 1976 Reform and Subsequent Reforms 231
The Lesson of the British Experience 234

10
Striking the Balance 237

The System We Have 237
Achieving Adequate Coverage of Special Needs and Emergencies 242
Balancing Standardization and Individualization 247

REFERENCES 249

SUBJECT INDEX 255

List of Tables

1.1 Six-Cell Stratified Sample of the 50 States 21
2.1 Special Needs Items Not Covered or Covered Minimally 29
2.2 Goals Listed on Executive Questionnaires and What They Measure 47
2.3 Welfare System Goals as Rated by State Welfare Executives 49
2.4 Welfare System Goals as Rated by County Welfare Executives 51
2.5 State Welfare Executives' Perceptions of Attitudes of Various Groups toward Specialized Programs 54
2.6 Local Executives' Perceptions of Attitudes of Various Groups toward Specialized Programs 56
3.1 Emergency Assistance and Special Needs Programs Provided by States 60
3.2 AFDC and AFDC–EA Caseload and Expenditures in One Year 63
3.3 General Assistance Data, February 1978 82
4.1 Correlation between AFDC Characteristics and Specialized Assistance 104
4.2 Correlation between Selected Goals and Specialized Assistance 107
4.3 Correlation between Selected Measures of Community Pressure and Specialized Assistance 111
5.1 State Mandates Concerning Informing Basic Grant Recipients about Emergency Assistance and Special Needs 121
5.2 State Requirements Concerning Exhausting Outside Resources before Receiving Assistance 122

5.3 State Requirements Concerning Verification of Applications 123
5.4 Coverage of Various Groups by State Specialized Programs 124
5.5 Items Constituting 81–100% of the Costs of State Specialized Programs 126
5.6 Circumstances Covered at Least in Part by State Specialized Programs 127
5.7 Forms of Specialized Aid Permitted in State Programs 129
5.8 Conditions of Specialized Aid Imposed by State Programs 130
5.9 Correlations of State Administrative Characteristics and Selected Measures of Emergency and Special Needs Program Size 134
5.10 Correlations of Measures of Public Welfare Policy and Administrative Characteristics in State Specialized Programs 139
6.1 County Rules and Procedures Concerning Informing Potential Recipients about Emergency Assistance and Special Needs 150
6.2 County Requirements Concerning Exhausting Outside Resources before Receiving Assistance 151
6.3 Items Usually Verified by County Programs 152
6.4 Coverage of Various Groups by Local Specialized Programs 153
6.5 Items Constituting 81–100% of the Costs of Local Specialized Programs 154
6.6 Circumstances Covered at Least in Part by County Specialized Programs 155
6.7 Forms of Specialized Aid Permitted in County Programs 155
6.8 Conditions of Specialized Aid Imposed by County Programs 156
6.9 Regression Model of County Program Costs Compared to AFDC Costs 161
6.10 Regression Model of Local Acceptance Rate of Applicants for Specialized Programs 163
7.1 Frequency of Various Types of Worker Behavior in Emergency Assistance Programs 171
7.2 Characteristics of State–County Communication 173
7.3 State Executives' Perceptions of Administrative Problems 174
7.4 County Executives' Perceptions of Administrative Problems 174
7.5 Designation by County Authorities of Problems with State Rules and Guidelines 175
7.6 Responses of State and County Administrators Concerning Adequacy of Specialized Assistance Coverage 177
7.7 Responses of State and Local Administrators Concerning Appropriate Coverage of Various Circumstances by Specialized Programs 179
7.8 County Administrative Response to Increased Demand for Specialized Assistance 184
8.1 Responses of Local Program Administrators Concerning Perceived Availability of Community Resources 192
8.2 Beliefs of Local Executives Concerning Action Taken in Absence of Public Specialized Aid Programs 194

8.3 Responses of Local Program Administrators Concerning Private Sources of Specialized Aid 195
8.4 Responses of Local Program Administrators Concerning Types of Clients Likely to Receive Specialized Aid from Private Sources 196
9.1 Supplementary Benefits: Composition of the Rolls, 1978 219

Foreword

Across the broad front of governmental action, from the conduct of monetary policy to the administration of welfare benefits, the choice between uniform rules impersonally administered and individualized responses at an administrator's discretion is being debated yet again. Uniformity is in the ascendancy, at least rhetorically.

This book examines how the welfare system now deals with emergencies and special needs in the U.S. system, which is vastly complicated by state and county administration, and where each jurisdiction's pursuit of uniformity results in enormous system-wide variability.

Niggardliness further presses each administrator to limit the focus of his or her beneficence to those few problems most urgent or most consistent with local mores. Variability is thereby further increased. Most of all, there is wide discretion because the life of welfare clients remains wildly unpredictable.

Handler is a lawyer, Sosin a social worker. Both have long and strong backgrounds in research on discretion, organizational processes, and client services. Yet, what they see outrages them.

> No one state claims to have all of the existing emergency assistance or special needs programs, but looking at the states as a whole, we find an impressive number of programs. These, however, are programs on the books.

> Within the limitations of the data, our general finding is that these programs are, in fact, small, variable, and discretionary in administration. Like weeds searching for cracks in a straight and unyielding concrete road, these programs struggle for existence against the dominant ideology of routinization and reduction of cost, error, and fraud. Overall the many fragmentary provisions for emergency assistance and special needs give little aid to clients, leave large gaps in coverage, and possess great heterogeneity. The budgets are extremely small when compared to the amounts states spend on their regular income maintenance programs. Thus AFDC–EA, one of the most important specialized programs, exists in less than half of the states, and the average expenditure for AFDC–EA in those states is only 1.5% of the average AFDC expenditure. Minnesota, one of the most generous states, spends about 3% of its welfare budget on specialized aid. Not many weeds are poking through [pp. 238–239].

Improvement must come from a change in attitudes. According to Handler and Sosin, "Individualized treatment in public welfare is not a necessary evil, but a necessary good, and part of the evaluation of any public welfare system must depend upon its willingness and ability to meet those needs that cannot be covered by the standardized grant [p. 12]." Perhaps that turnabout will be initiated by this book.

EUGENE SMOLENSKY
Director
Institute for Research on Poverty

# Acknowledgments

A study of this size and complexity builds up many debts. Irwin Garfinkel, during his tenure as director of the Institute for Research on Poverty, was the original catalyst. He encouraged us to pursue the topic and organized the excellent resources of the Institute to help us in the task. Throughout most of the study he provided valuable support and goodwill. His successor, Eugene Smolensky, assumed the same role. We not only received indispensable material assistance, but also benefited greatly from the Institute's tradition of scholarship and commitment. We would like to take this opportunity to express our thanks to the large number of people at the Institute who helped in various ways: Joyce Collins, Luise Cunliffe, Debbie Deininger, Janet Dewane, Michael Dunham, John Flesher, Marie Goodman, Nancy Rortvedt, and Jack Sorenson.

Many people worked directly with us on the project. Their work was of good quality, and they were fun to work with. Each in his or her own way contributed to the intellectual and pleasurable parts of the task. We thank Ray Berger, Deborah Bowen, Stephen Cole, Michael Daley, Martha Gordon, Randy Levinson, James Rowen, and Michael Sherman. We have a special note of appreciation for Rosemary Gartner and Susan McGovern. Throughout the entire project they made substantive contributions and became friends as well as valued colleagues.

Elizabeth Evanson and Elizabeth Uhr performed excellent editorial services.

We would also like to note the secretarial contribution of Violette Moore, a competent, cheerful person whom we shall miss.

The research was funded in part by Grant No. 18-P-00113-5-02 from the Office of Research and Statistics of the Department of Health and Human Services to the University of Wisconsin. The persons directly responsible for the grant were M. I. Pendell, Nancye Campbell, Wilbur Kerns, and David Arnaudo. We thank them for their encouragement, confidence, and support.

CHAPTER 1

Standardized Systems and Individual Needs

A characteristic dilemma in modern society is the attempt to provide humane services to citizens in large, bureaucratic structures. As bureaucracies take on many responsibilities and grow, they have to make rules to control workers, to ensure equity, and to minimize error. In other words, they strive to standardize their operations. At the same time, these rules cannot go too far. At the field level, where services are delivered, life is complicated and variable. Discretion is needed to make sure that services are appropriate, that needs are being met, and that the system runs smoothly. Bureaucracies are constantly dealing with the tension between standardization and meeting individual needs, whether in providing safe and humane care in hospitals, sensitive and competent education in city schools, or justice in urban courts.

Although it is commonly believed that an organization must either rely on standardizing rules or individualizing worker discretion, public bureaucracies actually must carry out both strategies at the same time. The system must have rules to ensure a level of fair and equal treatment to all citizens, and must at the same time allow for discretionary decisions in cases for which the rules do not completely apply. The difficulty is in molding together a system of rules and discretion that does not err too far in either direction. Rules must be definitive enough to avoid undue manipulation yet flexible enough to allow for actual differences in circumstances; a bureaucracy must strike some type of balance.

These tensions are quite evident in public welfare. Large-scale public welfare organizations have to deal with masses of clients; efficiency requires categorization and routinization, smoothing the wrinkles and bumps, minimizing error. But clients also have individual needs. Their world, too, is one of constant change. Families form and dissolve; children are born, grow, and leave home. Unemployment, accidents, sickness, fires, evictions all occur. Accordingly, there is variable but persistent pressure on public welfare programs to respond to situations that do not quite fit the rules.

This study looks at how large-scale public welfare programs respond to the conflicting pressures of standardization and meeting individual needs. In technical terms, it looks at the relationship between the basic income maintenance grants (standardization) and the provisions for emergency assistance and special needs (discretion). We examine this relationship in all of the major income maintenance programs in the United States—Social Security, Supplemental Security Income, Aid to Families with Dependent Children, Food Stamps, and General Assistance—as well as in Great Britain (Supplementary Benefits). Because the needy turn to private charity when public programs do not respond, we also look at the interaction between public programs and private charities. In all these areas we are concerned with the history and development of the conflict between standardization and discretion, the present balance that has been struck between these two pressures, and an evaluation of that balance. Are needs being met?

This chapter presents an overview of the issues involved in the conflict and sets a framework for analyzing the strategies that are available to government. It also describes the plan of the book and the methodology.

FROM DISCRETION TO STANDARDIZATION

Over the last 45 years there has been a gradual reduction in discretion in public welfare. The Social Security Act of 1935 reduced state and county discretion considerably by establishing categorical eligibility for aid (those who were blind, elderly, or had dependent children were eligible), by mandating nondiscrimination, and by establishing certain principles, such as the use of cash rather than in-kind payments (since modified). Gradually, over the course of the next decades, federal policies led to the formation of strong state administration of the AFDC and other categorical programs.

Nevertheless, until the 1970s a very large level of discretion remained. The income maintenance budgets, at least in theory and in legal form, were individualized: each family's resources and expenses were calculated, and determined needs were uniquely met (up to a standard). Upon application by recipients, many states also had special programs to meet additional needs.[1] Individual treatment, including special needs provisions (which also covered emergencies), served a number of purposes. It was supposed to result in equity. In real life, families have different needs and circumstances, and individualized calculations were designed to bring dissimilarly situated families up to a common standard. If a particular family lacked essential clothing, furniture, or bedding, extra sums would be provided to put it in the same position as a family that had the standard amount of these items. If a family had long-term special needs or suffered an accident, then the extra payment was to restore the family to equity.

There were other functions of the individualized budget. Welfare policy reflects society's moral judgments about the poor—why they are poor and what should be done about their poverty. The budget and the other components of welfare programs, such as man-in-the-house rules, suitable home provisions, and work tests, are instruments of this policy. Individualized budgetary decisions were historically used to punish and reward. Families could be forced to move because the welfare program (or individual caseworker) felt that certain accommodation were too commodious. Budgets for food, clothing, and furnishing may have reflected judgments about the character and behavior of particular families, and distinctions were made between the "deserving" and "undeserving" poor.[2]

Individualized treatment was the historic practice of public welfare until about the 1960s. Then the pressures for standardization began to build. Probably the most important reason for change was the sheer growth in the welfare rolls. All systems of administration must adopt routine to handle volume, and welfare is no exception. As rolls expanded during the 1960s, "administrative chaos" became the term used to describe AFDC, in particular. In the urban centers, it was im-

[1]For a description of the composition of the AFDC budget before the advent of the consolidated grant and the variety of special needs offered in at least one state, see Handler and Hollingsworth (1971, Chapter 4).

[2]See Handler and Hollingsworth (1971), and Handler (1972, 1973) concerning the use of money to influence client behavior.

possible to verify information, to periodically review cases, to make the required home visits, and adjust budgets as circumstances changed. Working conditions deteriorated in the major welfare agencies; error rates and administrative costs rose to what seemed alarming proportions, and the public perception of program integrity thus fell.[3]

In the face of these administrative difficulties, the supposed benefits of individualized treatment turned into vices. Treatment which had been designed to achieve horizontal equity—to restore families with dissimilar needs to parity in terms of basic necessities—instead worked in the opposite way. It was widely believed that error and mismanagement, the development of informal rules, the failure to process individual claims, and the lack of information led to gross inequalities in the administration of welfare. In special needs programs, for example, use depended less on individual need than on the availability of information, the advocacy resources and skills of the welfare recipient, and the willingness of the individual field workers to grant or deny the requests. Quite often, special needs programs became paper programs only.[4]

A consensus emerged that large-scale welfare programs such as AFDC had to be simplified to reduce error, fraud, mismanagement, and administrative cost. In the words of the Joint Economic Committee of Congress: "It is possible to streamline program operations, to reduce fraud and errors, and to reduce administrative costs as well. But to accomplish these worthwhile goals, programs must be simplified and consolidated where possible [U.S. Congress, Joint Economic Committee, 1974, p. vii]." During the 1960s and early 1970s scholars began to clamor for a reduction in discretion in budgetary calculations. The most famous proposal was Milton Friedman's negative income tax.

[3]Error rates, first collected and reported on a national scale in 1973, confirmed the worst fears. In AFDC (equated in the popular mind with "welfare"), more than 40% of the cases, accounting for 17% of the budget, were in error. The problem was largest in the high-population states; in New York, there were errors in more than half of the cases. In states with smaller programs, error rates were lower. In Maine and Arkansas, only 12% of the cases included an error. Error rates seem to go down when standardization is adopted, but also when administration costs increase, that is, if a state is willing to invest in monitoring, supervision, and auditing, error rates will be reduced. Although linked in the popular mind, there seems to be something of a trade-off between error rates and administrative costs (see Congressional Research Service of the Library of Congress [1977, pp. 218–219]). For an analysis of AFDC error rates, see Bendick, Levine, and Campbell (1977). For other aspects of error rates, administrative costs, and other administrative difficulties, see Galm (1977) and U.S. Congress, Joint Economic Committee (1974, Chapter 3).

[4]See Handler and Hollingsworth (1971, Chapter 4) for a description of the special needs program in Wisconsin.

Friedman (1962) argued that the disparate, state and local welfare systems should be replaced with one uniform national system. State differences in benefit levels would be eliminated, and individualized budgetary calculations would give way to a standard grant, based on income and family size and administered through the tax system. The negative income tax proposal was of more than scholarly interest. It seemed to promise an end to the moral judgments and control of clients inherent under the individualized system, while improving control over welfare payments. National experiments in the negative income tax were undertaken and a revised version of the scheme was suggested to Congress by President Nixon, under the title Family Assistance Plan.[5]

Equity

In time, simplification also came to be equated with equity. Martha Griffiths, Chair of a subcommittee of the Joint Economic Committee, put the matter succinctly: "Personally, I am for the law applying equally to all, and this is the purpose of the entire investigation of income maintenance programs. This work began because of the inequity in the law. It is dedicated to equality in justice [U.S. Congress, Joint Economic Committee, 1974, p. 10]." In the minds of many, horizontal equity had become incompatible with individualized treatment. Thus, the promoters of horizontal equity, a humanitarian concept, joined forces with those interested in reducing administrative costs and errors. The goal of simplification was quickly adopted and enjoyed widespread appeal.

The notion of horizontal equity in welfare is a form of rough justice. If families have different needs, then giving uniform grants according to family size and income achieves equity for certain purposes but not others. Individualized grants, at least in theory, were supposed to achieve equity through unequal grants. The definition of equity, then, varies if one chooses to focus on individual needs or the income and size of a family. For example, all children may be counted equally for the purposes of achieving administrative simplicity, even though teenagers have different needs from younger children and infants. What is equitable depends on what differences policymakers choose to recognize. Nevertheless, despite varying notions as to which differences in families and individuals should be recognized, it became commonly understood that a large-scale welfare system could not take account of

[5]In addition to Friedman's work (1962) see Moynihan (1973), Kershaw and Fair (1976), and Robbins, Spiegleman, and West (1980).

very many differences and still maintain acceptable levels of errors, costs, and fraud, and that equity could be achieved only through rough justice rather than fine tuning.

Legal Rights

Another impetus toward simplification came from changes in legal perceptions of welfare. During the 1960s, welfare ceased to be thought of as a gratuity. It became, in effect, a legal entitlement; and legal rights, in turn, need clearly stated rules and procedures. Discretion is the opposite of legal right. Discretionary decisions can be challenged, but only up to a point, and the remedy is usually unsatisfactory. Legal rights based on specific and clear rules operate differently. Applicants can demand to be treated according to the clearly stated rules. Rights-bearing citizens have a different status from citizens who depend on the discretionary judgments of officials. Those who favored legal entitlement thus joined the chorus for simplifying need determination.

It was during this period that legal advocates for the poor began to seize upon existing emergency assistance and special needs programs to help increase membership in welfare rights organizations. For a time, demanding assistance for special needs as a legal right was highly successful, particularly in large cities, when there was considerable urban unrest (Gellhorn, 1967, p. 300). When unrest subsided, policy-makers used the new trend toward simplification to wipe out special needs provisions and at the same time to mortally wound the welfare rights organizations. The concept of legal entitlement was used first to reduce discretion, and then against the legal advocates of the poor (Piven and Cloward, 1977, Chapter 5).

Social Services

The adoption of federal antipoverty policy, the "war on poverty," witnessed the last major emphasis on individualized treatment. In that epoch of reform legislation, the poor were supposed to extricate themselves from poverty through rehabilitation and self-help. As part of that strategy, social services were joined with public assistance, and the law required that every AFDC family have a social service plan (Mott, 1976, p. 3). Within a few years, serious questions began to be raised about the wisdom of uniting individualized programs of social service with the now swollen, administratively chaotic, public assistance programs.

Calls arose for the separation of social services from income maintenance, with public assistance handled by less trained clerical personnel (eligibility technicians). The implication was, of course, that assistance payments would be better managed in a simplified, more routine, "clerical" fashion. The separation arguments were put forth by those who not only wanted to free social services from the welfare system, but also proposed a changed conception of the AFDC program.

Program Responses to Pressures

Milton Friedman's negative income tax failed enactment, but the forces for standardization of public welfare continued to work their way. The ideology of horizontal equity and legal rights, combined with the strong policy goals of reducing errors and administrative cost in the management of high caseloads produced a new flavor in programs in the late 1960s and the 1970s. The Food Stamp program, instituted in the late 1960s, was a flat, in-kind grant in which only income and family structure are taken into account. In fact, the Food Stamp program is a universal program for all of the poor, whether they are old or young, married or single, childless or with children. In 1973, the income maintenance programs for adults—Old Age Assistance, Aid to the Blind, and Aid to the Disabled—were taken over by the federal government and consolidated into Supplemental Security Income. While states may supplement the federal payments (a hold harmless statute requires states to dispense supplements if the new program reduces grants), the federal contribution is in the form of a flat grant.

AFDC was not turned into a federal program or otherwise standardized directly by federal law, but the states were under pressures to simplify because of their own mounting caseloads and costs as well as federal demands. As early as 1959, several states could no longer tolerate the traditional method of adding up all the items needed by each welfare family and began to aggregate totals for basic items or groups of items—one total amount for food, clothing, and personal items, another total for utilities and household items. The process toward simplification was hastened by the attitude of the federal government in the 1970s. Legislation mandated that matching federal dollars for AFDC grants would be reduced for high error rates. As will be shown in Chapter 2, nearly all of the states now have some form of standardized flat grant for AFDC.

There was no national unification of public welfare in the United States, but incrementally, partially out of the failure of welfare reform, standardization seemed to be largely accomplished. In part, this was the result of direct federal efforts—Food Stamps, SSI—and in part, it was at the state level, responding to a variety of pressures (AFDC).

THE COUNTERTREND: EMERGENCY AND SPECIAL NEEDS PROGRAMS

One of the inevitable results of the trend toward standardization was to raise in importance the need for individualized treatment to meet emergencies and special needs. Why is this so? The basic income maintenance grant calculates a standard or average budget for eligible individuals and families. Programs differ in arriving at this average or standard budget. In some, it is a flat amount per individual or family; in others, the total budget may be the sum of the costs of major components of daily living—for example, rent, utilities, food, and clothing. Still others may include a fixed amount designed to cover miscellaneous expenses, special needs, or emergencies. The standard budget may be complex or simple, generous or miserly, realistic or inappropriate. But no matter what method is used, the basic grant is characterized by calculations based on average or standard estimates of needs. When the individual or family, in real life, cannot manage on the basic income maintenance grant, emergency or special needs assistance is required. The terms "emergency assistance" and "special needs" imply a difference from the "usual" needs provided for in the basic grant.

The core distinction between programs for emergency assistance and special needs on the one hand, and basic income maintenance grants on the other, can be illustrated by the example of an AFDC family rendered homeless by a fire. The family has suffered a loss that may happen to many people, but which is an unusual event in the lives of any one family. The basic AFDC budget does not take account of this contingency; the family's monthly allowance does not include an amount to cover a loss of such a nature.

What is the family to do? It may be that as far as the public welfare department is concerned, the answer is, Nothing. If the department has no funds or programs to pay for this contingency, the family will have to go elsewhere: for example, move in with friends or relatives or seek assistance from private charities. Conversely, the AFDC program may have legal authority and funds to pay for the emergency. This would be an emergency assistance program, a program that provides for events not normally considered to be covered by the basic grant and for which the recipient must make a special request. An emergency item is not automatically computed into a standard budget.

Emergency assistance may be a part of the AFDC program, it may come from nonpublic sources, or it may be provided through a separate public program. For the purposes of this study, a distinction will be maintained between emergency assistance programs that are publicly funded and those that are privately funded, since one of the key analytic and policy questions concerns the relationship between public programs and private charity. As will be seen, there is a fair amount of private charity to cover emergency assistance and special needs, and there is considerable interaction between the public and private systems.

Fires are usually regarded as accidents or "acts of God." Once we move from such clear-cut accidents or unexpected events, however, the definitions of emergencies and special needs become muddy. An example demonstrates a second category: an AFDC family has a member who is diabetic and needs a special diet. This kind of long-term special need is usually not provided for in the standard welfare budget. If additions are to be made to the family budget from public funds, they may come from a special needs program which, again, can either be part of the basic income maintenance program or a separate public program. In several important respects, the diabetes example is similar to the fire. Although such events occur often in society, they are not normally planned for and certainly are not in the standard income maintenance budget. Usually the recipients have to bring the special circumstances to the attention of the welfare department and make a special request.[6] Long-term special needs are varied. People may need laundry, "meals-on-wheels," housekeeping, transportation, or other services for daily living. Generous programs may also provide job training, day care, and education.

A third category of items covered under emergency assistance or special needs are those normally included in the basic grant. For example, the category includes cases in which a family runs out of food before the end of the month, faces an eviction, or is threatened by a utility cutoff. The need can be caused by mismanagement, loss of a welfare check, the use of the basic grant to cover unusual expenses, or a host of other reasons. Funds for this type of special need, which is the most troublesome, are called "double payments," since provision has already been made for them in the basic income maintenance grant.

The three types, while analytically distinct, all involve emergency

[6]In some income maintenance programs there are questions on the application form that cover long-term special needs such as diabetes. In this situation, one of the key elements of the definitions drops out—that the recipient has to make a special request. However, we believe that such coverage is rare, and that recipients do have to request money to meet most long-term special needs.

assistance and special needs. Historically, emergency assistance programs were meant to cover acts of God and double payments. Special needs programs involved long-term aid. In practice, states and counties often use these specialized programs interchangeably. We will not make much of a distinction between the two and we will often use the term "emergency assistance" in a generic sense to include programs covering all three types of need.

From what has been discussed so far, it can be seen that what constitutes emergency assistance and assistance for special needs depends to some extent on the composition of the basic income maintenance grant. In some AFDC programs rents are budgeted on actual cost, and a high rent bill is part of the basic grant. In other programs there is a standard rent allowance, and if a family has unusually high bills it either must get the extra money from some other source or apply for special need coverage. The same would be true for other items of daily living—utilities, clothing, or food. The extent to which the basic income maintenance budget can be adjusted blurs the line between special needs and income maintenance.

While the line may, to some extent, be an artifact of how the basic grant is calculated, there will always be a demand for emergency assistance and help with special needs arising out of the normal vicissitudes of life. Even with a stable social environment—that is, with no real or sudden changes in the general economy and the levels of support in the major income maintenance programs—people have accidents; they lose their grant checks; they suffer illness, unemployment, and theft; and they mismanage their money. But the social environment is rarely stable. Demands or needs will vary with changes in general economic conditions and the responsiveness of the basic income maintenance grants. When heating costs rise faster than income maintenance grants, then demands upon programs for emergency and special needs will increase, not only for heating supplies but also for other items, since recipients will often shift resources to meet immediate needs.

Economic problems can decrease individual resources and contribute to the need for emergency aid. Of course, recently economic problems have increased dramatically. During the decade of the 1970s, the Consumer Price Index rose by 112.3%. AFDC real benefit levels, calculated for a family of four (mother; three children aged 4, 9, and 14) with no other countable income and living in rented quarters, fell by 22% during this same period. For an AFDC family of two, the drop was 20%. Three-fourths of AFDC families also receive food stamps. Food stamps are adjusted semi-annually, and this helps cushion the decline. From

1974 (the first year the Food Stamp program was in operation in all of the states), the combined real benefits for both types of families fell by 15%. These are nationwide averages. There was great variation among the states. In California, benefits rose by 20%; in Texas, they declined by 55%. Other states that showed large decreases were Tennessee (46%), Virginia (45%), South Dakota (43%), New Jersey (41%), and Pennsylvania (40%). Forty-seven states showed decreases in real benefit levels. Not only have there been substantial declines, but it must be kept in mind that the benefit levels were not that generous to begin with. In 1974, combined food stamps and AFDC benefit levels were 84% of the poverty line; by 1980, they fell to three-quarters of the poverty level.[7] In other words, real AFDC benefit levels fell in most states and for the nation as a whole. Other programs, especially Food Stamps, helped cushion the decline, but did not close the gap entirely. In addition, large segments of the AFDC population did not receive all of the benefits potentially available, and, we would add, there are other populations of the poor that were perhaps suffering even more, especially those who were not eligible for AFDC.

In sum, the achievement of standardization in public welfare will inevitably raise demands for emergency assistance and aid in covering special needs, demands that were always present but previously incorporated in the administration of the individualized grant. Consequently, it comes as no surprise that even as the forces of standardization were carrying the day, separate specialized programs began to appear. One important emergency assistance program was enacted by Congress in 1967. This was the federal Emergency Assistance to Families with Dependent Children program (AFDC–EA), an option available to states. It was broadly defined, in that money payments or other kinds of aid could be provided on a temporary basis "to avoid destitution . . . or to provide living arrangements for a needy child under the age of 21 who is . . . without available resources."[8] The reception of AFDC benefits was not necessarily a prerequisite, depending on state definition. This aid was limited, however, to 30 consecutive days in any 12-month period. In the succeeding chapters the AFDC–EA program will be described in detail. For now, it is important to keep in mind that this program gradually came to meet some individual needs as flat grants were instituted. In ten years, roughly half of the states adopted an AFDC–EA program.

[7]The data on AFDC in the 1970s are taken from the following sources: U.S. Department of Health and Human Services (1980, 1981), U.S. Department of Health, Education, and Welfare (1969, 1970, 1972, 1973, 1974, 1975, 1976, 1977, 1978, 1979).

[8]Public Law 90-248, 81 Stat. 893, Section 406(e).

Other efforts to meet specialized needs also developed. While the flat grant in AFDC replaced the provision of special needs aid, some states began to establish special needs programs along with the flat grant. Modern special needs programs are separated from the AFDC grant administratively. Three-fourths of the states with special needs programs instituted them after 1968. A number of other programs developed. Some states and counties used General Assistance programs to meet individualized needs. Special needs programs exist in certain SSI grant systems. Even Food Stamps has a small program to deal with short-term food emergencies. The trend toward standardization produced a countertrend.

FACTORS SHAPING THE BALANCE

Emergency assistance and special needs programs grew in the late 1960s and 1970s, but this development was not the result of a well-thought-through deliberate social choice. The opposite was the case. The dominant, virtually exclusive ideology of the times was standardization, the flat grant, horizontal equity. Very few voices argued for meeting individual needs. Nevertheless, despite the lack of articulated, conscious support, emergency assistance and special needs programs arose of necessity; there had to be some provision to meet needs that a flat grant cannot cover and to cushion the blows of difficult economic times. Although born of necessity, as will be demonstrated in subsequent chapters, emergency programs are only grudgingly accepted; they are often miserly, illogical, and hedged with restrictions. In America (as well as Great Britain), they are viewed, at best, as a necessary evil.

We take a different approach. Individualized treatment in public welfare is not a necessary evil, but a necessary good, and part of the evaluation of any public welfare system must depend upon its willingness and ability to meet those needs that cannot be covered by the standardized grant. In practice, a public welfare system must strike some sort of balance between the need to individualize and the need to standardize; the two countertrends occur simultaneously and must be examined together. By focusing on emergency assistance and special needs programs, this book looks at the balance that is reached, in practice, rather than viewing public welfare as either entirely standardized or entirely discretionary.

The balance reached is due to more than the simple interplay of flat grants and the specialized programs. It is also defined by the broader contexts within which public welfare decisions are made, such as attitudes towards the poor, the division of power between federal, state, and local governments, and budgetary constraints. The major issues of welfare policy are captured in the budget decision—who gets what, under what conditions. Within these broader contexts, what patterns should be expected?

State-Level Strategies

We consider first strategies from the perspective of the state-level bureaucracy. Even in states that have some specialized programs, the most likely strategy that we would expect to find is *delegation and denial*. Historically, the individualized budget not only meant that large amounts of discretion were delegated to the field level but also that supervision of this discretion was weak. State and federal efforts at quality control of emergency programs have not been effective. In large programs the emphasis has been on gross program costs and error rates rather than on supervising individual budgetary decisions. Emergency assistance and special needs programs receive far less supervision than the basic programs.

Emergency assistance and special needs decisions are potentially politically dangerous insofar as they involve moral decisions about how the poor should live. Documentation is elusive, and the likelihood exists that a particular decision will be questioned by politicians or journalists on the grounds of waste or fraud. In dealing with political hazards, top-level supervisors can either take full responsibility and closely monitor every decision (or selected important decisions), reserving certain types of requests for their own approval, or they can set general policies and attempt to delegate the major responsibility for individual cases to the field level and hope that the problems stay delegated—that is, that all the heat is absorbed at that level.

One can find both strategies in emergency assistance and special needs programs, but, generally speaking, the first strategy, close supervision, is not likely to predominate, chiefly because the task of implementing an adequate information system is not worth the cost and is not likely to be effective. Even the largest emergency assistance and special needs programs rarely exceed 5% of the total income maintenance budget, and a tight monitoring system would not reduce grant expenditures by very much. Because of the highly discretionary nature of these individualized decisions, it would be difficult to devise and implement effective monitoring controls. Top-level managers, on a purely cost–benefit basis, figure that their time is better spent on the major policy decisions affecting the economically significant parts of the income maintenance programs.

Another important reason for the delegation of authority is the substantive difficulty of making decisions on emergency assistance and special needs. As noted, many of these decisions, particularly those involving double payments, are not easy to make; there may be a suspicion of fraud, but an emergency has been presented, a family is in need (or appears to be), information is faulty, and there is the risk of harm (or at least harmful publicity) if relief is denied. Just as officials fear the publicity of waste and fraud, they also fear stories of people dying of cold. Why not let the field staff handle these unpleasant choices?

Delegation might seem to be a dangerous philosophy, particularly if the lack of an emergency appropriation results in a critical and well-publicized situation for a client. But these situations are rare, and delegation itself limits the possibility of publicity occurring. Officials simply do not publicize the program or monitor it; public notice is thus uncommon. Further, if problems develop and rules are vague, state officials can pass the blame on to local offices or even individual workers.

The dominance of delegation is not absolute. The field staff feel pressure from making individual, discretionary decisions. If the number of claims increases sharply, individualized decision-making becomes intolerable, and rules inevitably develop. The field staff develop their own rules of thumb, but also demand that the policymakers give more guidance through rules or policy statements. In addition pressures on states arise if costs increase. From time to time, particularly as programs grow in size, uniform rules do appear.

The growth of uniform rules does not refute the theory of the delegation of discretion, because these welfare programs tend to minimize tight control by developing crude guidelines. This often involves setting limits on program costs or establishing rules that indirectly control costs. To the extent that the problem is capable of quantification and does not involve acute moral questions about individuals and families, specific rules emerge. To the extent that the problem is not subject to quantification or does involve acute moral questions, the policymakers may issue a rule, but one that is not specific and that, in effect, redelegates the issue back down to the lower levels of the bureaucracy. Only if the delegation is unsuccessful, that is, if the problem becomes visible again and continues to cause political or administrative trouble, will more rules develop. Then the solution will most likely take a quantitative, rough-justice form. A department may decide to cancel the program altogether, or it may decide to give a flat, fixed sum on a first-come, first-served basis, limit eligibility to some emergency needs or categories of clients, place a limit on the number of requests, and terminate the program when the money runs out. Departments worry a lot about costs, but they will tend to use blunt, either-or solutions to contain overall costs rather than thread their way through moral and factually indeterminate decisions. These solutions are still forms of delegation, but now the delegation is to other public agencies or nonpublic sources.

In sum, many structural and substantive reasons account for and shape the exercise of discretion in emergency assistance and special needs programs. Technical situations require individual determinations; organizational or political interests—of the policymakers, top supervisors, and the field staff—are served when risky decisions are made at low levels and well hidden. A large part of the story of the growth and development of emergency assistance and special needs programs can be viewed in terms of the tension between the need to know and control and the need not to know. In general, though, we expect the need not to know to predominate at the state level. We expect to find efforts to keep programs simple, to have weak information systems, and to contain the programs through spending caps.

Although this describes the expected *character* of programs, there can be other responses affecting the *size* of programs. Two sets of hypotheses develop. The move to the flat grant is a political decision, and in many states no doubt a controversial one, subject to the usual pressures and compromises. As we shall see, states vary in how flat the basic grant is, and what exceptions and special programs still remain. In states which have had a generous welfare tradition and support individualization, it could be that a *consistency* principle would still be operative (that is, the new flat grant package for emergency assistance and special needs would approximate the prior system in terms of the range of benefits still available to the poor). Perhaps less liberal states will simply not support emergency programs.

Another counterpressure is also possible. All of the states have felt pressures to raise the levels of basic grants. As we have seen, very few states have actually done so. Depending on the various incentives (matching formulas), some states with the most inadequate grants may relieve this pressure by increasing their emergency assistance and special needs programs. In this kind of a situation, we would expect to find larger numbers of recipients receiving fairly uniform amounts for emergency needs in states with limited flat grants. This would be a *compensation* strategy. As we shall see, both the consistency and compensation principles help explain which states offer programs, and which programs are larger.

County-Level Strategies

The state bureaucracies may delegate, and deny, but it is at the county level where the decisions have to be made. As noted, emergency assistance and special needs decisions are hard to monitor; from the perspective of the state, they are small programs. And lack of willingness to supervise is combined with conscious delegation. Consequently, we expect to find a great deal of discretion at the county level of administration.

Formally, the relationship between states and counties differs drastically around the country. Some systems are state administered and others are administered by the counties, with some state supervision. Much more autonomy should exist in the latter situation. Yet, in practice, counties have considerable leeway in all states. They may not decide on program rules, but they can interpret them. County decisions may elaborate on state rules, or even alter the rules to some degree.

County administrations have different welfare cultures and these result in different styles of administration. In some counties, with a humane, liberal tradition, officials will bend state rules to meet pressing need. In other counties, the system may be more restrictive than the state requires—for example, counties may use voucher or vendor payments not required by the state. Counties have to ration in a variety of informal ways. Classes of clients, or types of emergencies or needs will be excluded. Rules will be established to limit both dollar amounts and repeat requests. In some counties, public emergency assistance and special needs programs will be viewed as programs of last resort, requiring applicants to first exhaust private charity. At this bottom level, where needs are most keenly felt but where funds are short, the moral values of welfare policy become most prominent.

THE CHARACTER OF SPECIALIZED AID

This book places emergency assistance and special needs programs within the context of the broad, historical trends in public welfare. It argues that, in the American context, the balance struck between standardization and individualization has been far from ideal. A number of factors—the desire to delegate problems; concern over error, fraud, and cost; county strategies; and the strong trend toward standardization itself—have kept emergency and special needs programs very small and variable. This book documents and explains the current situation, suggesting in its concluding chapter ways in which the balance can be struck more successfully.

Chapters 2 and 3 examine the character of the income maintenance programs and the role played by the specialized programs. The reasons why the flat-grant system has come to dominate—both philosophically and administratively—are detailed. The emergency and special needs programs that develop in such a climate are found to be small, scattered, and insufficient to meet the inevitable needs clients face.

Chapters 4, 5, and 6 attempt to explain some of the patterns by focusing more specifically on differences among states and differences from county to county. Wealthier states with less of an emphasis on standardization, historically, are found to offer the largest range of emergency and special needs programs. Nevertheless, administratively as well as financially, attempts are made to reduce the discretion even in these programs, limiting eligibility and also reducing the effectiveness of the programs. Counties seem to go even further in the direction of careful control of the specialized programs than do states. As Chapters 7 and 8 point out, this results in specialized programs with few administrative problems but with small ranges and capacities. Private networks often must pick up the slack, though their ability to do so is limited.

Chapters 9 and 10 turn to policy implications. Chapter 9 demonstrates the British experience and argues that a balance can be struck with more of an emphasis on meeting individual needs but that balance must be flexible enough to adjust over time. Chapter 10 presents our model of a more adequate, but still well-controlled, network for emergency and special needs. It argues that such specialized programs serve not only to meet temporary needs, but to act as a gauge of problems in the welfare system as a whole.

METHODS OF STUDY

The research uses a multi-level and multi-method design. Two levels are needed in order to look at questions concerning the relation between state and local actions. Two methods are required to maximize the comprehensiveness of the study. A survey may be used to determine such issues as the general patterns of administration of emergency programs and the way in which community conditions affect the dispensation of specialized aid for emergencies and special needs. But only case studies can supply a range of data concerning such issues as changes over time and specific patterns of dispensing and withholding aid.

State Case Studies

One of our first research tasks involved conducting intensive case studies of two state offices. These case studies were intended to provide preliminary information for state questionnaires and for the more extensive county case studies, conducted in 1979 and 1980. One state was Wisconsin, which has rather generous AFDC and SSI grants, but which places little emphasis on meeting emergency and special needs. The second was Minnesota, which has a similar liberal tradition, but which continues to dispense relatively large amounts of emergency aid. It was hoped that the comparison of two states that are so similar in many ways would help uncover some of the causes and consequences of more and less generous patterns of emergency and special needs aid.

The state case studies included a review of available records along with interviews with officials in all parts and at all levels of the state welfare office. Typical topics for interviews included the history of the movement toward flat grants in AFDC and SSI, the relation of the flat grant to pressures concerning emergency and special needs programs, the rules and philosophies concerning the specialized programs, and community pressures. In Wisconsin, the case study also involved an intensive investigation of documents that traced the history of decisions concerning the specialized programs.

State Survey

Six state-level questionnaires were developed from the case studies. An executive questionnaire asked about the range of specialized programs, the nature of the community, and the nature of regular grant programs. Three detailed questionnaires concerned the administration of specialized programs (rules, procedures, and so forth). These program questionnaires concerned AFDC–Emergency Assistance, AFDC–Special Needs, and the largest state-funded emergency or special needs programs. Two less detailed program questionnaires covered the SSI emergency program and specialized programs in Food Stamps.[9]

[9]In the latter case it was quickly discovered that there were no emergency programs beyond those mandated by the federal government, such as Expedited Food Stamps,

The questionnaires were sent to officials in all 50 states and in the District of Columbia. The questionnaires were usually sent to the head of the income maintenance branch of the state agency that administered AFDC. Normally this agency also dealt with Food Stamps and General Assistance. Occasionally the SSI program was also administered by this agency. This official was asked to fill out the executive questionnaire and to distribute the others to the heads of the relevant programs. When some emergency programs were handled elsewhere, telephone calls helped locate appropriate individuals, who were then sent the specific questionnaires.

Forty-five out of the 51 executive questionnaires were returned, for a response rate of 85%. Many states did not return the program questionnaires because there were no programs on which to report. Judging from executives' responses concerning which programs were available, it appears that at least two-thirds of all relevant questionnaires were returned. The following tabulation shows how many of each of the program questionnaires were returned at least partially filled out:

Type of Program Questionnaire	*Number Returned*
AFDC–Emergency Assistance program	14
AFDC–Special Needs program	19
State emergency program	21
Food Stamps emergency program	25
SSI emergency program	9

Six states completed no questionnaires and ten others returned only the executive questionnaire. Both groups were analyzed to determine if they differed from responding states on such characteristics as welfare expenditures, adequacy of the AFDC grant, number of emergency assistance programs, restrictiveness of AFDC eligibility standards, and the poverty population of the state. The size of the sample precluded the use of measures of statistical significance, but a case analysis revealed that the six nonresponding states were almost an exact cross section of all states. The ten states which returned only the executive questionnaire tended to have fewer emergency assistance programs, less adequate basic AFDC grants, larger poverty populations, smaller welfare expenditures, and more restrictive eligibility standards. Because these states had fewer specialized programs it is understandable that they did not return program questionnaires.

which provides three days' worth of stamps to applicants who have no income. This questionnaire is not used heavily in the research.

Finally, some documentary materials were used to gather information concerning state populations, AFDC rules, AFDC grant size, and so forth. Six sources were used: *Characteristics of State Plans for AFDC* (U.S. Department of Health, Education, and Welfare, 1978), *A Public Assistance Data Book* (Urban Institute, 1977), monthly U.S. Department of Health and Human Service's *Public Assistance Statistics*, the *Statistical Abstract of the United States* (1979), the *Book of States* (Council of State Governments, 1976), and the *County and City Data Book, 1977* (U.S. Department of Commerce, 1977).

County Case Studies

Week-long case studies of six counties were also carried out. These were an attempt to obtain information on issues such as the reaction to state-level changes in welfare grant systems, the interaction between state and county programs, the nature of the emergency assistance and special needs programs, the relation between the welfare office and the community, and the nature of the private emergency assistance and special needs network. Interviews were conducted with a range of officials within all relevant public welfare offices and within private agencies (advocacy and aid-giving), as well. The interviews were conducted according to an interview schedule that listed the relevant topics but left the exact wording of the question to the interviewers. This was also the procedure at the state level. Most interviews were conducted by teams of two.

The interviews were conducted in six counties: Hennepin, Minnesota; Boulder, Colorado; Mercer, New Jersey; San Diego, California; Oneida, New York; and Jefferson, Texas. In some counties the case study focused on county programs; in the largest communities—such as Trenton, New Jersey—it focused on the largest cities. The six counties were selected to fit a number of research criteria concerning size, geographic location, and accessibility. In addition, they represented each of the six cells used to select a stratified, random sample for the county survey, as described below.

County Survey

Two questionnaires were sent to a sample of counties. One questionnaire, similar to the state executive questionnaire, asked the head of the county office that administered AFDC about the general nature of the community, the welfare program, and the network for emergencies and special needs. A second questionnaire asked about the administration of the AFDC–Emergency Assistance program, if it existed, or the largest other emergency or special needs program. Two additional pages of the program questionnaire concerned the AFDC–Special Needs program, if it existed. As in the case of the state program questionnaires, the county program questionnaire included questions concerning the rules and procedures in the program.

A two-step sampling process, which resulted in a stratified random sampling of 392 counties from 27 states, was conducted. Since a major endeavor of the study was to explore the relationships between the flat AFDC grant and the need for emergency assistance, states were stratified in terms of (1) "flatness" of the AFDC grant, that is, whether any characteristics but income, family size, and work incentives were allowed; (2) existence of an AFDC emergency assistance or special needs program; and (3) level of emergency assistance expenditures per recipient (see Table 1.1). This produced a six-cell table of classification within which all 50 states and the District of Columbia were categorized.

Counties with populations of less than 25,000 were excluded from the sample because the types of programs and number of emergency assistance cases would be too limited to provide adequate information.

TABLE 1.1
Six-Cell Stratified Sample of the 50 States

States with AFDC–Emergency Assistance Programs	States with No AFDC–Emergency Assistance Programs
Flat-grant AFDC programs with high emergency assistance expenditures 1. Maryland, West Virginia, Washington, D.C. 2. Minnesota 3. Ohio	AFDC–Special Needs programs and flat-grant AFDC programs 1. North Carolina 2. Iowa, North Dakota, Colorado, Nevada 3. Rhode Island, Hawaii, Maine
Flat-grant AFDC programs with low emergency assistance expenditures 1. New Jersey 2. Oklahoma 3. Connecticut, Delaware, Nebraska	AFDC–Special Needs programs and non-flat-grant AFDC programs 1. California 2. Indiana 3. Louisiana
Non-flat-grant AFDC programs 1. New York 2. Oregon 3. Pennsylvania	No AFDC–Special Needs programs 1. Arkansas 2. Florida 3. Texas

However, about 400 counties were needed to ensure a county sample large enough for statistical analysis. Since states or state units were to be sampled from each of the six cells (producing 18 state units), each state had to consist of at least 22 counties with over 25,000 population. If a state had fewer than 22 counties with a population of over 25,000, it was then combined with another state (or states) to form a state unit, in order to reach the minimum level of 22 counties. Three states or state units were then randomly selected. To ensure that each county had an equal chance of getting into the final sample, state units were given a probability of falling into the sample proportionate to the number of counties over 25,000 they included. This sampling strategy resulted in the selection of state units detailed in Table 1.1. The final step in this sampling procedure was randomly to select 22 counties from each unit using a table of random numbers. In this final selection stage, two units still fell short of the minimum of 22 counties with a population of 25,000: New Jersey had only 21 counties, and Oregon only 19 counties, with populations over 25,000. This resulted in a final sample of 392, rather than 396, counties.

Almost every county that responded returned both questionnaires. A total of 240 counties eventually responded, for a response rate of 61%. Each of the 18 state units had an average of 13 respondents, out of a potential 22; the only unit with fewer than ten respondents was Oklahoma, and 14 of the 18 units had better than 50% response rates. Questionnaires were relatively thoroughly filled out, except for data on caseloads and expenditures. In sum, the number and completeness of responses to the county questionnaires fulfilled the objectives of obtaining detailed data from a cross section of counties above 25,000 in population throughout the United States.

Information from the *County and City Data Book* concerning demographic characteristics of each county was added to the material obtained from the questionnaires. Thus at the county as well as the state level, a comprehensive survey emerged of emergency and special needs programs and the organizational and community environments of the welfare offices within which they are contained. This book uses these data and other written work to explore the trend toward the flat grant and the role of emergency assistance and special needs programs.

CHAPTER 2

The Impact of Standardization on Basic Welfare Programs

The demand or need for assistance for emergency and special needs is the function of four interrelated factors: (1) the normal, expected vicissitudes of life which produce these demands or needs; (2) "hard times" in the general economy; (3) the failure of basic income maintenance grants to keep up with the cost of living; and (4) the structure of the basic income maintenance programs, that is, their capacity to take account of and meet special demands and needs. This chapter focuses on the last factor—the routinization of the basic programs and what this means for the provision of emergency assistance and special needs.

HOW THE MAJOR CONSOLIDATED PROGRAMS DEAL WITH EMERGENCIES AND SPECIAL NEEDS

During the 1960s, the move to routinize welfare began to grow with various proposals to federalize the categorical aids. The adult programs were eventually federalized in the Supplemental Security Income (SSI) program (1974) and considerably routinized into a flat-grant system. Although AFDC remained a state grant-in-aid program, the movement continued here as well. By 1974, more than half of the states had adopted a consolidated grant for AFDC. Two years later, the move was nearly universal: forty-six states, including the District of Columbia, reported that they had adopted the consolidated grant (Campbell and Bendick, 1977, pp. 89–93).

What does the consolidated grant cover? Does it wipe out all provision for variation, for emergencies, for special needs? How flat, in fact, is the flat grant? To what extent do provisions for special circumstances or special needs still exist to provide flexibility, to meet unexpected needs caused by the failure of the income maintenance grants to keep pace with rising costs?

In this section we will first examine the AFDC program. We will try to determine the degree of flatness in AFDC and the availability of special circumstances and emergency assistance. Then we will turn to the three other major income maintenance programs: SSI, Food Stamps, and General Assistance. In the final section of the chapter, we will examine the ideology of state and local officials and community pressures, which, along with the structure of the income maintenance programs, create the political context in which certain types of emergency assistance and special needs programs are likely to develop.

AFDC and Its Special Assistance Component

From its early days, AFDC, both in theory and in structure, was a fine-tuned, individualized program. Originally known as Mothers' Pensions, it carefully discriminated not only the needy, but also the worthy. Families, in addition to being poor, also had to be fit and proper (Bell, 1965). The budget was individualized. Each family's resources were matched against a standard, and the difference constituted the welfare grant. As circumstances fluctuated, so did the budgets; and there were special needs and emergencies. This was the general pattern although there were exceptions. Some states had maximum grants; others only gave a percentage of need with or without maximum grants; and others did not make any provisions for special needs or emergencies.

As noted in Chapter 1, the system of individualized budgets broke down as AFDC rolls swelled. Starting in the 1960s, states began to consolidate basic items of the budget—for example, lump sums would be given for food, clothing, and personal items; or utilities and household items. At the time of this study (1978), consolidation of the basic budget was virtually complete. In the program supporting 10.8 million people at a cost of $12.7 billion, 46 states reported having changed over from the individualized system.

This does not mean that the 46 states have taken a uniform approach as to what is included in the consolidated grant. There are a number of possibilities. The consolidated component of the grant can cover only some basic need items—for example, food, utilities, and clothing—but leave to individual determination other items, such as rent or special needs. According to documentary material, in two states—New York and Oregon—the consolidated grant does not include shelter costs (U.S. Department of Health, Education, and Welfare, 1978). These costs are computed separately. In all the other states, the consolidated grant not only covers the basic components of the income maintenance grant (food, shelter, utilities, clothing) but also a great many items that were formerly considered special needs or special circumstances. Virtually all the states report that their consolidated grant now covers such special items as high, continuing shelter costs, household needs other than furniture or appliance replacement, utility bills, food shortages, clothing needs, and personal needs. In many states (20), the consolidated grant also covers medical expenses and educational expenses. To a lesser degree, the consolidated grant also covers appliance replacements, special diets, chore services, rehabilitative and recreational needs, and security deposits.

What does it mean when a state says that these items are covered in the consolidated grant? Probably not much. It clearly does not mean that these items are separately budgeted. What it probably means is that at the time that the state converted to the consolidated grant, these items were eliminated as separately budgeted items, and were considered to be included in the consolidated grant. For example, State A might have had a program which paid for the replacement of major appliances, whereas State B had no such program. State A and B announce a consolidated grant of say, $275 per month for a family of four, and State A says that its program for major appliances is eliminated because this item is now included in the consolidated grant. The families in State A and B are in the same position. One family does not necessarily receive more money because the state lists more items included in the consolidated grant.[1] The only thing that matters is the level of payment that is made to each family.

[1]For example, in 1977 the State of Rhode Island's consolidated standard included many items that were considered special circumstances items in New York. Rhode Island's standard grant excluding food for an AFDC family of two was $254.74; New York's standard grant excluding food was $309 (shelter area, New York City) for a family of two. Rhode Island's consolidated grant ostensibly covered the following:

food		
clothing	utilities	telephone

The list of items is probably the articulation of what at least some of the states were doing when they moved to the consolidated grant. It is an expression of legislative intent only, and a weak one at that. The mere fact that a state said that it intended to include a particular special need or emergency in its consolidated grant does not necessarily mean that these needs are no longer covered by other programs in that state. That depends on how comprehensive the whole range of state programs is—that is, whether provisions for special circumstances remain and whether emergency assistance components are present in other programs in the state. In other words, it is the size and range of the total package that counts.

In Chapter 1, emergency assistance and special needs were defined as items (1) which were not automatically calculated in the budget; and (2) which, in the usual situation, clients had to request. Prior to the introduction of the consolidated grant, AFDC–Special Needs fit this definition. At least on the books, funds were available for nonrecurring needs (e.g., furniture replacement) or recurring needs that were not applicable to most families (e.g., special diets, unusually high heating costs). With the adoption of the consolidated grant, how many of the special needs programs were retained?

---

shelter
life insurance
school lunch
home closing costs
household supplies
household service
medicine chest supplies
personal services due to illness
personal care items
prosthetic devices
household equipment
indebtedness
transportation.

Separately provided grants for special circumstances covered only costs and emergency needs arising from catastrophe. New York's consolidated standard, on the other hand, covered the following:

food
clothing
utilities
household supplies
household furnishings
fuel for heating (when not included in shelter)
education expenses
transportation.

Special circumstances that were covered at least theoretically in this "flat grant" were supplies for college or training school; camp fees; attendant care; life insurance premium; home-delivered meals; household moving expenses; restaurant allowance; rent deposit, brokers/finders fees; replacement of clothing lost in fire, flood, or other catastrophe; purchase of essential furniture required for establishment of a home; repair of essential heating equipment, cooking stove, and refrigerators; property repair on own property; storage of furniture and personal belongings; temporary shelter in hotel/motel; allowance to meet increased needs of a pregnant mother.

According to documentary sources, most states (35) have retained some variations as supplements to the consolidated grant. States call these variations either "special circumstances" or AFDC–Special Needs. Sixteen of these states list both special circumstances and special needs; usually, the terms are interchangeable for the same program, but not always.[2]

The significance of these variations depends not only on how many states provide some coverage for special needs, but also on how extensive the programs are in fact (i.e., the number of items covered) and expenditures. Unfortunately, data are quite sketchy on these issues. Some of the programs do not fit into our definition (states may list federally required day care or work-expenses programs as special need items). Further, fourteen of the states reporting special needs programs only allow for one or two special items or situations, but seven states provide for six or more. The average number of special items for states with special needs coverage is 3.4. Depending on what the special needs are, and how much is spent, a state could have a consolidated grant in name only; the actual budgeting process could very well resemble the old, individualized AFDC budget. Although we do not have complete data, New York appears to be such a state; it covers the most special needs (15) of all the states with a consolidated grant, and our case study of Oneida County shows that 25% of total AFDC expenditures covers the special needs type of individualized aid.

But how broad is the coverage in terms of items? Do the special circumstances or special needs programs cover a wide range of needs or only a few? In our survey, 19 states gave coverage-of-item data for AFDC–Special Needs and the answer is clearly that programs are highly specialized. All 19 states said that 81% to 100% of their AFDC–Special Needs program was restricted to a single item or circumstance—for example, lost or stolen checks, or temporary shelter costs. Most items that were traditionally covered by individualized or AFDC payments (before the days of the consolidated grant) were not covered at all by current AFDC–Special Needs programs. Food shortages and special clothing needs are barely covered—only two states provide such coverage and the items account for 10% or less of special needs expenditures. There is no particular pattern of specialization. Four states (the highest number) specialize in replacing lost or stolen

[2]For example, in the District of Columbia there is both a special circumstances and an AFDC–Special Needs program, but the latter is restricted to a $49 monthly allowance for people in a non-WIN training program.

checks, three states in day care expenses, two states each specialize in housing-related needs, the need for household items, or winterizing. The remaining four states specialize in natural disasters, special services such as chore services, needs related to unborn children, and educational expenses and unemployment needs.

Looking at all of the states, one sees many programs for special circumstances and special needs. Many different items are covered at least somewhere. But this is a misleading picture. Within each state, few items are covered, and those which are covered are often hedged with many restrictions.

Turning to the counties, we find that nearly half of the counties in our questionnaire-respondent sample (100 out of 240) have an AFDC–Special Needs program, and over 90 counties reported data. As with the state data, the initial impression is of a broad range of items covered. *Some* coverage of each of a list of 15 items that are normally considered emergency assistance or special needs is provided by 45% of counties. This percentage is slightly deflated by the existence on the list of items that are more likely to be covered by other programs—for example, special winter needs (covered in 40% of the counties), which may be covered by federal energy aid. But other standard items are covered by about half of the counties, and sometimes by more—e.g., natural disasters (58% cover); lost, stolen, or delayed checks (62%); need for appliance, furniture, or other household items (60%).

But that is one side of the coin. The other is that most of these items are only minimally covered. Consistent with the state data, programs here are also specialized. If we combined the figures for "not covered" with "covered but less than 10% of the total special needs expenditures," we find the high percentages shown in Table 2.1. In more than three-fourths of the counties, standard special needs items are either not covered or covered only minimally.

Are there any patterns in coverage? In states where data are available, there is a curious blend between particular needs and more general ones, sometimes with fixed small maximum dollar amounts per recipient request or item. One program, for example, provides up to $100 for educational expenses, day care, lost checks, and moving expenses to obtain employment; up to $150 for special clothing needs for foster children and persons in state institutions; up to $4 a month for needs related to unborn children; and up to $500 for special winter needs. In one state, the only special need item is educational expenses, which on the surface appears broad and general, but is in fact restricted to students in nonpublic schools (up to $1200 per year per student—

TABLE 2.1
Special Needs Items Not Covered or Covered Minimally (Less than 10% of Total Special Needs Expenditures), by Counties

Item	Percentage of Counties
Natural disaster	81%
Lost, stolen, or delayed benefit check	71
Temporary shelter or moving & security deposits	68
Grants covering basic needs for pending cases	85
Need for appliance, furniture, or other household items	64
Unpaid utility bills	74
Food shortage	85
Special clothing needs	80
Special diet needs, laundry service needs, or medical expenses	71
Special services such as chore services	80
Day care	76
Unborn-child needs	81
Educational needs	84
Employment needs	68
Special winter needs: winterization, shelter repair, other (please specify)	85
Average percentage of counties in which items are minimally covered	77
N = 90	

exceedingly generous as far as these programs go!) and $50 per student per year in the State School for the Deaf. Why this particularity? Why the differences in dollar restrictions? The clear impression is that programs covering special needs and special circumstances do not arise through any systematic inventory of people's needs and how they should be met. Instead, the programs appear to be afterthoughts or the result of lobbying for particular interests or clients.[3] Consistent patterns of items covered are not to be found across states or even within states.

At the county level, one can discern a few patterns in coverage. As discussed in Chapter 1, the classic double-payment items, those considered covered in the flat grant, are the most difficult to justify in terms of equity and morality. They include coverage of food shortages

[3]In New Mexico, for example, the special needs program provides (1) once a year, in September only, special clothing allowances for school-age children; (2) special board and room rates when an AFDC recipient must arrange for board and room for special reasons; (3) layette allowances (one time only) to pregnant women in need of layettes.

and utility bills. In about 60% of the counties, there is no provision for meeting these needs. In contrast, coverage is highest for lost, stolen, or delayed checks; natural disasters; replacement of appliances, furniture, or other household items; and special diet, laundry services, or medical expenses. On the average, 60% of counties covered these items. Why? Lost, stolen, or delayed checks are easily verifiable and controlled; if the check turns up, it is deducted from future grants. Appliance, furniture, and other household needs, while they can be considered borderline double payments, are invariably vouchered and tightly controlled. Special diets, laundry expenses, or other medical expenses are also easily verifiable, and since the client population requesting them is more "deserving" (the aged and the ill), the moral hazard is smaller, as is true for victims of natural disasters.

Chore services, day care, unborn-child needs, and education and employment needs are not available in most counties in our sample. Only 40% of the counties cover these items at all—as low as the coverage of double-payment items. Why are these items in disfavor? They are probably considered less necessary than the others, or are thought to be covered by other programs, which might be true for day care and education and employment needs.

At the county level, then, some patterns in coverage are present though somewhat shadowy. But it is important to recognize that the above analysis is based on coverage, not adequacy. If we look at the double-payment items, only 20% of the counties have coverage amounting to more than 10% of total special needs expenditures. For acts of God and so forth—where verification is greater and moral hazard considerably less—more than 30% have coverage on which more than 10% of their budgets are spent. For long-term special needs, however, the percentage of counties spending 10% of their budgets drops back to about 20%.

We cannot satisfactorily answer the question of how much the states spend on special needs, because costs and caseload figures for special needs are generally not tabulated separately from AFDC income maintenance data as a whole. Only four states reported caseload and expenditure data. AFDC caseloads for special needs in 1978 ranged from a high of 95,400 persons in California to a low of 4882 in Minnesota; payments per family ranged from a low of $10 in California to a high of $135 in Minnesota. Clearly, we cannot generalize from this small and incomplete amount of data; however, there is no evidence that these programs (with the exception of New York) are large.

How difficult is it for an applicant to get assistance through special circumstances or special needs? In general, in 15 of the 19 states reporting on AFDC–Special Needs, there are no differences between the certification procedures for special needs and the basic assistance grant. The same kind of verification is needed: supervisory approval and the requirement that other resources be first exhausted. On the other hand, there are numerous special rules for particular needs. For example, in one state, a client must use his available liquid assets before the agency will meet a nonrecurring special need (e.g., a utility bill), or a client must show that an item to be replaced cannot be obtained free from another source (i.e., a relative or private charity). Seven states require the client to attempt to use other public assistance programs or private emergency aid programs.

There are other restrictive rules governing AFDC–Special Needs. In 13 states, there are fixed maximum dollar amounts per needed item. For example, a grant of $150 might be given to obtain a used refrigerator. On the other hand, most (13) of the states do not have rules limiting repeat requests, nor do they impose additional state requirements or conditions on clients making repeat requests.

We have some information on how AFDC–Special Needs works in two of the local areas that were case studies, Oneida County (Utica), New York, and San Diego County, California. New York has a long tradition of high AFDC grants and generous provisions for special needs. Even when it adopted the consolidated grant in 1974, it still retained the largest list, by far, of the number of special needs allowed. In Oneida County, these special needs are referred to as "on category" aid. They are provided as part of the regular AFDC program, and expenditures are not separately maintained. However, it is estimated by local officials that 20% to 25% of the pending AFDC caseload receives "on category" aid. The state plan includes a long list of covered items, including not only standard items which appear in most emergency and special needs programs (e.g., losses from fire, flood, or other catastrophe) but also items which used to appear on the old "liberal" lists before the era of the consolidated grant—e.g., supplies for college or training, camp fees, purchase of essential furniture, storage fees, deposits, and similar items (see footnote 1).

In fact, however, Oneida County is a clear example of a program which, though liberal on the books, is administered very conservatively. The bulk of the special coverage is for basic needs, such as food shortages and grants for pending applicants; moderate amounts are spent for lost, stolen, or delayed checks, utility bills, temporary shelter, and moving expenses; and minor amounts are spent to cover losses caused by natural disasters, or to purchase appliances, furniture, or other household items, and needed clothing. The county Department of Welfare, in part responding to state pressure to hold down costs, and in part on its own initiative, limits special needs requests to very basic needs. In addition, clients are not told that these programs are available, contrary to state rules. (They usually learn about them from Community Action programs (CAP) or other client-oriented organizations.) Each request must be discussed with supervisors and approved by them. Some requests are provided on an "as-needed" basis, but others are subject to restrictive payment maximums. Even though the program is relatively large, the special needs component of the consolidated grant, as administered in this county, is quite different from the state plan.

California is another state that has, on the books, an extensive AFDC–Special Needs program. Until very recently, this program was supported entirely by the counties. As a result, San Diego County was reluctant to fund the extensive list of special needs mandated by the state. Now the state has agreed to pay for special needs in all counties, and counties are required to inform AFDC applicants of the availability of special needs. The state regulations describe recurring and nonrecurring special needs. Recurring special needs are authorized by income maintenance workers; approval of a supervisor is required. Most recurring needs are provided at actual cost and include therapeutic diets, special transportation, special laundry, chore services, special telephone service or equipment for the handicapped, and excessive use of utilities "when the county verifies that the excessive use is required for a reason not common to a majority of recipients and is essential for their support." The language of the regulations appears to allow for a good deal of discretion. Nevertheless, San Diego County administers the program which provides for recurring special needs in a conservative manner: the maximum amount granted is only $10 per month per person. Naturally, this kind of local rule limits the program.

Nonrecurring special needs are approved by the social service staff. The regulations allow for replacement of items lost or damaged as a result of an "act of God" or sudden or unusual circumstances beyond the family's control. There is a maximum dollar limit for a number of specified items, and the total grant may not exceed $300. Clients are required to exhaust available liquid assets first and the county may require verification of purchase. The California AFDC–Special Needs program, at least as administered in San Diego County, fits the Oneida County pattern—generous on the books, not so in practice. When it comes to limiting the program, in San Diego, state rules are most important, and in Oneida County, N.Y., local practices are key.

The conclusion we draw from the data is that the special circumstances or special needs component of AFDC is not very significant in most states, with the possible exception of New York. Few items are covered, and although specific systematic data on expenditures are not available, we would be surprised if large amounts are spent nationwide. Indeed we have no indication that this is the case, and such expenditures would be inconsistent with what we have learned.

SSI: The Special Assistance Component

Supplemental Security Income (SSI) is an entirely federally funded and federally administered program established to provide a minimum income for all eligible aged, blind, and disabled persons. On January 1, 1974, SSI replaced the locally administered but partially federally funded programs of Old Age Assistance, Aid to the Blind, and Aid to the Totally and Permanently Disabled. The objective of the SSI program was to establish uniform national requirements relating to income and assets, and payment standards for its clientele. The size of the federal benefit is determined by the applicant's income, living arrangements, and marital status. SSI payments are indexed at the cost of living. As of January 1979, the maximum monthly federal benefit was $189.40 for an individual and $285.10 for a couple.

The SSI program is basically a flat grant. Eligibility is both categorial and income-tested. Persons aged 64 and over, blind,[4] or disabled[5] are categorically eligible. The SSI benefit level determines the income limit for program eligibility. Twenty dollars per month of regularly *unearned* income and $65 per month plus one-half of the remainder of regularly *earned* income must be disregarded for the purposes of determining SSI eligibility and payment levels. Certain amounts of irregularly earned and unearned income received over a quarterly period must also be disregarded. Above these disregarded amounts the monthly benefit will be reduced a dollar for every dollar of income. Assets limits are set at $1500 for an individual and $2500 for a couple; certain other specified assets (which can total as much as $4200) are not counted in determining eligibility. In addition, SSI recipients may be eligible for food stamps (which may be "cashed out" and included in the SSI benefit check), Medicaid, and Title XX social services.

States choosing to supplement federal benefits may vary this supple-

[4]Defined as central visual acuity of 20/200 or less.

[5]Defined as "unable to engage in any substantial gainful activity by reasons of any medically determinable physical or mental impairment which can be expected to last for a continuous period of not less than 12 months."

ment within certain federal criteria: (1) by recipient type (e.g., larger benefits for aged persons); (2) by area (implying cost-of-living differentials within the state); and (3) by type of residence or living arrangement. States may also provide aid for special needs and social services to the SSI population. Federal "grandfather" clauses required states to supplement payments of those transferred from the former adult programs if benefits under SSI were lower for those persons. Because of the federal mandate to maintain the income level of former recipients of public assistance, most states provide supplements for at least some of the aged. The states can either administer the supplementation themselves or allow the federal government to perform this task. There are strong fiscal incentives for federal administration, and two-thirds of the states have taken this option. Because these states include those paying large supplements, nearly 90% of state supplement dollars are now handled by the federal government. The federal government merely adds the state portion to the federal check and the recipients receive one check from the Social Security Administration (Martin, 1979).

As of December 1980, more than 4,142,017 people received SSI payments. The largest category was the disabled (2,558,400) followed by the aged (1,807,776). Blind recipients numbered 78,401. Total benefits were $7 billion. Of this amount, $5 billion were federal dollars; the rest came from the states.

Ten states have an emergency assistance program as part of Supplemental Security Income. Nine of these states reported economic data in the state survey. Again there is variation, both in total state program expenditures and in average payment per recipient. (Data reported are for 1977 and 1978.) California has an enormous emergency assistance supplement for its aged population. It lists three separate SSI emergency assistance programs—one a loan program, one for "presumptive disability and presumptive blindness," and one for conventional emergency assistance and special needs. In the conventional program, California reports spending $87,582,725 in 1978. An additional $3,115,269 was spent in the loan program. Moreover, the average grant per recipient is high in the regular SSI emergency and special needs program—$605. Maryland's total SSI special needs expenditure for 1978 was only $150,000 with an average payment of $200. Excluding California, the average total state expenditure is $4,055,000 and the average SSI special or emergency payment per recipient is $219.

In contrast to the other emergency assistance and special needs programs, the SSI program is not specialized. Only one state reports that a single item accounts for more than 80% of the program; and only four states report that a particular item accounts for between 41% and 80%

of program expenditures. For all the other states, a variety of special needs and emergencies are covered.

There are some curious inconsistencies about emergency assistance for the elderly. Relatively few states have adopted SSI–Special Needs, as compared to AFDC–Special Needs, or, as we shall see in Chapter 4, AFDC–Emergency Assistance and special state emergency assistance programs. Does this mean indifference to or rejection of the plight of the elderly poor? Not necessarily. In the states which have adopted SSI–Special Needs, the programs are not crabbed and illiberal as are AFDC–Emergency Assistance, state emergency programs, or AFDC–Special Needs. Rather, the programs cover a range of situations and are somewhat generous. *As administered,* SSI–Special Needs does not reflect suspicion and hostility to those who "abuse the system." Indeed, the characteristics of the SSI–Special Needs programs confirm other research which points to a more kindly treatment of the elderly than of other poverty populations. There is less disagreement and controversy about the special needs of this group.[6] We take it, then, that the failure of more states to adopt SSI–Special Needs is either because in most states SSI is entirely federally administered, and it is unlikely that federal employees will administer a state-funded supplement, or because of inertia or other administrative difficulties, rather than a substantive decision rejecting the needs of this group. The Wisconsin state case study supports this contention; once the federal government assumed responsibility for SSI, state officials directed their attention to other matters and now tend to overlook the SSI population when deliberating policy changes.

Food Stamps and Special Assistance

The Food Stamp program started as an authorization to the Federal Surplus Commodities Corporation to purchase surplus farm products and distribute them to needy families; its purpose was to strengthen domestic agricultural markets (MacDonald, 1977, Chapter 1). Complaints arose over the distribution system, and a stamp program was enacted in 1939 which was designed to increase food consumption channeled through regular businesses. Approximately 4 million people

[6]For brief historical comparison of the different treatment that the various categories of welfare clients receive see Handler (1972, pp. 13–14). See also Handler (1980). This paper discusses different attitudes toward the elderly that were evident in administrators' eagerness to grant emergency assistance to this group.

participated in the program. In 1943, as unemployment and farm surpluses fell, the program was terminated.

Interest was renewed in the postwar years with the growth of surpluses. In 1958, a two-year pilot program was enacted, but it languished until the Democrats took office. President Kennedy, influenced by the poverty he saw in the West Virginia primary, started eight pilot programs. With the passage of the Food Stamp Act in 1964, the program became national. The federal government and the states shared responsibility. The United States Department of Agriculture established the purchase requirements (the cost of the stamps to recipients), but the states established the eligibility standards. Because participation rates were low and varied from state to state, there was political pressure for reform during the 1960s.

The program officially became a nationalized flat grant under President Nixon in 1971. Uniform national eligibility standards were established, and in 1974 the program became mandatory in all counties. The 1971 amendments effectively doubled the average benefits available to recipient households by eliminating the purchase requirements for the most needy and reducing it for others. As a result of these changes, as well as the 1974–1976 recession, the program grew rapidly. By 1975, more than 19 million people received food stamps; this tapered off to 16.7 million in 1977 as the economy improved, but as of 1980, more than 21 million received stamps at a total cost of $8 billion.

In 1977, the program was further standardized and changed in response to a number of criticisms. The requirement that clients purchase the stamps had been widely attacked as a barrier to low-income families who could not come up with the cash. In addition, the program had been considered overly complex. An extensive list of individually itemized deductions had made it difficult to place a clear limit on eligibility. Concerns about fraud and abuse had been raised as well, though they were of secondary importance.

The Food Stamp Act of 1977 for the first time provided for emergency issuance of food stamps, called Expedited Food Stamps. Prior to this federal policy, regulations did not specifically require emergency certification and issuance of benefits to households in immediate need of food assistance. It was left up to the states or local offices to decide how immediate needs would be met, if at all. Some states had adopted policies requiring provision of emergency food stamps (e.g., Wisconsin) one year before implementation of the new federal policy; other states left it to local discretion. The 1978 regulations required that "expedited service" be given "destitute" households or households with zero net income (after required deductions). A household was defined as "destitute" if (1) its only income for the month of application was received prior to the application date; (2) that income was from a source that was no longer available; and (3) the household did not expect to receive more than $25 from a new source for at least ten days. According to the federal timetable, expedited stamps were to be provided within three days of application.

Numerous other changes were made in the Food Stamp program. The USDA and HEW designed a new simplified uniform national application form, and required that eligibility determination be combined with the intake process of the major public assistance programs. Standardized computation of benefit and expense deductions replaced a more individualized system that was based on actual figures. The purchase requirement was eliminated in favor of a system whereby recipients received the "bonus value" of stamps at no cost.[7] Elimination of the purchase requirement was intended to increase program participation. The "bonus value" benefit is not intended to entirely cover the cost of an adequate diet; rather it is regarded as a supplementary benefit, and recipients are expected to make up the difference from other sources. Another new provision ended categorical eligibility by basing eligibility solely on income, set at the federal poverty level. All Food Stamp standards (the Thrifty Food Plan and standard deductions) are geared to keep pace with inflation through adjustments made twice yearly. Thus, Food Stamp reform has features consistent with the overall trend towards simplification and standardization in welfare administration as well as a feature counter to this trend—the provision for expedited service to meet exceptional, emergency needs.

Even though an Expedited Food Stamp program is a federal requirement, only 26 of 46 reporting states claim to have one, and 21 of these states completed program questionnaires. The program is, in effect, a method by which applicants for regular food stamps can get emergency stamps pending approval of the application. Unfortunately, only four states supplied any financial information. In two of these states—Colorado and New York—the Expedited Food Stamp component amounts to 15% and 25% of the entire Food Stamp expenditure. In the other two states—Nebraska and Utah—the emergency portion is quite small.

The same variation appeared in the case studies. In Oneida County, New York, Expedited Food Stamps was considered a "very important component" of the emergency assistance program. However, the pro-

[7]The "bonus value" is determined by taking 30% of the household's net income after deductions and subtracting that amount from the USDA Thrifty Food Plan allotment for that household's size. (The Thrifty Food Plan is the standard on which Food Stamp benefits have always been based.)

gram is limited to new applicants—emergency food stamps are not available for current recipients. When ongoing Food Stamp clients claim their stamps or vouchers are lost or stolen, the replacement procedure is complex and not as speedy as the expedited service. If the initial notice informing the client to pick up the stamps is lost or stolen, the client must sign an affidavit for replacement. If the client claims that the notice never arrived, the client generally must wait five days after the expected arrival date to ensure that the problem is not simply a mail delay.

Stolen stamps can be replaced if a police report is filed, but such replacement requires an interview with a worker, whose decision is discretionary. Claims of stolen stamps near the end of the month often are rejected. Lost stamps are rarely replaced. Such decisions are discretionary, but the Food Stamp intake supervisor in Oneida County felt that informal rules have developed among workers through meetings, discussion, and observation so that the patterns of decision-making have become fairly clear and uniform.

In Trenton (Mercer County, N.J.), the Expedited Food Stamps program is occasionally available for recipients who claim that their food stamps were lost or stolen. For other emergencies, food stamp recipients either go to AFDC–Emergency Assistance, if it is available, or to private charities. In Trenton, new Food Stamp applicants can receive expedited food stamps within three days, or, if eligibility is determined, within a day. There are two basic criteria for this service: lack of any income, which can usually be determined, and a "true emergency." This is a discretionary decision, but a state of homelessness or an impending eviction will qualify.

General Assistance: The Residual Program

Historically, General Assistance (GA) is the original welfare program, inherited from England during the colonial period. It was then (and still is, in many states) administered locally—in the townships and municipalities. The basic administrative characteristics throughout its history have been local funding, local administration, large amounts of discretion, and, consequently, great variability. Until recently, there was practically no systematic information about the operation of General Assistance.[8] Findings that emerged from the few scattered studies

[8]An excellent study of a local General Assistance program was included in the State of Michigan's series, Studies in Welfare Policy, No. 5 (Dahler and Savage, 1975).

Several studies of GA were undertaken as a result of the Carter administration's 1978

and much anecdotal information generally showed that there was extreme variation in eligibility requirements, conditions of coverage, and size of grants, not only from state to state, but within states, and even within counties. Quite often, each township or other local unit of government operated under its own formal or informal set of rules. It is probably fair to say that in most cases grants were small, usually for one-time-only items, and in the form of vouchers to clients, payments directly to vendors, or in-kind transfers.

As welfare programs began to grow during the latter part of the nineteenth century and more rapidly in the twentieth, General Assistance received little attention. State and federal programs were developed for favored categories of the poor (e.g., the blind and the deaf, dependent children, the elderly). The general, the undifferentiated poor, who did not fit in these categories, were left to rely on General Assistance wherever and however it existed at the local level. In welfare history, General Assistance remained unaffected by the great expansion of welfare programs.[9]

We look at General Assistance from two perspectives. In this chapter, we ask: To what extent does it function as an income maintenance program serving those poor who are not eligible for state and federal programs? In the next chapter: To what extent does it function as an emergency assistance and special needs program—and if it does, is it for GA recipients alone, or does it fill the needs and gaps for people receiving aid from other programs?

Over time, there have been changes in General Assistance, principally with increased state funding and increased state control. Administrative and funding differences are important. The more state control and responsibility for General Assistance, the more uniformity there is in standards, size of grants, and conditions. While the trend in General Assistance towards greater uniformity and standardization is consistent with overall changes in the public welfare system, the rate of change is slower than in the categorical programs. Currently, the structure of General Assistance is as follows: (1) it is state supervised, ad-

---

welfare reform effort. The "Better Jobs and Income" proposal included federal money for the GA population, and HEW needed data about recipient characteristics and potential costs of assisting this previously unserved population. One HEW-contracted study was done by Urban Systems Research and Engineering, Inc. (1978). Also in 1977, an Indiana citizens' group published a comprehensive study of the poor relief system in that state, and made recommendations for reforms in their report (Citizens' Study Commission on Poor Relief, 1977).

[9]See Piven and Cloward (1971). Chapter 1 provides an overview of the early history of relief-giving.

ministered, and funded in 21 states (three of these states have partial county funding but state administration); (2) it is state supervised, may be funded not at all, partially, or completely by the state, but is administered by counties in ten states; (3) it has county or local supervision and administration in 18 states (Koppell, Murphy, and Craig, 1977).

Perhaps the most extensive study of General Assistance is a survey of 20 states published in 1978 (Urban Systems Research and Engineering). The survey selected one General Assistance program in each state, so that it does not represent all of the available programs. Nevertheless, the selected programs were meant to be the most "significant."

According to the study, most of the states primarily dispense assistance to meet continuing, basic needs. Only two of the programs are primarily "one-time only" programs and only seven dispense some "one-time only" emergency grants. On the other hand, some programs have time limits. In six of the states the average number of months in which an individual received General Assistance was six or less.

The size of the grants varies significantly. The range in cash grants is from $55 a month to a maximum of $188 a month. There are also some earmarked, in-kind grants. Significant expenditures occurred in the earmarked category, primarily to meet medical needs, because General Assistance recipients are seldom eligible for Medicaid. In most instances the typical recipient is a single adult, although this is not always the case.

A more detailed study of Wisconsin's program, General Relief, which is locally administered, has recently been completed (McGovern, 1979). Much of the information in this section is from that study. In Wisconsin, as is true in most of the other states, the principal modern function of GA is to meet the needs of the "gap" population—young and middle-aged single persons; older parents whose children are grown; and childless couples. With the exception of childless couples, these groups have a higher risk of unemployment. Middle-aged former homemakers constitute a growing segment of the GA population, apparently due to rising divorce rates and lower mortality rates for women.

The state of Wisconsin has no supervisory role in GA, which is administered by 656 different units. Forty-eight counties have countywide administration; two counties have the "group system" (the county Department of Social Services contracts with local units to administer GA), and 22 counties are on the "unit" system, meaning that each city, town, and village in the county, regardless of population size and resources, is responsible for administering relief. Even within the unit system a variety of forms of administration exist, including part-time administration by volunteers or public officials, administration by full town boards or welfare committees, or agency administration by full-time welfare administrators.

For FY 1977–1978 (July–June) the statewide GA expenditure total was $13,355,936, a decrease of about 18% from the previous year. However, rates were not uniform across the state, and some counties' costs increased by as much as 50%. For June 1978, the monthly average statewide caseload size was 4862. The ratio of caseload to county population not only varies from county to county, but may be inaccurate or underreported.[10]

In response to a state survey (1978), 8% of county-system respondents reported that GA benefit levels were "usually less" than AFDC payment levels. Milwaukee County, which serves approximately 43% of the state's GA recipients, reported monthly grants of "approximately $215 for one person for food, shelter, and clothing; persons over age 60 receive an additional grant of $28 monthly for fuel and utilities." The basic Milwaukee AFDC monthly allowance for one person is $184, not counting the value of the medical assistance and other benefits available to AFDC recipients.

Almost all of Wisconsin county-survey respondents said GA limits on income and assets were "more stringent" than AFDC limits in determining eligibility. Coverage is even more limited under the unit system. Almost half of the unit-system respondents reported no active GA program. In these jurisdictions the only aid available to the GA population would be food stamps, or perhaps fuel loans.

Many Wisconsin GA programs do not provide for some of the most basic needs; for example 9% provide no food aid; 18% no shelter, 53% no clothing; 14% no fuel aid; 27% no aid for other utilities; and 57% no aid for transportation. Some local programs grant only one-time or short-term assistance, regardless of the actual needs of applicants. On the other hand, there are exceptions. A few jurisdictions follow monetary standards equivalent to or more generous than AFDC or SSI. In these programs large vouchers for fuel, shelter, and medical bills may be granted, but usually only once.

Job search and other work requirements vary. Some agencies have either no rules or have minimal registration only; others are more stringent. Some jurisdictions offer only work relief. Wages paid in 1978 for work relief ranged from $1.60 to $3.50 per hour.

Exacerbating the problem of stretching limited resources at the local

[10]For example, small-town boards may not consider a one-time emergency grant as a GA "case," and it would not be reported as such.

level is the increasingly burdensome cost of providing emergency medical care to indigent persons, especially for agencies that have hospitals in their areas. Under the law hospitals can charge GA for emergency services, and some agencies report that 40% to 50% of their expenditures are for medical needs. Agencies have little choice but to pay; as a result, GA in Wisconsin is, to a considerable extent, a medical-aid program with expenditures going to hospitals and physicians.

The unit-system agencies are within the jurisdiction of county departments of social services, which often means that clients are shuffled between agencies. Shuffling is sometimes caused by agencies trying to save money by forcing clients to apply to other agencies (e.g., AFDC applicants are referred to GA for emergency food vouchers instead of being granted expedited food stamps). In addition, part-time relief administrators are often difficult to reach, even in emergencies; in most similar jurisdictions there is no public office where applicants may go to apply for assistance, so they must apply either at the director's residence or his place of business.

In general, eligibility criteria are extraordinarily vague, and the determination of the amount of the assistance grant is left to the discretion of the relief officials. For example, one administrator reported that before granting eligibility "we check with the applicants' neighbors as to patterns of life and living." A substantial number of relief administrators are unaware of the applicable statutes. Several court decisions regarding welfare administration in general and Wisconsin GA in particular were not reflected in many relief agencies' practices. For example, federal court rulings dating back to 1970 established the recipient's right to written procedures, such as written notice of the right to appeal adverse decisions,[11] yet two-thirds of the active unit-system programs did not give written notice of denial of aid, and less than 20% of the rejected applicants were notified in writing of a right to appeal. Only 20% of the unit systems had written eligibility standards, although almost 80% of the county systems did obey this rule. The Wisconsin study concluded that there was a pervasive pattern of neglect of procedural rights in the GA programs, but that the problem did not lie with the individual relief directors so much as with the inadequate structure

[11] *Goldberg* v. *Kelley*, 337 U.S. 254 (1970) established procedural rights for all welfare recipients. *Alexander* v. *Silverman*, 356 F. Supp. 1179 (E.D. Wisconsin, 1973) established the right to written notice of denial plus a notice of the right to appeal for general relief clients. Uniform compliance with court decisions can be achieved through voluntary compliance (which so far has not occurred), or by bringing suit against each noncomplying agency, or by legislative revision of the statutory language to concur with the court decisions.

and financing of these programs, especially in the more rural areas. The relief directors have to deal with different cases—clients who cannot qualify for the more established programs—yet these officials have inadequate preparation, virtually no previous experience, other time-consuming duties, and very little money. In the jurisdictions with larger populations, of course, GA is administered differently. Directors tend to be professional; there are GA offices, line-item budgets, and more procedural regularity.

The Wisconsin General Relief study was statewide and developed information on the smaller jurisdictions spread throughout the state, thus filling a much-needed gap in empirical work on General Assistance. The case studies in our study deal with the administration of General Assistance in somewhat larger areas and with significant variation among communities.

In New Jersey, General Assistance programs are administered by each of the 567 municipalities, rather than by the counties. In 1979 there were an estimated 25,000 GA recipients in the state. In Mercer County, each of the 20 municipalities has its own separate GA program. The City of Trenton Welfare Department administers the county's largest program, from offices in a dilapidated, ancient clapboard building. General Assistance in Trenton is an example of a flat-grant income maintenance program, although the local officials consider it to be emergency assistance because applicants must demonstrate a dire need to qualify, and the program has stringent requirements, and is of short duration.

The financial staff of the city's welfare department administers GA; there are 35 full-time workers, 16 of whom are CETA employees. Staff salaries are paid solely by the city, whereas the state reimburses the city for 75% of the monies spent on grant expenditures. In 1979, Trenton's GA expenditures totaled $261,026. Caseload figures were not easily available, but the director of city welfare estimated that there were about 1000 GA recipients in Trenton. Clients were unemployed, single or married adults with no minor children, all of whom should be eligible for food stamps as well. About 75% were black, 60% were male, and most, in the city welfare director's opinion, were employable. The director held the view that many were "drug addicts or alcoholics or close to it" who supplemented their GA grant by selling their food stamps.

When a client applies for GA, there is a strict verification process that allows for no discretion. There must always be a referral from the Food Stamp office to show that the person has applied or is applying for food stamps, plus verification of address, amount of rent, last place worked, doctors' notes, social security number, etc. If the person claims to have been evicted and therefore has no address, the welfare director requires a rent receipt from the last month to verify that the applicant did have a Trenton address and paid rent. She says she instituted this rule because so many people were giving false addresses or were transients.

Every new case must be reviewed by an intake supervisor before being transferred to the services section. A city quality-control person comes in regularly to check for errors. The most common worker error is likely to involve verification of employment termination; people who quit a job are ineligible for GA for 90 days immediately following such termination, and the agency suspects them of falsifying the "quit" day. Ongoing cases are strictly reevaluated every six months, however, to further reduce the chances of errors, overpayments, or fraud. The welfare director estimated that fraud occurs in about 2% of the cases; most of this she labeled "productive" fraud (i.e., a client who in fact, has a job), which the director showed little concern about controlling.

The basic GA grant is $119 a month for each client. The grant is flat; there are no special allowances, loans, advance payments or supplemental grants. Clients are expected to live on this plus food stamps. There are no emergency assistance provisions; GA itself *is* considered emergency assistance (although not by our definition), since most people don't apply unless they are experiencing an emergency. GA clients appear to discover quickly that there are no additional sources of emergency aid at city welfare; each month only about fifteen ongoing clients come in to request emergency aid, in the form of a loan, advance, or additional grant. Standard staff procedure in such cases is to refer clients to a private agency, such as the Catholic Welfare Bureau, or to the Social Security Office in the case of SSI recipients.

The most common emergencies involve housing, because of the severe housing shortage in Trenton. Many evictions occur when clients withhold rent in response to substandard housing. In the winter months utility cutoffs also become a major source of requests for aid. In either case, the most direct action the GA office will take is to send the landlord or utility company a voucher indicating that the client has a guaranteed income of $119 from welfare and suggesting the client and the landlord or company work out a payment plan. Occasionally, when the case worker knows and trusts a client, he or she may attempt direct, informal negotiation with the vendor to forestall cutoffs or evictions; but this clearly is not standard procedure.

The Trenton GA program is narrow, inflexible, and hostile. The administrator of this program makes no apologies. She views her task as administering a meager program in an equitable manner, which means under clear, sharply defined rules, with no exceptions, to those who are clearly in need. She is proud of the agency's record in keeping fraud and abuse to a minimum, restricting aid to residents, and encouraging people to help themselves.

THE POLITICAL CONTEXT OF THE CONSOLIDATED GRANT

Attitudes of Welfare Officials at State and Local Levels

We have seen the increased emphasis on standardization in the structure of the grant in AFDC, SSI, and Food Stamps. In addition, many General Assistance grants are also standardized. This emphasis has greatly altered the patterns of behavior in state and county welfare offices. Some of the more obvious manifestations reflect national changes: the separation of services from income maintenance, the adoption of the flat grants in AFDC, the separation of AFDC programs from programs for the disabled and elderly, and the emphasis on quality control. Less obvious but equally significant changes have also occurred. There has been a significant increase in administrative efficiency. For example, the use of the computer has increased dramatically, especially since the 1970s.[12] At the time of our study, over a third of the states and counties had adopted monthly reporting systems in which certain public welfare recipients must report their income and circumstances every month rather than every six months. Monthly reporting, now mandatory, is a further step toward creating a standardized system that looks closely at income and family circumstances in calculating benefits.

To what extent do these trends dominate state and local offices? What other pressures do executives feel, and how do these relate to the provision of aid for emergencies and special needs?

The trend toward standardization can be seen in the basic operating principles adopted by states and counties. One way of gauging these commitments is to ask officials about organizational goals—the state of affairs the leader of an organization is trying to bring about (Etzioni, 1975, Chapter 1). Goals involving horizontal equity, error control, and administrative efficiency represent the organizational expression of the trend toward standardization. The extent to which the goals are sup-

[12]Of 38 states responding to a question on the matter, 35 claim to use a computer for keeping records and nine claim to use a computer in order to determine eligibility.

ported indicates how far state policies of standardization have been accepted.[13]

We distinguish between *actual* and *desired* goals (Gross, 1968). It is conceivable that welfare officials may wish that they and their staffs were free to work for different ends from those they are currently required to carry out.

In the state and county survey, welfare executives were asked to rate, on a six-point scale, how important a list of goals are at present, and how important executives believe the goals should be. The list of goals (Table 2.2) attempts to specify the major commitments of welfare policy, as outlined in Chapter 1. The equity and efficiency commitment—the trend toward standardization—is measured by three goals: (1) simplifying procedures; (2) verifying client statements; and (3) making sure that clients are treated equally. The trend toward the flat grant is an attempt to maximize simplification, efficiency, and equity.

The traditional policy orientation involving the opposite of standardization—individualized aid—is measured by three goals: (1) dealing with unique financial characteristics of clients; (2) maintaining the flexibility to deal with cases that do not quite fit the rules; and (3) avoiding welfare dependency.

Chapter 1 stressed the importance of the distinction between the deserving and undeserving poor. In one sense, the issue is restrictiveness. Some states and counties consider clients in general less deserving than do other states and counties. They favor restricting aid as much as possible. Two goals measure the policy commitment to minimize the use of the public program: (1) encouraging applicants to use private resources; and (2) restricting aid to those who need it most.[14]

We also decided to add a dimension that is seldom measured in

[13]Over the past decade, goals have gone out of favor as a topic of research. One claim is that goals are not important because they merely *reflect* pressures that an organization must deal with, rather than independently *affecting* organizational performance. To us, this objection is not a problem. We are using goals as an indicator of broader pressures with which the welfare agency must deal, such as federal pressures for a flat grant. It is irrelevant whether goals affect broader policy commitments or whether they reflect them, as long as goals and policies are consistent. We merely claim that variations in these goals, whatever their source, help measure current welfare practices and commitments. See, for example, Simon (1964) and Yuchtman and Seashore (1967).

[14]The differences between individualization and restrictiveness should not be stressed too strongly, as many claim that they represent similar concepts. Stress on individualization may be consistent with a restrictive orientation, as both imply carefully determining whether some clients are actually "undeserving" and not eligible for aid. This ambiguity is unavoidable, but as we will see, the analysis in a later chapter finds differences in the way measures of the two concepts relate to the emergency assistance system.

TABLE 2.2
Goals Listed on Executive Questionnaires and What They Measure

Goal	Underlying Concept
1. To make sure all the basic financial needs of clients are met	Part of philosophy of "flat grant"
2. To be sensitive to the unique financial circumstances of each client	Traditional value underlying a discretionary system
3. To make sure that some clients are not treated more favorably than others in similar financial situations	The basic equity goal underlying administrative standardization
4. To keep application forms and procedures as simple as possible	Administrative rationality: creating an easy-to-administer system
5. To carefully verify client needs and resources	Standardization measure—to help ensure uniformity and reduce costs and errors
6. To restrict aid to those who need it most	Central part of philosophy of keeping benefits low
7. To avoid the encouragement of welfare dependency	A traditional goal, based on model of individual change
9. To encourage applicants to get help from private sources before applying for public funds	A means of keeping benefits low
9. To increase the efficiency and control the costs of program administration	Central "flat grant" goal for administration
10. To provide workers the flexibility to make decisions that do not quite fit the rules	Part of the traditional, discretionary approach
11. To obtain comparable working conditions for the staff	Internal organizational maintenance
12. To obtain high staff salaries	Internal organizational maintenance
13. To keep staff turnover low	Internal organizational maintenance
14. To keep channels of communication open	Internal organizational maintenance
15. To maintain ties with outside groups and organizations	External maintenance, keeping interest-group support
16. To make sure the public is not misinformed about the welfare program	External maintenance, keeping public support
17. To lobby actively for changes in legislation	External maintenance, improving conditions

studies: organizational maintenance, or the tendency of an organization to protect and enhance its functioning. This dimension contains two components, the attempt to maintain pleasant working conditions for staff (internal maintenance) and the attempt to maintain satisfactory relations with external groups (external maintenance).[15] These maintenance goals lead organizations to attempt to control clients (Piven and Cloward, 1971). Control is useful because it avoids community complaints about client behavior—complaints that directly affect ties with external groups and indirectly may threaten the budget of the agency. Maintenance goals may have repercussions on emergency and special needs programs. For example, executives may believe that emergency and special needs programs compromise maintenance by creating administrative difficulties. In addition, because specialized programs create situations in which errors or cases of abuse may occur, they may threaten relations with the community. The study of this dimension is consistent with our desire to determine how preexisting values affect decisions about specialized programs.[16]

Table 2.3 presents the mean scores on the goal items at the state level. Four current goals are tied for the highest rank: meeting basic financial needs, making sure clients are treated equally, increasing administrative efficiency, and verifying client needs and resources. These are the central aims of the trend toward standardization—to provide a basic, constant, easily administered welfare system. The goal ranking fifth, keeping forms as simple as possible, is also in line with this common point of view. There is thus a strong emphasis on administrative rationality.

While the fit is not quite perfect, goals concerning maintenance of the organization fall into the middle ranks. Goals involving internal communication and communication with the public tie for the sixth rank, maintaining ties with outside groups is in a tie for eighth, and keeping

[15]At the county level, one item asked of state officials that is often beyond control of local executives is omitted: the goal of keeping staff salaries high.

[16]Some may claim that goals cannot be adequately measured by questionnaires, and there is truth to the argument. But we tested the validity of measures of goals by correlating them with more "objective" behavioral indices. The results support the use of the goal measures. For example, we correlated the goal of carefully verifying needs with a "verification scale" for AFDC developed in *A Public Assistance Databook* (1977—see Section IV, p. 198). The two correlated ($r = .33$), increasing confidence in the goal measure. There were other correlations involving indices from this book: maintaining flexibility correlates negatively to the index of verification ($r = -.25$), the goal of being sensitive to the unique circumstances of clients correlates with having face-to-face interviews ($r = .41$), a restrictive orientation correlates with the percentage of AFDC cases denied ($r = .36$).

TABLE 2.3
Welfare System Goals as Rated by State Welfare Executives

Goal (Shortened Descriptions)	Mean Score of Existing Goal (Rank)	Mean Score of Desired Goal (Rank)[a]
Meet basic financial needs	5.0 (2.5)	5.4 (1)
Make sure clients are treated equally	5.0 (2.5)	5.1 (6)
Increase efficiency, control costs	5.0 (2.5)	5.3 (2.5)
Verify needs and resources	5.0 (2.5)	5.1 (6)
Keep forms and procedures simple	4.8 (5)	5.2 (4)
Keep communication channels open	4.7 (6.5)	5.3 (2.5)
Keep the public informed	4.7 (6.5)	5.1 (6)
Maintain ties with outside groups	4.5 (8.5)	4.8 (9.5)
Restrict aid	4.5 (8.5)	4.8 (9.5)
Avoid welfare dependency	4.3 (10)	5.0 (8)
Keep staff turnover low	4.2 (11.5)	4.7 (11)
Lobby for legislation	4.2 (11.5)	4.6 (12.5)
Obtain comfortable working conditions	4.1 (13.5)	4.6 (12.5)
Be sensitive to unique financial circumstances	4.1 (13.5)	4.4 (14)
Obtain high staff salaries	4.0 (15)	4.3 (15)
Provide worker flexibility	3.8 (16)	4.2 (16)
Encourage use of outside resources	3.0 (17)	3.2 (17)
N = 44		

Note: Scores on a scale of 1 to 6; 6 is "absolute top priority." Decimals indicate ties.
[a]Order follows rank of previous column.

turnover low, lobbying for legislation, obtaining comfortable working conditions, and obtaining high salaries range in rank from eleventh to fifteenth.

Significantly, items involving the more traditional perspectives in public welfare generally rank low. Avoiding welfare dependency ranks tenth; being sensitive to unique financial circumstances of clients is in a tie for thirteenth, and providing flexibility ranks sixteenth. Restrictive coverage is in a tie for eighth, and obtaining aid from private resources is seventeenth out of the seventeen goals.

There is a high agreement between the desires of the executives and their perceptions of the goals of the existing system, particularly if we concentrate on ranks. This is most true among goals ranked as the lowest seven priorities. Keeping turnover low ties for eleventh as a current goal and ranks eleventh as a desire; lobbying actively for legislation ties for eleventh as a current goal and ties for twelfth as a desire, and so forth. There are only three moderately large discrepancies in rankings: keeping communication channels open is more a desired than an existing goal, and verifying needs and treating clients equally rate a bit lower as desires than as current goals. However, even here, differences are within a similar general pattern. The important point is that state welfare executives seem to accept the efficiency and equity notions inherent in the trend to the flat grant, rating these items as the highest desires and rating the more traditional goals as less important.

The basic agreement between current goals and desired goals of executives might indicate that the organizational priorities are highly institutionalized—accepted by top officials as well as part of daily practice. Therefore, one might not expect large conflicts between existing commitments and the pattern of conduct designed by executives. In keeping with historical trends, executives want to focus most heavily on goals relating to standardization. Individualism and restrictiveness, more traditional orientations, seem to be stressed to a smaller degree. The standardization principle thus seems quite well established in public welfare bureaucracies.

Table 2.4 presents the desired and actual goals as reported by the county respondents. These goals are quite consistent with those of state officials in that the difference in the mean score on any goal item is never more than three-tenths of a point, and the ranks follow the same general pattern. Four of the five most highly ranked goals support the emphasis on standardization: making sure clients are treated equally, verifying needs and resources, increasing efficiency and controlling costs, and making sure that basic financial needs are met (a tie). Keeping forms and procedures simple, which ranks fifth with state officials, ties for eighth among local officials. Also in keeping with state-level results, the goals involving organizational maintenance occupy middle ranks (tie for third, sixth, seventh, tie for eighth, twelfth, and thirteenth). Again, significantly, most of the goals related to maintaining flexibility and restricting aid rank the lowest.

There are a few discrepencies between state and county responses. While organizational maintenance occupies the middle ranks according to both groups, county officials rank some items higher.[17] Another difference is that the goal of being sensitive to the unique circumstances of clients is ranked somewhat more highly by the county execu-

[17]The high rank given by county officials to the goal of keeping open channels of communication—a tie for third—is the prime example. As opposed to state officials, local officials thus appear to be somewhat more interested in the internal functioning of the organization.

TABLE 2.4
Welfare System Goals as Rated by County Welfare Executives

Goal (Shortened Descriptions)	Mean Score of Existing Goal (Rank)	Mean Score of Desired Goal (Rank)
Make sure clients are treated equally	5.3 (1)	5.5 (1)
Verify needs and resources	5.2 (2)	5.3 (4)
Increase efficiency, control costs	4.9 (3.5)	5.3 (4)
Keep communication channels open	4.9 (3.5)	5.4 (2)
Meet basic financial needs	4.7 (5.5)	5.2 (7.5)
Keep the public informed	4.7 (5.5)	5.2 (7.5)
Maintain ties with outside groups	4.6 (7)	5.0 (10)
Keep forms and procedures simple	4.5 (8.5)	5.3 (4)
Keep staff turnover low	4.5 (8.5)	5.2 (7.5)
Be sensitive to unique financial circumstances	4.4 (10.5)	4.9 (12)
Avoid welfare dependency	4.4 (10.5)	5.2 (7.5)
Obtain comfortable working conditions	4.3 (12)	4.9 (12)
Lobby for legislation	4.0 (13)	4.9 (12)
Restrict aid	3.8 (14)	4.0 (14.5)
Provide worker flexibility	3.4 (15)	4.0 (14.5)
Encourage use of outside resources	3.2 (16)	3.7 (16)
N = 232		

Note: Scores on a scale of 1 to 6; 6 is "absolute top priority."
Decimals indicate ties.

tives. Further, the goal of restricting aid to those who need it most is ranked at a much lower level by county officials.

On the other hand, county officials share with state officials the ranking of their desires to keep forms and procedures simple and be sensitive to the unique circumstances of clients. But in terms of current goals, county officials rank the goal of simplifying procedures lower than do state executives, and the county officials rank being sensitive to unique circumstances higher. Another finding is that county officials tend to rank lower—as a current goal—meeting all of the financial needs of clients.

Although one should not make too much of the differences—they are the result of rather small discrepancies in mean scores—many of them seem to fall into a pattern. County officials may report somewhat different scores for some current goal as a response to the actual pressures and difficulties they face. For example, while state officials believe that forms are simple, county officials may find this not to be the case. Seemingly simple state forms and procedures may be complicated to apply to individual clients. Or county officials may find that they must be sensitive to unique circumstances if their programs are to work, despite their feeling that sensitivity should not be an important goal. Perhaps county officials are forced to deal with the varying needs of clients much more than they would wish to. Further, county officials appear to be more aware of the fact that benefits are low: they rank the goal of meeting basic financial needs of clients at a lower level than do state officials, apparently conceding that it currently is not accomplished. Perhaps the pressures and complaints that clients bring to bear on county officials lead to an increased awareness of financial problems. In other words, the real problems of clients, which often vary from individual to individual and are often a response to limited welfare benefits, apparently inhibit the acceptance of the ideology of standardization at least a small degree.

Attitudes of Those Who Influence the Welfare System

If one looked only at the policies and attitudes of welfare officials, one would expect to find very limited, well-controlled emergency assistance and special needs programs. The actual and desired goals of these officials stress standardization, equity, and a reduction in error. The discretionary nature of specialized programs, however, compromises these goals. In addition, owing to the number of individualized decisions that are required in the specialized programs, emergency assistance and specialized aid may be inconsistent with organizational maintenance: more staff time is taken up and more complaints about error and fraud are likely to occur if the discretionary program is adopted. A next step is to determine how those who influence the welfare system view emergency assistance and special needs programs—as reported by those who filled out our executive questionnaires.

State and local executives were asked to rank which individuals and groups, in their opinion, might affect emergency and special needs programs. At the state level, these groups included federal and regional officials, service providers, public welfare interest groups, officials in other units of government, as well as public welfare officials. At the county level, similar groups were included, although local officials were added and some state-level groups were excluded. We were particularly concerned with three issues. We wanted to ascertain how much influence various groups have on the nature of emergency assistance programs, since this will reveal the extent to which each group may affect policy. We further wanted to find out what size program each group thought was appropriate, as the answer to this question reveals much about the nature of the program for which each group might lobby. And we wanted to estimate the concern each group felt over error and fraud in the emergency programs in order to determine whether this important issue indirectly affects the operation of emergency programs.[18]

Table 2.5 lists the mean score on a five-point scale of each group on the three issues at the state level. The groups are listed according to perceived influence, since the desires of a group must be weighed against the influence the group has.

As noted in the first column, at the state level the perceived influence of agencies seems to be ranked in a manner that is consistent with common sense. Executives believe that the legislature and the governor have the most influence over emergency programs, that the state welfare officials have the third highest influence, and that the state budget office and the county offices are next in line. These groups represented those who directly deal with expenditures by law (legislature and governor) or administration (budget office), and those who deal with the emergency program on a day-to-day basis (state and local welfare officials).

Somewhat less influence is attributed to federal program administrators, welfare rights groups, the welfare advisory board, and regional offices of the federal government. These are groups that probably either indirectly control policy or lobby for their own interests. Groups with some concern about emergency assistance but with fewer direct relations to the welfare system were assumed to have the least influence. These groups include private charities, the press, the general public, other social service agencies, and individual clients.

One might expect the emergency assistance program to reflect the interests of those groups with the most influence, and such groups

[18]Once again, it is important to note that the measures are not perfect. We do not have independent information about community pressure. We rely on the perceptions of executives.

TABLE 2.5
State Welfare Executives' Perceptions of Attitudes of Various Groups toward Specialized Programs

Group Scored by Executive	Mean Score for Influence on Program (Rank)	Mean Score for Desired Program Size[a] (Rank)	Mean Score for Concern over Error and Fraud[a] (Rank)
Governor and staff	4.0 (1.5)	2.9 (9)	4.6 (1.5)
State legislature and legislators	4.0 (1.5)	2.6 (11)	4.6 (1.5)
State welfare agency staff	3.8 (3)	3.3 (4)	4.5 (3.5)
State budget agency	3.7 (4.5)	2.3 (13)	4.4 (5)
County welfare agency	3.7 (4.5)	2.8 (10)	4.5 (3.5)
Federal program administrators	3.4 (6.5)	3.1 (6.5)	4.1 (7)
Welfare rights and advocacy groups	3.4 (6.5)	4.4 (1)	2.7 (12.5)
Welfare advisory board	3.1 (8)	3.2 (5)	4.0 (9)
Private charitable agencies	2.9 (10)	3.7 (3)	2.7 (12.5)
The press	2.8 (11)	2.5 (12)	4.0 (9)
The general public	2.7 (12.5)	2.2 (14)	4.2 (6)
Other state social service agencies	2.7 (12.5)	3.1 (6.5)	2.8 (11)
Individual clients	2.4 (14)	4.1 (2)	2.5 (14)
Mean	3.26	3.09	3.83
N = 44			

Note: Scores on a 1 to 5 scale; a score of 5 means high influence, or large program size, or great concern.

Decimals indicate ties.

[a]Order follows rank in column 1.

seem to favor relatively small programs, according to the executive questionnaires. For the five groups with the highest influence, the average program size desired is somewhat below "moderate" on the five-point scale (2.78 with moderate = 3), and also somewhat below the average desired size. With the exception of the state welfare officials, those groups with most influence desire the smallest programs. Of the 14 groups, the governor's average desire regarding program size ranks ninth, the county welfare agency ranks tenth, the state legislature eleventh, and the budget office thirteenth.

According to the executive questionnaire, those who desire a much larger than average emergency assistance program tend to be scattered throughout the lower ranks in terms of influence. Understandably, the three groups ranked highest in terms of the desirable size for such a program are welfare rights groups, private charities, and individual clients. The first group is ranked intermediate on influence, the latter two are ranked low. Groups assumed to desire a small program, such as the press and public, and those presumably desiring an intermediate program, such as the regional offices, also are ranked as having low and intermediate influence.

It seems conceivable that the desired size of an emergency program will vary with concern over error and fraud, given the potential for abuse that an emergency assistance program might have. Perhaps (this will be tested later) the higher the level of concern over these issues, the smaller the program desired. And indeed the five groups ranked as having the greatest influence on emergency assistance are also those who are judged by welfare executives to be most concerned about error and fraud: the governor, the legislature, state welfare officials, the county welfare agency, and the state budget agency.[19]

The results imply that concomitant fraud and error are important issues in emergency assistance. The average concern with error and fraud is quite high, 3.83 on the five-point scale. Moreover, the groups ranked highest on influence score either 4.5 or 4.6 on concern over error and fraud.[20]

One prediction is that concern with fraud and error influences the size of the program that groups and individuals desire. This appears to be true for some groups.[21] Concern over error and fraud relates to a preference for smaller programs on the part of the county agency ($r = -.23$), the regional office ($r = -.38$), the legislature ($r = -.24$), the press ($r = -.42$), and clients ($r = -.35$). For these groups it appears that a desire to avoid fraud and error reduces the desire for a large emergency program.[22]

At the state level, external pressures thus appear to be structured in a clear pattern. The groups with the most influence in public welfare generally are said to desire small emergency programs. They also are

[19]There are a number of "ties" in scores among other groups, so there is little difference in concern with error and fraud between groups that rank medium and low on influence.

[20]In fact, the scores of the groups judged to have greatest influence are so close to the maximum that they appear to be almost a constant between states. The concern over error and fraud may limit the size of all emergency programs, but it does not predict why some states will have larger programs than others.

[21]We use a .20 correlation as a cutoff point for substantive significance.

[22]In other cases, concern with error and fraud does not correlate with desired size, but it is possible that the near constancy of such concern across states is the reason. There is one positive relation: The state welfare officials, themselves, evince more concern with error and fraud when they desire a larger program ($r = .53$). This last result may indicate that executives believe that a large program causes difficulties for an administrator.

TABLE 2.6
Local Executives' Perceptions of Attitudes of Various Groups toward Specialized Programs

	Mean Score for Influence on Program (Rank)	Mean Score for Desired Program Size[a] (Rank)	Mean Score for Concern over Error and Fraud[a] (Rank)
State welfare agency staff	4.1 (1)	3.2 (6)	4.4 (2)
State legislature and legislators	3.9 (2)	2.7 (9)	4.2 (4)
Governor and staff	3.7 (3)	2.9 (8)	4.1 (5)
Local executive and staff	3.4 (4)	3.4 (4)	4.6 (1)
Welfare rights and advocacy groups	3.2 (5)	4.5 (1)	2.6 (12)
Local elected legislature	3.0 (6)	2.5 (10.5)	4.0 (7)
Local elected executives (such as mayor)	2.8 (7)	2.5 (10.5)	3.9 (7)
Local welfare advisory board	2.7 (8)	3.0 (7)	3.7 (8)
Local social service agencies	2.6 (9)	3.6 (3)	2.8 (11)
The press	2.5 (10.5)	2.6 (12)	3.6 (3)
The general public	2.5 (10.5)	2.2 (13)	4.3 (3)
Individual clients	2.4 (12)	4.2 (2)	2.4 (.3)
Private charitable agencies	2.3 (13)	3.3 (5)	2.9 (10)
Mean	3.01	3.12	3.65
N = 232			

Note: Scores on a 1 to 5 scale; a score of 5 means high influence, or large program size, or great concern.
[a]Order follows rank in column 1.

judged to have rather high levels of concern over possible error and fraud. If these pressures dominated, one might expect to find small, carefully controlled emergency programs.

There are only small differences in the perceptions of community demands held by state and local officials. Table 2.6 notes local welfare officials' perceptions (following the state-level form in Table 2.5) of various groups' influence, the program size they desire, and their concern over error and fraud in emergency programs. Local welfare executives rate the average size of the emergency program desired by all groups at 3.12, close to the state average of 3.09 (on a five-point scale). Concern with error and fraud is perceived as slightly lower at the local level, averaging 3.65 compared to 3.83. However, the local executive questionnaire does not list the state budget office, an agency whose concern over error and fraud is thought to be quite high, and groups listed in both questionnaires are ranked similarly on the issue of concern with error and fraud by executives at the local and state levels. Local officials rate their own concern at 4.6, quite close to the state executives' self-rating or 4.5 on the five-point scale.

There are also similarities in the relations between influence on the one hand, and both the desired size of the emergency program and concern over error and fraud, on the other. At both the state and local levels, those groups thought to have the most influence are usually perceived as desiring small programs and as having much concern over error and fraud. Three of the four groups rated as having the highest influence at the local level were also rated to have the highest concern over error and fraud (state welfare agency, state legislator, local executive). The four highest-rated groups in terms of influence are said to desire, on the average, a small emergency program. In other words, the perceived incentives at the local level are similar to those at the state level, usually favoring a small, well-controlled emergency program.

The Standardization Ideology

The standardization ideology appears to be deep-rooted. At both the state and county levels, officials believe that equity, standardization, the control of error, and even concerns about simplifying forms and procedures are prime goals. Individualized concerns and a restrictiveness that may be associated with theories concerning the undeserving poor are ranked low. The general pattern is somewhat less obvious at the county level, where pressures toward individualization are stronger, but the county discrepancies are only minor. The nature of external pressures from interest groups, as perceived by welfare officials, also seems to support policies that favor standardization over individualization. Most of the groups presumed to have high influence are also presumed to favor a small emergency and special needs program and to demonstrate a high level of concern over error and fraud.

Everyone seems agreed. In such a situation, the public welfare system is bound to remain standardized to a large degree: pressures favor limiting the individualized emergency and special needs programs. Thus, an observer who believes that the emergency and special needs network will tend to be consistent with general demands and pressures would predict that a limited specialized network, at best, would evolve.

CHAPTER 3

Reactions to Standardization: Attempts to Fill the Gap

Not only has standardization been enacted legislatively, it has also been embraced ideologically, implying small, well-controlled emergency assistance and special needs programs. In this chapter, we see what programs have survived. Here, we look at emergency assistance and special needs programs that are formally separated from the income maintenance programs. The distinction is an artificial one, since what we are concerned about is the ability of public and private resources to provide emergency assistance and meet the special needs of the poor, regardless of the formal structure of the program. Conceptually, however, emergency assistance programs and special needs programs have arisen as a result of the flatness of the income maintenance programs—the consolidated grants. It is for this reason that we first looked at the programs for emergency assistance and special needs that are incorporated in the basic income maintenance programs (Chapter 2) and now look at the remaining programs that try to fill the gaps. In the rest of this book, when we discuss programs that provide for emergencies and special needs, we include those mentioned in both of these chapters.

RANGE OF PROGRAMS DEALING WITH EMERGENCY ASSISTANCE AND SPECIAL NEEDS

Forty-five states listed one or more statewide programs for emergency assistance or special needs on the state executive questionnaire

TABLE 3.1
Emergency Assistance and Special Needs Programs Provided by States

Program	Number of States
AFDC–Emergency Assistance	22
AFDC–Special Needs	18
State Emergency Assistance	17
Federal Emergency Fuel	23
Expedited Food Stamps	26
Title XX	24
SSI–Special Needs	9
General Assistance	26
Other[a]	7

[a]Because of semantic differences, some of the programs specified in the "other" category actually belong under one of the listed categories. For example, South Dakota's County Emergency Assistance (grocery orders, fuel) probably should be categorized as "General Assistance"; the District of Columbia's Consolidated Emergency Assistance program could be categorized under "State Emergency Assistance." Nebraska's State Catastrophic Illness program could be classified under "State Emergency Assistance." Other responses to this category are as follows: Maryland cited "twelve EA programs in 24 local departments," 11 funded by the county, in Baltimore part of the cost contributed by the state; Wisconsin cited CAP Emergency Assistance and private agencies; Michigan noted that all the EA programs available in the state are combined into one state EA program.

(Table 3.1). In fact, the *number* of programs per state is surprising—the 45 states *average* four separate programs. (All state data include the District of Columbia).

These programs, of course, vary in coverage and expenditures. Some are statewide and of general applicability—AFDC–EA, AFDC–Special Needs, and state emergency assistance. Some are statewide but for specific items only—for example, the federal and state fuel programs. The SSI–Special Needs program is for all those receiving SSI and is statewide. As we have seen, the emergency portion of the Food Stamps program is, in fact, only an expedited service of the basic Food Stamps program. Though it is a widespread service covering one of the most important emergencies and is broadly applicable, it is a one-time-only program, available only for applicants.[1] As such it could be excluded altogether from a definition of emergency assistance on the grounds that other income maintenance programs (e.g., AFDC and SSI) sometimes provide prepayment before eligibility is finally determined. Ex-

[1]Three respondents commented that their Expedited Food Stamps program was used only in cases of disaster.

pedited Food Stamps is not available for those already on the Food Stamps program who run short.

It should be noted that there are discrepancies between various sources of data. Eighteen executives report that special needs programs exist and there are 19 responses to our special needs programs questionnaire, whereas documentary materials report 35 such programs. Perhaps many programs are so small that executives do not believe they are relevant. For example, four programs cover only basic financial needs of pregnant women. In addition, some programs, such as work-related day care, are listed in documents as special needs programs but do not fit our (and perhaps respondents') definitions. At least three programs fall into this category. Finally, at least two states abolished their special needs programs between the time the documentary material was collected and the time that the questionnaire was mailed out. Similarly, 17 executives report a state emergency assistance program, but we have 21 completed questionnaires. In this case, the explanation is that 10 such programs are AFDC–EA programs with extended eligibility; some executives simply do not report these extensions on Table 3.1.

Title XX is not usually considered an emergency assistance or special needs program as such. Rather, it is a form of revenue sharing to the states that may be used for a wide variety of social services under broad grants of discretion. Several states apparently use some Title XX money for such items as laundry services, chore services, transportation fees, and other items that are within the ambit of emergency assistance or special needs. Assistance is in the form of in-kind services provided by social workers or through contractual "purchase-of-service" arrangements with other agencies; cash assistance is rare. We will discuss its role below.

As noted, many states list General Assistance as a program available for emergency assistance and special needs. General Assistance, as income maintenance, has been discussed in Chapter 2; here we will consider it as emergency assistance. It should be noted that in some states where short-term General Assistance is provided to meet basic needs, the program is nevertheless classified as emergency assistance.

With these categories of emergency assistance and special needs programs in mind, we find that of the 45 states who responded, all but 9 have, on the books, at least one statewide emergency assistance program of general applicability. The most popular program is AFDC–EA, present in 22 states at the time executives responded (states are constantly discarding old programs and beginning new ones). The states that have AFDC–EA usually also have other programs—either other statewide general programs (e.g., AFDC–Special Needs or state emergency programs) or specialized statewide programs—emergency fuel and Expedited Food Stamps.

COVERAGE IN EMERGENCY ASSISTANCE AND SPECIAL NEEDS PROGRAMS

What do the programs cover? How much is spent for various needs and various types of clients?

AFDC–Emergency Assistance

As distinguished from AFDC–Special Needs, which, in some states, seems to have survived the conversion to the consolidated grant, AFDC–EA is a recently adopted program. Although it is part of the basic AFDC program, with federal cost-sharing and the accompanying HEW (now HHS) regulations, it is an optional program. At the time of the questionnaire, 22 of the states had AFDC–EA programs.

There are federal requirements for AFDC–EA. The most important ones restrict eligibility to families with dependent children and limit the number of requests to one period of 30 consecutive days within any given year. But beyond these, the legislation is very broad and the states have great latitude, particularly in the most crucial areas of how much assistance to dispense and for what purposes.[2]

Table 3.2 presents AFDC–EA data from the states reporting figures in 1979 (21 of 22) and compares EA grants with AFDC grants and expenditures. The most prominent feature of the data in the table is the great variation in extensiveness among the states. Several states treat AFDC–EA as a more-or-less regular supplement. Wyoming is an extreme case of this tendency, with AFDC–EA grants 92% as large as the AFDC caseload,[3] but in several other states the proportion of AFDC clients receiving EA seems to be high for what one would consider an exceptional aid program. (In West Virginia it is 55.0% as large as the caseload; in Ohio, 56.5%; in Connecticut, 38.3%; in Minnesota, 33.7%;

[2]Prior to 1978 Supreme Court decision, *Mandley* v. *Quern*, 436 U.S. 725 (1978), lower federal courts had prevented states from imposing additional restrictions on AFDC–EA. The *Mandley* decision, however, overruled these restrictions, and except for the few federal limitations, the states have wide latitude in administering AFDC–EA. See *Bacon* v. *Toia* 648 F.2d 801 (1981).

[3]Wyoming's AFDC–EA program covers medical needs only, and may be used to supplement or substitute for the Medicaid program in that state.

TABLE 3.2
AFDC and AFDC–EA Caseload and Expenditures in One Year (March 1978–February 1979)

	AFDC–EA				AFDC–EA	
State	No. of Families	Average % AFDC Caseload	Average Payment per Family	AFDC Average Payment per Family	Expenditures	% of AFDC Expenditures
Conn.[a]	17,537	38.3%	$135.38	$328.50	$ 2,374,167	2.0%
Delaware	3,093	27.9	45.98	214.57	142,240	0.4
D.C.	6,025	19.3	181.41	233.53	1,093,018	1.2
Kansas	4,786	20.3	153.82	236.87	736,224	1.1
Kentucky	17,852	29.6	212.86	167.89	3,800,089	3.1
Maryland	15,695	21.4	176.84	197.49	2,775,646	1.6
Mass.	49,396	39.5	273.51	315.59	13,510,599	3.1
Michigan	48,906	24.0	151.00	350.00	7,384,999	0.8
Minnesota	15,863	33.7	219.56	303.17	3,482,964	2.0
Montana	393	6.5	80.99	215.23	31,828	0.2
Nebraska	1,544	12.5	180.00	256.44	277,949	0.7
New Jersey	6,799	21.4	296.34	293.11	2,014,859	0.4
New York	80,295	22.0	214.00	379.93	17,183,759	1.0
Ohio	93,304	56.5	168.94	225.20	15,763,701	3.5
Oklahoma	3,409	12.0	203.28	218.91	693,007	0.9
Oregon	5,585	12.6	122.38	275.54	683,513	0.5
Penn.	2,857	1.4	138.12	292.36	394,605	0.05
Virginia	1,477	2.6	132.67	204.41	195,956	0.1
Wash.	12,480	25.0	345.28	313.47	4,309,085	2.3
W. Va.	14,344	55.0	74.30	170.69	1,065,820	2.0
Wyoming	2,156	92.0	82.31	225.00	177,462	2.8
Average		27.3	170.90	257.99	3,718,000	1.4
Median		24.0	176.84	236.87		1.1

Source: *Public Assistance Statistics* (Washington, D.C.: U.S. Department of Health, Education, and Welfare), March 1978–February 1979.

[a]Figures are not for a full year: Connecticut suspended its AFDC-EA program on July 1, 1978, and restored it on December 1, 1978.

and in Massachusetts, 39.5%.) Moreover, there is no immediately apparent explanation for these data. West Virginia is a state with a low income and low average AFDC grants. It would therefore face greater demands for emergency assistance and special needs. Massachusetts, Minnesota, and Ohio, however, have high average AFDC grants (they rank 15th, 10th, and 8th respectively, in the nation) and are in the higher two quintiles in terms of average income. Looking at the opposite end—at the states which use AFDC–EA the least—again there is no obvious pattern. Pennsylvania has the lowest proportion of AFDC–EA to caseload, 1.4%, but the program was just getting under way at the time of our study. The other states having EA caseloads proportionately far below the national median are Virginia, Montana, Nebraska, Oklahoma, and Oregon. In subsequent chapters, we will look more closely at the states to determine what accounts for differences in EA programs.

When states do choose to give an AFDC–EA grant, the grant seems to be fairly substantial. The average AFDC–EA grant is approximately three-quarters of an average monthly AFDC grant. In fact, in some states (e.g., Washington and New Jersey) the average AFDC–EA grant is larger than the average AFDC grant. ("Substantial," of course, is a relative term; if a family is burned out of their home, then an emergency grant of $177 [the median] would be a pittance.) Because AFDC–EA can only be given once a year and for a period not exceeding 30 days, it is probably used for a substantial loss or need rather than for the small amounts that are often repeatedly requested. Our guess is that when families run short of food in a particular month, they are not encouraged to use their once-a-year AFDC–EA eligibilities for $20 worth of food. Rather, those amounts are sought from other sources. This is the situation in one of the case studies, Hennepin County, Minnesota, and probably elsewhere.

The last column in Table 3.2 shows the size of AFDC–EA annual expenditures relative to what the state spends on the AFDC population. The average proportion is about 1.4%, indeed a tiny amount. Ohio, apparently with the largest AFDC–EA program relative to AFDC (excluding Wyoming), spends a proportion three times higher than the median, but its proportion is still only 3.5%. Compared to the AFDC budget, AFDC–EA is a small item. Compared to a state's total social welfare expenditures (which, of course, include much more than AFDC), AFDC–EA is even more insignificant. From a budgetary point of view, at the state level, these programs cannot have much salience. Yet they seem to have a political or social salience, an issue we defer until later.

Fourteen states and 92 counties responded to specific questions about AFDC–EA administrative procedures. Most (12) states said that either EA requires less rigorous certification procedures than AFDC or there are no differences. At the local level, 26% said there are no differences, but 47% said that AFDC–EA requires *less strict* verification procedures. Apparently, with a one-shot grant program not costing that much money, there is little concern about error and fraud when determining eligibility.

On the other hand, although certification procedures may not differ from AFDC, there usually are special rules applying to applicants for

AFDC–EA. One group of rules requires applicants to exhaust other resources. Ten of the 14 respondent states have such rules, although they vary considerably. Aid is usually given immediately in disaster cases. Some states require referrals to other agencies, the exhaustion of "real resources," application to other welfare programs (e.g., Food Stamps), and "any resource that can be made available to meet the need," intending that EA should serve as a last resort. These rules appear to be more stringent at the county level. Seventy-eight of the 92 counties listed at least some requirement for exhausting other resources as an eligibility condition for AFDC–EA. About half the counties listed as available resources, private aid (e.g., Salvation Army), Food Stamps, AFDC, SSI, Unemployment Insurance, and Social Security.

Our questionnaire also elicited opinions on how clients learn about AFDC–EA. In only two (of the 14) states are clients automatically advised of the availability of AFDC–EA—that is, the information is contained on the basic AFDC application form; and this information, of course, only reaches those who are applying for AFDC, not those who are otherwise eligible for AFDC–EA. In the rest of the states, AFDC applicants must rely on the welfare office to supply the information either in writing or orally. In only two states are notices posted. And in 13 of the 14 states, there are no rules, guidelines, or policies for informing nonrecipients about the availability of the program.

Concerning financial eligibility standards, the picture is mixed. In most states there is no difference between AFDC and AFDC–EA when it comes to monthly income and property assets. Just as many states reported that in one program eligibility criteria relating to income and property assets were higher as reported they were lower. But although about half of the states reported no differences in restrictions on liquid assets, most of the other states had more stringent requirements for AFDC–EA in this respect.

Although AFDC–EA is available in some states for non-AFDC recipients, not surprisingly, most of the recipients of this program in our sample are also AFDC recipients. The 92 counties report that 47% of the EA cases are on AFDC and another 13% are in the AFDC–Unemployed Parent program. The next highest percentages are nonparticipants in any program (19%), and food stamp recipients (14%). AFDC–EA recipients, however, are treated differently from AFDC recipients in a number of ways. One is the form of payment. Whereas the cash grant is the norm in AFDC, in AFDC–EA it is the exception. As administered at the local level (the 92 counties), over 70% of the AFDC–EA grants are either vouchered or vendored. Less than 30% are in cash. On the other hand, other conditions, such as a protective payee requirement (the client's expenditures would have to be approved by a third party), work requirements, or budget counseling, or other kinds of counseling are rarely imposed (less than 10% of the cases).

Rules vary as to the amount of emergency aid that an eligible family can receive. Few of the local jurisdictions in our sample have flat maximums per family (6%), or maximums based on the type of emergency situation covered (13%). Most (53%) report fixed amounts for some emergencies, and coverage for others as needed; a larger share (42%) report that the amount of the grant is generally determined on an "as-needed" basis.

Data from the case studies support the general conclusion about the great variation in AFDC–EA. Even within states and counties, AFDC–EA is constantly changing, principally by responding to powerful shifts in community conditions. One of the most interesting situations is in Mercer County (Trenton), New Jersey. This is a liberal department (AFDC–EA is administered by the social services unit, not the income maintenance unit) led by an energetic, experienced supervisor, with good staff morale, considering the hard times. Originally, AFDC–EA was limited to need caused by "homelessness," which meant victims of natural disasters or other emergency situations over which the individual had no control, who experienced a substantial loss of shelter, food, clothing, and/or furnishings. There were various rules governing amounts that could be paid. For example, food could be paid for at $1.50 a day, or $4.50 if no cooking facilities were available, but emergency shelter would be reimbursed at actual cost or "the most reasonable rate available."

Over time, the department stretched the definition of "homelessness" to include victims of domestic violence, applicants for other income maintenance programs who were homeless within the 7 days prior to their application, and those who lacked an "appropriate" home because of utility shutoffs or other conditions. These liberalizing changes were responses to several changes in the environment. At about the time the consolidated grant came in (1971) and requests for emergency assistance began to increase, a statewide housing shortage developed. In Trenton, a lack of public housing, with inadequate, substandard high-cost private housing, meant that for a great many welfare recipients, high rents could no longer be financed out of the basic welfare grants. This led, in turn, to an increasing number of housing- and utility-related requests. New blood came into the welfare department, and in response to the increased demand, the department stretched the rules.

This was one side of the coin—the liberal side. As far as actual grants are concerned, as per the law, clients could still only receive one payment a year (with some exceptions), and 75% to 85% were in the form of vendor or voucher payments. Furthermore, the average payment in Trenton in 1978 was $110 per recipient, which is considerably below the national average. The liberal local department was sharply constrained by available funds and the rules.

We have, then, all of the elements of variety in AFDC–EA described earlier. There is the combination of specific rules (e.g., payment maximums) with vague rules (e.g., payments according to "actual cost" or "a reasonable amount"). There is a liberal department pushing for an expansive interpretation of the rules to respond to severe environmental pressures, there are few conditions imposed, few special controls for fraud, and a considerable amount of local discretion. On the other hand, practically all grants are in the form of vendor or voucher payments, the actual cash values of the grants are quite small, and, it must be remembered, available only once a year. Despite the existence of a liberal agency and large amounts of discretion, the program is still restricted by the rules. Emergencies relating to natural disasters, the placements of victims of domestic violence in hotels, and some food emergencies can be handled easily. But only the last item involves a direct payment of cash to the client. The rules prohibit paying for security or utility deposits, delinquent utility bills, temporary shelter (except in rare cases), or the giving of food assistance to people who have run out before the end of the month. A great deal of time, then, is spent negotiating with vendors and landlords and trying to get clients aid from other sources. AFDC–EA, in Trenton, contains a sharp mixture of generosity and strictness.

A contrasting situation obtains in Oneida County (Utica), New York. Initially AFDC–EA (called Emergency Assistance for Families, EAF) was quite a liberal program used to meet a broad range of emergency situations, with a great deal of local discretion. Syracuse, for example, used the program primarily to meet the first month's needs of pending AFDC and Home Relief applicants. New York City used the funds for nonrecurring emergency needs of current AFDC recipients, and Utica spread the funds for a variety of emergencies and special needs.

During the past few years, New York State has become increasingly concerned both about error and fraud and about controlling costs. As a result, AFDC–EA has been sharply curtailed to prevent it from expanding into a broad system of supplementary grants for persons receiving AFDC. The major concerns were that AFDC–EA grants too often duplicated regular grant payments and that clients abused the system. The changes in New York now provided (1) the automatic denial of emergency assistance in the form of cash to all families eligible for AFDC; (2) the automatic denial of EA in all cases of loss, mismanagement, or theft of a regular public assistance grant; and (3) the automatic denial of EA to replace or duplicate a public assistance grant already made to AFDC and Home Relief cases.

In the early days, the Utica EAF program was open-ended and the agency used it to cover, in the words of the county director of income maintenance, "everything." But then, according to local officials, federal instructions prohibited the use of AFDC–EA for emergencies where the regular grant provided coverage. This eliminated almost 90% of Utica's EA cases. As of 1980 the Oneida County AFDC–EA program has become almost exclusively an emergency fuel program. An entire season's fuel bills are paid up during the one yearly thirty-day eligibility period. Apparently this is now done administratively, that is, without specific application by the AFDC family, and the regular AFDC fuel allotment is deducted from the basic grant. Although other emergencies can be covered, they are "exceptional"; only emergencies caused by fire or floods or, on occasion, housing condemnations, are now covered by the EA programs.

On the books, the AFDC–EA program in Oneida County is still reasonably liberal, more so than Mercer County. In practice, however, the attitudes of the two agencies are very different: in Oneida, the program is quite restrictive and those who administer it are suspicious of welfare recipients. Utica's income maintenance director, for example, reported that some AFDC clients would request EA at the end of each year, claiming lost or stolen checks, in order to get their once-a-year grant. In his opinion, clients either run out of funds that month because of Christmas, or realize that this is their last chance; but whatever the reason, there is abuse of the system.

In part, the restrictive attitude in this county is the result of recent state pressures to control costs and error, but local observers say that the county administration began cutting back on emergency assistance long before the state began to exert pressure. The director acknowledged that the inadequacies of the basic grant gave rise to increased emergency requests, but nevertheless thought that these needs should be met through the use of private charity. As will be discussed later, this practice is becoming the norm not only in this county but throughout the areas that we have studied. The director seemed quite attuned to his role as guardian of public monies, ever alert for possible client abuse of the system.

Hennepin County (Minneapolis), Minnesota, represents still a third variant: a liberal program experiencing increasing pressure (as is true all over), but so far managing to resist the pressure fairly successfully. Minnesota has had a long history of generous special needs programs. Prior to the separation of social services from income maintenance, each case was assessed individually, and there were no limits on spending from a long list of available special needs items. With the separation, Hennepin County established a separate unit (eventually called the Financial Crisis Unit) solely to administer special needs through what was called the Special Supplemental Payments program; later it administered AFDC–EA as well. Originally, only pending AFDC cases were eligible for AFDC–EA, but coverage was extended to ongoing cases and two separate administrative units were established, one to administer ongoing AFDC cases, one for nonrecipient and pending AFDC cases. The Financial Crisis Unit administers emergency assistance funds from other sources as well as AFDC–EA.

A 1974 federal review of Hennepin County's EA program expressed concern over double payments. Apparently a large amount of EA money was spent on items theoretically covered by the basic grant. The federal audit also noted reliance on EA to meet applicants' basic needs the first two months, rather than speeding up processing of AFDC applications.[4] In addition to the federal audit, there was also state pressure to tighten up EA and make the program more consistent. There was a feeling that federal and state guidelines were too vague, allowing programs to be too open-ended. The attempts to set limits were welcomed, and the changes—presumptive eligibility and more uniform administration—were satisfactory to the county agency.

State rule prohibits emergency assistance to aid clients living beyond their resources. For example, if a mortgage is so high that the AFDC family could not normally pay it, emergency aid for repairs for the house will not be given.

A major discretionary area lies in deciding whether the applicant's request should be met from AFDC–EA funds or some other source, bearing in mind that AFDC–EA must be rationed, since it is limited to one 30-day period in any year. Thus, if a client comes with a small need at the end of the month, such as a food shortage, EA will not be used;

[4]At that time, Hennepin County had a pending case backlog of 600 to 800 cases, and the county was attempting to reduce the backlog by granting immediate payments from AFDC–EA, despite the fact that EA cost it more than AFDC. In addition to saving time through use of EA, with its simpler application and verification process, the county may have reduced AFDC applications, as some EA recipients did not return to request ongoing assistance. After the audit the state instituted presumptive eligibility, allowing immediate payments from AFDC funds, and the number of pending cases receiving EA dropped dramatically.

rather, small grants (up to $35) will be given from county funds to tide the recipient over. If applicants are expecting a paycheck within a few days, they are referred to private agency "food shelves." In other instances, it may be more appropriate to refer the applicant to regular AFDC. Normally funds that are chiefly from noncounty sources will be used first, but red tape or restrictions placed on the use of funds influence the decision on which funds to use. In general, Hennepin County first utilizes its allocation from the state for special needs, then AFDC–EA; only after those funds are exhausted will county resources be tapped.

When AFDC–EA and state funds for special needs are used, the office attempts to make large payments in order to get as much as possible from the once-a-year allotment in the use of AFDC–EA and to maximize use of noncounty matching funds from both programs. This practice sometimes results in what the director of assistance payments believes are gross inequities—when some clients receive grants totaling thousands of dollars for major home repairs, for example, and others receive comparatively small grants for minor emergencies. The special needs program has been particularly subject to very large payment requests because of the nature of the items it covers—major home repairs and the replacement of furniture and appliances. Thus far, the issue of large payments has been treated with some ambivalence. Concern over inequities conflicts with the desire to get as much mileage as possible from noncounty funds.

Hennepin County administrators believe that emergency aid should not be governed by inflexible rules. (Some items, however, such as refrigerators, have a set replacement price.) In place of rules, constant supervision promotes consistent administrative practice. Workers consult routinely with supervisors about difficult case decisions. All EA grants over $500 must be approved by an immediate supervisor. Payments over $1000 require higher-level approval, and negotiations all the way up to the state commissioner are not uncommon.

The agency is not overly concerned about the issues of fraud, abuse, or deserving/nondeserving clients. Yet the use of vendor payments, protective payees (voluntary only), and compulsory counseling on money management is increasing. Nearly all cases receive vendor payments now, although theoretically clients have a choice regarding form of payment.

While the agency's figures show that one-third of all AFDC cases get emergency aid each year, these figures include some repeat requests. In the staff's view, a small percentage of clients simply cannot make it on the regular AFDC grant. One worker said she can detect when the situation is not a true emergency by looking at past records of EA use; if EA is used often by the individual, it may be a supplement to the grant for continuing, not emergency, needs.

In sum, Hennepin County's emergency assistance program appears more liberal than most, limited somewhat by fixed appropriations for the state special needs program, or federal restrictions in the case of AFDC–EA, and by some pressure from the state on all programs, but largely remaining free of restrictive conditions. A mild tightening of EA administration began a few years ago and continues to the present: more specific guidelines and reporting requirements, increased use of vendor payments and voluntary protective payees, and more rules limiting worker discretion. There is concern about inequities caused by large payment amounts; but, although every large payment is carefully assessed by supervisors, the payments are usually made.

State Emergency Assistance Programs

After AFDC–EA, the next most frequent statewide program is State Emergency Assistance (the uniform term we use to cover a variety of program names), present in 17 of the 45 states in our reporting sample according to one measure and 21 according to another. This program, however, is considerably smaller than AFDC–EA. Only eight states supplied caseload and expenditure information on their state emergency program. Three of these states also have AFDC–EA. Maryland is the only state in which the emergency program is larger than AFDC–EA. The states with the next largest State Emergency Assistance programs are Kentucky and Oklahoma, but the annual expenditures for these programs are less than 20% of what is spent for AFDC–EA. In most of the other states, yearly expenditures and average grants per family are small. The average state expenditure for AFDC–EA in 1978 was \$3,718,000; for State Emergency Assistance, it was \$978,000. Apparently, State Emergency Assistance is not considered a significant program at the county level, for only 4 counties (out of 240) reported data on this program (we asked counties to report only the largest program).

In 10 of the 21 states, State Emergency Assistance is a separate program; in the others, it is combined with either AFDC–EA and/or other state and local programs. As with AFDC–EA, there do not seem to be special eligibility requirements. Nearly all report that certification procedures are either less strict than (i.e., less verification needed) or no different from AFDC. Information about the availability of the program is not automatic (i.e., it is not contained on the AFDC application form) but must be supplied by the agency either orally (10 states) or in writing (5). Two states use the media or posters displayed in various community centers. Five states have no rules or guidelines on how information is given to applicants.

In most (15) of the states, applicants for State Emergency Assistance must exhaust other resources before funds from the program will be granted. "Other resources" usually means welfare (AFDC, Food Stamps, General Assistance), but in seven states applicants must exhaust private charities as well.

As with AFDC–EA, state emergency aid tends to be specialized. Fifteen of the states list only one type of emergency or special need as accounting for more than 80% of the program's expenditures, but from state to state, no particular favorite use or pattern of use was found.

Most of the states (15) have written rules providing for maximum amounts that applicants can receive regardless of the type of emergency. The amounts range from $70 to $250. Of the states reporting economic data, the average grant amount was less than $100. In most states, apparently, there are no formal limitations on how many times an applicant can request emergency assistance from this program. Only six states had rules regarding repeat requests.

Title XX

Of the 45 states reporting to us, 24 listed Title XX as one of the programs available for those requiring emergency assistance or having special needs in their state. Title XX provides funds to states for a broad range of social services. In effect, it is a revenue-sharing program: the requirements on the states are minimal, and the states can choose what services they will provide, under what conditions.

One does not normally think of Title XX as an emergency assistance or special needs program. It is a social program; it does not distribute cash; and it is not considered to be part of the income maintenance package.[5] In fact, however, the line between Title XX and what are considered to be emergency assistance and special needs programs may not be all that clear. Most emergency assistance and special needs programs also do not deliver cash, but they do deliver close substitutes—vouchers, vendor payments, and sometimes expedited food

[5]Although to some extent Title XX stems from the separation of social services from AFDC, this is a different conceptual and policy development from the issue of routinization vs. individualized treatment in income maintenance.

stamps. It is true that there are some emergency needs that are met with in-kind goods and services only—items of food, temporary shelter—but this is rare. In the programs that are the subject of this study, needs are met either through cash or its close substitute. Title XX services could also be considered substitutes for cash. This is certainly true at a budgetary and policy level, but it also may be true at a practical level. To the extent that a good Title XX day care program is available, there is less need for cash to cover day care costs. The problem with this approach is that one cannot tell how much Title XX money is spent for items that are the equivalent of emergency assistance and special needs and how much for regular, ongoing traditional social services. For example, in 1977 (the latest year in which data are available), $163,203,266 was spent on "day care children." Much of this money could have been spent for traditional emergency assistance or special needs—for example, an AFDC mother needing short-term day care to help maintain family functioning when she is ill. On the other hand, the money could also be used for day care centers for people not receiving welfare and those above the poverty line. In a sense, day care is a special need, but using such a definition, any public service that clients do not completely pay for can be considered as meeting a special need.

Because of the structure of Title XX and the accounting practices, it is very difficult to know what its monies are spent on, let alone whether these monies are used for emergencies and special needs, as we have defined them. Under Title XX, a certain sum is allocated to the states for the provision of social services to meet five broadly stated federal goals (e.g., reducing dependency, preventing neglect and abuse, reducing inappropriate care). The states are given a great deal of flexibility in how they spend the money. They must have at least one service directed toward each of the five federal goals and at least three services available to SSI recipients. Eligible recipients include AFDC and SSI recipients and others whose income is less than 90% of the state's median income. The states can also designate "group" eligibility if 75% of the people in the group have incomes less than 90% of the state median.[6] The states decide which services are available for which groups and individuals, and they have an option to provide a sliding-scale fee. The federal government pays 75% and the state 25% of the total cost. At the local level, social services administration is usually divided into separate units, one serving the adult population (primarily the elderly and the disabled), and another primarily providing services

[6]In Wisconsin, for example, designated Title XX groups include all persons over 75 years of age, migrants, Native Americans, and adult developmentally disabled persons.

to children or families; in some areas, additional separate units exist to serve other distinct client populations, such as those needing employment-related services.

In Wisconsin, Title XX is administered by the county departments of social services. These agencies either provide services directly or contract with other public or private agencies. In Wisconsin, state supervision over the counties has been minimal. Exact data on how Title XX funds are allocated are not available at the state level. Among the reasons for lack of specific information given by the state officials is that local caseworkers do a variety of things, part of their salary is paid by Title XX funds, and it would be impractical for them to keep a running record of what they do during the day and estimate what proportion is allocable to Title XX funds. Reporting is better for purchased services, but again, only for limited purposes. A county may report the purchase of 1000 hours of counseling, but will not report how many persons or what categories of persons received the counseling.

In Wisconsin, at least, officials claim that Title XX is used to pick up the special needs that were eliminated with the consolidated grant. However, because of the lack of systematic records, one does not know whether this actually occurs. Moreover, estimated expenditures projected for 1979–1980 show that the bulk of the money is not being spent for emergency assistance or special needs. Major expenditures are for child day care for AFDC recipients and income eligibles (around $7 million); counseling services (around $7.5 million); day services for those who live in their own homes, usually the handicapped (around $20 million); planning, placement, and supervision, mostly for AFDC recipients (around $10 million); and sheltered employment, mostly for income-eligible handicapped (around $20.5 million). Only $25,000 is projected for emergency shelter, the one "true" emergency assistance item covered under Title XX in Wisconsin. Other possible emergency assistance or special need items are chore services (around $4 million); court services (around $4 million); and supportive home care ($2.8 million).

San Diego County, California, has a wide variety of social services funded by Title XX with matching funds from the state as well as other sources. Social services are provided under three administrative divisions: children, employment, and general services. The children's division includes the following: (1) respite care, which provides day care for up to 24 hours to prevent child abuse and neglect (total budget for 1979 was $480,000); (2) child protective placement; (3) other services: day camp, tutoring, money for return of out-of-state runaway minors, emergency shelter, adoptions, foster home licensing. The employment division administers WIN, employment services, Indo-Chinese Refugee Training Program, and CETA training for General Relief clients. The general services division provides adult protective services, conservatorship (managing a client's property), homemaker, chore, and a variety of other Title XX-type services. All clients must be eligible for another public welfare program to qualify for social services, and verification is required for all programs.

In Mercer County (Trenton), New Jersey, the adult services unit considers its homemaker service and emergency nursing home placement service as significant emergency services for the adult population. The type of service varies according to client need, but 4–8 hours of homemaker services per day are available. These are contracted out by the adult unit (all homemakers are ex-AFDC clients). This is an expensive program, and because of the recent cutbacks in Title XX funds, it will soon be completely eliminated. At the time of this research (1979), there was already a 50% reduction in the homemaker staff.

Oneida County, New York, offers 21 different social services to clients, but few could possibly be classified as emergency assistance. One is protective services for children. The state Registry for Child Abuse accepts requests for immediate aid and provides information and referral over a toll-free telephone hot line. Referrals are also made from the Foster Care Services Office, courts, schools, and other public and private assistance agencies. There are self-referrals as well. Child-abuse cases require constant monitoring, which consumes much of the resources the social services office receives from the state, according to the director. A new state rule demanding 24-hour response capability has had a deleterious effect on the office's ability to provide other services. This requirement, along with inflation and the federal ceiling on Title XX spending, increasingly limits the ability of the agency to meet a range of needs for social services. Currently, more and more Title XX money supports crisis intervention; less goes to preventive services such as counseling, respite day care, and other supportive sources.

Some adult protective services cases can also be considered emergency cases. Deinstitutionalization programs have given rise to increased needs, and battered women are emerging in greater numbers than in the past to request assistance from social service agencies.

The social services office also provides some services that can be regarded as special needs assistance, but such services are quite limited. Homemaker services are available to a very limited number of clients. Chore services would be provided if purchase-of-service provider agencies existed in Utica, but none presently exists. The Adult

Protective Services section does provide aid in money management to public assistance recipients who are unable to manage their resources. A large number of the cases handled by the Adult Protective Services section are recently released patients from mental hospitals.

The shortage of funds in Oneida County, as elsewhere, was reflected in referral patterns. A local survey of requests for aid from public agencies indicated that the largest number of requests were for (1) transportation; (2) health-related services; and (3) housing-locating services. Although transportation was the number one request, the county office provided transportation service to only four persons in 1977–1978. Health-related services were granted to only 12 persons, and services in locating housing were not even included in the county's service plan for that year. The social services office considered that its primary function relating to these service needs was to provide information and referral to programs such as Medicaid and the Older Americans Act program, which actually provide the services.

The data from Wisconsin and the other case studies have shown how difficult it is to assess the importance of Title XX in providing emergency assistance and meeting special needs. It is a huge program when compared with more typical emergency assistance and special needs programs. However, at least on the basis of the case studies, it is doubtful whether much money from this program is spent on emergency assistance or special needs.

Fuel and Winterization Programs

In the span of less than five years the federal financial commitment for fuel assistance to low-income persons has grown from about $242 million to $1.6 billion, and expenditures are expected to increase. In the same number of years the basic character of the federal fuel-related programs has changed as well, from loosely structured "crisis assistance" programs governed by relatively few regulations, to a more structured system providing fuel-cost supplementation and governed by increasingly specific regulations. The primary locus of responsibility for administering fuel programs has changed too, from the Community Services Administration (CSA) to Health and Human Services (HHS).

For the 1979–1980 heating season, Congress appropriated $1.6 billion for three energy-related assistance programs, including $800 million to be distributed to the states in block grants collectively titled the Energy Assistance Payment (EAP) program. The states had several options for the use of the EAP block grants. They could select an HHS-developed plan for making a lump-sum payment in January or February to all recipients of AFDC, or, within broad guidelines, they could opt to submit plans of their own design for distributing the funds.

According to the federal regulations, different plans called for different forms of payments—ranging for direct payments to recipients, to vendor payments, or a vendor line of credit. Income eligibility was set at 125% of the poverty level, except for those households already determined eligible for AFDC, food stamps, or General Assistance. State plans were required to give priority to households experiencing significant increases in fuel costs between 1978 and 1979.

The data from the case studies on the administration of the fuel programs contain themes common to the other emergency assistance and special needs programs—namely, considerable local variation, small amounts of help under varying restrictive conditions, and preferential treatment for the aged poor. But there are also themes special to a new and hastily enacted program—confusion, unevenness, bad timing, and regulations and incentives working at cross-purposes. An obvious problem with the fuel programs thus far is that quite often by the time funds become available, the winter may be half over and clients will have used other resources to pay fuel bills. The continued uncertainty of the federal program has also taken its toll on state and local planning.

Another difficulty, which is not so obvious, has been the tendency to move important administrative powers from local agencies (e.g., Community Action Programs—CAPs) to state agencies either to standardize the programs or, as is more likely the case, capture more federal reimbursement for administrative costs. But the unfortunate result is that this has lessened the power of the local agencies to bargain with utility companies to withhold cutoffs. In the early days of the programs, the local agencies had the ability to guarantee checks to the utility companies within short time periods. Now they are losing this power, and many state agencies thus far have been unable to deliver in a timely and efficient manner, with the result that the companies are less willing to withhold sanctions.

In Boulder, the emergency fuel assistance program, called Crisis Intervention, is administered by the local CAP office. Families with incomes not greater than 125% of the poverty line are eligible, with the elderly targeted as a high priority. Local administrators felt the previous year's (1978–1979) federal regulations were very cumbersome and excluded many of the needy. For instance, clients were required to present a utility shutoff notice as a condition of eligibility. The new regulations do not require presentation of a shutoff notice and allow for more flexible use of funds. The maximum grant has been set at $300 in Colorado. A small weatherization program is administered by the local housing authority, rather than CAP.

To date, New York has no state-funded fuel assistance program, but the state has imaginatively used the federal aid programs to provide as much fuel assistance as possible to as many people as possible. The Emergency Assistance for Families program is virtually a supplementary fuel assistance program serving AFDC recipients, and one of the federal fuel aid programs, Energy Crisis Assistance (ECAP), by state directive, serves eligible nonrecipients. In the past AFDC and SSI recipients received the lion's share of federal fuel aid. The state hoped that by broadening fuel assistance coverage, some individuals could manage to avoid applying for AFDC.

Oneida County received an allocation of $345,000 for ECAP on November 1, 1979. Administrators estimated that at least twice that amount would be necessary to meet the total demand. One-time grants of $300 or less per household were given on a first-come first-served basis, and funds were exhausted long before seasonal requests ceased.

Implementation of the 1979–1980 federal energy aid program was hampered by delays and organizational complications. The old federal aid program was administered entirely by CAP along with its weatherization program and other assistance to low-income persons, but this year responsibility for ECAP was transferred to the Oneida County Department of Social Services, which had to hire and train new personnel to administer the program. The program was further complicated by the state's insistence that eligibility be determined at the state level. This was apparently a strategy to capture federal funds to cover some of the state's general welfare-related administrative cost. CAP staff claim that the cumbersome processing system, while it may save the state money, has resulted in poorer service for clients needing immediate aid. When CAP had control of the program, it had developed a cooperative working relationship over time with the utility companies and small, independent dealers. It was able to negotiate with the companies to ensure continuation of service while fuel aid applications were processed. Now that applications are processed in Albany, payment can no longer be guaranteed by local client advocates. The same problem was reported by CAP agencies in Trenton.

On the other hand, Oneida County officials were pleased that the new federal program provided better coverage. In the past, aid was provided only when an emergency, such as a prolonged cold spell, was declared. In 1979–1980, funds were provided to meet normal winter fuel needs.

CAP in Oneida County administers a winter weatherization program serving low-income persons. In the Utica area the program serves 25 to 30 housing units per month. Ninety percent of weatherization is done for homeowners, on a first-come first-served basis, although the elderly and disabled are given "extra consideration." Clients must usually wait for service, but crews are sent out immediately in emergencies (e.g., to repair broken windows during cold spells).

United Progress, Inc. (UPI), a private, nonprofit agency administering many CAP programs, is the City of Trenton's own CAP agency. As a multi-purpose service agency, UPI has more than a dozen components, including both the federally funded emergency fuel assistance and weatherization programs. Federal funds did not become available until March 1979 and had to be spent by June 1. A total of 2700 families out of 3000 applicants were served in this 3-month period. UPI hoped to have funds for the 1979–1980 winter available by the beginning of October, but it was not until mid-November that Trenton was allocated $202,000.

Within the first three days after UPI received the late 1979 energy aid grant, 1100 applications were accepted, and when 700 of the applicants were ruled eligible, the funds were exhausted. The maximum emergency fuel payment allowed was $400, and although most applicants did not receive the maximum, they were eligible to reapply for aid when need arose, up to the $400. Assistance amounts were primarily determined by the size of the delinquent fuel bills the family owed. Income standards set by the state ranged from $4200 for a single person to $11,000 for a family of six. Senior citizens were given top priority. In fact, while senior citizens constitute only 12% of Trenton's population, from 25% to 30% of the people who received emergency fuel assistance were senior citizens.

UPI also administered the weatherization program for Trenton. This program provides a maximum of $560 per home for supplies only; the labor component is not covered by the program. As with the emergency fuel assistance program, weatherization of homes of the elderly receives priority. Because the income eligibility standard is somewhat lower than that for the fuel assistance program, 95% of weatherization clients are also public assistance recipients.

In Wisconsin, as elsewhere, there was disorganization in the administration of the fuel program prior to the 1979–1980 heating season. In 1979–1980 both CAPs and counties administered the program, but in 1980–1981 the counties assumed more responsibility. One reason for the change, according to state officials, is that CAPs do not necessarily overlap with the welfare population. People have to be aware of the program and come to the agency to apply for aid.

On the other hand, the system the state developed for making Energy

Assistance Payments (EAP) completely misses the nonrecipient population. In Wisconsin, there is an automatic welfare payment system called the Computer Reporting Network (CRN). The computer automatically issues a flat payment check to public assistance recipients, who are categorically eligible for the fuel aid payment. Each recipient family receives a $200 grant. If they heat their homes with fuel oil, they are eligible for an additional $200 "supplement" for which they must apply. Payments are not intended to cover recipients' total energy costs, but rather to offset rising fuel costs. Funds were received on December 28; checks were sent out in January, and by mid-January $20 million in fuel assistance was in the hands of recipients.

In the 1979–1980 year only food stamp and SSI recipients received the automatic payment (most AFDC recipients are also food stamp recipients). There are 60,000 SSI recipients in Wisconsin, and in 1979–1980 only 16,000 applied for the second supplementary payment. In 1980–1981 all SSI recipients received both payments automatically. However, renters, who constitute about 40% of the caseload, received only the first payment of $200.

Recently, state legislators, suspecting that EAP money is not being spent on fuel, have called for two-party checks. If that system is implemented, each check will be made out to both the recipient and the fuel provider so that checks cannot be used for any other purpose. However, SSI recipients will continue to receive one-party checks, because their checks are issued through the federal Social Security Administration office.

In 1980–1981 eligibility for the federal fuel program was expanded. Persons with incomes at or below 125% of the federal poverty level had been eligible; persons with incomes at or below 140% to 175% of the BLS Lower Living Standard became eligible in 1980–1981 (the applicable percentage range depends on family size).

In Wisconsin, as is true with the other case studies, the major complaint with the federal fuel aid programs has been the lack of continuity from year to year. Federal appropriations are voted on each year, and there are different regulations every year, creating planning and hiring difficulties. For instance, administrators originally expected funding for the 1980–1981 program to be extended for three years, but, again, it was cut back to one year.

General Assistance as Emergency Assistance

Twenty-six states listed General Assistance as a program available for emergency assistance and special needs. In addition, 24 counties returned questionnaires reporting General Assistance as the most important emergency assistance and special needs program in their jurisdiction. An additional 19 counties returned questionnaires for local programs that are funded entirely by the county. Although not specifically designated "General Assistance" by the respondents, those programs are probably the functional equivalent—the residual welfare program—and we have classified them with the General Assistance responses. In analyzing these data, as well as the data from the case studies, we will try to determine whether these are emergency assistance and special needs programs for GA recipients, if they fill gaps from the other income maintenance programs, or if they serve both functions.

Federal statistics on General Assistance programs must be treated even more cautiously than data on other programs. There is no federal funding for General Assistance and no federal regulatory authority. Hence state and local incentives to comply with federal requests are weaker than with other programs. Furthermore, record keeping is notoriously lax in social welfare programs, especially at the county and local level. With these caveats in mind, we present in Table 3.3 data for all General Assistance expenditures of the states that have listed General Assistance as available for emergency assistance and special needs, and for which expenditure data are available. If we assume that all GA programs were exclusively emergency programs, total expenditures, on the average per state, seem high—for example, eight times higher than the average amount spent by states on AFDC–EA. On the other hand, a study of General Assistance finds that only seven of twenty studied programs have an emergency component and that the specialized aid represents only 5% of the caseload (Urban Systems Research and Engineering, 1978). In other words, although GA accounts for a considerable amount of money and serves a great many recipients, "average" grant figures may mean very little in determining the adequacy of emergency programs. Perhaps GA only deals with emergency matters in the 26 states so reporting, and only a small part of those programs are consigned for emergencies.

County data on emergency GA programs were collected from 43 locations. As might be expected, GA and the similar county programs are even more restricted to "basics" than other emergency assistance programs. There is virtually no coverage of such items as special services (e.g., chore services), day care, educational expenses, and special winter needs, and there is only minimal coverage of needs related to unborn children, employment needs, and needs for appliances, furniture, or other household items. Grants from these programs are more for the bread-and-butter items; GA and similar programs spend their resources

TABLE 3.3
General Assistance Data, February 1978

States	Number of Cases	Number of Recipients	Payments	Average Payment per Case
Alabama	21	21	$ 262.50	$ 12.50
Alaska	–	–	–	–
Arizona	2,340	2,340	229,425	98.04
Arkansas	–	–	–	–
California	43,857	46,621	5,530,826	126.11
Colorado	399	971	32,083	80.40
Connecticut	–	–	–	–
Delaware	1,419	2,125	79,899	56.30
D.C.	6,114	6,372	984,781	161.06
Florida	–	–	–	–
Georgia	1,536	2,855	93,990	61.19
Hawaii	8,222	15,131	2,157,399	262.39
Idaho	–	–	–	–
Illinois	70,676	84,240	9,662,909	136.72
Indiana	–	–	–	–
Iowa	–	–	–	–
Kansas	5,752	6,153	892,494	155.16
Kentucky	–	–	–	–
Louisiana	2,707	1,790	161,989	59.84
Maine	4,189	11,972	320,470	76.50
Maryland	19,669	20,780	2,207,328	112.22
Massachusetts	20,203	22,099	3,179,498	157.37
Michigan	42,291	56,880	7,645,579	180.79
Minnesota	13,197	15,798	1,859,547	140.90
Mississippi	1,119	1,335	17,454	15.60
Missouri	4,656	5,110	312,986	67.22
Montana	757	1,247	54,582	72.10
Nebraska	–	–	–	–
Nevada	–	–	–	–
New Hampshire	1,897	3,916	231,996	122.29
New Jersey	27,954	37,677	4,252,904	152.14
New Mexico	327	333	31,314	95.76
New York	143,069	184,373	28,199,868	197.11
North Carolina	3,152	7,210	139,917	44.39
North Dakota	101	258	9,307	92.15
Ohio	41,075	47,778	3,809,929	92.76
Oklahoma	512	1,270	15,970	31.19
Oregon	5,069	8,674	617,952	121.91
Pennsylvania	142,172	168,464	23,380,639	164.45
Rhode Island	4,163	7,205	627,068	150.63
South Carolina	1,014	1,098	56,478	55.70
South Dakota	551	1,480	35,668	64.73

(continued)

TABLE 3.3 *(Continued)*

States	Number of Cases	Number of Recipients	Payments	Average Payment per Case
Tennessee	–	–	–	–
Texas	–	–	–	–
Utah	1,658	2,164	289,402	174.55
Vermont	–	–	–	–
Virginia	7,605	11,988	854,994	112.43
Washington	12,446	14,217	1,899,301	152.60
West Virginia	4,308	12,893	215,321	49.98
Wisconsin	5,442	7,810	655,023	120.36
Wyoming	372	685	30,109	80.29

Source: *Public Assistance Recipients and Cash Payments by State and County* (Washington, D.C.: U.S. Department of Health, Education, and Welfare, 1979), "Statistical Report on Numbers of Recipients and Amounts of Money under GA, by County, February 1978."

Note: Dashes indicate that no data are available.

primarily for needs caused by food shortages, utility bills, basic needs pending application to other programs, and special diets, laundry services, and medical expenses. General Assistance also provides some coverage for temporary shelter and to aid victims of natural disasters.

As we found with the other emergency assistance and special needs programs, the certification procedure for these programs is less strict than for AFDC. Two-thirds of the 43 county respondents reported that emergency assistance requires less strict verification procedures and the approval of fewer supervisors than AFDC. On the other hand, these are programs of "last resort." More than three-quarters of the General Assistance administrators insist that applicants first go to other income maintenance programs (i.e., AFDC, SSI, Unemployment Insurance, or Social Security); half require an application for Food Stamps, and about a third require applicants to go to private charity first. As a result, little aid is given to recipients of other programs. For example, only about 10% of these recipients are reported to be on AFDC, and less than 20% are reported on Food Stamps.

For those receiving General Assistance, there are various restrictive conditions. All of the counties have rules requiring higher-level supervisory approval for requests above certain dollar amounts (a mean of $118.40 and a median of $140.00), or repeat requests, or certain types of requests, or other conditions.

There seem to be somewhat fewer rules in GA and the similar local programs than in AFDC–EA specifying the *amount* of aid that an eligible family can receive. AFDC–EA is fairly flexible—most emergencies are handled as needed—and GA is more so. On the other hand, most aid is given in voucher or vendor payments (73% of total grants), rather than cash, a characteristic shared with other programs for emergency assistance and special needs. These programs also have more conditions on their grants than AFDC–EA. For example, more than 20% of their cases have a work requirement as compared to less than 10% of AFDC–EA cases. Twenty-five percent of their cases are required to sign repayment agreements, as compared to only 2% of AFDC–EA cases. And twice as many of their grantees (about 35%) repay their loans in whole or in part as compared to AFDC–EA grantees.

The General Assistance program in Hennepin County, Minnesota, currently represents the most liberal and comprehensive program among the case studies, and the only one thus far that has been able to withstand restrictive pressures. In part, this is due to the liberal traditions in Minnesota and in part because the recession has not been as severe in this county as elsewhere.

Minnesota's GA program has an emergency component called Emergency–General Assistance (E–GA), but GA as a whole may be seen as a crisis program, at least in Hennepin County, since 98% of the applicants receive a GA check and food stamps on the day of application. Hennepin County's unique intake system for GA has the effect of minimizing the income maintenance caseload and maximizing the one-time-only, immediate-aid caseload. The GA office has developed a two-step eligibility certification process. First, new applicants are given immediate aid based on presumed eligibility, and second, appointments are made for a second, formal eligibility review, to take place from four to twenty days later. Applicants are asked to bring required documentation to the second appointment. The amount of the immediate grant depends on the length of time until the second appointment—if the second appointment is within 5 days, the grant is $20 plus food stamps; if it is twenty days later the grant is $100 plus food stamps. Clients are allowed to repeat the presumptive-eligibility procedure twice and receive prorated grants before being declared ineligible for further aid. About 40% of presumptively eligible recipients do not return for formal certification and ongoing aid.

Emergency–GA and presumptive eligibility grants are not the same thing; although both are emergency assistance, all new GA applicants receive immediate aid based on presumed eligibility; ongoing GA recipients faced with emergencies are eligible for E–GA. The most common emergencies covered are "threatened eviction, utility crises, stranded transients, and paying actual cost beyond the standard."

E–GA also includes partially state-funded special needs items equivalent to those provided in the AFDC program, such as repair or replacement of essential household goods. Major home repairs are not funded by the state, but are provided from county funds.

Since 1974, Minnesota GA programs are funded on a 50/50 funding match (state and county) but actual state appropriations are "sum certain" (that is, a maximum appropriation is set and determined according to past expenditures). When caseloads are high, therefore, the counties end up paying more than 50% of the costs. Minneapolis caseloads shot up in 1974, when the recession hit, to about 7000, and funding restrictions forced staffing cuts, causing long lines and delays. These shortages resulted in administrative policies considered more restrictive than those currently in operation. In any event, problems quickly subsided when the economy improved. When the interviews were conducted in 1979, the GA caseload in Minneapolis was about 4000.

A generally pro-recipient spirit reigns in this agency, an attitude which reflects the general tone established by the state. Much of the GA manual is concerned with protecting clients' rights. A state-employed full-time client advocate assists clients and guards against any possible punitive agency actions. The GA director recognized that some clients abuse the agency's good faith, but felt such abuse was within tolerable limits, or at least it was not a problem which concerned him.

The families who receive GA are either those who do not qualify for AFDC, or AFDC recipients who have exhausted their once-a-year AFDC–EA grant and need emergency assistance. AFDC families are specifically excluded from GA coverage by state rules, but assistance is still provided from GA funds when no other resource can be tapped. There is some uneasiness about this use of GA funds, partly from a belief that GA for AFDC recipients constitutes duplication of payments.

General Assistance is seen as a program of "last resort," and concerted efforts are made to tap other community resources. Thus, workers attempt to determine eligibility for CAP fuel assistance funds or any other federally funded program. They negotiate payment arrangements with utility companies and intervene with clients' landlords to forestall evictions. Nevertheless, only 5–8% of applicants are denied assistance, a substantially lower denial rate than for any other county studied.

Despite the liberal orientation, controls are exercised. One eligibility technician said she considered questions such as, How did they get there? What was done to prevent it? and What will their resources be? in evaluating emergency situations. The degree of client voluntarism in creating the emergency situation definitely affects her decisions. Written rules are not helpful, as "each case is considered on an individual basis." Supervisors are consulted frequently, and the amount of money involved determines how far up the chain of command decisions are taken.

About 40% of cases received vendor payments, most on a voluntary basis. The law provides for compulsory vendor payments only if evidence of misuse exists, but Hennepin County developed a voluntary vendoring system that received state approval. In the words of the agency director, "It is especially used for halfway house cases. If the client signs the form, we vendor the check. They permit us, [but] somebody could challenge us." To date there has been no legal challenge. Compulsory vendor payments are used frequently as well. "We've got a lot who do [misuse payments]; they don't pay their bills; these people have problems or they wouldn't be here." The vendor system helps clients obtain housing, the director believes, because landlords are assured of rent. "If they stop to get a six-pack on the way home, they don't have enough money for rent."

In contrast to Hennepin County, the GA program in Boulder and San Diego counties are under stress and show what has happened to formerly liberal programs in the current recession.

In Boulder, General Assistance is the major emergency assistance program, primarily serving recipients of other public assistance programs. It is administered along with other income maintenance programs by the county department of social services. GA is 100% county-funded, with state reimbursement for medical and transportation expenses, and is used exclusively for emergency assistance. In 1978 the average monthly caseload was about 420, and grant expenditures totaled $207,238.

Intake and certification functions for GA, as well as for the other income maintenance programs, are not specialized; they are performed by both the eligibility technicians and supervisors. Eligibility for emergency assistance through the GA program requires verification of income and assets, as well as a verified emergency. Clients are also required to apply for federal and state programs (Food Stamps, AFDC, SSI, Unemployment Insurance, the state supplement to SSI, and private aid where applicable). However, as noted in other jurisdictions, certification for GA tends to be less strict than for the basic income maintenance programs. Higher-level approval is required when the amount of aid exceeds a standard amount for a given family size, and when the request is for a rental deposit or transportation. In the last three years GA has been expanded to include people not otherwise eligible, if there is a need for "protective services" (i.e., cases of domestic violence).

One of the major functions of GA in Boulder is to cover medical and medical-related expenses, since Colorado has a poorly funded and restrictive Medicaid program. The items most frequently covered by GA are emergency burial, special diets, laundry, eye and dental care, drugs, medical transportation, and other medical expenses. Less frequently covered by GA are lost checks, temporary shelter, security deposits, utility bills, food, clothing, needs related to unborn children, employment needs such as work clothes, and shelter repair.

Workers are directed to make GA decisions based on the type of emergency rather than the type of client. Because GA is only an emergency program, having no ongoing caseload, and single adults (unless aged or disabled) are ineligible, almost all GA cases are recipients of other forms of public assistance. Sixty percent of GA cases are on AFDC, 20% on SSI, 5% on AFDC–UP, 4% on old age payments (a local program). Nonrecipients make up only 10% of the cases, and migrants, 1%. Almost all aid is in the form of vouchers or vendor payments. Ten percent of GA recipients are required to sign a repayment agreement, and 20–30% of these repay. For some covered emergencies, there are specified fixed amounts. For others, the amount of aid is determined as needed, which allows for a fair amount of worker discretion.

Discretion, and the resulting inequities, are issues of genuine concern for Boulder administrators. They are aware that the "squeaky wheel gets the oil." Partly as a result of this concern, in 1979 the county was rewriting its entire GA policy to keep better track of how GA funds are expended and to reduce inequity.

Some groups of needy persons are underserved by the GA program, in part because no outreach efforts are made, in part because some are specifically excluded from program coverage. And there are individuals who are unwilling to apply, out of pride. Most probably, officials believe, the elderly and the handicapped are in this group.

Those already on public assistance are more likely to become aware of GA through their caseworker or through word of mouth among other recipients and their acquaintances. A nonrecipient family, especially in a rural area, is less likely to have information or access. The one specifically ineligible group, even at private agencies, is the "employable single adult," which in Boulder seemed to be a code phrase for transient. The public agency's policy not to serve this group reflects community pressure, and administrators were not always comfortable carrying out the policy.

Consistent with the idea that there exists a core of recipients who are especially knowledgeable about GA, repeat requests for GA are high. Between 35 and 50% of requests are from clients who made a previous request the same year. An attempt in the past to exclude repeaters led to so many complaints that this policy was soon dropped. The outcome of a repeat request now depends on the particular worker's discretion.

Almost all GA is in the form of vouchers or vendor payments. Landlords, motel managers, food store owners, or other providers are often unwilling to accept vouchers because it takes two to four weeks for the welfare office to redeem them. Although the public utilities have accepted this system, it has been hard to find providers of other services who will accept it.

In San Diego County there are two programs of General Assistance, one for non-AFDC cases and one to supplement AFDC. The 100% county-funded General Relief (GR) program is for those not eligible for AFDC. Benefit levels for the basic (nonemergency) program are well below these of other major programs and a 30-day residence requirement must be met. The basic grant for an individual is $120 per month. "Interim assistance" is often provided from GR monies to cover SSI applicants for one month, while they are awaiting SSI benefits. Employable recipients may not receive more than one month's assistance without reapplication, but unemployable persons can continue as ongoing cases for extended periods.

General Relief does administer a small emergency loan program, available only to SSI recipients with not more than $50 in liquid assets. About one-sixth of the money is eventually repaid.

Until severe budget cuts this year, the major emergency assistance program for AFDC recipients in San Diego County was County Supplemental Assistance (CSA). Generally, AFDC–Special Needs funds were tapped first to meet AFDC emergency or special needs, but CSA was used as an extensive secondary source. CSA coverage tended to supplement rather than match coverage under Special Needs. CSA had been a liberal program, in the range of needs covered (for example, transportation, child care, household items, shelter, and security deposits) as well as in the size of the grants. Appropriations varied from year to year but were generally about $100,000. In 1977, they rose to $200,000. However, as a result of Proposition 13 (passed on June 6, 1978), this program was cut drastically. In 1980 the county board allocated an initial $5000 and then another $5000 when that money ran out, after about a month. No more was forthcoming for the year. Furthermore, these monies must be divided among 16 to 19 local district offices. In one office, the CSA appropriation for 1980 was $250. As a result, all grants are now limited to a few dollars. The maximum grant has been cut from $300 to $50. CSA funds are limited to AFDC (80%) and AFDC–UP recipients (20%).

In short, as the result of Proposition 13, CSA was suddenly transformed from a liberal, highly discretionary program into a very minimal, conservative program. Now all emergency requests from this fund must be justified in terms of need of the family. Previously, decisions regarding eligibility and benefits had been made by line workers with approval of the supervisor in the local office. Monies are divided among the local district offices and every office rations in its own way—dividing the funds up by weeks or months.

CSA is administered by social service workers, not eligibility technicians. The CSA cutbacks have also had an indirect negative effect on utilization of social services. In the past, applicants who were referred to the social service offices for CSA were offered social services as well. With no emergency funds available, fewer cases are referred to the services side, and without referrals services cannot be offered.

The AFDC–Special Needs program has not been able to pick up needs formerly covered by CSA, partly because CSA was designed to cover items not covered under the AFDC program. As we have noted (see Chapter 2) Special Needs is itself a very restrictive and conservative program. Recurring special needs are limited to $10 a month per person in San Diego County.

The cutbacks described above have had a substantial effect on clients and private agencies. Families undergoing an emergency find it more difficult to stay intact. For instance, if a family is evicted for failure to pay rent, CSA no longer provides any backup. Consequently, children are taken out of otherwise suitable homes and placed in foster homes when an eviction or lack of funds threatens the family. (Cutbacks in funding for temporary Respite Care for Children has also resulted in more placements in foster homes.) CSA was also a major way to forestall utility cutoffs. Cutoffs may result in families living without utilities.

Boulder and San Diego represent formerly rather liberal GA programs that attempted to fill the emergency assistance needs and the special needs of recipients of other income maintenance programs, and which are now devastated by cutbacks in public funds. Beaumont, Texas, on the other hand, is the opposite case—a program designed from the beginning to do the absolute bare minimum.

The State of Texas has never allocated funds for any county-administered General Assistance programs. The result is a wide range in the availability, size, and type of county welfare programs in Texas. The 15 counties near the city of Beaumont have very different programs aimed at different populations and different needs; in at least three counties, there are no GA programs at all. Jefferson County, which contains Beaumont, has a medium-sized county GA program in comparison with other counties in the region, but it is very restricted, designed to fill the medical assistance gap left when, in 1967, the single hospital in Jefferson County terminated services to indigent and low-income people. Medical aid is still the primary concern of the county welfare department, although other forms of aid are given to people with medical problems.

The primary, and only inflexible, eligibility criterion is that all clients must have a medical disability which renders them unemployable for at least a calendar week. Clients applying for assistance must furnish a statement from their doctor supporting their claim of medical disability, or submit to an examination by one of the staff doctors or nurses at the county welfare offices. After eligibility is determined, there are also income eligibility standards, which are somewhat stricter than the income standards for other forms of assistance. There is also a vaguely worded residency requirement. The net result is that almost anyone, including transients, who can prove a medical need, can receive some medical services, but not necessarily anything else.

What medical services are provided? A county-run clinic—staffed by doctors from the nearest hospital which has services for indigent persons—provides obstetrical and gynecological care, eye care, X-ray and lab service, and prescriptions. Medical transportation is also provided by the county.

The financial basic needs unit of the county department of health and social services provides supplementary services to clients with medical problems. The initial application for aid is fairly long, and verification procedures are strictly spelled out and followed. If a client satisfies the medical and income eligibility standards, the client can also be considered eligible for basic needs assistance. Basic need items are considered to be primarily shelter and utilities, though sometimes clothing and food are covered, if the person is ineligible for food stamps (a rare situation). There are strict guidelines regarding maximum amounts for each item: for example, rent for 1 or 2 people is $60 per month; for 3 or 4 people $85. Delinquent rent or utility bills cannot be paid, and current bills are always paid through vendor payments. Food orders are occasionally given to people who have to wait for food stamps, and nonfood vouchers are sometimes issued for miscellaneous items. The only cash given directly to a client is gas money to drive to the hospital, and a social worker always verifies whether the money was spent on gas. The county provides 100% of the funding, except for the services of the staff doctors from the hospital.

Most clients are middle-aged (younger persons are less likely to have medical problems), and a majority are black. A large number are single, unemployable males who do not qualify for other forms of aid. Very few are elderly. New applicants for other forms of public welfare who are awaiting their first benefit check can also qualify for aid, if medical need exists.

Both the director and a social worker emphasize that county welfare was originally, and still is, intended as a program of last resort; they therefore view almost all of their work as emergency assistance. Aid is designed to be temporary; rarely will a case remain open longer than a month, though a client may reapply frequently. The program is not meant to maintain an ongoing or active caseload.

The amount of aid given is not a discretionary decision in that it never exceeds the maximum standards (which are meant to apply for a monthly period). However, in certain situations, the social worker may confer with the supervisor about stretching the rules; this usually involves giving basic needs assistance to clients who aren't strictly eligible, and such cases almost always involve clients with children or single clients with particularly acute medical problems. County government does not monitor the staff members' decisions, as long as the programs stay within budget.

Any expansion or redefinition of the state and county public welfare programs in Beaumont and throughout Jefferson County seems unlikely; if anything, cutbacks in these already limited sources of aid appear more likely.

Local Programs for the Elderly

In the case studies, the other major area of emergency assistance specialization on the local level was for the elderly. In all of the case studies, there was some program for the elderly. Beaumont, Texas, is the polar case of a minimal public emergency assistance or special needs program, but it does provide four state-authorized services for the SSI population through the federal Title XX program—homemaker service, chore service, day care, and foster care. These services are administered at the county level through the protective services unit, and are supported by a 75% federal contribution.

In the other areas studied, there was a more complete range of programs available to the SSI population. California, as noted, is one of the states with a large and varied supplementation program for SSI, and a variety of special allowances and emergency programs are available. The size of the supplement varies with category (aged, blind, or disabled) and living arrangements—for example, there is a $33 "restaurant allowance" for those without cooking facilities. The SSI–Special Needs program is called Special Circumstances Payment (SCP) and provides a one-time allowance for unusual needs. Needs covered are (1) replacement of furniture, clothing, and similar items lost in a catastrophe; (2) housing repairs necessary for health and safety; (3) emergency moving expenses; and (4) food for guide dogs for blind recipients. There is also a small state program for blind people who are ineligible for SSI solely because of the value of their homes.

In Oneida County (Utica), New York, an Emergency Assistance to Adults (EAA) program is available to SSI recipients only. It closely follows the AFDC–EA pattern. For example, requests are limited to one in a 12-month period. However, in contrast to AFDC–EA, this program covers many typical emergency situations for SSI recipients that are not now covered for AFDC families. The most commonly occurring emergencies are for replacing appliances, furniture, and clothing. Next are needs arising out of lost, stolen, or delayed checks, and the need for temporary shelter. Minor amounts are spent for needs arising out of natural disasters, unpaid utility bills, and special services such as chore services. Eighty-five percent of the payments are vendored or vouchered. SSI recipients constitute about 25% of the entire emergency assistance caseload in the county.

Whereas emergency assistance requests require the approval of immediate supervisors, payments of more than $100 and second payments within the 12-month period require higher-level approval. Other than clothing replacement and food, where the maximums allowed are $84 and $21.70, there are no maximums on other requests. The average EAA payment falls between $100 and $150. Larger payments can be made to cover utility bills, moving expenses, back rent, and to replace major appliances.

The county also has an emergency loan program for pending SSI applicants. The federally administered $100 emergency advance payment is rarely used because the county loan system works more efficiently. Under the county system, the applicant signs an agreement to repay the loan from future SSI checks. If the applicant turns out to be ineligible, he does not have to repay the emergency advance. The county will also make loans to cover lost, stolen, or delayed checks. Clients who do not repay the loans immediately must agree to "direct deposit of income" arrangements (usually the agency deducts a percentage from the SSI check).

Mercer County (Trenton), New Jersey, does not have a special needs component of the SSI program, but the SSI population is eligible for an emergency assistance program similar to the basic AFDC–EA program. The adult services unit, which handles the SSI cases, limits eligibility according to the same restrictions covering AFDC–EA families, namely, emergency needs caused by "homelessness," but Title XX services specifically for the SSI population, such as homemaker services and emergency nursing-home placement, are also available from this unit.

Colorado has no statewide emergency assistance or special needs programs, but in Boulder County provisions are made for the SSI population through Title XX services and a state supplement to SSI handled by the department of social services. All SSI recipients are eligible for the state supplement if they meet a means test. The supplement varies by category; this state supplementary program also provides for some special needs: $73 for "essential spouse" (the spouse must be home to care for the client) and $217 for "home care" allowance.

THE HODGEPODGE OF STATE AND COUNTY PROGRAMS

At state level, one sees great variability and unevenness in coverage of emergency assistance and special needs. Almost every state has something, but that is the only generalization that can be made. There is no uniformity among the states or even within the states. The largest and most commonly adopted program, AFDC–EA, has been adopted in less than half of the states. In all of the cases, even at the state level, there are bits and pieces of programs—state emergency, SSI–Special Needs, Expedited Food Stamps, Title XX, and so forth.

Not only is there lack of uniformity as to type of programs, but there is also diversity and uneven coverage within programs. They are characterized by large amounts of discretion and uneven administration. Some programs, such as federal fuel assistance, seem to be administered in a fairly uniform, first-come first-served basis, but most appear to have been quite variable, at least as far as data permit such inferences. Moreover, with the exception of the federal fuel program, there is no indication of any general trend towards uniformity or comprehensiveness. Indeed, the trends would indicate the opposite. The Supreme Court decision in *Mandley* v. *Quern*[7] allows the states even more flexibility in administering AFDC–EA, which was the only program that contained the possibility of consistency. Furthermore, cutbacks in state and local funds have taken a toll on state and local

[7]436 U.S. 725 (1978).

programs, leading to further restrictions. At the state level at least, there has been no significant effort to cover the needs left uncovered by adoption of the consolidated grant in income maintenance programs.

Despite the paucity of our information, we think it unlikely that General Assistance plays a large role in covering emergency assistance and special needs at the local level. Available evidence indicates that of all the publicly financed programs, this one is most uneven and variable. As the Wisconsin state study points out, the program does not even exist in many small jurisdictions. In those areas where it functions, one cannot generalize about its characteristics. Although the Hennepin County (Minneapolis), Minnesota, program is comprehensive and liberally administered, within the limits of General Assistance, the officials there thought that the cash grants were by no means adequate for the recipients. Still, in comparison with what we found elsewhere, the Hennepin County officials did the best they could with their resources. The program was designed to assist those not receiving other public assistance, though it was sometimes stretched to cover AFDC families in trouble.

The programs in Boulder and San Diego represented different functions for GA—in these counties, the programs were available specifically to fill the gaps of the income maintenance system. Most of the GA recipients in these two counties were AFDC families. Prior to the economic recession (and Proposition 13 in California), these were fairly liberal programs, again by GA standards, though more restrictive than AFDC, in that more grants were vendored and vouchered, there were more regulations, and groups such as transients and single adults were excluded for moralistic reasons. Recently these programs have been gutted, and are so small (particularly in San Diego), that they barely serve as bandaids.

It is our guess that until there is a significant turnaround in the economic health of the states, most General Assistance programs will rapidly shrink to the Boulder, if not the San Diego, size. Within the states and counties that listed General Assistance as an available emergency assistance and special needs program, the programs were specialized and restrictive, and grants were small. There are no federal funds for these programs, and the recipients of GA historically have been the most politically impotent of all of the poor. There will probably continue to be funding for dire emergencies that are highly visible, such as the health needs in Beaumont, or emergency fuel. The public would demand coverage to prevent women dying in childbirth and people freezing to death. Such circumstances do not raise too many moral objections.

Although there are meager resources for emergencies and special needs, the picture is brighter for some of the elderly poor. We noted in Chapter 2 that SSI–Special Needs was a liberal program (compared to the other emergency assistance and special needs programs) but was adopted by only 10 states. At the local level, however, we see what seems to be a determined effort to help the elderly poor. Even in the more conservative counties, such as Jefferson County (Beaumont) and Oneida County, the emergency assistance and special needs programs for the elderly stand in sharp contrast to what is available for the rest of the poor. Trenton, which has a very restrictive program, still manages to provide additional aids for the elderly. It would therefore appear that moral judgments are at work in determining who does and who does not have access to emergency assistance and special needs programs. This is no more clearly brought out than in how the elderly fare as compared to the others.

CHAPTER 4

The Influence of State Public Welfare Policies on Specialized Programs

CONFLICTING COMMITMENTS AND PRESSURES

The nature of emergency and special needs programs—specialized programs—seems to reflect conflicts over basic commitments in public welfare. The previous chapter notes that national policy and state and local beliefs favor a standardized approach and that specialized programs, by forcing the welfare system to adopt some individualization, may threaten to undermine recent standardizing reforms. Emergency and special needs programs are also problematic due to concern over the error and fraud that might occur within them. On the other hand, officials seem aware that the low level of benefits in the grant programs results in the need for additional assistance, and that, in any case, there always are individual needs. States and counties have thus set up some programs to meet serious needs, even though the other sets of concerns guarantee that programs are small and scattered.

This is the general picture. However, there are some variations among the programs: For example, the AFDC–EA program in Minnesota is many times the size of the program in other states, and the number of specialized efforts in this state doubles that found elsewhere. Why is this so? Most programs are adopted at the discretion of states. If our belief that emergency and special needs programs are an important indicator of the balance between standardization and individualization is correct, then differences in programs should reflect the various reactions of states to the national pressures to reexamine the balance. The specific policy commitments (goals), community pressures, and existing welfare system in each state should determine the balance between standardized benefits and meeting individual needs with an emergency assistance or special needs program. Thus an analysis of state differences helps further specify how the various pressures operate, while it indirectly indicates whether the factors we have stressed are indeed important.

Chapter 1 mentioned two principles that might account for variations in the implementation of the emergency assistance and special needs programs: consistency and compensation. The principle of consistency is based upon traditional social science concepts (Selznick, 1949; Zald, 1970). According to this principle, the response of any organization to a new input tends to reflect preexisting patterns of action. Thus states that are accustomed to programs much like emergency assistance and special needs, or that have long-standing beliefs that are consistent with the philosophy and operation of the programs, will make greater efforts to maintain these programs.

This perspective leads to specific hypotheses. One can argue, for example, that those states which are most liberal in providing basic welfare benefits will also be more willing to provide emergency aid. If this is the case, states with a higher basic grant, a higher standard of need (that is, the standard that states set as representing an adequate income is high) and a more complete willingness to meet the standard of need will have larger emergency programs. Further, states pay a varying percentage of AFDC grant costs, with the federal government providing a larger match for states with lower per capita incomes. It can also be argued that a state with a lower federal match, demonstrating greater wealth and thus an ability—and perhaps willingness—to support emergency programs, will have a larger emergency effort.

The principle of consistency also suggests hypotheses about basic goals. It is clear that the move to a flat grant is prevalent. Most AFDC grants are now flat, or at least have a reduced number of individualized items. Other major programs, such as SSI and Food Stamps, also allow relatively limited individualization. The consistency prediction is that the movement to a flat grant symbolizes a new set of administrative goals that are not conducive to the development of emergency programs. The standardized grant is meant to increase horizontal equity by ensuring that individuals with similar incomes and family arrangements receive similar entitlements. It also helps to reduce administrative errors and to increase the ability of the administrators to control costs and local eligibility decisions. If policymakers and administrators support the ideologies inherent in the movement to the flat grant, they may attempt to limit emergency assistance. Emergency programs threaten to reintroduce an element of horizontal inequity by providing special aid to some, but not all, families. These programs also necessitate some discretionary decision-making that seems to increase error and decrease state control. The trend toward the flat grant thus may both increase the need for specialized programs and reduce the desire to provide them.

Despite the trend toward the flat grant, states remain committed to other approaches that may also influence decisions made about emergency assistance. Some states retain an element of the more traditional, individualized approach. For example, in some states counseling interviews are required of all applicants, in order to assess what social services are needed and make individualized plans. Some states are also more prone than others to discourage applications for public assistance. Each of these approaches, if part of a general set of welfare goals, could affect the provision of emergency assistance. An individualized approach may be consistent with emergency assistance and special needs programs which match grants to special conditions. A restrictive orientation toward basic grants may be consistent with limiting emergency assistance and special needs programs, in the belief that many clients are undeserving and that benefits should be few.

The principle of compensation, which contrasts with consistency, is not as strongly based on social theory; instead it is specific to the welfare system at present. It suggests that states are aware of the limits in the welfare systems as a whole, and use the specialized programs to make up for specific problems—in other words, to fill gaps. If any social theory is relevant at all, it is the perspective that, within a given culture, institutions tend to adopt behaviors that mitigate the most severe problems brought about by other social choices.

Compensation proponents would hypothesize that states with lower basic grants will utilize emergency assistance more often, in order to provide some aid to those very needy individuals who do not receive adequate monthly benefits. If this is the case, states with more unmet needs will have large emergency programs. Accordingly, higher emergency payments will be a consequence of a lower basic grant, a lower standard of need, and a failure to meet the standard in the monthly payments. States with a higher federal match, having lower average incomes and thus fewer resources, may also have larger programs.

A further hypothesis based on compensation is that the move to a flat grant encourages emergency assistance. No matter how generous they are, flat grant programs cannot by themselves meet emergency needs.

Individuals may have particular medical problems or other special needs not covered in the basic grant, and sudden expenses that cannot be financed out of the standard appropriation may arise periodically. Perhaps states use emergency programs as a means of compensating for these difficulties by providing some support that can be geared to individual circumstances.

The compensation point of view may also apply to basic welfare commitments as measured by goals. For example, the trend toward equity, standardization, and error control results in a grant with very little discretion. If states desire to compensate for this trend they may adopt large programs to cover emergency assistance or special needs. A restrictive orientation implies low basic grants, and a state that attempts to compensate for low grants may adopt specialized programs. On the other hand, states with a firm commitment to individualization may find a specialized program an unneeded luxury.

Community pressures are also likely to affect emergency assistance programs in contradictory ways (although the predictions are not precisely based on the two theories; instead they appear to involve only consistency). In the face of emergency needs, it seems likely that welfare advocacy groups and other civic groups will attempt to lobby to increase assistance. But the programs cost money, and concerns over cost should be expected to have the opposite effect. Somewhat distinct from monetary policy are perceptions of program error, fraud, and abuse. A high concern over these issues may reduce the emergency effort, because emergency programs are highly discretionary and may be perceived as particularly prone to these problems.

SORTING OUT THE INFLUENCES: MEASURES OF WELFARE COMMITMENTS

Which of these many themes seem to operate? An empirical analysis can provide some answers. Thus, three factors are said to influence the provision of special aid; the nature of the AFDC system, goals of state welfare systems, and community pressures. Variables can be developed to measure these factors, and to measure aspects of the emergency assistance effort to which they may be correlated.

The Nature of AFDC

As mentioned in the introductory section, the AFDC program is often most closely linked to emergency assistance and special needs aid. Four measures of the AFDC grant collected from 1979 figures seem relevant in indicating welfare system characteristics that might be related to emergency and special needs programs: the grant size for a family of four, the state standard of need, the percentage of that standard that is met by the grant, and the percentage of the AFDC grant that is paid by the federal government (the federal match). The first two items measure state generosity. The third may be a measure of unmet needs. The last, as has been mentioned, can represent the ability a state has to adopt a program. It may also be a measure of state incentive: States with a high match on AFDC may be less likely to use emergency and special needs programs, for which they receive less in the way of matching funds.

The Goals of the Welfare System

The goals of the welfare system that will be correlated to the specialized efforts have already been described in general. But correlating each to the nature of the specialized systems is cumbersome. Accordingly, we developed indices. These are calculated by taking the average score of some goals (as reported by welfare executives) that were highly related. Both logic and correlations between goal items were used to make the choices.

One index measures the current emphasis placed on treating clients equally and efficiently—the central organizational attributes designed to achieve equity and standardization. This index averages five current goals: meeting basic financial needs, making sure clients are treated equally, keeping application forms and procedures simple, verifying needs and resources, and increasing efficiency and controlling costs. We call this index "current equity and standardization index."

The second and third indices measure internal and external maintenance, respectively. In these cases, the measures rely on desired goals, under the assumption that desired, and not actual, maintenance will affect the decisions of program administrators. Internal maintenance includes obtaining comfortable working conditions, obtaining high staff salaries, keeping staff turnover low, and keeping channels of communication open. External maintenance includes maintaining ties with outside groups, making sure the public is informed about public welfare, and lobbying actively for legislation.

The five goals representing traditional orientations did not correlate with each other highly, and are analyzed separately. These include restricting aid to those who need it most, being sensitive to the unique circumstances of clients, avoiding welfare dependency, encouraging applicants to use private resources, and providing workers with flexibility to make decisions about cases that do not quite fit the rules.

Community Pressures

Two indices take the mean of community attitudes, as measured by the executives' perceptions. One averages all scores on the desired size of the specialized assistance program. The second averages concern over error and fraud in emergency assistance and special needs aid. But because groups differ in their desires concerning specialized programs, measures of influence were divided into smaller combinations. One index—influence of political groups—averages the influence of groups with some political control over welfare policy: the governor and staff, the state legislature, the state budget office, and the welfare advisory board. A second index—influence of interest groups—includes groups with a vested interest in client services: welfare rights and advocacy groups, private charitable agencies, individual clients, and other state service agencies. The influence of the press and general public were combined in another index—influence of public groups. The last index averages the influence of the central and regional offices of HEW (now HHS).

The influence of two groups—state welfare officials and county welfare officials—seemed distinct enough to keep as separate variables. Both types of officials directly affect welfare programs, and their desires would seem to merit special attention in the analysis.

Measures of Specialized Assistance

The correlation of the measures of welfare characteristics with measures of the specialized assistance effort helps determine how welfare policy commitments relate to specific emergency and special needs programs. But one overall measure of the emergency and special needs effort cannot be developed; we simply do not have enough data on costs for all such programs, because states seldom responded to our request for these data. Less complete measures are necessary, and some important decisions must be made in order to develop them. For example, one possible measure of emergency assistance and special needs aid is the number of these programs a state has. But the number and size of programs may not be related to each other, so it is also necessary to look at costs and caseloads. Another choice occurs because such statistics must be compared to some base in order to avoid the dominance of the larger states, and the choice of a base is significant. Comparing program size to the poverty population places the specialized effort in the context of possible need, but it ignores the fact that many programs deal primarily with current recipients of income maintenance grants. Yet comparing the size of specialized programs to the size of the current welfare effort may provide higher scores for states that are less generous, in general, since these states have smaller AFDC programs.

In order to maximize information, we decided to rely on multiple measures that have somewhat different implications. These measures include the following:

1. The number of emergency and special needs programs, as reported by the executive. This measure provided some idea of the range of programs each state provides.
2. The caseload of the AFDC–EA program compared to the number of poor people in a state. This measure involves one of the most important cash programs, AFDC–EA. It compares the caseload to the poverty population in order to place the emergency assistance effort in some relation to need.
3. AFDC–EA costs compared to AFDC costs. This measure is meant to compare the emergency assistance effort to the most relevant basic grant program. It attempts to compare the emergency program to the population most likely to make use of it.

The second and third measures together attempt to get at the size of emergency assistance efforts. They involve only AFDC–EA. This is the only program within our definition of emergency assistance for which complete national data exist. Admittedly, other programs may have different correlates, and only about half of the states use AFDC–EA; yet the AFDC–EA program is a reasonable focus, because it is often the largest cash emergency effort in a state.

THE RELATIONSHIP BETWEEN CHARACTERISTICS OF THE AFDC SYSTEM AND SPECIALIZED ASSISTANCE

In order to help determine the relation between specialized assistance efforts and characteristics of the basic grant program, Table 4.1 reports correlations between measures of these two types of assistance. Because our data involve a population, not a sample, statistical significance is not entirely an appropriate concept. Therefore, the text generally refers to relations above .20 as worthy of discussion, regardless of statistical significance. Nevertheless, for those who desire to use statistical measures as a guide, they are provided in the table.

TABLE 4.1
Correlation between AFDC Characteristics and Specialized Assistance

	Size of AFDC Grant (Family of 4)	Size of AFDC Standard of Need (Family of 4)	Percentage of Need Standard Met by AFDC Grant	Federal Match for AFDC Grant
Number of programs for emergencies and special needs in a state (45 states)	.47**	.57**	.41**	−.50**
AFDC–EA caseload compared to the poverty population (22 states)	.35*	.22	−.17	−.26
AFDC–EA costs compared to AFDC costs (22 states)	−.14	−.35*	−.47*	.55**

*$p < .05$
**$p < .01$

As the table indicates, there are a number of large correlations involving the first index, the number of programs. States with larger numbers of specialized assistance programs tend to have higher AFDC grants, higher standards of need, and a larger percentage of that standard met. The number of specialized programs is higher when the federal match is lower.

In general, the relations seem to support the argument for consistency between general policy commitments and the nature of the emergency and special needs effort. Thus, the results imply that there are more programs in those states which have more generous attitudes toward public assistance, as measured by the grant size, standard of need, and percentage of the standard met. Apparently states that are more generous in general also tend to provide more specialized programs.

The fact that the federal match is lower in states with more programs may also be explained by the consistency principle. Perhaps states with a lower match, having (by definition) a higher average income, can more easily afford specialized programs. Or perhaps the lower match reduces the cost of providing specialized assistance relative to the cost of increasing the size of the basic grant. (In states with a higher match for AFDC, the federal emergency program might seem a poor deal compared to expanding the basic program, because AFDC–EA matches state funds with federal funds on a 50–50 basis, which is the lowest match for AFDC basic grants. Most states receive a higher percentage of federal funds for the basic grant.)

The correlations are quite different when the measures of AFDC characteristics are related to AFDC–EA costs per AFDC costs. The results involving AFDC–EA costs (compared to AFDC costs) are most extreme, being exactly the opposite from those mentioned above. The measure is related to lower grants, a lower need standard, and a lower percentage of the standard met. Higher costs also relate to higher federal match.

The relationship between the AFDC–EA caseload (compared to the poverty population) and the four characteristics of the AFDC grant are approximately halfway between the other two sets. For example, the correlation between the emergency caseload and the size of the AFDC need standard is .22. This is about halfway between the correlation of the need standard with the number of emergency programs (.57) and the correlation of the need standard with the measures of emergency costs (−.35).

Why do measures of the number of emergency programs correlate with the characteristics of the AFDC program so differently from measures of the size of specialized programs? Unfortunately, some of the differences in our results may be statistical artifacts. The denominators for the measures—the number of poor individuals in a state and the AFDC costs—in themselves correlate closely to the grant size, need standard, and percentage of the standard met. This causes a statistical problem. The reported correlations may in part simply reflect correlations between the denominators, not the numerators, and the independent variables. Thus, it is difficult to interpret the results.

The federal match, however, does not correlate closely with the denominators used in making indices for the emergency effort. Therefore, the fact that this measure tends to be associated with higher AFDC–EA costs compared to AFDC costs is probably not a statistical artifact. The correlation may have to do with need. States with higher federal AFDC matches tend to be poorer ones. When these states begin a specialized program, the high level of poverty might increase the number of emergency situations or special needs requests, and states may be forced to expand any program that is established. (It is even possible that the correlation between costs and the match helps explain why states with a higher match provide fewer emergency programs; these states may realize that high demands will develop, and they may thus attempt to limit costs by having fewer programs.) In sum, while relations involving the *number* of specialized programs indicate consistency between general welfare policy and emergency assistance, relations involving the *size* of emergency programs, at least in part, indicate some compensation for low basic grants.

THE RELATIONSHIP BETWEEN THE GOALS OF THE SYSTEM AND SPECIALIZED ASSISTANCE

Table 4.2 reports the correlations between the selected goal measures and the specialized assistance effort. These correlations measure the relationship between emergency and special needs assistance and general welfare policies. Although the correlations are not as consistent as those between characteristics of the AFDC grant and the specialized assistance effort, they are often quite large, and they also imply some very significant differences between the way in which general policy relates to the size of the AFDC–EA program and the way it relates to the number of programs.

The number of programs is most closely related to three goals. In each case the relationship is a negative one—that is, there are more programs when the goals are stressed less often. Thus, Table 4.2 indicates that when the index measuring equity and standardization is lower, there are more special programs. In addition, less stress on both the internal and external maintenance indices is consistent with more programs.

These three relations are in keeping with the consistency principle. First, as we argued earlier, the equity and standardization goal is part of the aim of the trend to a flat grant. This particular goal index is meant to represent a belief in a basic grant system in which all clients with similar incomes and family structures are treated equally. Thus, if the consistency view held, a state with this belief would have fewer special programs, because emergency and special needs programs in effect give some individuals more aid than others who have the same income and family structure.

The consistency principle is also supported by the fact that stresses on both the internal and external maintenance goals relate to fewer programs. Specialized programs require discretion, which leads to questions, administrative difficulties, and complaints. Apparently, when officials stress internal maintenance, they avoid specialized assistance because of what it entails administratively.

TABLE 4.2
Correlation between Selected Goals and Specialized Assistance

	Current Equity & Standardization (Index)	Desired Internal Maintenance (Index)	Desired External Maintenance (Index)	Current Goal: Restricting Aid	Current Goal: Considering Unique Circumstances	Current Goal: Avoid Dependency	Current Goal: Use Private Resources	Current Goal: Flexibility of Use of Rules
Number of programs for emergencies and special needs in a state (45 states)	−.20	−.43**	−.24*	−.17	−.19	.15	.17	.13
AFDC–EA caseload compared to the poverty population (22 states)	.24	−.16	−.35	.29	−.76**	.16	−.08	.20
AFDC-EA costs compared to AFDC costs (22 states)	.38*	.03	.06	.17	−.36	.07	−.30	.12

*$p < .05$
**$p < .01$

External maintenance may be consistent with fewer programs for similar reasons. Perhaps executives fear that the programs will cause public criticism, given the potential for complaints about abuse in such discretionary programs. Executives with a desire to avoid trouble in the community may attempt to accomplish this goal by limiting the number of specialized aid programs.

The size of the AFDC emergency program, as measured by caseloads and costs, relates most closely to goals in a very different manner, although the table shows large correlations between a number of the goals and one or the other measure of size. A high score on the equity and standardization index, on the current goal of restricting aid, and on the current goal of using rules flexibly relate to a larger AFDC–EA program. A stress on external maintenance, the goal of considering the unique circumstances of clients, and the goal of using private resources relate to smaller AFDC–EA costs and/or caseloads.

Why do these relations occur? Whereas relations between goals and the number of emergency programs seem to support the consistency principle, some of the relations between goals and the size of the AFDC–EA program seem to support the compensation principle. Most notably, stress on the equity and standardization goal relates to a larger AFDC emergency program. Stress on this index apparently indicates that a state has a basic grant system that does not meet the varying needs that individuals with similar incomes and family structures may have. When needs are not met in the basic grant program, perhaps clients simply apply for emergency assistance more often. This explanation is supported by the fact, not reported in a table, that the existence of a flat grant (as found in state plans), while not related to the number of emergency programs ($r = -.06$), relates to larger emergency caseloads ($r = .32$).

Another interpretation of the positive relationship between the goal of equity and standardization and the size of AFDC–EA is that consistency is at work here in the application of the rules. Simple rules applied to all may not distinguish between AFDC recipients and others in need. Thus the AFDC–EA program could be accessible to many more people in a state where distinctions are kept to a minimum. In fact, a high score on the goal of equity and standardization does relate to providing AFDC–EA to General Assistance clients who are not AFDC recipients but who fall within federal guidelines for AFDC–EA eligibility ($r = .77$). And, as the next chapter will point out, the breadth of aid that is provided has an influence on the costs and caseload of emergency programs.

Questioning the Effect of Traditional Goals

According to Table 4.2, the restrictive goal is consistent with a larger AFDC–EA program. The correlation seems to represent a case of the compensation principle at work. States with an emphasis on the restrictive goal apparently limit access to the AFDC system, so when AFDC–EA exists, many clients have unmet needs and attempt to use the emergency program to meet them. It is even possible that state officials intentionally use the emergency program as an alternative to providing basic benefits. We have found that in AFDC–EA programs, the restrictive goal correlates with providing aid to poor individuals who do not receive AFDC ($r = .73$).

Relations between goals and the size of the emergency assistance effort are complicated, however, by the fact that some correlations support the consistency principle. For example, a high score on external maintenance correlates with lower AFDC–EA caseloads. This seems to support the notion, noted above, that executives who stress maintenance desire to avoid emergency programs in order to minimize public criticism.

More important, Table 4.2 indicates that when one type of individualization is stressed, emergency programs tend to be small: that is, there is a very large negative correlation between the AFDC–EA caseload (compared to the poverty population) and the goal of considering the unique characteristics of clients. This traditional goal, in fact, explains about 58% of the variation in caseloads. Why this correlation?

The consistency principle provides a likely explanation. Perhaps discretion in the overall system encourages states to allow more discretion in emergency assistance. And, such discretion may result in a tendency to approve fewer emergency grants; workers may use their discretion to decide more carefully when clients are more or less deserving. For example, this goal is stressed more in AFDC–EA programs in which more verification is required ($r = .30$).

Supporting this explanation, this traditional goal is also consistent with a philosophy that restricts coverage. We find, for example, that General Assistance clients are covered less often in AFDC–EA programs where the "uniqueness" goal is stressed ($r = -.41$). Many authors have maintained that traditional welfare orientations separated out the deserving from the nondeserving, giving aid only to the former (Handler and Hollingsworth, 1971). General Assistance clients are often considered nondeserving. Perhaps, then, the goal of treating clients uniquely represents the tradition, and special programs deny benefits to General Assistance clients because they are deemed unworthy.

Other measures of traditional welfare orientations are not so clearly related to the emergency effort, with one exception: The goal of encouraging the use of private aid is consistent with lower AFDC–EA costs. Perhaps this relationship occurs because in states that encourage the use of outside resources in general, such requirements are used to restrict eligibility for emergency and special needs aid as well.

THE RELATIONSHIP BETWEEN COMMUNITY PRESSURES AND SPECIALIZED ASSISTANCE

Table 4.3 reports the correlations between specialized assistance and the measures of community concerns. It helps suggest how the emergency assistance effort relates to external demands. The correlations are quite scattered; it is rare for a measure of community pressure or sentiment to demonstrate a large correlation with more than one of the measures of the emergency program.

The number of programs seems closely related, negatively or positively, to four measures: (1) the program size desired by the community; (2) the influence of public groups; (3) the influence of federal and regional welfare administrators; and (4) the influence of political groups. When the influence of public groups is high, there are fewer programs. In the other cases, higher scores on the community measure correlate with more programs.

Those relations involving federal officials and regional officials may be at least partly artificial. These individuals deal with specialized programs on a day-to-day basis. Their influence may be higher as a *result* of a larger effort; when there are more programs, these officials have more to do. Accordingly, relations involving these groups should not be stressed too much in an attempt to explain why states vary.

The correlations between the number of programs and both the size of the emergency program that the community desires and the influence of the public groups seem to indicate that the emergency network does respond to public pressure. The fact that the influence of public groups correlates with fewer programs is consistent with one of our general themes. As Table 2.5 made clear, the press and public were perceived to have considerable concern over error and fraud. Perhaps when the influence of these groups is high, officials begin fewer emergency programs for fear of complaints about error and fraud.

TABLE 4.3
Correlation between Selected Measures of Community Pressure and Specialized Assistance

	Influence of Political Groups (Index)	Influence of Interest Groups (Index)	Influence of Public Groups (Index)	Influence of Federal and Regional Offices of HEW (Index)	Influence of County Welfare Officials	Influence of State Welfare Officials	Concern with Error & Fraud (Index)	Program Size Desired by Community (Index)
Number of programs for emergencies and special needs in a state (45 states)	−.01	.20	−.33*	.28*	−.03	.29*	−.15	.51**
AFDC–EA caseload compared to the poverty population (22 states)	−.08	.36	−.22	.25	.13	.21	−.10	.38
AFDC–EA costs compared to AFDC costs (22 states)	.47*	.14	.15	.38*	−.06	.32	−.14	.12

*$p < .05$
**$p < .01$

This possible role of fraud and error might seem to be refuted by the fact that the average concern of community groups over error and fraud does not relate to the number of programs. But one explanation is statistical; this direct measure of concern has such a limited range of scores that it cannot relate to other factors. In other words, those groups with the most influence over the program share a high concern over error and fraud across states, and the existence of a constant level of concern makes prediction difficult.

Measures of the caseload of the AFDC emergency program relate to different variables. When federal, regional, and state officials have more influence, caseloads tend to be larger. Caseloads are also larger in two other cases—when interest groups have more influence, and when the index of the program size desired by a community is high.

The relationship between influence of public officials and the caseload may, again, merely indicate that when programs are larger, officials have more influence over them. The fact that a general demand for a larger emergency program relates to a higher caseload is self-explanatory. Most interesting, the influence of interest groups also relates to larger caseloads. This probably occurs (as Chapter 7 explains further) not because the interest groups are able to change program rules, but because they are able to convince clients to apply more often to whatever emergency program exists. That is, the relation implies mobilization of demand by interest groups.

Some of the groups included in the measure of interest groups clearly have a direct stake in mobilizing demand. Client and advocacy groups, in particular, have this function. Other groups in the index may have less obvious reasons for mobilizing demands, as the index includes measures of the influence of public and private social service agencies. These agencies probably wish to mobilize demand for emergency programs in order to protect themselves; if the public welfare system did not handle the emergency cases, more of a burden would be placed on these client-serving agencies.

Emergency costs (compared to AFDC costs) appear to be linked to the influence of political groups (as well as to the influence of groups that advocate for clients, for reasons explained above). This relationship is surprising; these groups tend to desire smaller programs and are concerned about error and fraud; yet when they have more influence, costs are higher. Two explanations are likely: Either the influence of these groups may reduce the welfare effort in general, so that the emergency assistance system faces more unmet needs; or political groups may attempt to control programs only when costs are larger.

REGRESSION ANALYSES

We also calculated regressions between the three measures of specialized assistance (the dependent variables) and various measures of the public attitude toward welfare. Our technique was to use the .05 level of statistical significance as a guideline, eliminating variables until a final equation was reached in which all variables were statistically significant. Then, other variables that seemed to increase the explained variance were added.

The use of statistical significance is of course only a guideline, and our procedure tends to be somewhat atheoretical. Nevertheless, it seemed necessary in order to avoid using a cumbersome number of variables in the equations. Using this technique, a large proportion of the variance in each measure can be explained by a small number of variables.

Fifty-five percent of the variance in the number of programs is explained when three independent variables are used: the state need standard ($\beta = .36$); the average size of the program community groups desire ($\beta = .43$); and the desired internal maintenance goal ($\beta = -.38$). When two other variables are added, 60% of the variance is explained: the influence of the general public ($\beta = .19$) and the federal match ($\beta = -.14$). These two variables, however, do not quite have statistically significant relations by themselves.

These regressions seem consistent with interpretations developed up to this point. But there is a notable exception; direct measures of the trend toward standardization are not included in the equation. However, it is often the case in regressions that when more than one variable that represents a concept are included, any one will be entered in an equation. In the present case, the equity and standardization goal is closely correlated to the low state need standard ($r = -.76$), perhaps indicating that, in terms of this equation, the two are polar opposite measures of similar concepts. So the failure of the equity and standardization goal to be included in the final equation may indicate that more "liberal" states also tend to be those that resist the trend toward standardization.

Sixty percent of the variance in the emergency caseload (compared to the poverty population) is explained by the current goal of treating individuals uniquely ($\beta = -.70$). When this goal is stressed, the caseload is much smaller. The explained variance increases to 68%—although the added relations are not quite statistically significant—when the influence of interest groups ($\beta = .23$) and the average size program community groups desire (β = .19) are added to the equation. Thus, according to the regression, the reliance on traditional, unique handling of cases plays an important role in limiting the size of the specialized programs. Apparently, as predicted, a more standardized approach reduces the ability of a state system to pick and choose among clients in the specialized program. The results demonstrate that direct community desires play a limited role, as well.

Fifty-seven percent of the variance in emergency costs (compared to AFDC costs) is explained by three variables: the federal match (β = .38); the influence of political groups (β = .44), and the percentage of the need standard met (β = .43). Again, these results are consistent with general explanations of the tendency of states with reduced AFDC benefits and a higher proportion of AFDC costs paid for by the federal government to have a larger AFDC–EA program. As has been mentioned, the influence of political groups may be something of a statistical artifact. As noted earlier, the failure of the direct measures of equity and standardization to find their way into the equation may indicate that this philosophy is closely related to such objective characteristics of the AFDC system as the percentage of the standard met or the federal match; less wealthy states that meet the standard less well also tend to favor standardization.[1]

[1]To gain confidence in the statistical results, simple correlations between a number of the more "objective" measures of a state's welfare commitment and the three dependent variables were also carried out. In general, the results provided few surprises; many of them are consistent with the previously reported correlations and regressions. For example, the number of emergency programs is higher when administrators spend more of their time in administration (r = .24), when counseling interviews are required (r = .26), when verification, as measured by a verification scale, is reduced (r = − .22), and when public attitudes toward the poor, as measured on previous sample surveys, are less harsh (r = − .30). All relations seem to indicate that more liberal, less standardized states have more programs. In contrast, the number of emergency cases compared to the population in poverty is greater when administrative costs are smaller (r = − .47), when counseling services are not required (r = − .38), when face-to-face interviews are not required (r = − .55), when there are more cases per worker (r = .64), and when attitudes toward poverty are more harsh (r = .41). On these measures, states with an interest in standardization and a less liberal environment tend to have a larger AFDC–EA program. Similarly, AFDC costs are higher when there are more cases per worker (r = .39) and when public attitudes toward the poor are more harsh (r = .46). All of the above relations are statistically significant at the .05 level.

One underlying assumption, that equity and standardization goals are consistent with a low error rate, is confirmed by Mills (1981). He notes that error rates are lower when the grant is consolidated, when there are more workers compared to cases, and when grants have a maximum payment, regardless of family size. In other words, the standardization concept is consistent with lower error rates.

THREE TYPES OF STATES

In sum, the basic policy commitments in public welfare outlined in earlier chapters strongly affect decisions concerning emergency and special needs programs. The consistency principle seems to explain the *number* of programs a state chooses to provide. The basic commitment to standardizing the bureaucracy seems to lead to a reduced emphasis on providing specialized programs, whereas individualization seems to be consistent with more programs. Perhaps states that have tended to resist the trend to standardization view emergency assistance and special needs programs as ways of maintaining part of the traditional, individualized orientation.

Other commitments interact in this basic struggle. There are more programs in states with unusually high AFDC benefits, a low federal matching rate, little emphasis on internal and external maintenance, and more pressure from external groups to provide specialized aid. Many of these relationships are not necessarily independent of the basic struggle between individualization and specialization. For example, states with high AFDC benefits and a low ranking on the maintenance measures also tend to be those that are less committed to standardization (see footnote 1). To some extent the argument that standardization inhibits the adoption of programs is the same as the argument that states with less "liberal" AFDC systems adopt fewer programs, because these are the same states. Nevertheless, some measures of standardization appear to have independent effects on the number of specialized programs a state adopts.

A somewhat more complicated pattern is found with respect to the size of the AFDC–EA programs. Those few states with a commitment to standardization and a low AFDC grant that have the AFDC–EA program tend to spend relatively large sums on the program. Apparently, this is partly due to a compensation principle: these states tend to rely on AFDC–EA to deal with the worst problems that their policies might cause. States that have more need—as demonstrated by the percentage of the need standard met by the AFDC grant—also have larger programs, when they have any program at all.

To complicate matters, it is possible that the fact that states with standardized programs are bound by the rules of their programs contributes to the size of their AFDC–EA programs. Standardization may imply permitting more categories of clients to obtain benefits, which by itself increases costs. Nevertheless, the principle of compensation, based on greater need for specialized programs, appears to be at least partly valid.

One way of summarizing some of these results is as follows: there are three types of states. One type has many emergency and special needs programs but a small AFDC–EA program. These states seem to distrust standardization and provide high benefits. The adoption of many programs seems to be consistent with the emphasis on meeting individual needs and providing reasonably adequate benefits. The low expenditures for AFDC–EA may at least partly reflect relatively limited needs for such programs in these states.

A second set of states has few specialized programs, but spends relatively large sums on AFDC–EA, when such a program exists. In these states we find a strong belief in standardization and lower than average AFDC grants. Apparently the lack of interest in providing a large number of programs stems partly from the belief that such programs compromise the trend toward standardization, and partly as a response to an inability, or unwillingness, to provide many benefits. However, the AFDC–EA costs are relatively high, at least partly because of high need, and perhaps partly owing to the nature of rules such states tend to have.

Finally, a third group of states provides few programs and has no AFDC–EA program at all. Most of these states also have highly standardized, low-cost welfare systems. Apparently, in these states aid for emergencies and special needs is viewed as inconsistent with basic welfare policies. It is even possible (and in our estimation, likely) that such states have no large specialized programs that compensate for the inadequacies of the basic grants.

CHAPTER 5

Rules, Procedures, and Delegation in State Programs

Because there is room for much discretion, it is the states that shape the character of most emergency assistance and special needs programs. States must determine such issues as eligibility rules, conditions that must be met in order for aid to be received, and the balance of authority between state and county administrators. These decisions are not arbitrary; they are made within the context of the general welfare policies of states and the specific goals of programs providing emergency assistance and special needs aid.

Some of these decisions reflect the dilemmas inherent in providing specialized assistance within the context of increasingly standardized state welfare systems. As Chapter 1 pointed out, the discretionary nature of specialized programs can in theory work at cross-purposes with the income maintenance system. Whereas basic income maintenance programs stress standardization, horizontal equity, and the control of errors, the specialized programs often encourage the opposite traits. They seem to demand dispensing decisions on a case-by-case basis, awarding differential grants to individuals with the same income, and making decisions which require judgment and therefore are subject to error. As the first chapter notes, there are thus pressures toward delegating many decisions from the state officials to county and line workers. When state officials make fewer decisions, they can deny blame either for inequities that may arise or for complaints concerning fraud and error.

Despite this overall desire to delegate, state officials want to retain control over some aspects of the individualized programs. Most important, state officials usually desire to keep costs within budgetary limits. In some cases, however, they may make conscious decisions to use emergency or special needs programs to compensate for limits in basic grants and may attempt to ensure that at least some funds are spent. In Minnesota, for example, state officials appeared to be in a paradoxical situation, encouraging larger expenditures for specialized programs in some counties while attempting to control their costs in the major metropolis.

As the consistency theory suggests, the administrative philosophies in the overall public welfare system in a state may also influence the rules and procedures adopted in specialized programs. One such philosophy is the distinction between the deserving and undeserving poor (Handler and Hollingsworth, 1971). Traditionally, states mandate that aid must be dispensed mostly to clients in need because of circumstances beyond their control—the so-called deserving poor. Officials are more reluctant to provide aid to people whose problems may seem to stem from personal failings, or even from fraud and abuse—the undeserving. It may be that states that are more restrictive in their philosophy as a whole believe that most applicants for specialized aid are undeserving, and thus that restrictive rules should be adopted in the specialized programs. It may also be the case that some types of clients are viewed as particularly undeserving. Traditionally, individuals who are physically able to work, who do not belong to a nuclear family, or who appear to have problems budgeting are most often deemed to be responsible for their own failings and thus less deserving of support.

Obviously, prevalent beliefs may play a role in administration. For example, states in which officials believe in individualized treatment may adopt rules that allow more careful screening; the belief in standardization may result in a certain level of standardization in the specialized program; and community pressures concerning error and fraud may result in more careful control within the agency.

This chapter looks at patterns of administration, keeping these themes in mind. First, it provides an overview of the rules and procedures in specialized programs in order to demonstrate the balance states strike between delegation and control and between the various possible goals and philosophies. These topics were briefly covered in earlier chapters, but whereas the emphasis in Chapters 2 and 3 was on the functioning of each of the individual programs, the emphasis here is on rules of all programs taken together.

Second, the chapter looks at how these various administrative mechanisms relate to the costs and caseloads of specialized programs. This section helps indicate exactly what elements of administration affect the overall size of the program. The answer is not obvious. While it might seem likely that restrictive rules (e.g., more strict verification requirements, fewer circumstances covered, and so forth) reduce the size of the program, it is unclear just which rules or procedures will have such an effect.[1]

STATE RULES AND PROCEDURES IN SPECIALIZED PROGRAMS

This examination requires developing a list of rules. Even though the literature concerning how organizations function often considers rules, it is seldom very specific about what types of rules and procedures are most important in dictating the character of a program.[2] In constructing questions about rules we used organization theory to develop some basic categories—such as the distinction between procedural rules and monitoring—but we relied chiefly on variables that seem to be most useful in clarifying both patterns of delegation and distinctions between the deserving and undeserving poor. Six sets of variables were developed. *Access rules* involve the extent to which states mandate that potential recipients must be informed about the existence of a specialized program. *Resources and verification rules* define what resources clients must tap before being eligible for specialized assistance, and the extent to which need must be proved. *Client-eligibility rules* concern which types of clients (such as SSI recipients, the unemployed, and so forth) are allowed to obtain aid. *Circumstances* involve the types of emergencies—such as special diets or rent arrears—for which coverage is allowed. *Special requirements and conditions* involve unusual obligations incurred by clients who obtain aid. For example, clients may be required to accept budget counseling (a special requirement), or clients may be given a voucher and not cash (a condition). Finally, *monitoring and control devices* involve the extent to

[1]Very little of the literature concerning complex organizations speaks to such a subject (see Piliavin, Masters, and Corbett, 1979, p. 318).

[2]One summary of the literature is Hall (1977).

which the states oversee programs, and the extent to which counties are free to interpret, and even adjust, rules and procedures as desired.

To analyze these rules and procedures, individual program questionnaires were sent to administrators of three state-level programs: AFDC–EA, AFDC–Special Needs, and a state-financed emergency program. Not all states have each program; and not all programs are represented by a completed questionnaire. We obtained information on 14 AFDC–EA programs, 19 AFDC–Special Needs programs, and 21 state emergency programs. Ten of the 21 state emergency programs are partly financed by AFDC–EA.

The questionnaires vary by program because certain questions are irrelevant in some cases—for example, because AFDC–Special Needs cannot be used for those who do not receive AFDC, the list of the basic grant recipients other than AFDC clients who can obtain aid is irrelevant. Nonetheless, many identical questions are included in each of the three questionnaires, or at least in two of them. Therefore, for descriptive purposes, responses to identical questions may be combined in this discussion. When systematic differences in the responses from each type of program seem important, this is reported in the text. However, discrepancies are quite rare.

One caveat: Rules represent intentions, not actual behavior. As a later chapter demonstrates, local areas often alter program rules, thus acting in a manner that is not reflected in responses of state officials. It is necessary to be cautious in asserting that these rules actually define behavior, even though it is clear that they influence behavior to some degree.

Access Mandates

Even though outreach is important in informing some individuals in need about the existence of an emergency assistance or special needs program, it seems that state mandates offer very little guidance to local areas in this regard. Individuals who are not currently receiving AFDC, SSI, or General Assistance (GA) grants are eligible for many AFDC–EA or state emergency programs (but not AFDC–Special Needs), but little is done to inform nonrecipients about the specialized programs. In fact, in the 34 responses to this question, only two programs claim to provide any outreach at all. The outreach consisted of notices sent to community groups (in both programs) and a media campaign.

There are a few more mandates involving informing current recipients of income maintenance grants about specialized programs, as Table 5.1 points out. Thirty-eight out of the 52 responses to the question on our program questionnaires claim there are *some* such mandates. Yet only a small minority of programs include questions about emergency or special needs aid on the application for public assistance, few mandate that counties post written notices, and only a small number mandate the provision of a written statement about the availability of a specialized program.

The only form of information that is mandated in more than half of the programs is that of verbally informing applicants for basic aid about the existence of emergency assistance or special needs support. Unfortunately, this form of mandating access apparently is of limited utility. Most applicants are not likely to remember any oral statement about the availability of specialized aid that is given during the long, complex, emotionally charged application process. Moreover, apparently such a regulation is often overlooked in the attempt to gather all the information that is needed to verify eligibility for the regular income maintenance program. In two of the case studies, mandates involving informing applicants about a specialized program were not obeyed.

The lack of outreach mandates may indicate a belief that many potential recipients of emergency or special needs aid are undeserving. State officials may feel that the lack of many access-providing mandates ensures that individuals who would demand specialized assistance if they knew about the program—even if the need for aid was not intense—do not have the information. Instead, the suggestion of specialized aid is usually left to caseworkers, if they are made aware of an unusual need that they believe is legitimate.

TABLE 5.1
State Mandates Concerning Informing Basic Grant Recipients about Emergency Assistance and Special Needs

Mandate	Number of Programs	Percentage of Programs
Basic grant application contains questions concerning eligibility for emergency aid	7	13.5%
Grant applicants must be verbally informed about emergency aid	27	51.9
Written information about emergency aid is given to basic grant applicants	13	25.0
Notices about emergency aid must be posted	2	3.8
There are no rules	14	26.9
$N = 52$		

Note: Multiple responses are possible.

The paucity of outreach effort may also indicate the extent of delegation in the individualized emergency and special needs programs. Perhaps state officials, in an attempt to avoid responsibility for a time-consuming, value-threatening issue, often prefer to keep their hands off specialized programs, letting counties decide on outreach by themselves.

Resources and Verification

States may also mandate a number of procedural requirements. Tables 5.2 and 5.3 present some information concerning two types of requirements, the exhaustion of outside resources by clients, and the verification by external sources of client claims concerning circumstances and needs. As Table 5.2 shows, in about 60% of the programs, clients must apply for some other type of aid before receiving specialized assistance. Slightly less than a third of all programs demand that clients exhaust resources from private charities before receiving emergency aid. These programs greatly limit eligibility for aid. The implication in these programs is that specialized aid must be looked at as a backup to the private system—a system that usually has very limited resources.

The majority of programs seem to require that clients apply to one or more of a number of relevant public programs. Because specialized assistance may be only temporary, generally application to other public

TABLE 5.2
State Requirements Concerning Exhausting Outside Resources before Receiving Assistance

Requirement	Number of Programs	Percentage of Programs
No requirements	20	39.2%
Exhaust private aid	14	27.4
Apply for Food Stamps	12	23.5
Apply for General Assistance	7	13.7
Apply for AFDC, if applicable	18	35.3
Apply for SSI, if applicable	13	24.1
Apply for Unemployment Compensation, if applicable	16	31.4
Apply for social security, if applicable	16	31.4
Other	20	39.2
N = 51		

Note: Multiple responses are possible.

TABLE 5.3
State Requirements Concerning Verification of Applications

Item Verified	Number of Programs	Percentage of Programs
No verification	3	5.8%
Income	30	57.7
Assets	32	61.5
Existence of the emergency	40	76.9
Family structure	12	23.1
Attempts to obtain public assistance	22	42.3
Attempts to obtain private assistance	15	28.8
N = 52		

Note: Multiple responses are possible.

programs ensures that continuing needs are met. In fact, it is possible that when an emergency assistance or special needs program does not require an application to other public resources, the specialized program is viewed as a way of keeping basic grant caseloads down. For example, in Minneapolis, the emergency system was altered when a 1974 federal audit of the AFDC emergency program seemed to indicate that emergency aid tended to reduce the number of AFDC applications; clients would receive a one-month check and would not return.

Although some programs may adopt resource requirements to restrict access, Table 5.3, which reports the items that workers must verify in emergency applications, suggests that the requirements are usually not so strict. All of the programs that require the exhaustion of private resources demand that this fact be verified, and these programs are obviously quite restrictive. But only 22 of the programs demand that the use of public programs be verified. Apparently, in at least some programs, applications to other public programs are encouraged in order to ensure continuing aid, but are not verified.

In general, it appears that verification is not particularly strict in the majority of programs when compared to typical procedures mandated by the state for basic grants. Although it is not reported in a table, the majority of state program administrators (30 out of 49) claim that verification requirements for emergency and special needs programs match those in the basic grants. Fourteen claim that requirements are less strict than are those for the basic grant, and only 5 programs have more strict requirements for the specialized program. Table 5.3 thus indicates that verification requirements for the existence of an emergency (such as presenting a utility bill) are quite common, as are requirements for verifying income and assets. Beyond that point, verification requirements are not widely mandated, although a minority of programs have some other verification rules.

Although a minority of programs have very restrictive resource and verification regulations, which imply that many clients are undeserving of aid, the general picture is thus one of fairly typical requirements. It might seem that a consistency explanation is key—states tend to use mandates similar to those already established in the rest of their public welfare programs. An attempt to minimize the administrative difficulties of the emergency or special needs programs is implied. States appear to take the easiest road, simply borrowing rules and regulations from the traditional grant programs in setting up specialized programs.

Client Eligibility

Respondents were asked whether certain groups of clients are specifically eligible for programs—SSI recipients, migrants, and so forth. Table 5.4 reports our results. It also gives the estimated percentage of the caseload of recipients from each category. These figures probably provide a fairly accurate picture of the intentions of states to cover certain groups, though the percentage breakdowns are often estimates and may be somewhat inaccurate.

In the 21 relevant programs, four of the seven categories of recipients

TABLE 5.4
Coverage of Various Groups by State Specialized Programs

Group	Number of Programs Including Group	Percentage of Programs Including Group	Average Percentage of Group in Caseload[a]
AFDC recipients	18	85.7%	37.1%
AFDC–UP recipients	7	33.3	4.2
SSI recipients	10	47.6	4.5
Food Stamp recipients	12	57.1	10.2
General Assistance recipients	10	47.6	9.7
Nonrecipients (of a basic grant)	14	66.7	29.7
Migrants and transients	14	66.7	6.1
N = 21			

Source: Sosin (1982, Table 1).

Note: Question not asked in AFDC–Special Needs questionnaire.

[a]Average of participation reported in the responses. Because of the reporting discrepancies and missing data, column does not add to 100%.

are eligible over half of the time. AFDC recipients are eligible in all but three programs, and these three programs are state emergency programs that are specifically targeted for the elderly. Perhaps surprisingly, nonrecipients and migrants and transients are eligible in two-thirds of these state programs. Food stamp recipients are eligible in the majority of programs, as well, although coverage of this group falls off to some extent.

SSI recipients, General Assistance recipients, and AFDC–UP recipients are the least likely to be covered. Often, the limits on coverage may be beyond the control of the state program. For example, SSI recipients usually are excluded from AFCD–EA programs, but they are included in all state emergency programs except one. The exclusion from AFDC–EA programs is probably due to federal regulations, which stipulate that only families with children are eligible. Many states do not have an AFDC–UP adjunct to the state AFDC program, perhaps thus limiting the potential for eligibility for emergency programs as well. A similar explanation seems warranted in the case of General Assistance clients, who are virtually never included in AFDC–EA programs and are also ineligible for AFDC.

However, the differences are not completely artifacts. Further statistical breakdowns indicate that one-third of the state-funded specialized programs also do not cover General Assistance cases, even though federal rules are not an issue. Indeed the fact that AFDC–UP cases are often excluded, though this mirrors decisions made in the basic grant, is a meaningful comment about how these types of clients are perceived. Decisions concerning who should be covered in both instances indicate some restrictiveness. The lack of coverage of AFDC–UP and General Assistance cases in some programs is consistent with the typical belief that "able-bodied" workers should not receive aid.

With the exception of some groups often considered to be less deserving, however, the general picture is one of provision of aid to many categories of clients who are in need. This certainly does not imply that needs are met adequately or that all clients in a group receive aid—our earlier overview of the programs paints a rather different picture. The main point here is that state rules in a majority of programs do not appear to be designed to limit eligibility by group.

Circumstances Covered

Despite the problems in defining emergency situations, most programs make some attempt to list the sets of circumstances for which emergency or special needs aid is available. We have decided to report the defining situations in two ways. Table 5.5 reports the number of programs with a specialized focus—that is, the number in which one type of situation is stressed. It lists the frequency with which an item from our predetermined list is said to represent at least 81% of program costs. Table 5.6 lists how frequently programs cover items to any degree.

Table 5.5 indicates a perhaps surprising degree of specialization. Thirty-seven of the 51 program officials responding to the question include one item that represents at least 81% of the cost of the program. In other words, while emergency and special needs programs can, in theory, cover a wide range of situations, in practice this is not the case. Rather, states focus on only a smaller segment of need (perhaps a circumstance in which some special interest has been expressed by a member of the legislature). This specialization is one possible indication of how states separate the deserving from the undeserving in emergency assistance and special needs programs. In most states a small number of circumstances are considered legitimate; other types of needs are not supported.

It is difficult to find patterns in such a small number of specialized programs, but it is interesting that special winter needs, lost or stolen checks, and chore service are most likely to be the central focus. These items seem to be less "morally hazardous" than many others, because

TABLE 5.5
Items Constituting 81–100% of the Costs of State Specialized Programs

Item	Number of Programs	Percentage of Programs
Special winter needs	8	15.7%
Lost or stolen checks	6	11.8
Chore service	4	7.8
Disaster aid	3	5.9
Need for appliance	3	5.9
Moving expenses	2	3.9
Educational expenses	2	3.9
Unborn child needs	2	3.9
Special diets	2	3.9
Clothing needs	2	3.9
Food shortage	2	3.9
Unpaid utility bill	1	2.0
Total programs with specialization	37	72.5
N = 51		

Source: Sosin (1982, Table 2).

TABLE 5.6
Circumstances Covered at Least in Part by State Specialized Programs

Circumstances	Number of Programs	Percentage of Programs
Temporary shelter, moving expense	33	64.7%
Natural disaster	31	60.8
Unpaid utility bills	29	56.9
Need for appliances, furniture	28	54.9
Food shortage	26	51.0
Special clothing needs	26	51.0
Other	22	43.1
Lost, stolen, delayed checks	20	39.2
Grants covering pending applicants' basic needs	18	35.3
Special winter needs	16	31.4
Employment needs	16	31.4
Special diet needs, laundry needs, medical needs	14	27.5
Day care	13	25.5
Unborn child needs	12	23.5
Educational expenses	9	17.6
Special chore services	6	11.8
N = 51		

Source: Sosin (1982, Table 2).

they involve needs that clients obviously cannot meet by themselves, and they are easy to verify.

Programs seem to be less likely to specialize in items that are normally considered to be covered by basic welfare grants—such typical basic needs as food emergencies and threatened evictions resulting from nonpayment of rent. It is possible that, in these cases, moral concerns about the undeserving arise. Perhaps officials are reluctant to expend specialized resources on items that in theory should have been covered by the recipient's monthly check.

Table 5.6 reports the items covered, at least in part, by the specialized programs, despite the predominant focus on one item. Six of the items are covered in a majority of programs, and three more are covered in at least a third of the programs. Apparently, despite the propensity to focus on one item, the programs occasionally meet a variety of other needs.

Natural disasters are covered in a large number of programs. Perhaps these situations are so obviously beyond the control of clients that many policymakers and administrators regard them as an acceptable expense. Yet the other most frequently covered items involve basic needs—moving expenses, utility emergencies, food shortages, clothing needs, and other furniture needs—that are also included in regular grants. These needs are more commonly met than are needs of pending applicants or even emergencies resulting from lost checks. Basic need items seem to represent a small component of many programs.

Interviews conducted with officials suggest that basic needs are provided because there are bound to be unpredictable situations in which clients do not have the wherewithal to survive, and because officials have difficulty in controlling the use of programs designed for other purposes to meet such need. Nearly all definitions of emergency assistance can be stretched to cover them, and given the rather low level of most basic grants, state and local officials often allow this expansion to occur. As we mentioned earlier, in New Jersey, emergency assistance under the AFDC–EA program is limited to cases in which homelessness is threatened, but Mercer (Trenton) County claims that a threatened eviction or utility cutoff constitutes homelessness, and the state has not objected. As a result, the emergency program has, in effect, slightly expanded to encompass some basic needs.

It is unclear why certain items, such as special services not normally covered in basic income maintenance programs, are seldom covered. Many of these items are covered in the Medicaid programs and in Title XX, and perhaps officials perceive that such needs are more likely to be met by other sources. It is also possible that these special services are less likely to work their way into programs that do not intentionally include them. Perhaps they can easily be excluded by judiciously defining the circumstances to be covered by specialized programs.

In general, the tendency to specify the circumstances for which aid is available is an exception to a pattern of delegation. That is, while in most cases states develop very general rules or simply use rules designed for other programs (such as in the case of verification requirements), many programs are quite strict in defining circumstances. It can be assumed that states control circumstances as a means of keeping costs in line, while delegating other responsibilities—a point of view that is supported by some of the data reported later in this chapter.

Special Requirements and Conditions

Emergency and special needs programs may establish a number of special requirements and conditions. Some of these mandate the form in which aid is disbursed, others mandate that clients accept counseling or a protective payee, and still others call for special handling of repeat requests.

Table 5.7 reports the form in which aid is given. In order to deter-

TABLE 5.7
Forms of Specialized Aid Permitted in State Programs

Form	Number of Programs Using Form	Percentage of Programs Using Form	Average Percentage of Clients Aided[a]
Cash	38	100.0%	59.7%
Vendor payments	25	65.8	36.2
Voucher payments	9	23.7	17.3
In-kind; social services	1	2.6	0.6
N = 38			

[a]Column does not add to 100% because sample sizes differed slightly and there were some inconsistencies in reporting.

mine how often a form is permissible by state law, the table reports the number of programs in which each form may legally be used. Percentages of the caseload, according to estimates of state-level officials, are also provided.

The table makes it clear that the three most common forms of aid are cash, voucher payments, and vendor payments. In-kind payments or social services are rare forms of emergency aid. Cash is the most common form. It is claimed (although not reported on the table) that cash is used at least 95% of the time in about half of the reporting programs. In nine of the programs, cash is said to be used less than 5% of the time. On the average, 59.7% of recipients are said to receive cash. As we will see in the next chapter, however, local behaviors are not consistent with these perceptions of state officials.

Vendor payments, used in 25 of the 38 reporting programs, are the second most common form of aid according to our questionnaires. AFDC–Special Needs programs rely on this form least often—no Special Needs program claims to use vendor payments more than 25% of the time. There are some other programs in which vendor payments are said to be always used. On the average, vendor payments are said to be less common than cash, used 36.2% of the time.

Voucher payments appear to be somewhat more rare; they are used in only nine of the programs. When used, vouchers are apparently often relied on extensively, as in six of the nine programs, vouchers are said to be the payment of choice.

We were interested in why the form of payment differs, and we asked program administrators about this. They report that the most common reason for varying the form of payment is the judgment that the client is incompetent. This leads to changes in the form of payment in 28 programs. The form varies with the emergency or special need situation in 20 programs. For example, immediate food shortages may be handled by a cash payment, whereas utility bills may be covered by a voucher. Sixteen of the programs vary the form of aid with the category of client—for example, AFDC–UP clients may receive vouchers while others receive cash. Only nine state administrators report that programs change the form for repeat requests.

Table 5.8 reports state administrators' perceptions of the conditions under which grants are given, using the same mode of presentation as Table 5.7. Only three of the programs rely on budget counseling, and only two use repayment agreements—turning the appropriation into a loan. For statutory reasons, repayment agreements are not used in the AFDC–EA program, although a few other programs mandate a repayment agreement or budget counseling in 100% of the cases. Work requirements (that is, the condition that a client must work to receive benefits) are a bit more common, but they are still used in only 10 of the programs. When used, work requirements are mandated for a minority of recipients.

The only common condition is the requirement of a protective payee, utilized in 21 programs. Even in those states where it is used, the protective payee is a rarely applied condition. AFDC–Special Needs programs are most likely to utilize protective payees, perhaps because they are used in the basic grant to which special needs programs are often attached. In general, administrators report that decisions on the condition of payment reflect the type of emergency or the competence of the client.

For programs other than AFDC–EA (which is restricted to one request per client per year), three-fourths of those responding to our questionnaire allowed repeat requests. And only eight programs out of thir-

TABLE 5.8
Conditions of Specialized Aid Imposed by State Programs

Condition	Number of Programs with Condition	Percentage of Programs with Condition	Average Percentage of Cases with Condition
Protective payee	21	60.0%	2.3%
Work requirement	10	28.6	9.3
Budget counseling	3	8.6	7.3
Repayment agreement	2	5.7	5.3
N = 35			

ty-three have additional rules for repeaters. These are likely to take the form of a protective payee or the use of vouchers. Higher-level approval for repeaters is rare, required in only four programs. Thus state-level rules do not generally imply that repeaters are not deserving. Perhaps it is more common to rely on workers to informally screen out applicants who seem to be using the specialized programs too often.

As a whole, special conditions and forms of aid are thus fairly uncommon. This again appears to be consistent with a theory of delegation; state rules do not mandate types of procedures that make the emergency or special needs programs complicated. States seem to prefer that cash be dispensed and few conditions imposed.

Control and Monitoring

Once eligibility and access rules are developed, states must guarantee compliance by monitoring local performance. Control and monitoring are also needed when officials find that the rules are insufficient and that day-to-day adjustments are needed.

State program officials apparently believe that the rules themselves leave little room for discretion: Twenty-three say that there is little or no discretion at the local level; 22 claim there is a moderate amount; and 7 claim that there is a great deal of discretion. One would guess that state officials try to limit local discretion by writing very definite rules.

Yet, there is little evidence that these rules are monitored closely or that many adjustments are made. One way state officials could monitor local decisions and adjust rules would be to communicate regularly with local offices, but communication is rare. State officials say that they consult with counties about emergency assistance, on the average, slightly more often than once a month—a figure that, per county, is obviously less than this. Of 52 reporting programs, only 5 report communication once a day or more often. At the other extreme, 15 communicate no more than a few times a month and 19 communicate once a month or less frequently. Consistent with the theory of delegation, state program officials do not contact local offices frequently.

A quality control system to review decisions is another way of controlling the programs, but such reviews are apparently uneven. Although 29 state programs report some review, the distribution varies by the type of program. Fourteen out of 19 special needs programs have some quality control review. Only 15 out of 35 reporting AFDC–EA or state emergency programs have reviews. The high coverage for special needs programs probably reflects the fact that the grants from this program often are dispensed along with the basic AFDC grant. Therefore they are monitored along with the AFDC program.

The error rates give some notion of how thoroughly the reviews are carried out, and rates are quite low. Only four program questionnaires report an error rate at all; most respondents simply state that it is not known. When reported, the error rate is generally in the 1% or 2% range—clearly a rate that indicates a rather limited review.

Although any interpretation of our data would be speculative, the nature of control devices seems to indicate a high level of delegation. State officials attempt to establish fairly rigid rules, but they do not communicate often with local agencies or have a sophisticated quality control program. It would appear that state officials prefer to let local offices deal with the complicated, day-to-day problems that go beyond the rules in emergency assistance and special needs programs. And perhaps by limiting quality control, state officials are able to avoid the need to attempt to regularize this very individual, discretionary type of aid.

RELATING RULES AND PROCEDURES TO COSTS AND CASELOADS

Despite the common patterns, there are differences in administrative characteristics across states. A more detailed analysis of specific state-by-state policies can be gained by determining which rules and procedures actually affect the costs and caseloads of the emergency or special needs programs. To help answer this question, many of the rules and procedures described above were correlated with two independent variables: the number of emergency or special needs cases compared to the poverty population, and the cost of the specialized program compared to AFDC costs. These measures are analogous to those used in the last chapter, but they are not identical, because they combine responses from all three program questionnaires—in other words, "emergency cases" are not restricted to AFDC–EA. Responses are combined in order to increase a very low sample size and thus to make the analysis more meaningful. Such a combination was not attempted when community pressures were correlated with emergency costs and caseloads (in Chapter 4) because that analysis would be particularly vulnerable to incomplete data. When more than one program exist in a single state, sampling problems develop.

There were so many administrative variables that all could not be used in the correlations. Whenever possible, items were combined in indices or eliminated if they demonstrated little variance. Table 5.9 reports the relevant correlations, many of which are quite large. Clearly, administrative variables strongly influence the size of the emergency program. However, relations are so complex that it is necessary to summarize the most important results rather than reporting each correlation separately. We will consider correlations of .20 or above as substantively significant, although statistical significance is also reported in the table.

Costs and Caseloads: Possible Causes

A small number of administrative traits seem to determine the size of specialized programs as measured by caseloads compared to the poverty population and costs compared to AFDC costs. Three, in particular, seem important:

1. The number of special circumstances covered in the emergency program explains almost 40% of the variance in the caseloads (squaring a correlation indicates the variance explained), and it is also correlated with program costs. As predicted, restricting the circumstances under which aid is given appears to be one of the prime ways in which states control the cost and caseload of the emergency program. In fact, although the table does not report it, practically every one of the individual circumstances listed on the questionnaire correlates to larger costs and caseloads. Exceptions are disaster aid and winterization.
2. The number of repeat requests allowed explains about one-fourth of the variance in both measures of the size of the program. This relationship makes sense; when repeat requests are allowed, clients are eligible for specialized aid more frequently. And the larger the pool of eligible clients, the larger the costs and caseloads.
3. Coverage of some categories of clients correlates with larger costs or caseloads. This is true for the eligibility of General Assistance recipients and migrants and transients. It seems that when more categories of clients are eligible, the pool of potential recipients is increased, thus affecting costs and caseloads.

There is one correlation that appears to reverse the common trend: the eligibility of AFDC–UP recipients relates to lower costs and caseloads. However, this relation appears to be spurious. States with higher grant levels tend to provide aid for AFDC–UP clients in the emergency or special needs program ($r = .46$) largely because these states are also prone to cover AFDC–UP clients in the basic income maintenance

TABLE 5.9
Correlations of State Administrative Characteristics and Selected Measures of Emergency and Special Needs Program Size

	State Emergency and Special Needs Programs	
Characteristic	Caseload Compared to State Poverty Population	Costs Compared to AFDC Costs
Have some rules for informing current recipients	−.02	.07
Verbal information required	−.22	−.33*
Basic grant application includes questions, information about emergency aid	.44**	−.06
Have at least some requirements to seek other resources first	.17	.15
Number of resource requirements	−.02	.12
Require exhaustion of private aid	−.21	−.17
Have at least some verification requirements	.05	.20
Number of verification requirements	.04	−.09
Verify use of public aid	−.12	−.10
Verify use of private aid	−.21	−.17
AFDC recipients eligible	.08	.19
AFDC–UP recipients eligible	−.24	−.39
SSI recipients eligible	.16	.17
Food Stamps recipients eligible	.21	.09
General Assistance recipients eligible	.35	.19
Nonrecipients eligible	.10	.15
Migrants, transients eligible	.19	.34
Number of special circumstances covered	.64**	.28
Vendor payments used	.20	.03
Voucher payments used	−.09	−.06
Protective payee used	−.11	−.09
Work requirement	−.19	.16
Budget counseling	.00	−.14
Repeat requests allowed in a year	.48*	.51*
Added conditions for repeaters	.67**	.28
Discretion	−.27	−.14
Communication	−.22	.11
Have a review	.08	.05
N varies from 19 to 32		

Source: Sosin (1982, Table 3).
*$p < .05$
**$p < .01$

program. And, as the Appendix, which follows this chapter, demonstrates, these states also apparently have fewer requests for specialized aid, owing to the high basic grant, and thus a somewhat reduced level of need. Therefore, AFDC–UP eligibility may relate to lower costs and caseloads because it is more common in states in which there is less need for specialized assistance for other reasons.

Costs and Caseloads: Secondary Factors

Three factors seem to play a secondary role in controlling costs and caseloads. These factors demonstrate correlations above .20, our cutoff point. But the correlations usually involve only one of the two indicators of the size of the emergency program, or are only slightly above .20. In particular, when applications for basic grants include questions about the need for emergency aid, the caseload tends to be higher (but not the costs); when the exhaustion of private aid is required, costs and caseloads tend to be slightly lower. And when recipients must be informed verbally about the existence of the emergency program, costs and caseloads are slightly lower.

Each one of these relationships makes some sense. The mandate that the basic grant application include questions about the specialized program must increase the number of applicants, because it guarantees that all of those who have emergency needs at the time of application to the basic grant program will be able to apply for emergency aid. The correlation may be small because there are many continuing AFDC clients who also have emergency needs, and these clients are not affected by questions on the application form.

The requirement that private resources be exhausted before emergency aid is offered must reduce the size of the emergency program because it limits the pool of eligible clients to those who have carried out a rather difficult search for private aid. The only surprise is that the negative correlation is not larger. Perhaps this requirement is more common in programs that are more likely to be large for other reasons; this mandate may offset a number of pressures operating in the opposite direction.

The fact that the state-level mandate concerning verbally informing applicants about the availability of specialized assistance correlates with lower costs and caseloads fits earlier perceptions. As noted above, this mandate is not a very powerful one in increasing client access to the emergency program. The negative correlations, however, probably indicate that verbal information is mandated in programs that—for other reasons—have lower costs.

Costs and Caseloads: Apparent Effects

A small group of variables appear to be effects, not causes, of high costs and caseloads. For example, there are some requirements to seek other resources and some verification requirements when caseloads and costs are a bit higher. Apparently as programs get larger, state officials attempt to rationalize the system by mandating more requirements. Proof of this is that officials report less discretion at the local level when caseloads are higher ($r = -.27$).

The most notable such relation is that, when costs and caseloads are higher, restrictive conditions for repeat recipients of aid are more common. The most likely explanation is that conditions are added in order to distribute the aid more fairly once repeaters are allowed and the cost and caseload rise.

The same phenomenon seems to explain the moderate correlation between caseloads and vendor payments. When the caseload is higher, vendor payments are more often used. Apparently, as costs rise, administrators become more concerned about the program and make more attempts to ensure that emergency grants are used only to meet the established need. Looking at this correlation and the lack of relations involving most other conditions and forms of payment, it might be noted that there is little evidence that clients apply to programs less often when the form of aid changes and conditions are imposed—although work requirements correlate with slightly lower caseloads.

Table 5.9 also indicates that communication is more frequent when programs are smaller. This one correlation at first glance might seem to indicate that frequent communication has a small tendency to result in tighter controls and thus a smaller program. But it is equally possible that state officials only rely on direct supervision when the program, for other reasons, is small. When there are larger numbers of cases, officials may prefer to rely on rules, thus ridding themselves of troublesome work.

This explanation has some support. The amount of discretion in rules has a negative correlation to the amount of communication ($r = -.27$), and as the table suggests, there is a small tendency for rules to allow less discretion in the larger programs. (There is a negative correlation between discretion and the size of the program.) Perhaps there are two models of programs: a small program that is regulated by day-to-day communication and allows a moderate amount of discretion, and a larger program with less supervision but a little less discretion.

The possibility that the size of the program is a *cause* of variation in some aspects of administration could be important. It may indicate that there are some common ways of administering larger programs in public welfare. In particular, perhaps the use of some rules increases along with the program costs, in order to ensure that all local areas dispense emergency aid in a similar manner. A slightly different argument may explain the positive correlation between certain conditions and larger programs. Larger programs may generate fear of client abuse, which is dealt with by establishing more conditions.

All things being equal, it is possible that more conditions or other rules would reduce applications, and thus limit costs and caseloads. But all things are not equal; larger programs even seem to impose special conditions more often. Some caution is thus needed: a cross-sectional analysis cannot explain unequivocally the effects rules and procedures have on the size of a specialized program in a longitudinal study.

ADMINISTRATIVE PURPOSES OF RULES AND PROCEDURES

While the last chapter looked at special needs programs and emergency assistance as products of broader environmental constraints, this chapter views the programs as a series of administrative procedures directly linked to the size of the program. Although the analysis is complicated, two points stand out.

First, there are some typical patterns in the style of administering specialized programs. For the most part, administration seems to be in a relatively lenient tradition, in which repeat requests are often allowed, verification requirements are relatively mild, and so forth. When more strict administration is employed, it is usually achieved by defining emergency circumstances, and, secondarily, by restricting the number of client groups eligible. Apparently, in keeping with the idea of delegating responsibility, officials stress strict administration in only a few administrative areas, while continuing to limit program costs. However, about one-third of the programs are very restrictive. In these programs fewer categories of recipients are eligible, verification is much more strict, and many more conditions and requirements are attached to the reception of specialized assistance.

Second, the variations in administration apparently are linked to the costs and caseloads of the emergency or special needs program. Of particular importance are the number of emergency circumstances allowed, the extent to which repeat requests are allowed, and the eligibility of categories of clients. The use of special conditions and the overall number of verification and resource requirements seem to be effects, not causes, of the size of the specialized program.

A small number of general themes seem to be implied by this analysis. One is a tendency to delegate responsibility for individualized programs. In most cases, states seem to expend the minimal effort on a specialized program. They do not monitor it closely, and they have few unusual rules. Often they simply follow a pattern of regulations established in the standardized income maintenance programs. This apparently enables officials to avoid facing consequences of providing individualized aid within a standardized welfare system.

The desire to consciously affect costs is another theme. States seem to be concerned with defining the general nature of the circumstances and client groups covered, and these rules relate fairly closely to costs and caseloads. In fact, as the Appendix suggests, in many cases states intentionally expand coverage to compensate for limits in the flat grants: the individualized program may be viewed as a way of ameliorating the worst consequences of standardization within inadequate budgets.

The deserving–undeserving distinction apparently also plays a role. Clients and circumstances that seem to threaten more moral hazard are less often covered. This is a traditional theme in public welfare.

APPENDIX:
RULES AND THE WELFARE POLICY CONTEXT

One more analysis question is, How do program rules relate to the public welfare policies discussed in Chapters 2 and 4? Such an analysis helps clarify how welfare policies affect costs of specialized programs, since administrative rules are the mechanisms by which policy decisions are worked out. Table 5.10 reports the correlations between selected measures of policy and administrative procedures and rules. The rules and procedures in the table were selected primarily on the basis of the correlations shown in Table 5.9. Those variables that seem to be particularly important in predicting program costs compared to AFDC costs or the caseload compared to the poverty population are of special interest, although one or two other variables not in the previous set of correlations are included because they help explicate key points. Ad-

TABLE 5.10
Correlations of Measures of Public Welfare Policy and Administrative Characteristics in State Specialized Programs

Administrative Characteristics	Welfare Policy Characteristics									
	AFDC Grant Size	Percentage AFDC Need Standard Met	Federal Match for AFDC	Equity and Standardization Goal Index	Goal: Treat Clients Uniquely	Goal: Restrict Aid	Public Group Influence	Interest Group Influence	Desired Size of Program	Concern over Error and Fraud
Some verification requirement	−.09	.01	.06	−.35	.53	−.03	.06	−.17	−.03	−.19
Verify exhaustion of private resources	.01	−.16	.05	.03	−.03	.28	−.06	−.05	.16	−.28
Verbal information mandate	−.07	.05	−.24	−.02	−.16	−.13	−.03	−.10	.28	−.17
Number of circumstances covered	.01	−.12	−.28	−.06	.18	.20	.02	.25	.39	−.05
Cover basic needs for pending applicants	.17	−.44	.28	.37	.24	.41	−.13	.10	.21	−.20
Food Stamp recipients eligible	−.02	−.39	.56	.24	−.29	.23	−.24	.07	.34	.06
General Assistance recipients eligible	.10	−.61	−.01	.23	−.48	.42	−.21	.07	−.04	−.23
Nonrecipients eligible	.25	.03	.59	−.06	.20	.44	−.30	−.27	.12	−.13
Migrants and transfers eligible	.07	−.25	.51	.06	.15	.70	−.05	.08	−.03	.15
Repeaters allowed	−.05	−.12	−.27	−.09	−.04	−.10	−.24	−.36	.29	−.21

N varies from 19 to 32

mittedly, the results lend themselves more to speculation than to proving a case. It is for this reason that we are setting this material off as an appendix. However, a few themes stand out.

Financial Policies

As shown in Chapter 4, three variables that seem to measure less adequate state financing or higher level of need relate to larger AFDC–EA costs or caseloads. When states have a higher score on the current goal of restricting aid in the basic grant program, the AFDC–EA program is larger. It is also larger when the federal match is larger—that is, when the state has a lower per capita income. Further, when the AFDC standard of need is less adequately met by the basic grant, the AFDC–EA program is larger. The relationships are of moderate size.

The reason for these correlations was left a bit unclear in Chapter 4. One possible explanation of them is that a restrictive orientation, a standard of need which is not met, or a low state per capita income simply increases the demand for specialized aid on the part of clients. A second possibility is that states having any of these three characteristics *intentionally* use their specialized programs as a means of compensating for an inadequate basic grant program by providing a short-term emergency grant.

If the relationship were a result of demand, one would not necessarily expect to find correlations between the restrictive orientation, the size of the basic grant, and the federal match on the one hand, and administrative procedures on the other. Client demands, rather than rules, would be the prime cause of the high costs and caseloads. However, if the relations were a result of intentional strategies, some correlations would exist. In particular, the intentional use of specialized aid to compensate for limits of the basic grant is consistent with providing aid to groups of clients who are *not* eligible for the basic grant. Thus, the restrictive goal, the size of the basic grant, and the federal match would relate to the eligibility for emergency aid of those not receiving the basic grant. In addition, the three factors might relate to the eligibility in the specialized program of those who have pending applications for the basic grant program, since dispensing emergency aid to applicants can improve the immediate situation and thus forestall or avoid an addition to the basic grant program.

The correlations in Table 5.10 support the second point of view (intentionality of program use), because the three factors relate to the eligibility for emergency aid of nonrecipients and individuals with cases pending. The goal of restricting aid relates quite strongly with the eligibility of basic grant applicants, and with the eligibility of all listed groups of clients. It also relates to the coverage of more emergency circumstances. A higher federal match also is linked to coverage for pending applicants to the basic grant, and to the eligibility of all but one category of recipients. The relations involving the state standard also concentrate on coverage of applicants for the basic grant and eligibility of many categories of clients, although the direction is reversed, indicating that eligibility is more common when the standard is less well met.

In other words, poor and restrictive states intentionally develop rules for emergency and special needs assistance that result in the use of this program as an alternative to the basic grant. It is unclear whether administrators and policymakers desire to adopt this less expensive form, or whether political issues dictate an attempt to increase aid through a specialized program rather than through extensions or increases in the basic grant. In either case, the effect is the same.

The tendency to compensate for small basic programs with larger specialized grants does not indicate a desire for lenient administration. Thus, two of the three indicators of a restrictive AFDC policy relate to variables that tend to decrease the size of the specialized assistance program. When the restrictive goal is stressed, exhaustion of private resources is verified more often. And when the federal match is higher, fewer circumstances are covered and repeat requests are allowed less frequently. In turn, the exhaustion of private resources, allowing few circumstances, and restricting repeat requests for aid relate to smaller programs. Apparently, beyond the purpose of substituting emergency aid for the basic grant, states that are particularly restrictive do not desire a large program.

Equity and Standardization

In Chapter 4 we showed that the equity and standardization index relates to a larger AFDC–EA program. Two explanations were offered. One was that stress on this goal led to a less flexible basic grant program, so that more emergency aid is needed to compensate for the inadequacies of the basic grant. The other explanation is that equity and standardization in the basic grant lead to the adoption of standardized rules in emergency programs, and that these rules lead to a larger program because they do not permit workers to be selective.

At first glance, it might appear that the former explanation is supported by correlations with administrative variables, because the equity and standardization index correlates with the eligibility of groups who are not necessarily included in a basic grant program, namely applicants for basic grants, food stamp recipients, and General Assistance recipients.

However, a closer look at these correlations supports the second explanation, that equity and standardization promote standardized rules that have the effect of increasing the size of the program. For when equity and standardization are stressed, a state apparently relies on a universalistic philosophy that encourages uniform benefits for all individuals who receive any public aid. Universalism implies that, if any basic grant recipients are eligible for emergency aid, *all* should be. Notably, this point of view does *not* imply granting aid to clients who are not eligible for basic welfare benefits.

If the second explanation were valid, then equity and standardization would only correlate to the eligibility for specialized programs of current or pending recipients of the basic grants. This is the case. The equity and efficiency index correlates with the eligibility of current recipients of food stamps or General Assistance, or applicants for a basic AFDC grant, and it does not relate to the eligibility of nonrecipients of basic grants, or migrants and transients, groups not normally covered by the public welfare system.

The second argument is also supported by a further correlation that seems to indicate that equity and standardization encourage rules that expand the specialized program. The equity and efficiency index thus relates to a less frequent use of verification requirements, and the philosophy represented by the goal complex again seems to explain the relationship. Equity and efficiency encourage administrative simplification, and, given the small amount of money involved in most emergency programs, verification is not consistent with the efficient use of resources.

Traditional Social Welfare

We also saw in Chapter 4 that the goal of treating clients uniquely (i.e., considering individual circumstances) related to much smaller caseloads and costs of the AFDC–EA program. Two explanations were offered. First, the relation may be a result of the traditional philosophy of dealing with clients that this goal orientation implies. The goal of unique treatment seems to be part of the traditional, professional philosophy that stressed collecting a careful social history for public welfare recipients. Collecting a history takes time and is a barrier to processing large numbers of cases.

The second possible explanation is that the goal of treating clients uniquely is consistent with another alleged component of traditional social welfare: the tendency to distinguish deserving from undeserving recipients. According to this point of view, probing specific circumstances enables caseworkers to weed out the undeserving poor, thereby reducing caseloads and costs.

Correlations with administrative procedures should resolve the argument. If treating clients uniquely is related to spending time assessing a client's background, then it should correlate with procedures that take time. For example, more strict verification requirements might be found when the goal of treating clients uniquely is stressed. If treating clients uniquely is a matter of separating the deserving from the nondeserving, this goal should be consistent with refusing aid to categories of clients who, historically, are considered nondeserving—General Assistance recipients and food stamp recipients, for example.

Both points of view are supported by the correlations. The goal of treating clients uniquely correlates with the existence of verification requirements. Lower costs and caseloads may therefore occur in programs that stress treating clients uniquely, because the goal is consistent with procedures that take more time and thus allow fewer applications to be processed. But treating clients uniquely also relates to excluding General Assistance cases and Food Stamp cases from specialized programs. So weeding out the "undeserving" may also be a factor in keeping costs and caseloads down. The correlation reported in the previous chapter thus seems to be the result of a combination of effects.

Table 5.10 also reveals that pending cases and nonrecipients of a basic grant are eligible for aid more often when stress is placed on treating clients individually. At first, this may seem surprising. But the relation may be consistent with a traditional philosophy. Even if the deserving and nondeserving are distinguished, some individuals who have applied for assistance, and some nonrecipients, may obtain aid as long as they are classified as deserving.

Concern over Error and Fraud

Concern over error and fraud was shown in Chapter 4 to have a small negative relationship to the size of a specialized program. In addition, the perceived influence of a group with a high concern over these issues—the public group—relates to smaller AFDC–EA programs.

Apparently the correlations operate largely through eligibility requirements and rules concerning repeated requests for aid. Thus the influence of the public group is higher when food stamp recipients, General Assistance recipients, and nonrecipients are less frequently eligible for aid. It is also higher when rules prohibit repeat requests. Similarly, high concern over fraud and error correlates with restrictions on the eligibility of General Assistance cases and rules prohibiting repeat requests.

Concern over error and fraud does not seem to reduce costs and caseloads by creating barriers to the acceptance of eligible applications. The influence of the public groups does not relate to verification requirements at all, though concern over fraud and error seems to relate to a tendency to avoid mandating verification of the use of outside resources. Perhaps concern over error and fraud results in controlling program abuse in the simplest way—by restricting eligibility to fewer groups and by rejecting repeat requests. These techniques focus on controlling variables that many believe relate to program abuse, since repeaters, as well as General Assistance recipients, food stamp recipients, and nonrecipients, are often thought to be particularly untrustworthy.

Demand for Specialized Assistance

We also found that the AFDC–EA program is larger when the influence of interest groups that deal with clients on a day-to-day basis is higher, and when the perceived average desire of all community groups favors a larger program. Table 5.10 notes how these two variables relate to administrative characteristics.

The perceived average desired size of the specialized program seems to correlate positively with both of the administrative characteristics that relate most closely to program costs and caseloads: the number of circumstances covered and giving repeated aid. In addition, the score on desired size tends to be higher when food stamp recipients are eligible for the specialized program and when the specialized program covers needs of applicants for a basic grant. The desired size is also larger when verbal information on available specialized programs is mandated—a requirement that (according to an earlier result) is consistent with lower program costs.

Summing all of these together, perhaps community desires for a larger specialized program encourage states to expand the circumstances and number of groups covered and to allow repeat requests. However, these rules apparently expand the pool of applicants as much as is desired, so that the states subsequently adopt the sorts of mandates for informing clients about specialized assistance that do not expand the programs further.

Table 5.10 also reveals that the influence of interest groups relates to two administrative variables in ways that might both increase and decrease costs. It is higher when more emergency circumstances are allowed, but it is also higher when repeat requests are not allowed.

This may indicate that the bureaucracy responds to pressure from interest groups in a complicated manner. It may increase the number of emergency items for which clients are eligible if interest groups lobby for a larger program. But it may prevent expansion by simultaneously eliminating the possibility of repeat requests.

Because the two relations cancel each other out, it might seem that the influence of interest groups should have no effect on the size of a specialized program, overall. Yet Chapter 4 pointed out that the influence of interest groups relates to a larger AFDC–EA program. Perhaps interest groups affect the size of a program by less direct means. They may mobilize clients, convincing more to apply for specialized aid, thus increasing the caseload by increasing demand.

A similar logic seems to apply to correlations involving the size of the AFDC grant. It will be remembered that larger size related to slightly lower AFDC–EA program costs, even though it related to more programs. As Table 5.10 demonstrates, the size of the AFDC grant bears few correlations to administrative characteristics, only relating above the .20 cutoff to the eligibility of nonrecipients for emergency aid. As we speculated earlier, AFDC–EA costs may be lower when the AFDC grant size is higher because a higher AFDC grant reduces the need for specialized assistance. Thus, there appears to be some trade-off between a higher grant and a need for specialized aid.

Chapter 6

County Administration of Specialized Programs

Organizational theorists have documented that line workers may in practice alter the rules and procedures established by higher-level officials. The workers may ignore rules, substituting their own priorities, or they may use rules in ways that modify the original intentions. Resistance is most likely to occur when higher-level mandates threaten lower-level interests (Mechanic, 1962). For example, the resistance of lower-level participants has been implicated in the failure of some mental hospitals to implement forms of treatment that threaten to reduce the power of attendants (Scheff, 1961) and in the failure of due process guarantees that can reduce the power of court officials to be effective (Stapleton and Teitlebaum, 1972). The principle extends beyond line workers; subtle changes may occur as rules filter down each level of a hierarchy.

These general considerations suggest that the behavior of workers and officials in local welfare offices may affect the operation of programs dispensing emergency assistance and providing for special needs, despite the fact that many of the rules are set by state officials. Local officials and line workers may ignore state regulations, supplying instead procedures that are based on their own interests and desires. It is also possible that state rules, though followed in a formal sense, may be manipulated in a manner that alters their consequences. For example, local officials may expand the meaning of the term "emergency" beyond what is intended by the state. In still other cases there may be only vague state rules that need to be further specified by counties, while some programs are purely a county initiative and must be administered at lower levels.

As Chapter 2 pointed out, there are reasons to suspect differences in the character of rules at the two levels of government. Even though state and county officials share many sentiments and organizational principles, there are some differences in motivation that can affect action. At the county level, the commitment to equity, standardization, error control, and careful restrictions of the emergency and special needs programs is challenged by other priorities. For example, local officials rank goals involving individualization somewhat higher than state officials.

County officials also appear to feel more keenly the intense problems of clients. They tend to thus rank the *actual* goal of meeting client needs lower than do state officials. This difference is also apparent in sets of questions involving desires concerning specialized assistance (to be summarized more fully in Chapter 7). Among the local officials responding to our executive questionnaire, 75% say that emergency and special need coverage of basic goods, such as food and shelter, is insufficient, whereas the corresponding figure for state officials is 37%. Pressures to meet such needs must motivate county officials to adopt individualized approaches that can meet such needs at least occasionally, instead of the theoretically favored standardized approach. This may explain why county officials rank some of the goals involving individualizing treatment somewhat higher.

Even when there is theoretical agreement between state and county officials, lower-level officials may be forced to find different ways to deal with problems, because the pressures on these "front-line" officials often call for responses that higher-level executives can avoid (Smith, 1965). Thus state officials express their concern about error and fraud by keeping individualized assistance programs small, thereby limiting the potential arena in which these problems may occur, and by delegating responsibility to control error and fraud to counties. But local officials are usually the target when community groups complain about error and fraud; limiting the budget is not a sufficient response, and further delegation is impossible. Local administrators and welfare workers also directly confront individual situations in which fraud and abuse seem likely, so that their desire to control the problems is quite strong. County officials, from executives to line workers, are therefore more inclined to attempt to deal with this issue by setting rules that control potential client abuse, rather than by attempting to keep programs small.

The manner in which the pressures involving both needs of clients and concerns over error and fraud may be met—within a framework in which standardization is still highly valued—can be understood by comparing the operations of emergency assistance and special needs programs at the county level with state-level administration. In order to understand local administrative characteristics, program questionnaires were sent to local officials who administer specialized programs. Officials were asked to respond on the basis of the AFDC–EA program if it existed in the county, or to respond on the basis of the largest emergency or special needs program if there were no AFDC–EA program. Replies with useful information were received from officials in 110 AFDC–EA programs and in 124 other programs.

The questionnaires covered many of the same administrative issues that were summarized in Chapter 5—access, rules involving exhausting outside resources, verification requirements, and so forth. In most cases, local officials and state officials referred to the same program, so differences in the pattern of responses may indicate a tendency of local offices to alter state rules. However, local officials were asked only about their largest program, whereas state officials were asked about three programs. And, on occasion, local officials referred to a locally funded program.

It is possible that sampling biases cause differences in patterns of responses. A preliminary look at the results suggests this is unlikely, because responses from each type of program at the local level demonstrate nearly identical mean scores on almost all of the items reported below. Nevertheless, to deal with the potential problem, county responses to questions about administrative issues are first compared to state responses, descriptively; the reasons for differences and similarities between local and state responses are analyzed in some detail separately.

COUNTY RULES AND PROCEDURES IN SPECIALIZED PROGRAMS

Access Rules and Procedures

Evidence is strong that local areas provide far more information to potential recipients of emergency assistance or aid for special needs than state programs require. Outreach programs are reported by 23% of the county agencies, and half of these agencies have hired at least one worker for the task. This should be compared to the lack of outreach in 32 of the 34 reporting state programs.

At both levels of government it is equally likely that *some* mandates exist for informing basic grant recipients about specialized programs. Local areas have a mechanism for informing current recipients about specialized assistance in all but 28.2% of the programs (see Table 6.1). The comparable state figure is 26.9% (Table 5.1). However, local areas use more forms of outreach. Particularly notable is the attempt on the part of half of the county programs to automatically consider basic grant recipients for an emergency or special needs appropriation.

The county offices probably have some other forms of outreach that could not be tapped in our questionnaire. The case studies suggest that many clients who receive specialized aid are referred by the service worker or eligibility technician. Although workers will refer fewer clients when program costs must be cut (as in San Diego), in general the informal referral network is an important source of clients.

Resources and Verification

While local areas generally expand access, they often mandate more strict procedures concerning resources and verification than state rules imply. In our survey, 77% of the county programs required that emergency assistance or special needs applicants seek outside aid before

TABLE 6.1
County Rules and Procedures Concerning Informing Potential Recipients about Emergency Assistance and Special Needs

Procedure	Number of Localities Using Procedure	Percentage of Programs Using Procedure
Media campaigns	33	15.8%
Notices and posters	75	35.9
Applicants for the basic grant are automatically considered	105	50.2
Applicants for the basic grant are verbally informed about emergency aid	96	45.9
No special attempt is made	59	28.2
N = 209		

TABLE 6.2
County Requirements Concerning Exhausting Outside Resources before Receiving Assistance

Requirement	Number of Programs	Percentage of Programs
No requirements	44	23.7%
Exhaust private aid	65	34.9
Apply for Food Stamps	84	45.2
Apply for General Assistance	34	18.3
Apply for AFDC	103	55.4
Apply for SSI	95	51.1
Apply for Unemployment Compensation	94	50.5
Apply for social security	88	47.3
Other	58	31.2
N = 186		

receiving a specialized grant. This contrasts to 65% of the state programs. The mandate to require an application to other public programs seems to be more common at the local level as well; over half of the local programs (compared to a third of state programs) demand such applications. Table 6.2 summarizes these requirements.

We did not ask county officials about verification of the requirement to first seek other public aid, but Table 6.3 shows that verification in other areas is quite strict. A very large percentage of the programs mandate verification of income, assets, living arrangements, and the existence of the emergency. Proportionately, about 10 to 20% fewer state programs have such mandates.

Despite their somewhat greater restrictiveness, county agencies perceive their policies in specialized programs as relatively lenient. Thus, 48% of the local program administrators believe that the verification procedure for specialized programs is less strict than the procedure for the basic grant, whereas the state figure is 27%. This probably occurs because the procedure for verification of the basic grant at the local level is much more strict than the state demands.

Client Eligibility

According to local officials, eligibility of client groups in county programs expands state-level coverage (see Table 6.4). Although some client groups are excluded from a majority of state-level programs, each

TABLE 6.3
Items Usually Verified by County Programs

Item Verified	Number of Programs	Percentage of Programs
Income	137	76.5%
Assets	118	65.9
Existence of the emergency	138	77.1
Family structure	89	49.7
Living arrangements	94	52.5
Attempts to use private aid	66	36.9
N = 179		

group is covered in the majority of local programs. Particularly noteworthy is the coverage of SSI recipients and General Assistance recipients in a large percentage of the county programs. However, county administrators report somewhat lower coverage for migrants and transients than do state administrators.

The apparent expanded coverage for some groups is actually consistent with the case studies. Many local line workers told us that they attempt to stretch coverage to client groups that are not explicitly covered by the state programs. State officials are not necessarily aware of these decisions, given the limited monitoring of the programs. Perhaps counties report these clients to state officials as "nonrecipients"; the average percentages of various groups in the caseload are similar for states and localities, except that states report a higher percentage of nonrecipients, while counties report more AFDC–UP and SSI recipients.

The reduced coverage of migrants and transients at the county level also seems consistent with the case studies. Workers in Boulder, for example, reported that coverage of these groups was politically unpopular. Perhaps many communities pressure local officials to reduce coverage of migrants and transients in order to avoid creating a dependent, "undeserving" client group.

Circumstances Covered

Just as state programs often focus on only one type of circumstance, so do local programs. Of the 180 reporting county programs, 145, or 81%, claim that one item constitutes at least 81% of emergency costs.

The corresponding state figure is 72.5%. However, whereas natural disasters are often covered by specialized programs at both the state and county levels, problems involving unpaid utility bills are stressed more often at the county level. As Table 6.5 reveals, utility bills rival lost, stolen, or delayed benefit checks for the second most common area of specialization. Other basic needs, such as food shortage, also are the main component of many more local than state programs. In other words, even though local areas continue the pattern of specialization found at the state level, they more frequently specialize in coverage of basic needs. This is consistent with the keener awareness at the county level of the inadequacies of the basic income maintenance grants.

A larger number of needs are covered to some degree by county as compared to state programs. Coverage for basic needs often rivals, or even surpasses, coverage for disasters or similar emergencies; counties demonstrate an unusual propensity toward providing double payments (see Table 6.6). As is the case with state programs, special, continuing circumstances, such as day care or educational expenses, are often not covered in county programs.

One might wonder how priorities at the county level can differ from those at the state level, assuming reporting involves the same program. Perhaps local agencies, attempting to "fit" cases into state guidelines, use somewhat different categories when reporting to the state than they do for their own purposes. More than state rules imply, counties apparently try to find ways to use specialized programs to cover situations that leave members of the community in need of basic necessities.

TABLE 6.4
Coverage of Various Groups by Local Specialized Programs

Group	Number of Programs Including Group	Percentage of Programs Including Group	Average Percentage of Group in Caseload
AFDC recipients	149	92.0%	36.3%
AFDC–UP recipients	96	59.3	9.2
SSI recipients	103	63.6	8.0
Food Stamp recipients	94	58.0	13.8
General Assistance recipients	100	61.7	17.5
Nonrecipients	103	63.6	15.0
Migrants and transients	88	54.3	3.7
N = 162			

TABLE 6.5
Items Constituting 81–100% of the Costs of Local Specialized Programs

Item	Number of Programs	Percentage of Programs
Natural disaster	26	14.4%
Overdue utility bills	20	11.1
Lost, stolen, delayed check	18	10.0
Food shortage	14	7.8
Temporary shelter, moving expenses	13	7.2
Grants covering basic needs, pending AFDC cases	11	6.1
Special diet need, medical need, laundry services	8	4.4
Need for appliance, furniture, household items	6	3.3
Chore and other services	6	3.3
Special clothing needs	5	2.8
Employment needs	4	2.2
Other	4	2.2
Day care	3	1.7
Special winter needs	3	1.7
Unborn child needs	2	1.1
Educational expenses	2	1.1
Programs with specialization	145	80.6
N = 180		

Special Requirements and Conditions

Although there are some similarities between state and local responses concerning special forms of aid, county respondents report a higher use of forms other than cash. Table 6.7 gives the county figures. Whereas 100% of state respondents report dispensing cash, only 68.5% of county respondents do so. The percentage of programs using voucher payments, in-kind aid, and social services is higher in local programs than state administrators believe. For example, 48.8% of county programs use vouchers, but only 23.7% of state programs claim to rely on this form of payment. Vendor payments are distributed similarly in both state and county responses.

County responses also reveal a reduced propensity to use one form of assistance to the exclusion of others (not shown on the table). For example, of the 168 responding county programs, only 22 rely almost exclusively on cash, 22 on vendor payments, and 18 on vouchers. Well

TABLE 6.6
Circumstances Covered at Least in Part by County Specialized Programs

Circumstances	Number of Programs	Percentage of Programs
Overdue utility bills	139	77.2%
Temporary shelter, moving expenses	135	75.0
Natural disaster	131	72.8
Food shortage	127	70.6
Lost, stolen, delayed check	120	66.7
Need for appliance, furniture, household items	107	59.4
Basic needs for pending AFDC cases	103	57.2
Special clothing needs	102	56.7
Special diet needs, laundry needs, medical needs	80	44.4
Special winter needs	63	35.0
Employment needs	62	34.4
Unborn child needs	51	28.3
Day care	46	25.6
Educational expenses	37	20.6
Other	34	18.9
Chore services	29	16.1
N = 180		

over half of the state respondents claimed that one form was used almost exclusively.

Table 6.8 reports conditions attached to receiving aid. Local and state officials estimate similar percentages of the caseload for which conditions are imposed. Thus protective payees are said to represent 5.4% of

TABLE 6.7
Forms of Specialized Aid Permitted in County Programs

	Number of Programs Using Form	Percentage of Programs Using Form	Average Percentage of Clients Aided[a]
Cash	115	68.5%	36.3%
Vendor payments	119	70.8	39.0
Voucher payments	82	48.8	22.2
In-kind aid	16	9.5	1.5
Social services	27	16.1	5.3
N = 168			

[a]Owing to rounding and to missing data, column does not add to 100%.

TABLE 6.8
Conditions of Specialized Aid Imposed by County Programs

Condition	Number of Programs with Condition	Percentage of Programs with Condition	Average Percentage of Cases with Condition
Protective payee	45	29.0%	5.4%
Work requirement	39	25.2	11.0
Budget counseling	51	32.9	9.1
Repayment agreement	39	25.2	8.8
Other	20	12.9	10.2
N = 155			

the caseload according to local statistics and 2.3% in state statistics; work requirements average 11.0% and 9.3%. As the figures indicate, there are slight tendencies for local areas to report a larger percentage of the caseload receiving conditional aid.

The use of conditional aid may be based on a number of different rules (not shown in the tables). About 10 to 15% of local officials claim that the imposition of conditions is governed by rules relating to the category of the client, the number of payments authorized, and characteristics of the client (e.g., incompetence). An equal percentage claim that there are no rules, that individual workers must decide when to impose conditions. About 26% of the respondents claim that specific needs (such as for utility payments) are more often handled with conditional aid.

Control and Monitoring

County reports concerning communication between local and state governments are consistent with state reports. In both cases, the vast majority of respondents indicate that communication is infrequent. Counties report a bit less communication, and this makes sense. Thus, if a state communicates with any office about specialized assistance once a week, each specific office will probably hear from the state less frequently than that. While 29% of state officials say that cross-level communication occurs a few times a month, and 37% say that it occurs once a month or less, county figures are 17% and 65%, respectively.

Half of the responding counties report an error rate, but it appears that the rate is seldom obtained from a thorough quality control review.

The average error rate is 1.9%, an unrealistically low rate for a welfare program. In fact, only 6% of the counties claim to carry out a quality control review. In the vast majority of programs, errors are found through normal supervision. This pattern is quite similar to that found at the state level.

STATE AND COUNTY DIFFERENCES: METHODOLOGY OR SUBSTANCE?

There are many differences between state and county responses. Why does this occur? As has been mentioned, one possible cause for the difference is the method we employed: the state focus on three programs may not be equivalent to county reporting of the largest program. Indeed, in a few instances this appears to be the case. The higher reported use of the protective payee arrangement in state statistics is apparently a consequence of the larger number of special needs programs in the state responses.

In order to determine if the sampling method explains all of the differences, we attempted to compare state and county responses to identical questions about the same program. In particular, we focused on AFDC–EA. Given the stratified sampling design, there were seven state-level AFDC–EA program questionnaires that matched up with county responses concerning the same program. Looking at these responses, we confirmed the existence of differences in rules and procedures between levels of government.

In Minnesota, for example, where there are 18 county responses and a fairly complete response to the state program questionnaire, state officials report that there are no requirements to exhaust other resources before applying for emergency assistance. Yet, one-third of the counties report that applicants are required to exhaust private aid before being considered for AFDC–EA. Further, about one-third of the counties report a number of eligibility conditions that the state does not report.

Minnesota is not a unique case; in fact, the case study of this state suggests that state-level officials have zealously attempted to control county discretion. Other state–local comparisons also reveal differences. In some instances, the data contradict the general trend toward more restrictive local rules. Although state officials in Oklahoma report that there are some requirements that applicants exhaust other resources before receiving aid, three of the seven reporting counties do not list any requirements.

Forms and conditions may also be used differentially. Oregon, according to the state questionnaire, has no work requirements. Most county programs claim to follow the state mandate, but 4 of the 16 local Oregon respondents claim to have such requirements, and one local area uses those requirements for 100% of the emergency caseload. In general, divergences were found in all state–local comparisons.

If they aren't methodological, why do these differences exist? Part of the answer is that compliance with state mandates is rarely guaranteed. If state officials were seriously concerned about compliance with each procedural matter, they would have to carry out case-by-case audits to determine if the circumstances local areas reported to them actually fit within the rules and if the clients receiving aid are actually eligible. They would also have to travel to local areas to ensure that verification requirements and conditions were handled in a manner that was in keeping with state priorities.

As the theory of delegation suggests, close monitoring of local agencies may be more trouble than it is worth. Considering the small size of special program appropriations relative to the cost of basic grants, attempts to review cases and otherwise check up on the county practices would be quite expensive. It is also risky, since the state agency would then bear responsibility for local decisions. Perhaps states often simply prefer to let counties interpret the rules as they see fit, as long as costs and caseloads are not out of line.

It seems that counties have motivations to alter rules when given some leeway, as mentioned in the introduction to this chapter. Many local officials told us that they felt pressured to meet the day-to-day emergency requests of clients, even if these requests did not fall within the rules in a strict sense. Local administrators obviously find it hard to refuse help to an SSI recipient who is out of cash, or an individual with no food, whether or not these desperate people are covered in state rules. Many of the discrepancies we have noted are thus consistent with the survey responses at the local level (summarized in the introduction to this chapter) claiming that grants are insufficient and needs must be met. In particular, the expansion of circumstances covered to embrace many basic needs and the expansion of groups covered must be reactions to such beliefs.

The introduction also pointed out that local administrators also often experience firsthand the problems that are inherent in a discretionary program. They may witness recurring problems as a small group of clients continue to run short of cash, and they see the individual cases of fraud or program abuse, such as clients "stopping on the way home for a beer'' with cash meant to meet an emergency need. The selective use of special conditions may be one way of handling these problems. With vouchers or vendor payments, clients are more likely to spend the appropriation for the intended purpose. Further, the use of work conditions, or similar constraints, is meant to ensure that only the needy clients are served; local officials may believe that those who have only a limited need for the special appropriation will not agree to a work program. Most of these conditions are a matter or local discretion, imposed only on those clients who appear to be particularly untrustworthy.

Strict verification procedures may provide further means for limiting fraud or abuse. Rather than relying on client claims, local agencies are likely to attempt to verify the need for the appropriation. They also may use requirements for the exhaustion of outside resources as means of ensuring that only the deserving clients are served.

COUNTY ADMINISTRATIVE CHARACTERISTICS AND PROGRAM SIZE

The discrepancies between county and state mandates lead one to wonder how the local rules affect the size of the specialized programs. Accordingly, a number of factors were correlated with two dependent measures, the yearly costs (i.e., benefits) of the county program compared to county AFDC costs, and the reported rate of acceptance of individuals who applied to the program. The acceptance rate (as estimated by county officials) averages 66%, but it varies across local areas from nearly 100% to only 1%. It was selected as a measure because it seems most under local control. A measure of caseload compared to the local poverty population, also constructed, had very few correlations with other factors.

These measures are correlated to variables equivalent to those used at the state level in Chapters 4 and 5. For example, the key question in Chapter 4 is how state-level programs relate to general policy commitments in public welfare. The characteristics of the AFDC grant, organizational goals, and community pressures were correlated with measures of the specialized assistance effort to determine the relationship. Accordingly, the measures of local emergency assistance and special needs efforts were correlated with such equivalents as the average AFDC grant size, measures of goals according to local responses, local perceptions of the average size of the program desired by a list of various external groups, the (perceived) average concern over error and fraud of these groups, and the influence the groups were said to have over the emergency assistance system.

Chapter 5 related the size of the state emergency effort to a number of administrative variables. Local responses to similar questions were also correlated to the size of the local program. Relevant variables include access, verification requirements, requirements to exhaust other resources, circumstances covered, categories of clients included, and so forth.

A brief inspection of the resulting correlations uncovered an interesting general result; the environmental and administrative factors did not usually relate closely to the size of the county program for emergencies and special needs, even though often such factors helped predict the caseloads and costs at the state level. Whereas the cost of the state AFDC–EA program related strongly to the AFDC grant standard of need, equity goal, and so on, the costs of the local program related in a statistically significant manner to only two environmental variables, placed in a regression: desired external maintenance (for definition, see Table 2.2), and the current goal of avoiding welfare dependency (also see Table 2.2). Only 14% of the variance is explained. The acceptance rate relates to the influence of local officials, the influence of state officials, and the current goal of encouraging recipients to use private resources before applying for public aid. These variables only explain 10% of the variance.

The administrative variables had similarly low correlations. At the state level the number of circumstances covered by the program correlated strongly with program size, as did the eligibility of various groups of clients (Table 5.9), but this pattern was not repeated at the county level. The correlation at the local level between program costs and the number of circumstances covered is −.08, far below the corresponding state figure (.64). No correlation involving any county-level administrative variables reported so far in this chapter was above .25.

We next looked at other indicators that came closer to representing actual county priorities and behaviors. We considered such variables as how often officials believed that dispensing emergency aid was used as an alternative to approving a long-term basic grant, how often workers attempted to forestall emergency situations by negotiating with creditors, and how often workers refused to dispense specialized assistance in order to avoid the possibility of committing an error. Other measures included how serious the administrators thought a number of problems involving the rules were, which individuals dispensed funds and approved the requests, and whether grant costs were fixed or variable.

(Some of these measures are discussed in Chapter 7.) The effects of the local financial match for the program were also assessed. These variables seemed more predictive. They were thus included in regressions explaining costs and acceptance rates.

Tables 6.9 and 6.10 report the resulting "best fitting" regressions. The regressions were constructed by placing all variables (goals, community pressures, administrative constraints, and behavioral measures) that had statistically significant zero-order correlations with a measure of the specialized effort into one equation, and eliminating from the regression those variables that did not demonstrate statistically significant partial correlations.

Although the sample size is small (few respondents answered our query concerning both expenditures for specialized programs and AFDC expenditures), the regression explains a quite respectable 54% of the variance in the measure of costs. Expenditures are higher (i.e., the programs are larger) when the rules are considered complex, when workers use specialized assistance as an alternative to the basic grant, and when the cost of individual items is more often fixed—i.e., determined by rules. Expenditures are lower when workers determine grant amounts, when the supervisor must approve the application, and when the external maintenance goal is high.

Why do these results occur? The relations involve quite different

TABLE 6.9
Regression Model of County Program Costs Compared to AFDC Costs

Variable	Raw Coefficient (*b*)	Standardized Coefficient (β)	*t* Score
How often emergency aid is dispensed as an alternative to a basic grant	.08	.40	4.04
Rules are complex	.04	.35	3.39
Some emergency items have fixed costs	.07	.22	2.16
No emergency items have fixed costs	−.05	−.20	1.98
Intermediate supervisors approve the application	−.15	−.22	2.17
External maintenance goal index[a]	−.09	−.39	3.81
N = 57			

Note: R^2 = 54. All coefficients but one are statistically significant at the .05 level; each adds significantly to the explained variance.

[a]See Table 2.2, in Chapter 2, for components of external maintenance.

variables from those demonstrating an effect at the state level, but many of the same general explanatory mechanisms seem applicable. For example, the state-level analysis revealed that the equity and efficiency goal index correlated with larger AFDC–EA programs (see Table 4.2). In looking at administrative characteristics, a three-step explanation for the correlations was suggested. First, it was claimed that equity and efficiency imply a universalistic philosophy. Second, in keeping with such a philosophy, more groups are eligible for the programs. Finally, eligibility of more groups raises program costs.

Assuming that costs are results, and not causes, of the factors, the results at the local level may have a similar explanatory principle. In particular, Table 6.9 notes that costs are higher when rules are thought to be complex, and when the cost of individual items is more often determined by rules. In some respects these results mirror the equity and efficiency argument. They seem to indicate that rule-bound programs have higher costs. That is, apparently (assuming that it is the rules that cause the costs and not the other way around) the existence of standardized rules leads to larger costs by reducing the ability of caseworkers to dispense aid to some at the expense of others and by providing minimum grants for some needs.

The results do not imply that rules *always* lead to larger programs; for example, at the local level rules specifying the number of circumstances for which aid is available have no effect on the size of the program. The point is that, at least in some instances, it seems that having a rule that dictates eligibility and amount of aid leads to higher costs than does leaving these decisions to the discretion of caseworkers.

A second explanatory principle at the state level is that a discretionary orientation (as measured by the goal of treating clients uniquely) reduces the size of the program by creating procedures that allow workers to distinguish deserving from undeserving clients. Consistent with this framework, local costs are lower when the cost of individual items is discretionary and when supervisors approve the application. In both cases, it appears that the driving force of control is worker and supervisor decisions, rather than written rules. Again, it seems that the existence of discretion in interpreting the rules is consistent with a smaller program. In other words, as the state analysis implied, local workers and supervisors appear to use their authority to limit aid when clients strike them as "undeserving."

State-level analysis also revealed that a restrictive orientation (goal) toward income maintenance basic grants increases costs of the AFDC–EA program. It was asserted that this occurs because a restrictive orientation in the basic grant implies that specialized aid is used as an alternative to the basic grant. Consistent with this explanation, the regression reveals that local specialized programs in general are larger when local officials use specialized aid as an alternative to the basic grant.

Finally, there is a relation between external maintenance and lower costs at both levels, although the state-level analysis did not discuss it in detail. It is likely that both state and local officials perceive specialized aid as a somewhat risky program. They may fear that dispensing aid will elicit community complaints about wasted money or fraud and abuse. Agencies concerned with maintaining friendly relations with the community probably limit aid as a means of minimizing external complaints.

Table 6.10 reports some of the correlates of the acceptance rate. This measure is higher when the specialized program dispenses cash. It is lower when a protective payee is used, when workers use negotiation strategies with creditors to forestall requests for emergency aid, and when the influence of the local government is high.

These relations do not mirror those at the state level. Rather, they indicate a number of concerns that appear to be distinctly local. The influence of county government may lead to lower acceptance rates because local governments, wishing to protect their funds, convince officials to be more chary in giving out aid. This explanation is supported by the fact (not reported on a table) that local government influence is higher when the local percentage match (that is, percentage of the costs paid) is higher ($r = .51$). In other words, the analysis indicates that the more that a program is financed from the local coffer, the

TABLE 6.10
Regression Model of Local Acceptance Rate of Applicants for Specialized Programs

Variable	Raw Coefficient (b)	Standardized Coefficient (β)	t Score
Workers forestall emergencies by negotiating with creditors	− 5.60	−.25	3.23
Cash used in the program	10.55	.20	2.67
Protective payees used in the program	−12.14	−.22	2.82
Influence of local government	− 5.31	−.22	2.92
$N = 148$			

Note: $R^2 = .20$. All coefficients are statistically significant at the .05 level.

greater is the pressure from local government to reduce the size of the program.

Other relations seem to indicate the importance of local desires concerning how much assistance to dispense. The relationship between the attempt to forestall the emergency by dealing with creditors and the acceptance rate seems to be a typical example of the role of local discretion. Local officials may decide to use procedures that limit the acceptance rate by first attempting to make informal agreements, such as an agreement with a landlord for gradual payment of back rent. Even though state rules rarely mandate any such attempts, local officials always have the option of using such informal means. In Minneapolis, for example, workers claimed to spend much of their time in attempting to deal with emergencies informally, through negotiations. This occurs even though Minneapolis has a generous program. Other local areas apparently use this technique even more often.

Indirect effects may account for programs being larger when cash is the principal form and smaller when a protective payee is used, since adding conditions is unlikely to directly reduce the acceptance rate. Perhaps the use of more strict forms or conditions is consistent with a more restrictive attitude toward expenditures which, in turn, leads to a higher rejection rate. Alternately, the use of conditions may be a result of a larger program—concern over abuse and fraud, and the perception that these matters must be controlled by conditions, may increase with costs. Chapter 5 contains a similar argument at the state level.

In sum, the acceptance rate seems to be affected by many local conditions and problems. It may give the clearest picture of the role of county discretion in the operation of specialized assistance. Its predictors largely include local concerns about costs and local desires to keep the program well controlled. It is not clear that all of these variables have equivalents at the state level, although it can be argued that some of the more rigorous verification requirements that appear to slightly reduce the size of the state-level program perform a function similar to the measures that correlate with the local acceptance rate.

DISCREPANCIES BETWEEN STATE AND COUNTY VARIABLES PREDICTING PROGRAM SIZE

The differences between the exact variables that predict the cost of the program at the state and local levels may seem to be a bit disconcerting, even though some of the same concepts are involved in both sets of relations. One might expect the same administrative factors that affect the costs of the state-level programs to affect specific counties; after all, for many programs county expenditures total to state expenditures, and state rules and pressures do influence the size of programs. However, the differences involving policy commitments can be explained by the distribution of power between the two levels of government. State policy commitments affect the state specialized assistance effort because these commitments are often translated into state-level regulations. Local policy commitments do not usually affect the emergency assistance effort (except for the concern over external maintenance), probably because local officials have limited control over state-administered or supervised programs. At least partly bound by state rules, they are less able to express their commitments in ways that indirectly affect the size of the specialized programs, even though they may slightly alter state regulations.

The fact that local administrative variables do not affect the size of the program appears to be more perplexing. Such variables as the number of circumstances covered influence the size of the program at the state level. Why do they not at the local level?

Perhaps the differences are more apparent than real. Although local agencies slightly bend or occasionally ignore specific state regulations, the *general spirit* or *tenor* of the regulations may continue to operate. If this is so, then even though counties may cover more types of emergencies and more types of clients than the state mandates (or fewer), they may retain consistency with the philosophy behind state policy. The local areas may use emergency assistance as an alternative to the basic grant when the state mandates such aid to pending cases; or localities may have a larger program when equity concerns (and thus standardized rules) are more pronounced, and have a smaller program when the traditional, discretionary model is utilized.

The explanation is supported by the fact that many of the concepts that affect state-level costs also affect costs locally—even though the variables that are involved differ. Apparently this occurs because general state policies affect county behaviors in indirect ways, even if exact rules are altered to some degree. Counties thus may alter state rules that increase access to specialized programs in restrictive states; the correlations between the type of client groups served (restrictive states, as has been pointed out, apparently expand the client groups served in order to dispense some aid to clients who are ineligible for the small regular grant program) and the size of the specialized program, reported for states in Chapter 5, thus will not occur at the county level. But the point of view of the restrictive states—using the specialized program to compensate for the low basic grant—is reflected in county policies that affect specialized programs. In fact, when the specialized program is viewed as an alternative to the regular grant, it is usually larger.

This explanation receives some support from the executive questionnaires. Both state and local officials were asked to rank the relative importance of items on a list of administrative characteristics such as state-level mandates, local mandates, informal worker contact, and so on. On the average, both state and local officials rate state mandates and state memos as most important.

This explanation also receives some support from the case studies. In Trenton, New Jersey, the AFDC–EA program is state-operated, but the county slightly altered some of the regulations. More funds go to SSI recipients and are used for basic needs (or double payments) than the state-level program suggests. Even though the Trenton officials are quite concerned about meeting the basic needs of individuals, they do not spend as much money as do local officials in Minneapolis, where the state has a more liberal program. True, the Trenton agency has extended homelessness to include cases of threatened utility shutoffs, but it only covers such problems when they are quite serious and when other alternatives are not available. Rules are bent, but the overall philosophy is still respected.

The countercase is Oneida, New York, a county with a restrictive attitude but with a fairly liberal state program. Despite attempts to establish restrictive eligibility rules, Utica has a relatively large program. The state program is designed to meet expensive fuel needs, and the county complies in a general way.

Another explanation of the discrepancies between state and county variables that correlate with program size lies in the budgetary process at the local level. Even though some *state* emergency programs are open-ended, this is not the typical *local* pattern. Almost every county we visited set a dollar limit on specialized assistance. Administrative styles and even agency values often had a limited effect because of the importance of the budget; no matter what local rules say, aid cannot be obtained when the money runs out.

The setting of a budgetary maximum does not completely negate the importance of state rules and even local discretionary policies, because the budget itself is based on history and on estimated costs. If state rules create a large program, the local budget will be larger. Indeed, if the budget is insufficient and counties convince the local administration that the state program must be carried out, a budget increase may occur in the following year. In Boulder, although the emergency program was locally funded and expenditures were limited by a budget, more money was appropriated each year as need expanded. The county government seemed willing to meet emergency needs as long as the county workers could prove that these needs were consistent with the purposes and regulations of the emergency program.

THE ADMINISTRATIVE RELATIONSHIP BETWEEN STATES AND COUNTIES

Not all of the questions are answered, but the data seem to present an overall picture of the relation between county and state administration of specialized assistance. Faced by a host of pressures both to curb abuse and to meet needs, counties tend to make small alterations in state rules—dispensing aid to more categories of recipients than the state mandates, adding coverage for circumstances involving basic needs, expanding outreach, but also encouraging more strict verification requirements and special conditions. To some small degree, pressures to simplify and standardize are modified.

Despite discrepancies, local areas apparently obey the general tenor of state mandates. Their programs thus reflect the most basic patterns found in the state-level study: the use of emergency aid as an alternative to the basic grant, the importance of uniform rules implied by equity and standardization, and the role of individualized, discretionary behavior in reducing costs.

The crucial role of state rules does not negate the importance of some county decisions. When programs are locally funded, more applicants are rejected. Further, local administrative fears concerning community reaction as well as the local practice of negotiating with creditors to forestall the need for aid affect the acceptance rate. State-level rules dominate in determining the size of the program, but counties have some autonomy. The pattern of restricting individualization is modified without being reversed.

Chapter 7

Administrators' Perceptions of How Well the Specialized Programs Work*

The administration of emergency assistance and special needs programs is the legal responsibility of a small group of officials who make the rules and monitor the disbursement of funds. These officials, particularly those at the state level, do not always place the specialized programs at the top of their list of priorities. In our executive questionnaire, state officials report that, on the average, 6% of the time of their staffs is spent on emergency assistance and special needs programs. The corresponding figure at the county level is 15%, and the difference indicates the higher saliency of the programs for those who are more directly faced with demands from clients in need. (In fact, when we carried out the case studies, state officials were often surprised that we were conducting an entire study about the small, specialized programs, whereas county officials generally greeted us with a statement on how important they considered issues raised by the special and emergency needs clients face.) Despite the differences, at both levels of government the limits of quality control reviews and the lack of monitoring probably result in somewhat less than systematic knowledge by administrators of exactly how these programs are utilized by line workers.

Nevertheless, the perceptions of administrators who deal with the

*Susan McGovern was a coauthor of this chapter.

programs are of value. These officials are affected by the conflicting pressures in public welfare. They are aware of—and may contribute to—the pressures toward standardizing not only the regular grants but also certain aspects of the specialized programs. On the other hand, they also may be faced with pressures to meet individual needs of clients for whom the standardized budget is not sufficient. Administrative perceptions, especially when validated by case-study material, help to further illuminate the way in which the cross-pressures are worked out in practice.

CHARACTER OF PROGRAM ADMINISTRATION

One set of perceptions involves the rules and procedures of the emergency assistance and special needs programs. The key issue is how these factors reflect the effort to reach a balance between standardization and individualization. Tables 7.1, 7.2, 7.3, and 7.4 report perceptions of administrators concerning the adequacy and utility of the rules and procedures. The tables are based on questions asked in the program questionnaires at both the state and county level, and often the county questions are a bit more refined.

Table 7.1 reports the frequency with which various kinds of behavior are used by social workers, in the opinion of administrators. The questions were designed to see whether administrators believed that workers bend the rules to try to increase their discretion to deal with individual problems, or otherwise engage in behaviors that might affect the generosity of the program (see Chapter 6). The table indicates that state and local officials have very consistent opinions concerning the frequency with which workers are more restrictive than the rules require. Very few believe that the problem "never" occurs, but even fewer believe that it occurs "often" or "always." "Sometimes" and "occasionally" are the terms commonly employed to describe its frequency.

We thought we could obtain more details concerning when this behavior is believed to occur by determining if workers have an incentive to deny emergency aid to avoid complying with complicated procedures. At both the state and the county level, the majority of respondents believed that this was not an incentive. Officials at both levels believe that emergency aid is seldom dispensed to noneligible recipients: "occasionally" and "never" are the typical responses. Emergency aid is also usually not perceived, at the local level, as a substitute for processing new AFDC applications.

The most commonly reported behavior is forestalling the need for

TABLE 7.1
Frequency of Various Types of Worker Behavior in Emergency Assistance Programs (Percentages of Responses)

Item	State (N = 48 or 49)					County (N = 181 to 187)				
	Always	Often	Sometimes	Occasionally	Never	Always	Often	Sometimes	Occasionally	Never
Workers are more restrictive than emergency rules suggest	0	4.1%	35%	51%	10%	0%	4%	33%	44%	20%
Workers dispense emergency assistance to applicants who are not eligible	0	2.1	10	56.3	31	0	0	9	52	39
Workers deny emergency assistance to avoid complying with procedural rules	0	0	2	35	63					
Workers deny emergency aid to lessen their chances of committing procedural errors			Not Asked			0	1	3	15	82
Workers use EA instead of processing new AFDC applications			Not Asked			1	2	8	14	75
Workers informally negotiate with vendors in order to forestall emergencies			Not Asked			10	52	16	13	6

Note: Owing to rounding, responses may not add to 100%.

emergency aid by negotiating with vendors. Among local respondents, 62% said "workers informally negotiate with vendors in order to forestall emergencies such as evictions and utility cutoffs" either "always" (10%) or "often" (52%). In fact some counties have written rules requiring such efforts. The case study of Mercer County, New Jersey, suggested that official restrictions on what AFDC–EA can cover have forced the workers to regularly resort to informal channels to service clients' needs. In Mercer County an estimated 50% of workers' time is spent negotiating with individuals outside of the welfare system on behalf of clients. As noted in Chapters 5 and 6, rules that deny assistance unless private resources are first exhausted are not common. Apparently, however, in an informal way, negotiations with vendors often occur, so that emergency assistance is viewed as a last resort, after other arrangements fail.

Table 7.2 reports perceptions concerning communication between local and state officials. An interesting finding is that the lack of communication does not appear to be a major difficulty on either side. Combined with the data involving the extent of communication in Chapters 5 and 6, this finding implies that local and state officials do not communicate often, and that both sides usually do not believe that lack of frequency is a problem. Perhaps state officials believe that emergency matters are appropriately handled, or that the programs are too small to monitor. Local officials may enjoy the autonomy a lack of communication creates.

Tables 7.3 and 7.4 report perceived difficulties in the nature of the rules. Based on our responses, problems with the rules are usually either only "occasionally serious" or "not at all serious." According to state administrators, there are few problems related to a lack of specific rules, too much discretion in interpreting rules, or a lack of enforcement of state rules. They are slightly more concerned with a lack of specificity than with the other two problems. Local officials view two of these issues as even less problematic; 70% or more believe that too much discretion or a lack of enforcement of state rules is "not at all serious." In addition, rather high percentages of local officials believe that local rules do not allow too much flexibility, do not allow too little flexibility, are enforced sufficiently, and are not too complex.

Two issues appear to be a bit more of a problem from the county point of view. Many county officials believe that "occasionally serious" or "somewhat serious" problems are caused by state rules that lack flexibility and are too complex. This may be a response to the typical pattern of control that seems to exist in larger programs; rules are viewed as relatively rigid, although other controls are not always

TABLE 7.2
Characteristics of State–County Communication (Percentages of Responses)

Item	State (N = 47 or 48)					County (N = 237)				
	Always	Often	Sometimes	Occasionally	Never	Always	Often	Sometimes	Occasionally	Never
Lack of communication between state and local staff	2%	0%	15%	60%	23%	9%	9%	16%	37%	29%
Too many questions from local offices	0	0	10	46	44			Not Asked		

TABLE 7.3
State Executives' Perceptions of Administrative Problems (Percentages of Responses)

Item	Very Serious	Serious	Somewhat Serious	Occasionally Serious	Not at All Serious
Lack of specific rules to guide local decisions	5.1%	12.8%	12.8%	33.3%	35.9%
Too much local discretion in interpreting rules	0	12.8	10.3	23.1	53.8
Lack of enforcement of state rules at the local level	5.1	2.6	12.8	33.3	46.2
N = 39					

TABLE 7.4
County Executives' Perceptions of Administrative Problems (Percentages of Responses)

Item	Very Serious (*N*)	Serious (*N*)	Somewhat Serious (*N*)	Occasionally Serious (*N*)	Not at all Serious (*N*)
Too much local discretion in *state* rules (concerned with emergencies)	1% (1)	2% (4)	4% (3)	23% (38)	70% (116)
Too much discretion in *local* rules	1 (1)	2 (3)	3 (5)	21 (36)	74 (128)
Lack of flexibility in *state* guidelines and rules	7 (12)	10 (16)	20 (34)	36 (60)	28 (47)
Lack of flexibility in *local* guidelines and rules	1 (2)	2 (3)	8 (13)	23 (39)	67 (115)
Lack of enforcement of *state* rules at local level	1 (2)	0	2 (4)	18 (29)	79 (131)
Too much complexity in *state* rules	7 (13)	21 (40)	16 (31)	21 (40)	36 (69)
Too much complexity in *local* rules	0	1 (2)	6 (11)	22 (37)	71 (122)

Note: Owing to rounding, responses may not add to 100%.

severe. In other words, local officials may be responding to intentional state strategies.

Although the above statistics demonstrate little general concern about administration of the programs, we also wished to look for more specific problems. We asked county administrators to indicate in what areas they would like more specificity in the rules or other additional state or federal guidance, and conversely, in what areas would they like less specificity and more local discretion in decision-making (Table 7.5). In response to the question regarding areas in which more rule specificity was needed, the majority reported either "none" was desired (30%) or left the question blank (31%). An additional small percentage said the rules were clear and workable; but half of those claimed that while the rules were fine, additional funding was necessary to adequately apply them.

About one-third of local respondents indicated dissatisfaction with the rules or other forms of guidance from higher levels. Some believe clearer guidance should be forthcoming to specify the way to determine eligibility. This includes desires for guidelines in computing income, resources and expenses, and desires for better definitions of what constitutes an emergency. Some officials desire comprehensive policy clarification. One administrator said "the local manual should read the same as the Quality Control manual." Miscellaneous general complaints range from a plea for "more encouragement in the use of EA" to requests for more restrictive rules on verification and conditions of aid. If there is any general theme at all, it appears to be the desire to reduce

TABLE 7.5
Designation by County Authorities of Problems with State Rules and Guidelines

Problem Area	Percentage Reporting (Figures Rounded)
Eligibility rules too vague	6.0%
Definitions of "emergency" too vague	7.0
Overall policy classification needed	5.5
Local/state procedural problems	2.5
Rules for new programs (e.g., fuel aid) need classification	2.0
Miscellaneous problem areas	9.0
Rules acceptable, need funding	3.5
No problems	30.0
No response	31.0
Not applicable (no state rules)	3.5
N = 192	

errors in determining eligibility. Many local administrators would like rules dealing with emergency assistance and special needs to be as clear-cut as rules about flat grants.

We also asked in what areas less specificity in the rules and more local discretion in decision-making was needed. Again, a substantial percentage said either no changes were needed (26%, 49 respondents) or did not answer the question (29%, 56 respondents). Typical comments from those desiring no changes emphasized the need for specific state rules to ensure equitable treatment of clients within their agencies and across the state. One wrote: "We need specificity so that each client receives the same treatment/benefits from our staff"; and another who specified no changes stated: "This state rule ensures statewide uniformity in applying the regulations. Therefore, decisions for eligibility are not based on individual cases." Although the desire for standardization is thus most common, 25% of respondents (48) desired increased discretion in administering the rules. Some advocated more individualized treatment of cases. Others wanted greater flexibility regarding particular rules or administrative areas, such as in determining how frequently emergency assistance could be issued, or in setting payment amounts. Only three respondents specifically noted a desire for more discretion to deny aid or to impose stricter conditions of aid.

Overall, administrators thus report few problems. Perhaps this is due to the specialized nature of most programs. Because few circumstances are covered and programs are kept small, there are few recipients and therefore few borderline situations that raise concerns about the rules.

ADEQUACY OF THE SPECIALIZED PROGRAMS

Groups Covered

Responses to our executive questionnaire provide a measure of the adequacy of emergency and special needs benefits, as perceived by officials. Both state and local welfare executives were asked to indicate what groups were eligible for specialized assistance in their jurisdictions, and which groups were "appropriately" served. Because the responses, given in Table 7.6, contain both descriptive and normative elements, it is important to avoid making too much of the results.

As noted in Chapter 6, local programs often give aid to groups not specified by the state, and, as a result, state executives may be unaware of the range of local programs. Our responses reflect this situation.

TABLE 7.6
Responses of State and County Administrators Concerning Adequacy of Specialized Assistance Coverage (Percentages)

Groups	Groups Eligible (N)	Not Served Enough (N)	Appropriately Served (N)	Too Often Served (N)
	State Executives			
AFDC cases	75% (33)	12% (4)	75% (25)	12% (4)
AFDC–UP cases	50 (22)	8 (2)	75 (18)	17 (4)
SSI cases	68 (30)	38 (11)	55 (16)	7 (2)
Food Stamp cases	66 (29)	10 (3)	90 (26)	0 (0)
General Assistance cases	70 (31)	23 (7)	70 (21)	7 (2)
Nonrecipients of public assistance	57 (25)	57 (15)	42 (11)	0 (0)
Migrants and transients	68 (30)	36 (11)	60 (18)	3 (1)
	County Executives			
AFDC cases	95 (209)	9 (19)	78 (166)	13 (27)
AFDC-UP cases	80 (144)	8 (11)	86 (126)	7 (10)
SSI cases	90 (189)	36 (70)	62 (120)	2 (3)
Food Stamp cases	91 (196)	15 (30)	72 (144)	13 (25)
General Assistance cases	88 (177)	18 (33)	77 (139)	5 (9)
Nonrecipients of public assistance	81 (165)	30 (53)	66 (115)	4 (3)
Migrants and transients	86 (174)	18 (34)	66 (120)	15 (28)

Note: Owing to rounding, responses may not add to 100%.

State executives are more likely than local executives to believe that nonrecipients of basic grants are not eligible for emergency assistance and special needs programs. They also generally are more likely to think that this group is not served often enough. We found that 57% of the state executives have this opinion, as compared to only 30% of the county executives. A third of the state executives think that migrants or transients are not served often enough, as compared to less than 20% of the local administrators. Conversely, a significantly higher percentage of local executives than state executives think that migrants and transients are "too often served" (15% to 3% respectively).

There is substantial agreement over the treatment of SSI cases. Although many more local administrators say this group is eligible for programs in their locality, more than a third of both county and state executives think that they are "not served enough," and very small proportions think that they are "too often served." These opinions may contain normative attitudes about the worthiness of the aged poor. The aged, particularly the SSI beneficiaries, normally do not raise moral questions; in fact, many believe that members of this group fail to take advantage of existing benefits. Therefore state and local executives agree on the utilization rates for SSI cases—relatively high proportions of administrators at both levels think that this group is not served enough.

Nevertheless, on the whole, administrators appear to be satisfied with the coverage of most groups. Very large majorities believe that the coverage of AFDC clients, AFDC–UP clients and Food Stamp clients is adequate. But significant minorities are concerned about a lack of coverage of migrants and transients, nonrecipients of a basic grant, SSI recipients, and General Assistance recipients. Few administrators believe that any group is served too often.

The case studies report actual gaps in coverage for certain groups of needy persons, and despite general satisfaction, these are the same gaps implied by some questionnaire responses. The single unemployed adult without children was consistently named as the most underserved and needy in nearly all the case-study counties, with the possible exception of Hennepin County. Even here grants to this population were considered inadequate by program administrators. This group is dominated by younger males, but it includes a significant number of older, borderline-disabled persons, who are ineligible for SSI. This group also includes the chronically unemployed or underemployed who are not seeking employment, as well as new arrivals to urban areas who are seeking jobs. Two-parent families in which the father is unemployed were noted as encountering many of the same problems as the single adults in states where there is no AFDC–UP program. Although our questionnaire responses note some concerns over meeting the needs of these individuals, most administrators indicate that at least *some* of the needs of each listed group are covered; the gaps often seem to be met in small part by one or two small programs.

Circumstances Covered

Table 7.7 reports the perceived appropriateness of the coverage of various circumstances. Although there are differences between the two groups of administrators, the table makes it clear that many at both levels feel that some circumstances are inadequately covered. The most troublesome emergency assistance or special need items apparently are the double payments ("inability to meet basic needs on the normal assistance grant"), which raise all of the issues concerning horizontal

TABLE 7.7
Responses of State and Local Administrators Concerning Appropriate Coverage of Various Circumstances by Specialized Programs (Percentages)

Circumstances	Situation Covered (N)	Requires More Coverage (N)	Appropriate Coverage (N)	Covered Too Extensively (N)
		State Executives		
Special one-time disasters such as flood or fire	75% (33)	35% (14)	64% (25)	0% (0)
Sudden one-time extra expense such as refrigerator breakdown	43 (19)	38 (1)	57 (17)	3 (1)
Lost or stolen checks	73 (32)	3 (1)	88 (29)	9 (3)
Lack of funds of pending applicants for other public assistance	66 (29)	34 (12)	60 (21)	6 (2)
Unusual, continuing circumstances such as special diets or laundry	32 (14)	56 (14)	40 (10)	4 (1)
Inability to meet basic needs on the normal assistance grant	25 (11)	35 (7)	47 (9)	16 (3)
		County Executives		
Special one-time disasters such as flood or fire	92 (208)	38 (82)	62 (134)	0% (0)
Sudden one-time extra expense such as refrigerator breakdown	51 (116)	53 (96)	45 (82)	2 (40)
Lost or stolen checks	84 (191)	16 (32)	79 (157)	5 (30)
Lack of funds of pending applicants for other public assistance	67 (147)	43 (78)	56 (102)	1 (2)
Unusual continuing circumstances such as special diets or laundry	40 (89)	57 (96)	43 (72)	0 (0)
Inability to meet basic needs on the normal assistance grant	23 (51)	75 (119)	24 (38)	1 (1)

Note: Owing to rounding, responses may not add to 100%.

equity, error, and waste. At both the state and county levels, it is reported that about three-fourths of the jurisdictions do not cover double payments. But the state executives appear to be more inclined than local officials to approve of denying additional aid to cover items in the basic income maintenance grant, or at least they are more sensitive to the budgetary implications of meeting basic needs through the use of specialized programs. Therefore, whereas 75% of the local officials want more coverage for the recipients who cannot get by on their grants, only 35% of the state officials are willing to recognize that more coverage is needed. And 16% of state officials believe there is *too much* coverage, compared to only one local official.

Very large percentages of our respondents believe that unusual continuing expenses and sudden one-time extra expenses are not covered. Fifty-three percent of the local officials want more coverage for sudden one-time expenses, such as an appliance breakdown, as compared to 38% of the state executives. On the need for more coverage for continuing circumstances, the figures are closer, involving 57% of county executives and 56% of state executives. About two-thirds of the respondents at each level say there is some coverage for needs arising out of lack of funds for pending cases, with 43% of county executives and 34% of state executives wanting more coverage. A large majority of respondents are satisfied with coverage for lost or stolen checks and for needs arising from natural disasters. Few believe that *any* circumstance is too extensively covered.

The specialization of programs reported in Chapters 5 and 6 has a price, according to these figures. Many items are simply not covered by *any* program in states and counties. In the majority of jurisdictions there is no coverage for basic needs or for special needs. A large percentage of our respondents believe that sudden, one-time extra expenses are not met, as well. It seems that items that in theory are covered by basic grants are often not covered in specialized programs—and many administrators are uneasy about this. Ironically, the specialization that probably contributes to satisfaction with administration may lead to dissatisfaction with coverage.

Sufficiency of Funding: Limited Money and Increased Demand

Perceptions of the sufficiency of funding and the certainty of funding were only examined at the county level. County officials said they were less certain of funding for emergency assistance programs than for income maintenance programs as a whole. Whereas 32% were "very certain" of income maintenance program funding; only 19% were "very certain" of funding for their emergency assistance programs. Ten percent were either "uncertain" or "very uncertain" of income maintenance program funding; 18% were either "uncertain" or "very uncertain" of emergency assistance program funding. Eighty-three percent placed themselves on the positive side of the scale of certainty for income maintenance funding; only 70% were so placed regarding emergency assistance.

The difference in the degree of certainty of receiving funding for the two different types of assistance programs may be explained by the differences in funding sources, or the extent of nonlocal contributions to the programs' costs. Generally, basic income maintenance programs receive a high share of funding from federal and state sources. Emergency programs, in contrast, tend to receive a high proportion of funds from the local property tax. The case studies, and comments on many local questionnaires, indicate a greater concern for holding down property taxes than for controlling other forms of taxation (Proposition 13 being the most obvious case).

On the whole one can still characterize administrators of emergency assistance and special needs programs as being fairly certain of receiving some funding to meet the costs of existing programs—70% expresses some degree of certainty. However, several comments on the questionnaires, as well as reports from the case studies, indicate that *inadequacy* of funding is the overriding problem for many administrators. As mentioned earlier, several respondents said that although the rules were acceptable, funds were insufficient to enable them to utilize the rules. Some who administered programs which were funded entirely from local sources advocated federal or state financial participation. Demand was reported to be increasing in 62% of the counties responding, and 7% noted an actual decrease in funds.

The following comments, excerpted from the case studies, underscore the point that programs operate under severe funding constraints.

> As one would expect, the biggest problem or complaint of the Mercer County welfare agency is the limited funding for what they see as vital programs. While funding for most of the major programs has been "moderately certain" over the past few years, there was agreement that the basic grant level is simply inadequate and therefore responsible for most emergencies clients encounter. With cutbacks in funding for some of the smaller supporting programs, more pressure has been placed on the major emergency programs.

> Everyone we spoke to in Boulder County and elsewhere reiterated the theme of "hard times." This is clearly a period of diminishing resources for public

> welfare. The slack is taken up with uneven results by private agencies, most of whom are experiencing hard times, too. . . . In past years the General Assistance program received a ten percent yearly decrease in funds. This year Colorado has passed a seven percent ceiling on the increase in public expenditures, which means that the amount of money available for emergency assistance will decrease in real dollar terms.
>
> Regarding insufficiency of funding, Jefferson County is a special case. The State of Texas has a low commitment to meeting the needs of the poor through public aid, indicated by a very low basic AFDC grant, which has not been updated since 1969. There is a lack of any public special needs or emergency assistance programs for AFDC or SSI recipients, except Title XX social services. GA is provided only in some parts of the state; in Beaumont only medically disabled persons are eligible for GA.
>
> Oneida County officials agreed that emergency programs are becoming more restrictive due to fiscal pressures emanating from both the state and local levels.

Most administrators perceive increased pressure on their agencies in the form of increased demand, but some are experiencing new pressures because of reduced appropriations. Comparatively few questionnaire respondents (7%) reported decreased appropriations during the past five years, but, as one respondent noted, inflation produces de facto reduction when appropriations remain the same. A few counties indicated *both* increased demand and decreased appropriations. One of the case-study counties, San Diego, confronted such an economic crunch in the wake of passage of Proposition 13.

> The effects of this limitation are to be seen everywhere in the human services system. . . . Our sources at the central office of DPW felt that the worst effects of Proposition 13 had not been felt because the State had used surplus revenues to partially bail out counties that otherwise would be severely strained by the property tax cuts. . . . Because of the limited local revenues the number of allowable staff positions for all county agencies was frozen at a ratio of one employee per 160 residents of the county. The staffing freeze has contributed to overwork, low morale, high turnover, and increasingly inferior service to clients.

There are also problems relating to specific types of shortages. Nearly 62% of local agencies reported increased requests for emergency assistance. Of those, 83% (144) reported increased requests for specific types of emergencies. Most were related either to the rising cost of energy, or to the decreasing amount of housing stock available to low-income persons. This supports case-study opinions that many emergencies were attributable to the inadequacy of basic grants.

Twenty-four percent of local agencies reported increased requests from specific categories of clients. Specified categories break down fairly evenly between basic grant recipients and nonrecipients, AFDC families and SSI recipients, and migrants and the unemployed. However, some agencies reported increases from a certain group because only that group is eligible for the program; consequently they may not have an accurate picture of actual new needy groups in their localities. Evidence from the case studies indicates a trend toward more applications for specialized aid from nonrecipient "working-poor" persons than in the past, primarily because of the rising cost of energy and other basic need items (but of course inflation in the cost of these items would affect welfare recipients as well). Trenton workers, particularly, emphasized that they were seeing increasing numbers of nonrecipient, working-poor individuals, for the first time. CAP staffs across the country report serving many more nonrecipient clients requesting fuel and weatherization assistance than in the past. In response to new demand, the State of New York recently modified Emergency Assistance policies in an effort to extend coverage to more nonrecipients.

ADMINISTRATIVE RESPONSE TO INCREASED PRESSURE

County administrators who reported either reduced appropriations or increased demand (170) were asked how their agencies dealt with the problem. Table 7.8 shows their responses, broken down into four general categories; (1) no changes (28%); (2) informal, unwritten procedural changes (57%); (3) formal, written rule changes (34%); and (4) staff and funding increases (24%). (The percentages total more than 100 because officials could check more than one response.) Many patterns emerge. Overall, most agencies' policies became more restrictive, either by informal or formal procedures. The majority of agencies (100) adopted informal methods of rationing resources, most commonly by screening each applicant more carefully and/or granting aid on a first-come, first-served basis. More restrictive written rules were adopted in over one-third (58) of the agencies. However, nearly one-fourth (41) did receive additional funding and staff; the theme of "hard times" is not universal.

The case studies provide more specific detail regarding agencies' responses to increased pressure. Mercer County began rationing overstrained AFDC–EA resources by screening each request more carefully at all levels, and by centralizing final decision-making regarding expenditures under the Director of the Social Services section. All supervisors

TABLE 7.8
County Administrative Response to Increased Demand for Specialized Assistance

Type of Response	Percentage of Responses (*N*)	
No changes	29%	(49)
Informal response (e.g., rationing)	57	(100)
Aid granted on a first-come, first-served basis until funds were exhausted	*19*	
Average size of grants was reduced without written rule changes	*3*	
Each request was screened more carefully	*32*	
More requests were denied for specific eligible applicants	*3*	
Staff/funding increases	24	(41)
Staff increases	*5*	
Funding increases	*19*	
Formal (written) response	34	(58)
Written rules were adopted to restrict demand	*17*	
Stricter conditions for receiving EA were imposed	*17*	
N = 170		

Note: Multiple responses are possible.

felt they encountered many cases that do not fit the strict standards of AFDC–EA regulations, which has resulted in efforts to develop alternative sources of aid. Alternative sources include their own "Sunshine Fund," raised from bake sales, raffles, and the operation of a food service in the welfare office building.

Boulder County's method of response has been highly pragmatic and adaptive. The agency director's approach consists in reviewing the nature and frequency of past requests for emergency aid, and then revising the rules to fit the demand, and trying to make them more specific. On an experimental basis, officials first tried providing General Assistance emergency aid on a first-come, first-served basis until funds were exhausted, rather than reducing coverage or setting up priorities among clients. Limits were placed on high-expenditure items as well, such as emergency dental care. In addition, alternate resources within the community have been developed by coordinated public–private efforts. Some rules have been established to reduce worker discretion, but as most emergency requests do not require supervisory approval, a greal deal of autonomy still resides at the worker level. Top administrators recognize that lack of specificity in the rules results in subjectivity and inconsistencies among workers. Thus the rules manual is currently being revised not only to meet new circumstances created by increased demand, but to enhance uniformity of client treatment. Some reductions in coverage or the establishment of priorities among clients may be included in the current revisions, again, as an experiment.

San Diego's welfare agencies faced a much more drastic blow to their budgets than other case-study counties, but their responses were not unique. Small emergency grants are given on a first-come, first-served basis from a decimated Community Supplemental Assistance Fund. Alternative resources had been developed previously by social services staff—the Children in Need Fund—but in the past, these grants had been used to cover items "essential to the social development of the child," such as music lessons or baseball uniforms. Because of Proposition 13, this special fund is now being used to cover such basic needs as food and clothing. As in Mercer County, decisions concerning eligibility in San Diego have been centralized as a result of reduced appropriations.

Oneida County's official response to increased pressures on the agency's emergency aid resources originated at the state level. Traditionally, the State of New York's approach has been to find ways to maximize the federal government's financial contribution to the state's welfare system, and recent policy changes initiated by the legislature are consistent with that tradition. The legislature wrote new rules limiting coverage and eligibility for AFDC–EA which effectively convert the formerly open-ended program into a fuel supplementation program. Total program expenditures are expected to jump, but half the additional cost will, of course, be borne by the federal government. Emergency assistance coverage of other basic needs of recipients, called "duplicate payments," were specifically prohibited by the new regulations. Thus, the state did away with the thorny problems surrounding double payments at the same time it addressed an ever-rising need, by limiting AFDC–EA coverage to routine fuel supplementation. However, even before these state policy changes were implemented, Oneida County had restricted emergency assistance coverage to burnouts and housing condemnation, primarily because of pressure from local elected officials concerned about costs and abuse.

THE TOUGHEST PROBLEMS

Housing

Although energy-related emergencies were responsible for most of the recent increases in emergency requests, few officials report that these situations create the most serious difficulties for local emergency assistance workers. Apparently, energy-related emergencies are being handled with some degree of adequacy by the new federal and state energy assistance programs, as well as government-imposed moratoriums on service termination during the winter months. Each northern state included in the case study review (Colorado, Wisconsin, New York, Minnesota, New Jersey) had instituted annual winter moratoriums on fuel and utility shutoffs.

There evidently has *not* been an adequate governmental response to a crisis created by the dwindling supply of low-cost housing. Housing-related emergencies, the second most common new type of emergency requests (including "evictions," "high rental costs," and "lack of availability of low-cost permanent shelter, especially for families"), were reported by the large majority of local respondents to be the single most difficult problem their staff must handle. There often is no housing available that poor families can afford.

While it is not strictly the welfare administrators' responsibility to locate housing for emergency assistance applicants, they may become involved because written rules may prohibit payment of rent until satisfactory arrangements have been made. There are many difficulties. For example, payment maximums or rules prohibiting coverage of more luxurious accommodations (e.g., furnished apartments) may restrict applicants to housing that is difficult to locate immediately, if at all. As we have seen, welfare workers frequently devote considerable time to informal negotiations with landlords threatening to evict tenants who have not paid rent. Often arrangements to budget payments are negotiated.[1]

Local officials interviewed during the case studies attributed the housing shortage to various trends developing over extended periods, among them the tight housing market, increasing demand, "uninhabitable conditions," abandonment of central-city housing by landlords, and, in particular, conversion of low-cost housing to condominiums for higher-income families. Four of the six counties included in the case studies had severe housing problems, and one other county had some problems. Most had some emergency shelter available intermittently, but not anywhere near what would be considered adequate to meet the need. Finding permanent affordable housing for families who must relocate after burnouts or evictions, or who have just arrived

[1]It appears that individual private-housing owners are providing a substantial amount of in-kind housing assistance to public assistance recipients across the country. The owners of low-income housing might consider these deferred-payment, free-credit arrangements to be a hidden cost of inadequate public housing and cash assistance programs.

in a city without resources, appears to create even greater difficulties for welfare agencies than requests for emergency shelter. Although hotels are expensive, people can be housed in them temporarily if no other resources are available. A brief description of the housing situation in each of the case-study sites shows varying degrees of public response.

While severe shortages exist, there is still some low-income housing available in Trenton (Mercer County), but much of it is in dilapidated, unsafe condition. Rents are high, even for this kind of housing. Some emergency shelter exists, but beyond that, not much has been done to alleviate the problem.

In Boulder, an extremely low vacancy rate, conversion of existing housing into condominiums, and the presence of a large university have all combined to make housing scarce and costly. A recently enacted freeze on new construction promises to make the problem worse. There are only a few public housing units in the county. Some of the past pressure on the county welfare department created by housing emergencies has been relieved through coordinated efforts by public and private agencies to develop alternate temporary housing resources. There are two emergency shelters, one for battered women and one for all clients needing immediate housing.

The housing situation in San Diego is very similar to that in Boulder, except in San Diego emergency housing and permanent low-cost housing, are both major unmet needs. The cost of housing in San Diego is among the highest in the nation, owing partly to the general attractiveness of the area, a very low vacancy rate, and a recent rush to condominium conversion.

Hennepin County, Minnesota, was the only site where housing shortages were not mentioned as a serious problem. Housing appears to be available, and low-income persons can afford it because the city of Minneapolis supplements the HUD Section 8 rental subsidy program with its own locally funded subsidy program.

In Jefferson County, Texas, there are long waiting lists for both the Section 8 rental subsidy and for public housing units. Recent changes in public housing rules have reserved more units for relatively higher income groups, further limiting space for welfare recipients. There is very little emergency shelter in Beaumont. City agencies reported increasing numbers of daily requests for emergency shelter, but at the time of our study the only movement toward alleviating the crisis was from private groups, and efforts were limited in scope.

Since in Oneida County, New York, destruction of dwellings by fire is basically the only emergency situation covered by emergency programs, relocating clients is the major activity of agency emergency assistance caseworkers. However, workers are unable to meet the demand. The need for services to locate housing was one of three major areas of unmet need identified by the county's social services plan last year. No new multiple-unit private housing was built in the most recent years for which there are published data.[2] Thus, rents for existing housing are high, and this results in increasing numbers of evictions of welfare recipients and others on meager fixed incomes.

Aid for Victims of Domestic Violence

Across the country there is an increased demand for services for victims of domestic violence. Because of the special, critical nature of the circumstances involved, the problem requires a response from agencies that is different from such administrative techniques as new rules or rationing procedures. Somehow coverage must be extended to meet the demand, even if it means raiding other programs and reducing services to other clients.

The Title XX social services program has been most affected by increasing demand for crisis-intervention services. Some social services offices are undergoing major structural changes in response to these urgent new demands. A common complaint of social services workers was that the necessity of developing a capability to meet the volume of requests for immediate intervention services prevented them from continuing to provide the more traditional, rehabilitative services. Staff time is the major resource provided by Title XX, and social workers are finding less time for the services which they consider "preventive" in the long run—therapeutic counseling, prenatal parental training, and so on. Many workers believe that if more preventive services had been provided, the crises they must handle could have been prevented.

Local communities differ in their response to the new problems, and there are varying degrees of success in handling the new situation. New Jersey responded by adding provisions to state statutes allowing AFDC–EA coverage to victims of domestic violence. Furthermore, the

[2] *The County and City Data Book, 1977* (U.S. Department of Commerce, 1977, p. 724) reports there were "zero" new multiple-unit (either 2 to 4 unit, or 5 or more unit) private housing structures authorized by building permits for either 1975 or 1976 in Utica, New York; all new housing for those years (totaling 35 and 18 units, respectively) were single-unit structures. In contrast, of the 372 building permits authorized by the City of Minneapolis in 1975, 54.5% were for multiple-unit housing, and in 1976 50.2% of a total 769 permits were for multiple-unit housing.

obvious urgency of such cases allows for more discretion in bending the rules to grant emergency assistance. In Boulder the General Assistance program was expanded to cover domestic violence cases. As in Trenton, social workers in Boulder focus on developing alternate community resources as a means of reducing the pressure on public agencies, and to that end they helped set up a privately financed emergency shelter for battered women.

Of all the social workers interviewed, Oneida County's social services director appeared to be the most frustrated—even bitter—about the use of Title XX programs for domestic abuse. A new state mandate that social services offices must respond within 24 hours to requests for assistance in child-abuse cases, and must continually monitor ongoing cases, has thwarted desires to provide a broader range of preventive services. "All kinds of preventive services and ongoing services have been cut back, including services to high-risk cases that later develop into protective cases where abuse has occurred." In the opinion of this worker, such "high-risk" cases require more than cash assistance, but that is all they receive from the county agency at this time. At the time of our research, groups were attempting to organize a shelter for battered women.

THE DILEMMA OF THE ADMINISTRATORS

The small, specialized nature of the programs that cover emergency assistance and special needs seems to create some paradoxes in the perceptions of administrators. Perhaps because the programs are so small, few administrators find problems in the nature of the rules, though many would prefer more standardized rules that ensure that clients are treated equally. Clearly the demand for horizontal equity in public welfare extends to the perceptions of administrators about the specialized programs.

Yet many of the complaints of the administrators stem from the problems that standardization and specialization cause in an era of hard times. In small, discretionary programs, hard decisions must be made. Administrators may be somewhat reluctant to deal with situations fraught with moral hazards—such as double payments. Yet there is great pressure to supply such basic needs as housing. Double payments put workers in the double bind of fearing abuse if they grant aid and fearing acute deprivation if they do not.

Administrators are acutely aware of many of the difficulties their clients face. They complain about the lack of emergency coverage for certain client groups and many items. Most notably, they find the lack of coverage of double payments in most programs a problem, despite the fact that the provision of aid for such circumstances might compromise standardization and ease of administration—goals that many officials desire.

There is no doubt that the major difficulty administrators face is simply lack of funds, not only for the specialized programs but for the basic grants themselves. There are increasingly severe budgetary limits in public welfare systems, and emergency and special needs programs reflect much of the pressure.

CHAPTER 8

Private Charity and Other Community Programs

Although there is great variety in public emergency assistance and special needs programs, most are small and specialized. Who, then, picks up the pieces? What happens to the poor who do not qualify for the public programs or who, even if they do qualify, do not receive sufficient aid to meet their needs? These are among the major unanswered questions in research on public welfare.

One answer that is often given to the question of what fills the gaps is private charity or other community resources. In this chapter, we present data on the availability and utilization of such programs of last resort. Since there is an extensive relationship between the public and private agencies, we were able to obtain information from county executives and program directors on the availability and use of private agencies. We also relied on data from the case studies on private and other community sources of aid.

RESPONSES TO INADEQUATE PUBLIC PROGRAMS

The responses of local officials to our program questionnaires, presented in Chapter 7, confirmed previous findings that needs are *not* being fully met by public programs. This is reflected in the local executives' call for more coverage for several different basic items, and especially to meet needs for items that are supposed to be covered by the basic income maintenance grant.

Table 8.1 presents data on the availability of community resources to meet needs. To the extent that these resources are available, emergencies and special needs may not arise, or, if they do arise, they can be met in whole or in part.

As seen in the table, community resources are reported to be available in a high proportion of the counties; however, in the opinion of the local program officials, in only about a third of the counties is there "extensive utilization." In a substantial proportion of the counties (average 28%) there is "minor utilization." Nevertheless, community resources are moderately available.

But what happens when needs are not met? One public response, if there is no adequate program in the area, is to deny the need for such a program. In part, the State of Wisconsin uses this technique. Senior state officials maintain that the basic grant is high enough to obviate the need for providing additional programs. They claim that if needs should develop over time, the appropriate response would be to raise the basic grant rather than institute programs to cover special needs or

TABLE 8.1
Responses of Local Program Administrators Concerning Perceived Availability of Community Resources (Percentages)

Resources	Available in Community	Extensive Utilization	Moderate Utilization	Minor Utilization
Goodwill Industries and other thrift stores	63% (114)	18% (19)	40% (40)	42% (45)
Public housing	75 (138)	39 (53)	36 (49)	24 (32)
HUD Section 8 housing subsidies	80 (145)	35 (51)	41 (60)	23 (34)
Multi-purpose neighborhood centers	45 (82)	24 (20)	49 (41)	27 (23)
Multi-purpose senior citizens' centers	75 (138)	30 (40)	43 (57)	28 (37)
Low-cost or free meal programs	89 (161)	32 (50)	39 (62)	29 (46)
Locally subsidized transportation	59 (106)	32 (50)	39 (62)	29 (46)
Other	16 (21)	36 (5)	43 (6)	21 (3)
N = 234				

Note: The numbers in parentheses are the number of people responding affirmatively. Owing to rounding, rows do not add to 100%.

emergencies. At legislative hearings in February 1979, in addressing the question of raising the state's supplement to SSI, the secretary of the Department of Health and Social Services testified that an increase was unnecessary, citing several "tiers of services" available to the SSI population—Older American Act programs, Title XX social services, etc. Whether SSI recipients in need actually receive assistance from these programs ostensibly designed to serve them was not discussed. This strategy effectively delegates the task of furnishing aid for any unmet needs to private charity, which a study of Wisconsin's Dane County (Madison) amply shows.[1]

The county respondents—who direct specialized programs at the local level—did not claim that needs are adequately met. When asked how people cope when there is no public emergency aid program in their locality, only one of these respondents out of 236 said that there are no persons with emergency needs. The overwhelming majority said that the people had to scramble: to rely on family or friends (38%), or seek aid from private charities (45%). (See Table 8.2.)

The relatively few studies that have been done on how the poor themselves cope not unexpectedly confirm the impressions of the county program officials.[2] For those on welfare, the basic grant covers most, but clearly not all, basic needs, and, of course, there is no reserve for emergencies or extras. Since the poor must borrow money from time to time, a portion of the welfare grant goes to pay off debts, and that means even less is available for day-to-day expenses. When clients come in for additional funds, they face a terrific amount of bureaucratic hassle: frequent trips, petty rules, home visits, often numerous verification requirements, frequent referrals, suspicion, and hostility. One must "go to a half-dozen places for aid." Emergencies caused by theft or loss are particularly troublesome because of suspicion on the part of the police and welfare officials.

When special aid is not available, both the welfare and nonwelfare poor rely on friends and relatives. There is a great deal of borrowing, sharing, helping out, bartering, and trading of food, shelter, clothing, and transportation. Merchants and landlords extend credit and ignore, at least for a time, missed payments. Welfare recipients also supplement their grant from earned (legally or illegally) income and gifts. It's a hand-to-mouth existence. In the words of one recipient, "You have to have help from everyone and anybody" (Stack, 1979, p. 28).

[1]United Way of Dane County Study, June 12, 1978.

[2]Reactions of clients are based on Gordon (1975), Sheehan (1976), Segal, Baumohl, and Johnson (1977), and Stack (1979), as well as our own case studies.

TABLE 8.2
Beliefs of Local Executives Concerning Action Taken in Absence of Public Specialized Aid Programs

Action Taken	Percentage of Executives Responding	Number of Executives Responding
Persons in emergency need obtain aid from church groups and private charities, such as the Salvation Army	45%	92
Persons in emergency need rely on family and friends for aid	38	78
Persons in emergency need apply for continuing income assistance	27	55
Persons in emergency need apply for public aid in other jurisdictions	7	14
There are no persons with emergency needs in this jurisdiction	5	1
Other	4	8
N = 204		

Note: First column adds to more than 100% because officials gave multiple responses.

AVAILABILITY OF COMMUNITY RESOURCES AND PRIVATE CHARITY

"Everyone and anybody" includes private charity, where it exists. When people turn to private charity, two questions are raised: Is it available? and Are certain types of people more likely than others to receive it? Ideally, one should make an inventory of what resources are available in a given community and who in fact is being served. Since that type of survey was beyond the scope of this study, we asked local program officials the key questions, on the assumption that they would have information based on their experience with the interaction between public programs and the private sector.

The survey of private agencies paints a bleak picture. It will be recalled that many of the public emergency assistance and special needs programs were considered "programs of last resort" and required clients first to seek out private sources. As reported in Table 8.2, the program officials in nearly half of the localities thought that people who do not receive public aid for emergencies and special needs obtain aid from private charities. According to these respondents, private aid, particularly church aid and the Salvation Army, does exist in most of the localities, but the amount of aid provided is small (Table 8.3). Only

TABLE 8.3
Responses of Local Program Administrators Concerning Private Sources of Specialized Aid (Percentages)

Private agency	Present in Community	Large Amount Provided	Moderate Amount Provided	Small Amount Provided	None Provided
Church aid	97% (176)	6% (11)	25% (44)	68% (120)	1% (2)
Salvation Army	89 (158)	13 (21)	35 (57)	51 (83)	2 (3)
Sectarian social services (e.g., Catholic Social Services)	67 (113)	7 (9)	26 (32)	57 (69)	9 (11)
Nonsectarian social services	56 (91)	8 (8)	24 (25)	52 (54)	16 (17)
Religious missions	39 (62)	14 (11)	18 (14)	38 (30)	30 (24)
Free clothing centers	77 (131)	15 (20)	31 (43)	48 (66)	5 (7)
Other	67 (46)	15 (7)	44 (21)	35 (17)	6 (3)
N = 234					

Note: The numbers in parentheses are the number of people responding affirmatively. Owing to rounding, rows do not add to 100%.

6% of the program executives said that the aid given by churches was a "large amount" as compared to 68% who said it was a "small amount." The replies for the Salvation Army were 13% for "a large amount" and 51% for "a small amount." The pattern holds true for both sectarian and nonsectarian social services.

Not much seems to be available from private sources. Who is more likely to get this aid? Table 8.4 shows that, according to the local program officials, some distinctions are based on the social characteristics of the recipients. The types of poor most likely to receive aid from private sources are persons experiencing a sudden catastrophe, those who are on SSI, and the disabled—that is, those who are usually considered morally blameless for their poverty. Those least likely to receive aid are the chronically unemployed, migrants, AFDC–UP cases, those with records of alcohol or drug abuse, and transients. Those least likely to qualify for public assistance programs are also least likely to be helped by private charity.

HOW COMMUNITY RESOURCES AND PRIVATE CHARITY WORK: CASE-STUDY DATA

This is the general picture. We turn now to the case studies for a better insight into how private charity and other programs of last resort

TABLE 8.4
Responses of Local Program Administrators Concerning Types of Clients Likely to Receive Specialized Aid from Private Sources (Percentages)

Type of Client	Most Likely to Receive Aid		Least Likely to Receive Aid	
Public assistance recipients				
AFDC cases	54%	(94)	46%	(79)
AFDC–UP cases	40	(59)	60	(89)
SSI cases	70	(122)	30	(52)
General Assistance cases	50	(80)	50	(80)
Food Stamp recipients	46	(77)	54	(90)
Nonrecipients of public assistance				
Mentally, physically, and emotionally impaired	84	(141)	16	(27)
Those with a record of alcohol or drug abuse	39	(67)	61	(103)
Victims of theft or vandalism	52	(85)	48	(79)
Persons experiencing sudden catastrophes (e.g., fires)	94	(165)	6	(10)
Persons with low incomes but ineligible for public assistance	62	(106)	38	(65)
Persons who have temporarily lost employment	52	(88)	48	(80)
Persons unemployed for long periods	32	(52)	68	(111)
Migrants	38	(63)	62	(103)
Transients	42	(73)	57	(98)

Note: The numbers in parentheses are the number of people responding affirmatively. Owing to rounding, rows do not add to 100%.

deal with emergency and special needs. The bulk of the case-study data will deal with private charities, since they are the most important in terms of amounts of money spent and clients served. They are also mentioned most frequently as an available resource by apologists for the public system. But there are other programs of last resort. Some communities are able to use parts of the income maintenance programs to meet dire need; in Boulder for example, Expedited Food Stamps is made available for single adults who qualify for no other relief program. There are also "sunshine funds," kitties to which administrators contribute small amounts of money to help people. These, too, will be discussed in the case studies.

Two broad themes will be considered in the case-study data in this chapter. One concerns relations between the public and private sectors. The cutbacks in the public funds, particularly but not exclusively General Assistance, have increased significantly the pressure on the private agencies. Demands are now made on them to fulfill emergency assistance and special needs functions which the private agencies feel is properly the job of public agencies. How are the private charities responding to this pressure? Are they demanding that the public sector reassume its proper burden, and if so, has this had any effect?

The second major theme concerns the relationship between programs of last resort and their clients. We have now come to the end of the line. What kind of aid is available for what types of people under what conditions? How is discretion exercised in these programs? Throughout all of the chapters, as we have moved from federal and state programs to local programs, we have seen that distinctions were made concerning the moral worthiness of the clients and their needs. The local officials were quite certain these distinctions also played a large role for those people who never made it past their door and had to seek the programs of last resort. What does happen at the bottom?

Boulder County, Colorado

Boulder is described as a "humanitarian" and "liberal" community, which is certainly reflected in the relative abundance of private sources of aid compared to other communities in our case studies. There appears to be a close relationship between the public welfare offices and the private agencies. Staff from all of these agencies have served together on interagency councils to coordinate all social services in the county. In part, this is possible because of the relatively small size of the community.

The county Department of Social Services (DDS), like several other public welfare departments we visited across the country, has used innovative ways to meet some of the needs not covered by the existing public programs. DSS maintains a small fund which is used for clients ineligible for any of the existing programs (e.g., someone stranded in town who needs gas money to drive back home), or to provide emergency aid to current recipients for items that cannot be paid for out of the grant. Two examples given were a woman on chemotherapy who needed a wig to replace lost hair, and a mother who needed to buy a reward for her troubled adolescent son who was doing well on a behavior modification program. In addition to this ongoing fund, there is a Christmas gift fund supported by community donations.

There are a number of innovative private programs that have been established in recent years, programs that have taken a lot of pressure off the county to provide emergency assistance. The interagency groups have provided a means to tie these private sources into public agencies; the county DSS, in fact, contracts for services with some of these private agencies.

The private agency providing the most significant amount of emergency assistance and maintaining the closest ties to DSS is Emergency Family Assistance (EFA). Funding for EFA comes from United Way, which allocated $36,000 in 1979, city/county funds totaling $11,000 in 1979, and private sources, including churches, community groups, and individuals. The 1979 budget was $72,000; an increase of over 100% in 1980 to $135,000 was planned to provide funds for a new temporary emergency shelter and a second office in Longmont, the second largest town in the county. The city and county funding is drawn entirely from revenue sharing rather than local taxes. EFA is the only private agency that dispenses direct services. The local Salvation Army, for instance, does not provide direct services, but gives money to EFA to dispense them.

EFA's approach to emergency assistance is to use cash aid for short-term needs and counseling and referral for long-term or ongoing cases. In the past, about half of EFA's budget went for food assistance, but with the increased budget over the last two years, there has been a trend to provide a greater diversity of aid. Money is provided for food, rent, deposits, transportation, prescriptions (for Medicaid recipients), furniture, and clothing. An emergency shelter facility, called Echo House, provides temporary housing to public assistance clients who were previously housed in motels at great cost to the county. Under a new contractual agreement with EFA, the county places emergency clients in Echo House and transfers a lump sum from General Assistance funds directly to EFA.

There was other evidence that EFA is filling in gaps that the county agency cannot cover. One-third of all referrals to EFA are from Social Services at DSS. Many EFA clients have applied for public assistance, for which they are eligible, but have no resources to help them through the waiting period. For instance, in the summer of 1979 there was an 8- or 9-day waiting period for food stamps. EFA is relied upon as the major provider of interim assistance.

The other local private agencies providing emergency assistance in Boulder tend to cover a relatively restricted number of situations or a limited range of clients in comparison to EFA. For example, the local Red Cross provides aid only to victims of natural disasters; the Citizen Advocacy Program serves the needs of the developmentally disabled through crisis information and legal advocacy, among other means; the Columbia Center houses victims of domestic violence for up to 30 days; the Colorado Migrant Council provides housing, food, health services, and child care services to migrants and farm workers whose incomes are below a certain level. Similar services are available in most of the smaller cities and towns throughout the county, so residents in outlying areas also have access to a relatively wide range of private sources of aid.

To coordinate the many public and private service agencies and organizations in Boulder County, United Way supports the Volunteer Information Center (VIC), whose primary functions are to act as an information and referral service and a volunteer placement center. VIC receives 30–50 calls a day, although only a few of these are requests for emergency aid. Many such emergency requests involve the need for immediate transportation, for which VIC can usually arrange a one-time volunteer ride. On rare occasions, VIC has also raised a few dollars for walk-in emergency requests, though it discourages publicity concerning such aid.

Despite the fact that a fairly high percentage (25%) of requests received by VIC are from public assistance recipients, the VIC directors did not feel that VIC was providing services that should come from DSS or SSI. This attitude was characteristic of private agencies in Boulder. There seemed to be a general perception that an inadequate public assistance basic grant is an immutable fact of life. Since the basic grant is so meager, emergency needs are inevitable; any unanticipated event such as a rent increase, a car repair, or an illness will always precipitate an emergency. Although VIC often acts as an advocate for clients with DSS in order to get help during emergencies, there was general agreement that the private agencies and churches will step in to help.

However small, the resources of these private agencies were important for groups not served by existing programs and for emergency needs of public assistance recipients trying to "get by" on a small grant. This trend toward aid by private agencies is increasing. A larger share of public monies is being funneled into private agencies from sources such as revenue sharing and contractual agreements with public agencies.

San Diego County, California

There are a large number and variety of private agencies in San Diego. About 60 private agencies have formed a group called the Coalition of Emergency Services Agencies (CESA). CESA was initially organized in 1974 over dissatisfaction with the Food Stamp program, and was successful in pushing for creation of a Food Stamp ombudsman position in the county. CESA is currently pressing a lawsuit against the county in an effort to make the General Relief grant more equitable and generous.

The head of CESA is also director of Lutheran Social Services (LSS), one of the major private providers of direct assistance. Although the primary purpose of LSS is advocacy for the welfare population, it does provide emergency assistance as well. Its funds come from three sources in about equal amounts: local Lutheran congregations, the national LSS office, and private contributions. Out of a budget of $100,000 in 1979, about $40,000 went to emergency assistance. LSS provides a 3-day food supply to needy clients who cannot get immediate aid from the Department of Public Welfare. Generally, these are clients for whom LSS is playing an advocacy role. The food aid is seen as one-time temporary aid to hold the person over until a regular resource can be found. LSS discourages repeated aid in favor of focusing on advocacy to help clients get aid from other sources. It does not serve clients who go from agency to agency seeking assistance. LSS receives a subsidy of $280 a month from Lutheran churches to stock this food bank, and individual churches also hold drives regularly to collect canned food.

In addition to advocacy, LSS provides refugee assistance, counseling for immigrants, and "community ministries" organized by Lutheran congregations to give the elderly poor in the community such services as meals-on-wheels, transportation, and friendly visitors.

About 3800 clients are served each year by two LSS offices in San Diego County, one located downtown, another in the South Bay area. Clients at the South Bay office are almost always families on public assistance. The downtown office sees primarily transients, single people, and "newcomers from the East." Clients here generally fall into one of three groups: (1) young, unskilled but employable men; (2) SSI recipients, especially those who are alcoholics, drug addicts, and physically disabled young men; and (3) deinstitutionalized individuals, who are concentrated in the inner-city area.

Repeaters have been a problem, especially at the downtown office. Young single men ("street people") are generally the ones who make repeated requests, and LSS rarely provides food or other tangible aid to this group.

Lack of food seems to be the most common complaint among those requesting help. There seem to be few requests for housing, but this is due primarily to the fact that people know such assistance is just not available, given the lack of reasonably priced housing in the area. However, families and battered spouses can get emergency shelter from the Salvation Army, which has a capacity of 64 people. Single men and transients are specifically excluded from the shelter on "nondeserving" grounds (in the Salvation Army director's words, they serve a "nicer," i.e., more middle-class, clientele). Space for single men is available at the Rescue Mission, if they are willing to perform certain tasks for the mission in return, such as fund raising.

The Salvation Army is a major source of emergency assistance in San Diego County. There is a large central office downtown, and five branch offices are located throughout the county. All of the army's emergency services are funded solely by Salvation Army funds, with the exception of "emergency lodging," which draws on some revenue-sharing funds as well. The director of the Salvation Army estimated that about $30,000 is spent annually on emergency services.

The national office sets some policies regarding temporary and emergency services and provides manuals which lay out regulations and guidelines regarding eligibility standards. There are income standards as well, which determine both eligibility for aid and the amount of aid received. However, there is quite a bit of flexibility within these standards; this flexibility, in fact, is an important aim of the Salvation Army program.

The emergency services provided are food, clothing, and shelter. Food is the most common request and the most frequent form of aid dispensed. Only rarely does the Salvation Army issue cash for food; in most cases it has vendor-payment arrangements with some grocery stores or it issues $20 food orders to specific stores. Other temporary emergency services include providing bus tokens to people who have job interviews, providing holiday toys and children's clothing, and in rare cases helping with other transportation needs, furniture, rent, and utilities.

The Salvation Army prefers to maintain a "crisis orientation" and, as such, will usually refer people elsewhere for ongoing needs. It also sees advocacy as a major service provided to people who come seeking emergency assistance; it will help people having trouble with public service agencies, landlords, police, utility companies, etc., by directly contacting and negotiating with other parties.

Clients of the Salvation Army are largely families, and about half are welfare recipients. This agency supplements public grants by providing emergency assistance to welfare recipients whose checks have been delayed or who have special one-time needs that cannot be met on the basic grant. It has a restrictive policy concerning emergency assistance to single men (occasionally a clothing order or bus token will be given out), usually referring them elsewhere, such as to the Rescue Mission or Travelers' Aid. Single men can qualify for the Salvation Army's adult rehabilitation program, which handles 90 men. The attitude of the agency is that single men can find assistance elsewhere, and are consequently not as much in need as others.

The emergency services program of the Salvation Army serves about 15–20 clients a day. After eligibility is determined, the client almost always receives some form of aid immediately. A complete file is kept on every client. Records are necessary to satisfy revenue-sharing requirements; they are also used to evaluate client needs and aid given. The Salvation Army sees repeaters often, but has a policy limiting aid to once in a month and no more than three times in one year. (It has made exceptions in cases involving infants, children, and the elderly.) Fraud is not a major concern. According to the staff, the many manipulators are easily screened out. When the same person requests aid several times, he or she may be confronted and pressured to accept some form of counseling or other services. Assistance is not conditional on accepting other services, however.

Some clients who come to the Salvation Army are referred by the Department of Public Welfare, but others come on their own initiative. The Salvation Army's reputation is widely known, so people tend to seek it out before trying other agencies. It also gets referrals from churches, schools, the police department, and other public and private agencies. It does no outreach or publicity for the emergency assistance program because it already has as many clients as it can handle, and "providing services is publicity in itself."

Another private agency that serves as a major source for emergency assistance is Crisis House. Crisis House is a social service agency with emergency-type services administered by a Crisis Intervention Program (CIP). This agency serves about 2000 clients a month. Its major emergency services are a telephone hot line, walk-in counseling, legal aid, and emergency food. It provides a two-day supply of food to clients from supplies donated by the community. The food program served 2400 clients in 1979. CIP also engages in advocacy with public assistance agencies, with agencies that provide emergency shelter, and with job-training programs.

Referrals to Crisis House come primarily from public social service workers, but also from churches and schools. Most clients (75%) are welfare recipients; others may be transients, victims of natural disaster, or people who have lost their jobs. There is little publicity, since Crisis House is already serving more clients than it can handle.

Crisis House refers clients to a variety of other local agencies and conducts a follow-up to see if services were received. Crisis House also educates people about welfare benefits, since many of its clients do not know they are eligible for benefits.

An additional emergency program, available in the east county area only, is called Focus. Established in mid-1979, Focus is a 24-hour emergency service mandated by the county Board of Supervisors and administered by the San Diego Department of Public Welfare (DPW). This multi-department project, designed to provide Emergency Response Services (ERS), operates out of the El Cajon social services office. The multi-department approach is seen in the staffing; there are, in addition to the director, public health nurses, a mental health worker, probation officers, and caseworkers on staff. The original intent of the program was to provide "integrated services" to families. However, because of the reluctance of the DPW staff to make referrals or cooperate in other ways, this original intent has not been carried out. Service workers tend to feel that Focus is unnecessary because it merely duplicates services they already provide. Focus supporters argue that the program is designed to deal with short-term or emergency requests and with after-hours problems, and, as such, it is a needed complement to the DPW bureaucracy. Presently, the primary service of Focus is carried out by its Information and Referral Unit, which is supervised and funded by Crisis House with money provided by Title XX allocations.

The tension and conflict apparent in the relationship between Focus and the DPW service staff at this east county office are indicative of the overall relationship among the county Board of Supervisors, DPW, and private agencies in San Diego County—it is characterized by struggle and dissatisfaction on the part of the private agencies. The Coalition of Emergency Service Agencies (CESA) and the Department of Public Welfare have been battling over the benefit level of the General Relief program. CESA and the San Diego Welfare Rights Organization brought a class action suit against the DPW in San Diego County and 19 other California counties to force them to raise the GR basic grant and end certain practices that client representatives consider illegal. The basic grant is \$120 month. In San Diego, which has the highest rents anywhere in the nation, even a single room in a rundown downtown hotel usually costs \$90–\$100 a month. This leaves only \$20–\$30 per month for all other basic needs. The suit was still pending by the time of the study.

Each private agency interviewed had serious complaints about its relationship to the public agency. Since the severe cuts in San Diego's County Supplemental Assistance program (see Chapter 3), there has been increased interaction between the private agencies and the Department of Public Welfare. Social service workers at DPW have had to refer many more clients to the private agencies for aid. LSS complained about the treatment of clients by DPW eligibility workers. There have been instances where an eligibility worker denied aid or held up the paperwork for some eligible clients, and attempted to "cool off" the clients by referring them elsewhere. Salvation Army staff complained of problems with DPW caused by a backlog of paperwork, verification requirements, the DPW staff's ignorance of available public resources, illegal residency requirements, and variable treatment of clients.

The cutbacks in public funds have had a substantial effect on the private agencies in San Diego. In the face of increased demand, private agencies, which in the past have been "unable" to cover such items as housing or appliances (they knew that county funds could be used), have suddenly managed to come up with the necessary funds. But the long-term impact will no doubt be a severe drain on resources of the private agencies. Although they are meeting some of the imminent needs created by cuts in public programs, the amount of money they provide is quite small compared to the amount that had been provided by the public sector. Certain items no longer covered by the public programs are not covered by the private agencies either (e.g., rental deposits and furniture).

Trenton (Mercer County), New Jersey

Of the 175 private agencies in Mercer County—most concentrated in Trenton—relatively few can be considered significant sources of assistance for the low-income population, and an even smaller number dispense any sort of emergency assistance or consider crisis intervention a major concern. However, for the borderline poor, those eligible for Title XX, single employable adults, transients, and lower-income persons or families experiencing a crisis, these agencies are the primary source of aid.

Only four or five were consistently noted by the public agencies as making a significant contribution to emergency assistance efforts for the low-income population. Mt. Carmel Guild, the Salvation Army, and Womenspace were cited as providing for a fairly specific clientele or need. Only United Progress, Inc., the CAP agency, and the Catholic Welfare Bureau are broadly based service agencies concerned with a wide range of client needs and offering a variety of programs and services.

The Diocese of Trenton runs a large social welfare complex called the Catholic Welfare Bureau, which provides services to an eight-county area. It operates two Family and Community Services offices in Mercer County (duplicating many public welfare functions); it runs an emergency shelter facility; it operates a crisis referral center for victims of domestic violence; it distributes food and clothing in the inner-city area.

The budget for the Family and Community Services program in Trenton is $300,000 per year. The director estimated that one-third of the clients are in the midst of "a real emergency" (i.e., a disaster); perhaps another five or six need immediate "physical relief"; perhaps another five or six a day walk in off the street with no appointment, simply seeking a specific item.

For the walk-in group, the Catholic Welfare Bureau does have a Physical Relief Fund which is used for food, clothing, medicine, and transportation needs. Public collections and donations from businesses are a major support system for this fund. There is also an allotment of $3000 a year from the diocese and a $200 monthly contribution from the *Trenton Times*, a local newspaper.

If the intake worker of CWB determines there is need for emergency assistance, aid is usually given on the spot. Eligibility standards per se are not really used; clients do not need to be Catholic (though about 50% are), nor have to prove destitution. Those in need of food and clothing are given supplies from CWB's stocks; requests for transportation or medicines are met by voucher payments.

Even though CWB does not publicize its Physical Relief Fund, there has been a recent upsurge in requests, which staff members blame on economic conditions. Once the monthly allotment of funds is exhausted, CWB will not dip into funds for the next month. Though there are no written regulations, when funds run short, workers tend to discriminate among requests more carefully. They see repeaters often; those requesting food are usually given aid, but "manipulative" people or those with "strange" requests will be denied aid. Aid is not made conditional on accepting other services, but repeaters are encouraged to accept budget counseling in order to "get to the root of their problem."

Although the director characterizes CWB's relationship with the county and city welfare department as "generally positive," CWB staff feel many client emergencies are the result of inadequate grants and "lack of timely and appropriate aid." The institution of the flat grant has also resulted in a greater potential for emergencies for welfare recipients, according to the staff. As a result of these increasing caseload pressures and continuing problems in the public welfare system, CWB has begun to consider expanding its role to include more client advocacy and political action.

Like Boulder, the Mercer County Department of Public Welfare has an emergency assistance fund raised by the agency staff. This Sunshine Fund has been in existence for approximately three years. The adult services unit began raising money through bake sales, raffles, lotteries, and solicitation of private donations. They also set up a small food service operation in the welfare building in order to provide a more stable source of income for the fund. There are no written rules, but it is well understood among workers that the fund is strictly for emergency situations for which no other coverage is obtainable.

The Sunshine Fund is not publicized at all. Usually a worker hears of a special problem from a client, makes a request to the supervisor, then informs the client of the "grant." Clients are told that the money is a one-time-only payment. Though no repayment requests are made, many clients, especially the elderly, do attempt to repay the money.

The average amount of money given out is $10–$15, but in rare cases clients have received as much as $100. Clients generally are given cash directly; workers said they are sure the money is spent on its intended purpose because the need is so great. Most recipients of Sunshine Fund money are the elderly; many are also eligible for Title XX. Rationing has not been a major issue: Since all workers help in raising the money, they have a sense of how much is available and are careful regarding how it is spent. Though it is not a large contribution to the emergency needs of the poor, the Sunshine Fund appears to help both worker and client morale.

Utica (Oneida County), New York

By New York State rules, clients must use all "available resources" before becoming eligible for emergency assistance, and Oneida County Department of Social Services includes private charitable agencies in the definition of "available resources." The agency director perceives private agencies, not public programs, to be the first-recourse emergency resources in the community. In his words, "local private agencies are there to help them, such as the Salvation Army or the Red Cross; local town Fire Departments have funds to meet emergencies from burnouts. If the resource is available in the community, why should taxpayers bear that burden? All we're trying to do is not duplicate those services." The policy regarding prior application at private agencies is not new, and would be reasonable enough if community resources were sufficient to meet demand. But the county director also admits that private resources are dwindling. For their part, the private agencies felt their primary function was not to provide first-line emergency assistance, but to get the public agencies to respond to the extent of their capabilities to meet emergency needs.

Catholic School Services, funded primarily by United Way and church donations, provides emergency assistance and social services to residents of Oneida, Madison, and Shenango counties. Emergency aid is usually limited to short-term food assistance, but occasionally it covers fuel bills or transportation expenses. The agency also provides information and referral and often intercedes with the county for clients eligible for public emergency assistance. Clients of CSS do not have to be Catholic, but they must reside within a CSS parish.

Most emergency requests are for food, but the agency thinks that at least half of those requests mask other unmet needs. In most cases people need food assistance near the end of the month because their rent is higher than the ADC (AFDC is called ADC in New York) housing allowance. Most of the emergency caseload is already on public assistance, and the reason for needing emergency assistance varies by program category: ADC and Home Relief (General Assistance) recipients often need emergency assistance because basic grants are insufficient to cover even basic needs; SSI recipients are most likely to need emergency assistance because of mismanagement of their resources due to "cognitive and emotional problems." Public assistance clients also end up at CSS because of time-consuming county verification requirements and eligibility conditions. Clients who ask for aid from CSS to satisfy the requirement that all available resources be exhausted before public emergency assistance is granted will always be referred back to the county, if only because the emergency resources of CSS are so limited.

The agency has a written rule limiting food assistance to three times a year. Persons making additional requests will be referred to other limited programs, such as the Food Bank (a stockpile of commodities collected by church groups). The Food Bank was repeatedly listed as a possible emergency food resource in Utica by county staff as well as client advocates, but CSS workers minimized its importance. Food stocks are unstable, the amounts allotted minimal.

Caseload statistics from CSS for 1978 show that of 902 "families and individuals" requesting emergency aid, 691 received financial aid and 211 were given information and referrals. In addition, 593 adults and 1407 children received Operation Sunshine Christmas Help. In 1979 the emergency assistance caseload jumped 30%. The agency director attributed the increase to cutbacks in the public emergency assistance program and inflation.

There are no written eligibility rules for CSS aid, but for each request an evaluation is made of how the need for emergency assistance arose. Questions are asked regarding food stamp usage, proper budgeting, and unnecessary expenses. CSS workers take great pains to "get at the root of the problem" through extensive counseling and negotiating with clients' creditors.

Because of limited resources, aid is granted on a priority basis. "There'll be more of an emphasis on mothers with children, senior citizens, and the handicapped," the program director said. Both cash and voucher payments are made; alcoholics and others who have difficulty managing their money are given vouchers.

In the past CSS and the county Department of Social Services had a cooperative relationship, but that relationship appears increasingly strained as CSS is forced to take over functions it feels the county should be performing. Recently Catholic Social Services agreed to assume administrative responsibility, along with other community agencies, for a new, generously funded community support program serving the large deinstitutionalized population in Utica. Emergency requests are up at a time when private social service agencies here and elsewhere would prefer to deemphasize cash assistance in favor of expanded rehabilitative services. CSS felt its appropriate role within the emergency assistance system was to advocate for clients to get the public agencies to respond as they should.

Beaumont (Jefferson County), Texas

The limited nature of public welfare systems and the traditional view that communities should "take care of their own" has forced a heavy reliance on the system of private agencies in Beaumont, Jefferson County, and throughout Texas. There was a clear consensus among welfare officials that the state should cover disaster relief and replacement of stolen or lost checks for ongoing welfare clients, that the counties should be responsible for providing short-term assistance to pending applicants for public welfare, and that private charities should cover all other needs and clients, including welfare recipients who are unable to meet basic needs on their assistance grants or who have continuing special needs. As for transients, migrants, and low-income people who encounter sudden, one-time expenditures, some officials felt the county should cover their needs, and a few felt these groups should fend for themselves. This, then, is the climate within which the private agencies operate. Public opinion does not clearly support the view that charities should fill the numerous gaps left by the public welfare system.

In Beaumont and in the rest of Jefferson County, there are hot lines for rape, suicide, child abuse, runaways, and family violence; there are as well various counseling services. The only sources of direct assistance for basic needs, however, are the Salvation Army, which provides limited emergency shelter and meals; Treasure House, a clothing distribution center; the Beaumont Association for Senior Citizens (BASC); and Some Other Place.

BASC, established in 1974, provides the elderly population in Beaumont with several services and programs. Among them are a telephone reassurance service, a day activity center, an escort program for the blind and handicapped, transportation, and information and referral services. Primary funding is from the governor's Office on Aging. Because BASC was required to raise an in-kind match in order to receive the 1979 allocation of $46,000, it is dependent on sizable, nonroutine private contributions, as well as city funds.

Given its service orientation, BASC offers little direct emergency assistance. As with adult services at the regional Department of Human Resources (DHR), most emergency work takes the form of tapping other private sources of aid. This involves contacting stores for contributions of furniture and appliances and finding private donors who will give money for food, utilities, medicine, clothing, and even telephone installation. Utility companies have been cooperative when BASC contacts them about deferred-payment plans. Most requests for emergency aid, however, are referred to the local DHR Protective Service unit or to Some Other Place. BASC follows up on 85% of such referrals, and characterizes its relationships with other public and private agencies as cooperative, symbiotic, and close. Directors and workers from other agencies serving the elderly and poor meet each month to plan programs and exchange information.

Agencies working directly with the elderly population attributed most emergencies to the inadequacies of the SSI and social security benefits. As was pointed out by the staffs of other agencies, the elderly tend to be hesitant about informing service agencies when emergencies arise. Requests for aid from BASC usually concern assistance with medical services and prescriptions. The director of BASC felt that high utility bills and inadequate housing contribute to emergencies directly and indirectly; elderly clients will often pay rent and utility bills before buying food and medicine. Such cases became so frequent that a small program has been established by a group of local churches enabling families in Beaumont to "adopt" an elderly person during the four winter months by paying the person's utility and fuel bills. Because BASC has a very positive view of its clients, there is greater concern about underutilization of services and unfilled needs than about client abuse of the system. As a result, repeat requests are neither discouraged nor ignored.

The only private agency in Beaumont providing any significant amount of direct aid to clients in emergency situations is Some Other Place (SOP)—the agency of "last resort." Founded in 1968 by the Methodist Church, SOP had an operating budget of $59,000 in 1980. Contributions from 24 Beaumont area churches constitute one-third of the budget; the remainder is raised through private contributions from individuals and local civic clubs and organizations. No federal, state, or local government funds are either requested or accepted, because of fears of bureaucratic red tape and restrictions on the use of funds. Staff consists of two full-time and one half-time paid positions (the director, a receptionist and two secretaries), and 40 volunteers a week, who do reception work or prepare and deliver the 65–70 meals-on-wheels.

SOP has managed, despite many outside pressures, to retain its original emphasis on providing temporary, emergency assistance, largely because of the director's steadfast commitment to this goal. As defined by the agency's rules, an emergency is an unexpected "crisis situation which cannot be met with an individual's private resources." The secondary goal of SOP is to help welfare recipients to break out of the welfare cycle through counseling, referral, and support. However, SOP fights a constant battle against being seen by clients and other agencies as "an alternate welfare system or a dumping ground for any and all problems."

During the first eleven months of 1979, 1351 clients were seen, which led the director to estimate that over 2000 people were served by SOP, since most clients had a spouse or dependents. Of the 152 people who walked through the door in November 1979, only 10 were denied aid, and these were referred to other agencies. Almost 75% of SOP's clients are welfare recipients, but because the director does not want SOP to function as an alternate welfare agency, she is trying to cut down on the number of welfare recipients served. Rules have been drawn up stating that welfare recipients who "want to stay on welfare" will not be eligible for SOP aid unless they or their children are ill. SOP will work with recipients to help them get skills and counseling, referring many to vocational rehabilitation programs. When welfare recipients show concerted efforts to "break their welfare dependency" by getting jobs or enrolling in training programs, SOP will then help them with direct aid. Determining when a client is making such an effort appears to be up to the discretion of the director.

Other people likely to be denied aid are transients, who are predominantly white males and viewed by the agency as "pros" at working the public and private welfare systems. They are usually referred to the Salvation Army. Repeaters may also be denied aid, because of SOP's emphasis on temporary assistance; however, repeaters whose cases involve medical emergencies, food shortages, or children will be given assistance.

Direct aid to clients takes several forms, including providing bus tickets (and occasionally money for gasoline), paying rent, utility bills, and druggist bills, and supplying foodstuffs. Only in rare instances does money change hands, most often \$5–\$10 for gasoline. In most cases, private vendors are contacted and agree to bill SOP for certain well-specified goods and services. An excellent working relationship exists between SOP and a variety of druggists, landlords, utility and telephone companies, and service stations. A supply of food is kept at SOP for daily use, but rules for giving it out have become much stricter, and now include some verification of need. SOP also operates a back-to-school clothing store in August; clients register at SOP and are given coupons for a certain number of items, depending on family size. The rules also specify a maximum expenditure of \$75 a year per client for all requests, though the maximum has been exceeded in some unusual cases, such as those involving medical and drug bills. Often, when a particularly large amount is needed for a special case, SOP will organize a fund-raising drive or ask a church to take over a case so that the SOP budget isn't taxed too heavily. While SOP never asks to be repaid for its services, some clients request aid in terms of a "loan," and 90% of such "loans" are repaid.

SOP is the only agency in Beaumont designed to provide a fairly wide variety of emergency services; it is also the agency with the most concern over abusers, manipulators, and repeaters. Perhaps the attitude of the staff toward clients tends to be cautious because, in serving as both a last and, in some cases, only resort for a wider variety of clients, they feel vulnerable to abuse. Even so, SOP is able to respond to crises in a rapid and thorough manner and has put its limited resources to the most efficient use possible, so that clients with "legitimate" problems (according to SOP guidelines) receive adequate aid. However, SOP can fill only a limited number of the gaps in the welfare network in Beaumont; there are still groups of clients who are inadequately served, and needs that are not receiving appropriate attention.

THE MISSION OF PRIVATE CHARITY

The major characteristics of the public emergency assistance and special needs programs are that they are small in size, variable across and within states, and highly discretionary. These characteristics are much more pronounced in the private sector. If one counts the number of private charity organizations and programs, there appears to be a great deal of aid available. A closer examination, however, reveals that the private sector's efforts to serve the emergency and special needs of the poor are uneven and inadequate.

Private charities dispense food, temporary shelter, referral services, and transportation. But there is great variability in all aspects of this distribution. Some localities have fairly extensive networks of private charity, and some degree of coordination or comprehensiveness in scope, such as we found in Mercer County (Trenton), but in other areas private charity is quite limited. Whatever the benefits—some agencies seem to specialize in small amounts of food, others in temporary shelter, and others in referral and advocacy services—the amount of aid is invariably small, it is rarely in cash, and there are few repeats (with some exceptions, e.g., the Salvation Army).

In all of the case studies, we found that private agencies have felt acutely the pressures arising out of the adoption of the consolidated grant, the failure of the income maintenance programs to keep pace with the rising cost of living, and the inadequacies of the publicly funded emergency assistance and special needs programs. In many of the private agencies, especially the larger ones (e.g., San Diego, Trenton, Oneida), most of the clientele are already on public assistance. A new role or at least an enlarged role has been thrust on the private agencies; demands are made on them to pick up the cases that are being abandoned or inadequately handled by the public agencies. Except in Boulder, where so far there has been acceptance of this relationship, the private agencies resent these additional tasks. In San Diego the private agencies are well organized and have been fighting back. Agencies in other areas are moving in the same direction. Thus we find that, increasingly, private agencies are engaged in advocacy services on behalf of clients to obtain benefits from the public agencies.

It is hard to predict what effects this reaction by private agencies will eventually have on the public sector. The forces leading to the cutbacks in public funds are very strong, at least at the present time, and the clientele of emergency assistance and special needs are far down the queue line in claiming political attention.

There is also the possibility of cooperation between the public and private organizations. We already noticed (e.g., in Boulder) a tendency for public money to be diverted to private agencies for emergency assistance and special needs, either through contracting for services or direct grants. This is a form of delegation, whereby public officials get rid of troublesome problems, and it may be that private agencies will be more willing to take on these tasks if more money is available. To the extent that cooperation becomes the norm, the private agencies will not become an active force in pressuring public agencies to be more responsive to the emergencies and special needs of their clients.

What impact does this increased role of private charities have on the poor? All social service agencies, but especially private ones, have a mission, a set of organizational goals which, for the sake of brevity, can often be summed up in the terms "reformation" or "rehabilitation." Most are not income maintenance organizations except insofar as providing income maintenance assists them in their work. They do not view themselves as adjuncts to the public income maintenance programs, and, as we have seen, they resent the burdens now being thrust upon them by the inadequacies of the public programs. What this means is that in allocating their scarce resources, in exercising their discretion as to which clients they serve in what amounts and under what conditions, the private agencies make choices in terms of their mission. They pick and choose clients and conditions in terms of their goals, and not in terms of public goals as reflected in laws and other public policies. Private agencies are under no obligation to provide procedural due process, to treat similarly situated clients equally, or even to refrain from imposing their notions of morality and right and wrong. The staff of Some Other Place, in Beaumont, Texas, not only feel no obligation to support those whom they judge to be unwilling to try to get off welfare, they feel that to support such people would be a serious misuse of agency funds. It is not a welfare agency; it is a social service agency whose mission is to help people to help themselves. The crucial point is that not only do private charities exercise discretion along moralistic, deserving–undeserving dimensions, but that this discretion is precisely what they are all about. It is rational decision-making in terms of their organizational goals. How this discretion is exercised depends on agency strategy. The Beaumont Association for Senior Citizens stands in sharp contrast to Some Other Place. The difference, of course, is the moral evaluation of the clients being served. The Salvation Army, in carrying out its mission, strains very hard to turn no one away empty-handed; it will always give something, if only a meal. No doubt the Salvation Army thinks that this is the best strategy for recruiting people for salvation. Most agencies, however, do not share this approach. Perhaps the polar opposite strategy is that used in dispensing "sunshine funds," the private donations of public social workers. These are secret funds, highly discretionary, given on a one-time-only basis and in very small amounts ($10–$20) to people who are really desperate.

Very few private agencies look for customers; they all seem to engage in careful screening. The small amount of relief they supply is conditioned. This is the bottom of the organized effort to help the poor in their need.

CHAPTER 9

A Comparative Note: Meeting Individualized Need in the British Supplementary Benefits Scheme*

Whereas the consolidated grant in the United States is relatively recent, the British adopted a uniform, national income maintenance program more than 30 years ago. Twice since then the British system became so warped by the pressures to meet emergency assistance and special needs that the entire scheme had to be overhauled. The British, for the entire period, have publicly, consciously, and seriously confronted the central issues in individualized treatment versus standardization in a major income maintenance program. This is in sharp contrast to the United States, where there has been very little public discussion, at least for the case of individualization.

THE BRITISH WELFARE SYSTEM

In Great Britain fundamental shifts in attitudes toward the poor and welfare policy grew out of the experience of World War II. As a result of

*This chapter is based on the research conducted by Joel F. Handler with funds provided by the German Marshall Fund in 1977–1978 and again in 1979. That support is gratefully acknowledged. Many people in Great Britain generously gave their time and commented on various drafts. Special thanks are due to David Bull, David Donnison, Alan Palmer, Martin Partington, and Michael Partridge. A more detailed version of this chapter is available as an Institute for Research on Poverty Discussion Paper (Handler, 1980).

the total war effort, the British government reexamined its existing welfare policies; modern social welfare in Great Britain can now be dated from the publication of the *Beveridge Report* (Beveridge, 1942).[1] The basic concept of the *Beveridge Report* was a national minimum floor of income below which no one would be allowed to fall no matter what the cause. The plan was univeral in that, with few exceptions, it would apply to all persons regardless of income, and all would make insurance contributions. The disruption of earning power by old age, sickness, or other vicissitudes would be guarded against by National Insurance. Family Allowances, payable for the second and subsequent children, would prevent the standard of living from falling as family size increased. For those not covered by National Insurance, the "safety net" or residual program would be Social Assistance, which was means-tested. There was also provision for a national health service.

The Family Allowance Act (1945) was financed out of the national treasury without a needs test or insurance contribution. Since it was thought undesirable to relieve parents of all financial responsibility for child rearing, benefits were fixed below what was considered a subsistence level. The National Insurance Act (1948) provided for loss or interruption of income for covered persons (employed, self-employed, and nonemployed) if the requisite number of contributions had been made and certain contingencies were met (i.e., unemployment, death, sickness, or old age).[2] Both contributions and benefits were at flat rates regardless of income. The government decided that benefits had to be reasonably related to contributions, and they were set below the subsistence levels calculated by Beveridge. The National Insurance (Industrial Injuries) Act (1946) covered loss of income caused by industrial injuries and diseases. It too was an insurance scheme; employers and employees paid into a common fund at flat rates. Benefits were paid for injury, disablement, or death.

National Assistance (1948), the predecessor of Supplementary Benefits, was the residual or safety-net program designed to fill the gaps left by the various insurance schemes. It was means-tested, with benefits at a subsistence level. It replaced the various social assistance programs, including the Poor Law, with a nationwide, uniform scheme. The program was administered by the National Assistance Board. Any person over 16 was eligible for support for himself/herself and dependents,

[1]For recent British social welfare history, see Marshall (1965); Mays et al. (1975); and McClements (1978).

[2]In addition to the basic pensions, there are many other benefits provided under National Insurance such as widows' benefits, guardians' allowances, and special allowances for children.

unless he or she was in full-time employment. National Assistance was primarily for those outside the insurance scheme—unsupported mothers, those who had exhausted or failed to qualify for insurance benefits, or those whose basic insurance grant was inadequate. Assistance was normally given in cash at rates fixed by Parliament. National Assistance officers did, however, have discretion to give higher grants to individuals with special needs or under exceptional circumstances.

This was the social security scheme set up in the post–World War II period at the national level. Our concern is with the development of the residual or safety-net program, National Assistance, which developed an emergency component. Before analyzing it in detail, we must describe briefly the characteristics of the British social security scheme as it matured, since the various parts of the major programs interact with each other and place constraints on the proposed reforms of Supplementary Benefits and its emergency system.

In *The Economics of Social Security* (1978), Leslie McClements summarized the social security sector in Great Britain.[3] The total population of the country, 56 million, has remained relatively stable in recent years, but the age structure has been changing. Since 1961, the population over pension age has increased (from 14.5% to 16.8% in 1974) and is expected to rise to 17.4% in 1981 before leveling off. As we shall see, this group has been one of the most important factors contributing to the size of the social security sector, as well as the problems of Supplementary Benefits. More than half of the population is dependent on social security. About half of this group are children below the age when they can leave school, and the other half—adults—are the aged, those not in the labor force (mothers, the sick, disabled, and unemployed) and students in higher education.

The social security sector itself accounts for 10% of the total economy or 20% of the public sector costs. In 1975, social security expenditures were £8918 million, about 10% of national income. The main source of the receipts is from National Insurance contributions; the central government contributes about one-third from general revenues. Insurance benefits account for 72% of expenditures; Supplementary Benefits grants are the next largest expenditure (12%), followed by allowances (6%), and other programs (e.g., war pensions).

The National Insurance scheme is large and complex. The most important beneficiaries, both in terms of numbers and expenditures, are the contributing pensioners. Until recently, benefits were paid at a flat rate, but under the Social Security Pensions Act (1975), pensions

[3]The figures that follow come from McClements (1978, p. 29).

became earnings-related; this should increase the sizes of many pensions; and the government hopes that when the scheme fully matures, in 1998, most pensioners will not also have to receive Supplementary Benefits to bring their incomes up to a subsistence level.[4]

Unemployment benefits are available to covered employees for up to 312 days, but can be withheld for up to 6 weeks if the claimant quits, was fired for cause, or refused suitable employment without good cause. The unemployment scheme also has an earnings-related supplement, and various kinds of sickness, injury, and maternity benefits.

Supplementary Benefits (SB) is the next most important program; it will be discussed in detail below. Whereas most National Insurance benefits are contributory and only available for well-defined contingencies (e.g., retirement, sickness, unemployment), SB is not contingency-based; it requires a detailed means test. SB levels, called the scale rates, are set by Parliament at what is generally regarded the official poverty line in Great Britain. The benefits are supposed to cover all normal living expenses, and they vary with the size and composition of the family (there is a "man-in-the-house" rule, governing the joint resources of unmarried, cohabitating individuals). SB claimants are entitled to other social benefits, such as free prescriptions, various health services, and free school milk and meals. On the other hand, SB claimants are not entitled to various housing benefits such as rent rebates and allowances.

Two other programs of importance are the Family Income Supplement, which supplements the incomes of family heads in full-time work (these benefits are taxed or "clawed back") and Child Benefits, which are paid for every resident child. There are also other small noncontributory programs, such as various war pensions and disability supplements.

THE OPERATION OF THE SUPPLEMENTARY BENEFITS SCHEME[5]

The Supplementary Benefits program was amended in 1966. The name was changed (from National Assistance) in the hope of making the scheme more palatable to the largest number of claimants, the aged.

[4]On the relationship between pensions and the Supplementary Benefits scale, see Atkinson (1970, Chapters 3 and 7); and Kincaid (1975, pp. 14, 115, 146–152).

[5]In addition to McClements, the description of the SB is based on Great Britain, Supplementary Benefits Commission (1975, 1976, 1977a, 1978); and Great Britain, Department of Health and Social Security (1978).

The other major changes were to introduce a legal entitlement to benefits and to reduce the number and amount of discretionary extra payments that had evolved under National Assistance, by increasing the level of payments to the aged and to those who had been in the program a long time.

Composition of the Rolls

In 1966, about 2.5 million people claimed Supplementary Benefits; and this number rose another half-million by the beginning of 1978. Counting the dependents of claimants, SB supports about 5 million people.

The distribution of SB recipients in 1978 is given in Table 9.1.

About 20% of all retired people are also dependent on SB. About half of the unemployed and single parents and about 20% of sick people who are receiving National Insurance or other benefits also receive SB benefits to bring them up to Britain's poverty line.

Although the total number of people claiming SB remains high, the composition of the rolls has changed over time. Because of changes in National Insurance benefits and occupational pension coverage, the number of pensioners, widows, and disabled receiving SB has been declining. The most significant change in the composition of the SB rolls has been caused by the rise in unemployment in Great Britain. In 1966, SB claimants who were unemployed numbered 179,000; by 1978

TABLE 9.1
Supplementary Benefits: Composition of the Rolls, 1978

Category	Number of People
Pensioners	1,736,000
Below pension age	1,281,000
Unemployed and registered for work	*677,000*
Single parents (not in other groups)	*331,000*
Sick and incapable of work	*222,000*
Widows with National Insurance pension	*23,000*
Required at home to care for aged or sick relative	*14,000*
Others	*13,000*
Total	3,017,000

Source: Great Britain, Department of Health and Social Security, "Social Assistance: A Review of the Supplementary Benefits Scheme in Great Britain," DHSS mimeo, 1978, p. 13.

this had increased to 598,000, which is about half of the registered unemployed (Great Britain, Supplementary Benefits Commission, 1978, p. 96). Unemployment is not expected to be reduced significantly during the next few years; moreover, even if the economy does improve, it is doubtful whether many long-term unemployed who are on SB will be able to find jobs. This large pool of unemployed is very likely to remain a significant proportion of the SB rolls, primarily because it is too expensive to extend unemployment benefits so as to reduce dependence on SB significantly.[6]

Single parents are the next most important SB group. This group is growing, not only because of changing social trends, but also because of declining employment opportunities.

Every British government since World War II has tried to reduce the number of people dependent on this means-tested program, but the costs of improving the other parts of the social security system sufficiently to reduce SB dependency are great. SB, in the foreseeable future, may therefore be expected to continue as a program of substantial size.[7]

The Benefit Structure

The size of SB benefits is determined by the scale rates. The basic legislation says that the scale rates are to cover "normal requirements" other than rent, but does not specify what items are covered.

The thrust of the scale rates, since the enactment of National Assistance in 1948, has been to achieve horizontal equity. The scale rates differentiate in terms of marital and household status and age. In all, there are eight basic scale rates, including four age classifications for children.

In addition, there is a long-term rate and a short-term or ordinary rate. This distinction was introduced as part of the 1966 changes; a higher rate (the long-term rate) was to be paid for pensioners and non-

[6]A 1978 government report estimates that it would cost £70 million to extend unemployment benefits from one year to two, even counting administrative savings, and that doing so would not reduce the number of unemployed on SB by even a third (Great Britain, Supplementary Benefits Commission, 1978, p. 16; Great Britain, Department of Health and Social Security, 1978, p. 15). See also Sinfield (1977).

[7]This is the conclusion reached by the recent Government Review Team (Great Britain, Department of Health and Social Security, 1978, p. 19), as well as almost every other commentator in Great Britain, including the present Conservative Government (Great Britain, Department of Health and Social Security, 1979).

aged claimants who were not unemployed and who had been on benefits for at least two years. This addition was originally designed to remove the growing number of discretionary extra payments for these classes of claimants. Though it failed to achieve that objective, it has been retained.

How adequate are the rates? The original rates were based on the "basket of goods" calculation of a minimum standard of living, and then periodically increased. Since 1966, in general, SB rates have been increased in the same amounts as National Insurance rates. There is no agreement (here, as elsewhere) on what is adequate, although it is apparent that the SB scale rates are far from generous. On average, for a family of four, the SB income is about two-thirds of the net income of the average male manual worker. Various household surveys have indicated that SB claimants are living on tight budgets, with "little cash to spare for nonessentials," have fewer durable goods than other lower-income families, and that for many, the scale rates are not sufficient to meet the "main requirements" of the claimants; for example, SB claimants, in general, were found to lack the minimum stock of clothing (Great Britain, Department of Health and Social Security, 1978, p. 16). The conclusion of a recent government review was that "the rates are, for the average family, below generally accepted measures of low earnings and comparable means tested benefits [Great Britain, Department of Health and Social Security, 1978, p. 51]."[8]

The Rise of Discretionary Payments in the Supplementary Benefits Scheme

The above description of SB emphasizes uniformity within classes of claimants, rather than individualized treatment, and that has always been the guiding policy of the Supplementary Benefits Commission and its predecessor, the National Assistance Board. Interestingly, this was not Beveridge's original conception. Since he thought that National Assistance would be a small, "essentially subsidiary" scheme for those who somehow failed to qualify for the basic, universal insurance schemes, it would take "full account of individual circumstances" (Great Britain, Department of Health and Social Security, 1978, p. 71). The enabling legislation reflected the board's view.

Nevertheless, despite board policy, discretionary payments began to grow almost immediately (Great Britain, Supplementary Benefits Com-

[8]See also Atkinson (1970, pp. 18–19; 1975); Kincaid (1975, p. 19); and Lister (1979).

mission, 1976, p. 89). The individual grants were small and were for such things as extra milk and eggs, window cleaning, and similar items, but as early as 1948, more than a quarter of the total National Assistance claimants also had a weekly discretionary addition. Most of the additions were for laundry and domestic assistance (59%) or special diets (32%).

The number of recipient units receiving weekly additions continued to grow. By 1965 the main items were fuel (30%), special diets (29%), and laundry and domestic help (35%). There was also a steady growth in the number of single payments for special needs. While the number of claimants doubled between 1948 and 1965, there was a threefold growth in the number of special need grants made, reaching a total of 345,000 per year.

When in 1966 National Assistance changed to Supplementary Benefits, one of the purposes was to reduce the number of discretionary payments. Long-term scale rates were raised by an amount roughly equivalent to the average amount of the discretionary addition that had been granted, in anticipation that any new discretionary payments to this group would only be for "exceptional circumstances."

In addition, the Supplementary Benefits Commission itself attempted to make more uniform and specific the circumstances under which discretion was to be exercised. It attempted to achieve greater uniformity by promulgating more and more rules to govern the exercise of field-level or "officer discretion."[9]

At first the 1966 changes were successful in reducing discretionary payments. The number of SB claimants receiving weekly supplements (now called Exceptional Circumstances Additions—ECAs), fell from 1,157,000 in 1965 to 594,000 in 1967 and continued to decline. But then the trend reversed, and by 1976 the number of claimants receiving ECAs was 1,431,000, or 49% of all claimants (Great Britain, Department of Health and Social Security, 1978, p. 72). ECAs were mostly given to those on the long-term rates. Sixty-six percent of all SB pensioners received ECAs; about a third of the sick and disabled and of single-parent families also received ECAs, as compared to fewer than 20% of the unemployed. ECAs were for a continuing expenditure for items either not considered covered by the scale rates (e.g., domestic assistance) or for additional expenses for items that were included (e.g.,

[9]Although the emphasis in this paper in on the discretionary authority to grant benefits, SBC also has discretionary authority to reduce or withhold benefits (see Great Britain, Supplementary Benefits Commission, [n.d.]).

heating). Grants for extra heating accounted for two-thirds of the total ECAs in 1976. The rules governing heating additions specify the precise amount of the payments that can be made, as well as the criteria.[10] Special diets were the next largest ECA item. They went down during the period from 1974 to 1975 but then rose rapidly to 386,000 in 1978. ECAs for laundry declined from 162,000 in 1974 to 143,000 in 1978.

In addition to the ECAs, discretionary lump-sum payments are given. These are called Exceptional Needs Payments (ENPs). These grew from 386,000 in 1967 to 1,199,000 in 1978. The bulk of ENPs are concentrated on a few items (clothing and footwear, bedding, fuel, furniture, moving expenses, and household repairs). Despite the fact that clothing and footwear are supposed to be covered by the scale rates, at least half of all ENPs were awarded for that purpose, and this has been true for the last ten years; in fact, the proportion of ENPs awarded for clothing continues to rise. Heaviest use for this purpose occurs in the beginning of the school year.

The SBC can impose "voluntary" savings deductions, and the money saved from the weekly allowance is eventually paid to the recipient in a lump sum for the special need request. The number of such savings deductions has been rising, from about 2000 in 1971 to about 120,000 in 1978; they have been used primarily for clothing. Whether and when to impose such plans on claimants is a discretionary decision, and it is normally used when claimants have repeatedly requested help for items considered to be within the scale rates. It is claimed that once a savings deduction is in effect, the claimant is less likely to receive additional discretionary grants.

Who receives ENPs? Although it is difficult to be precise, the SBC estimates that in 1975, of the 2.8 million recipients, 39% received ECAs and 17% received one or more ENPs during that year. Generally speaking, the ECAs go to pensioners. The distribution of ENPs is quite different. In 1976, the SBC estimated that 288,000 ENPs went to pensioners, 362,000 to the unemployed, and 415,000 to others (sick and disabled, single parents, etc.). About one-third of those who received ENPs did so more than once. Single parents had the highest proportion receiving an ENP (48%), and they, more than any other category, needed more than

[10]Examples (per week) include "mobility is restricted because of general frailty or advanced age"—70p; "chronic ill health (e.g., chronic bronchitis, rheumatism, severe anemia or chronic debility)"—70p; "housebound (or mobility . . . so restricted that [claimaint] is unable to leave house unaided)"—£1.40.

one ENP.[11] For all categories of claimants, the highest probability of receiving an ENP occurred during the first year of the benefits.

Neither ECAs or ENPs are very costly in terms of overall SB expenditures. During 1978, ENPs cost about £34 million, and ECAs £60 million (£45 million for heating alone), which overall is 6% of net SB expenditures (Great Britain, Supplementary Benefits Commission, 1976, p. 105). Nevertheless, there are other costs to the present administration of discretionary benefits. In recent years, there has been a large increase in the number of administrative appeals, and during 1978 at least 45% of the appeals involved decisions about discretionary payments. Both ECAs and ENPs are considered to be administratively intensive. It is estimated that ECAs use the time of about 600 field staff and ENPs require twice that number out of a total staff of 31,500 (School of Advanced Urban Studies, 1976, pp. 28–30). The proportion of staff time attributable to ECAs and ENPs is about 6% of the total SB staff time spent in local offices. Finally, there is considerable variation between offices and uneven take-up among claimants, raising problems of horizontal equity.

A number of explanations have been offered for the repeated and continued growth of ECAs and ENPs, including the rise of welfare rights and advocacy organizations which disseminated information and prosecuted administrative appeals. There was also an increase in the number of SB claimants, but this alone did not account for the increase in discretionary payments. Between 1968 and 1976, the number of SB claimants increased by 11%, whereas the number of ENPs increased by 137%. There were changes in the characteristics of SB claimants (i.e., more were unemployed) which would increase the number requesting ENPs but have little effect on the rise of ECAs. But whatever the reason, by the mid-1970s, Supplementary Benefits had come to resemble National Assistance, despite the 1966 changes that were designed to reverse the trend toward increased discretionary benefits.

The Supplementary Benefits Commission, concerned about the increase, began a study of the place of discretion in the administration of the program. As part of the study, the commission had its own inspectorate investigate the use of discretionary powers (Great Britain, Supplementary Benefits Commission, 1977b). Views were obtained from a large and comprehensive cross section of the SB staff to find out where discretion was exercised, staff attitudes towards the use of discretion,

[11]Great Britain, Supplementary Benefits Commission (n.d.). Families with children appear to have the hardest time managing on the basic scale rates (see Lister [1977a, p. 467]).

factors taken into account in making decisions, and what changes, if any, should be made in discretionary powers.[12]

The interviews with line workers revealed that, although most staff workers felt that ECAs went to people who clearly needed them because of ill health or disability, this was not the case for ENPs. Many of the staff expressed strong personal feelings about SB claimants. They were sympathetic toward parents of young children and the elderly and less sympathetic toward the unemployed.[13] The staff objected strongly to what they considered double payments of the scale rates simply because some claimants failed to budget properly. The staff did not feel that most requests for ENPs came from genuine need; they felt that because the vast majority of claimants were able to get along on the basic grant, the system worked unfairly. It rewarded those who "shouted the loudest." Compounding the difficulty, many of the staff were of the view that they lacked sufficient information to make discretionary decisions and often felt "conned." They wanted ENPs reduced drastically and they wanted detailed instructions on what the scale rates were supposed to cover.

In general the inspectorate confirmed what others had long suspected: that despite increasing efforts on the part of the commission to guide discretion by issuing more and more rules, large amounts of discretion continued to exist at the field level, with very unsatisfactory results. Discretion was exercised in variable, contradictory ways. Administration had become too complex for both the staff and the clientele. Administrative costs and inefficiencies continued to rise, and there were problems with participation and equity, and complaints of secrecy and unfairness.[14]

By 1976 major reforms were once again being called for, but the difference between 1966 and 1976 was that now, serious financial and political constraints reduced the available options.

[12]Interviews were held with more than half of the line workers, management, and regional staff from 24 local offices. Although the 24 offices were not randomly selected, and were located mainly in urban areas, there was considerable variation in the characteristics of the populations they served.

[13]Staff feelings are apparently communicated. The unemployed feel the hostile atmosphere (see Hill [1975, pp. 390–391]). On the other hand, David Donnison thinks that the unemployed probably have a more difficult time in demonstrating "exceptional" needs, since they differ little from others in low-paid work. The elderly are frail or live in hard-to-heat houses. The sick, disabled, and lone parents usually have all sorts of exceptional needs (see Donnison [1977, p. 215]).

[14]There are many accounts of how SBC discretion is exercised. See Stevenson (1973); the numerous publications of the Child Poverty Action Group; Bull (1975, pp. 201–205; n.d.); Lister and Carroll (1976, p. 16); and Tunnard (1976, p. 362).

REFORM PROPOSALS

Proposals for the reform of Supplementary Benefits came from a variety of sources. With David Donnison in the chair, the Supplementary Benefits Commission began to issue separate annual reports. The first report, in 1975, called attention to the problems of SB and invited public comment on what should be done. This was followed by a more detailed analysis of the issues, together with suggested remedies, in the 1976 report. Many groups and individuals responded to the SBC's invitation. One of the most prominent was the Child Poverty Action Group, an organization composed of intellectuals, academics, professionals, and community people that had a long, active history in advocating causes for the poor (Lister, 1975). A third source of suggestions was a special review team, established by the Department of Health and Social Security ministers to look at the Supplementary Benefits Scheme.

The Position of the Supplementary Benefits Commission

In its 1975 *Annual Report*, the commission stated its basic principles or priorities and identified what it considered to be the main issues facing the reformers of the scheme. The statement of principles was a reiteration of the philosophy that Great Britain adopted after World War II, namely, that the principal job of the program was to supply money for the poor and not individualized services. The commission put the matter as follows:

> Our first job is to ensure that people receive the incomes which Parliament laid down as their entitlement, leaving them as free as possible to spend this money in their own way. We should only be prepared to go beyond that and provide other services, such as shelter, help in finding jobs, payments for special needs and purposes, when it is clear that money alone will not fulfill our obligations. In such cases, we must beware of taking on tasks for which we are not well equipped. . . .
>
> The ideal towards which we would like to see policies directed would be a world in which large social groups, such as pensioners, the disabled and students whose needs are in total reasonably predictable, rarely have to rely on a last-resort means-tested, labour-intensive service for their incomes. Households of average size should rarely have to turn to supplementary benefit when drawing contributory unemployment and sickness benefits. . . . In shorter term, if our scheme develops as we think it should, those who must continue to rely on it ought to be able to discover, from a pamphlet which the great majority of people can readily understand, exactly what they are entitled to and in what kinds of circumstances—rare circumstances of fairly severe

potential hardship—some discretionary extra payments may be available [p. 17].

The first issue the commission identified was the growing use of discretionary extra payments. This growth was of concern because it reintroduced far too much emphasis on moral judgments by officials than should be present in a broad income maintenance program supposedly based on entitlements; it left claimants uncertain about what they were entitled to; it increased conflicts between claimants and officials; it unnecessarily politicized the program; it increased staff and administrative costs in a welfare program that was already too staff-intensive; and it was very problematic, at best, that there was an equitable distribution of extra discretionary payments.

Related to the growth of discretionary extra payments was the second major issue—the growing complexity of the scheme. In an effort to try to treat exceptional cases uniformly, the commission and the regional offices began issuing volumes of instructions to guide local decision-making. The result was a mass of complex, detailed instructions, together with frequent amendments and additions.

In its 1976 *Annual Report*, the commission reaffirmed the 1975 priorities and continued to address major issues. The first issue it dealt with was the adequacy of the scale rates. While acknowledging that the rates were quite low, and that many SB families were in hardship, the commission felt that public opinion demanded that there be a gap between the scale rates and the general level of wages paid lower-skilled workers, and that it would be unreasonable to expect any substantial rise in the scale rates unless there was also a rise in the incomes for this class of worker.

Again, major attention focused on the rise of discretionary payments. The commission viewed with dismay the record of discretionary payments since World War II and took it as a mark of failure that every decade the scheme had to be revamped to deal with what it regarded as the inordinate rise of discretionary addition. It hoped this time discretionary payments could be controlled so that the agreed-upon balance between the primary obligation of the scheme to provide basic income maintenance in an efficient and fair way and the need for some amount of discretion in a safety-net program could be maintained.

As to specific suggestions, the first task, according to the commission, was to make clear what the scale rates were intended to cover and what they were not. Food, clothing (including replacement), fuel, household sundries, and normal travel should be covered by the rates, but not major items of furniture, appliances, or furnishings. In addition, in considering items not covered by the scale rates (and therefore available for discretionary payments), the commission would distinguish between a recently unemployed claimant (who presumably would not need to replace items not covered by the scale rates) and a long-term unsupported mother with little or no prospect of employment.

For items outside of the scale rates, procedures could be simplified. For items covered by the scale rates, the commission would tighten up discretion considerably and allow exceptions only "in the exceedingly rare cases of 'fire and flood' and similar disasters [pp. 13–14]." But what about families who still could not cope, who found themselves without food or clothing at the end of the week or faced a utility cutoff or an eviction? This, of course, as the commission recognized, was the heart of the dilemma. The commission had no specific answer to this problem but offered the suggestion that all claimants be entitled to a lump-sum payment at regular intervals (e.g., once every six months) and that under normal circumstances, they would be required to wait until the lump sum was payable; but "where life or health are endangered," they would be permitted to draw against the amount that was held in their account.

This was the only concrete suggestion that the commission offered in the 1976 *Report*.

In framing the issues, the commission's fundamental point was that in any large welfare program there is a basic contradiction between a system of entitlements and large amounts of discretion and concomitant complexity; that in order for entitlements to work, there has to be a simple and clear explanation of what the system is about and what people are entitled to, and that they must be treated in a fair, equitable, and courteous manner. Perhaps as many as a million people, including 600,000 of the aged, were failing to take advantage of the benefits being offered. The SBC, under the persistent prodding of Donnison, posed the issue in terms of a hard choice between "creative justice" and "proportional justice." The former is the individualized discretionary system; the latter stresses uniformity and horizontal equity. Donnison insisted that only the latter was the proper choice in a large-scale income maintenance program.[15]

In response to the 1976 *Annual Report*, the government established a Special Review Team to consider the issues.

[15]As a result of the SBC position, there is now a lively debate in Great Britain on the meaning of proportional and creative justice and the trade-off between them. For a discussion of the distinction, see Stevenson (1973, p. 25); Bull (1976, 1977, 1980, pp. 22–56); Donnison (1977; and Jordan (1977, pp. 69–70).

The DHSS Review Team Report

In July 1978 the Department of Health and Social Security ministers published a report of the Special Review Team, suggesting ways to improve the Supplementary Benefits scheme (Great Britain, Department of Health and Social Security, 1978). In approaching its task, the Review Team decided that it would be unrealistic to consider proposals that would involve major, costly additions either for benefits to claimants or for increases in staff. An additional constraint had to do with the size of the program. The Review Team indicated that very large additional expenditures in scale rates would be required to reduce the size of the program in any significant manner; accordingly, it assumed that for the foreseeable future the scheme would have to continue to handle millions of claimants.

The Review Team recommended that the legal structure should state more precisely the conditions of eligibility. A certain amount of discretion would have to be retained, especially for unforeseen circumstances, but there, distinctions should be made between dealing with individual cases and issues of policy that would apply to broader categories of cases.[16] Along with a clearer legal structure, the Review Team emphasized that there had to be improved communications, and people had to be made aware of their rights. The two reforms are closely tied; it makes little sense to publicize either vague or overcomplex rules.

The Review Team had proposals for simplifying the basic scheme. They included some modifications in eligibility (a general tightening-up for regulations governing people leaving school, immigrants, and the aggregation of resources of individuals living together), an improvement in the rates for families with children, a better alignment of SB with National Insurance rates, simplification of procedures for short-term claimants, and a simplified treatment of resources.

The basic problem of discretionary payments, in the view of the Review Team, was that the scale rates, in failing to define "normal" requirements, made it difficult to know what "exceptional" circumstances are. Accordingly, the team suggested that some effort at definition, even if in general terms, should be made in the legislation.

[16]The Review Team favored a far more extensive use of administrative codes. For an analysis of the differences between a code and a regulation, and an argument in favor of the latter on the grounds that it strengthened claimant entitlements, see Levin (1978, pp. 202–205).

They made specific suggestions on how to deal with the heating costs and cut back other ECAs.

The thorny issue was that of ENPs for items supposed to be covered by the scale rates (i.e., double payments). The Review Team rejected the idea that these ENPs could be eliminated altogether on the ground that too much hardship would result, and was attracted to the idea of a lump sum, with advance payments and deductions. Special welfare officers would be assigned to those families who made repeated advance withdrawals or who still could not manage.

The approach of the Review Team was to try to specify in advance, as much as possible, the terms, conditions, and amounts of discretionary payments. It then addressed the question of whether officials should still have discretion to go beyond what was provided in the regulations or the administrative code. It concluded that such discretion should exist, that it was unwise to try to specify in advance all contingencies, but that this discretion ought to be subject to general guidelines, for instance, that "the need must be essential and the award necessary to avoid hardship, the amount of the award being limited to the amount which is essential [Great Britain, Department of Health and Social Security, 1978, p. 85]," but there should be periodic review, especially if awards exceeded certain amounts.

Reactions to the DHSS Review

Predictably, initial responses to the report of the Review Team either praised it for being more comprehensive than previous studies, or criticized it on familiar lines—the scale rates were too low and the proposed tightening of discretionary grants would cause too much hardship.[17] The Child Poverty Action Group argued that given the inadequacies of the scale rates, discretionary payments had to continue to relieve hardship, and the team's focus upon reducing complexity was really intended for the benefit of the staff and to hold down administrative costs. According to CPAG, when scale rates fall below changes in prices, as was the case when fuel costs increased rapidly, the exceptional needs of some claimants become more and more commonplace. Complexity occurs when the system tries to deal with exceptional cases in a uniform way across the whole country. Given the low levels of the rates, it is therefore wishful thinking to expect to reduce discretion and

[17]See, for example, Bradshaw (1978, p. 7); Bull (1978, pp. 14–18; 1980, pp. 22–56); Fimister (1978); Jordan (1978); and Lister (1979).

complexity, unless the scheme were to adopt draconian measures. One of the principal errors of the SBC as well as the Review Team was that they failed to recognize that a "last resort" income maintenance program like SB had constantly to readjust to changing circumstances. This would be especially true as long as scale rates remained low. Despite the hopes of the SBC and the Review Team, ways would continue to be found to meet hardship, and the failure of the 1966 attempt to reduce discretion would be repeated. Furthermore, if the scheme were really serious about keeping discretion down, SB recipients who could not meet their emergency or special needs on the basic income maintenance grant would have to turn to the social service departments of local authorities; these would then become the "safety-net" welfare program.

The Supplementary Benefits Commission also published a response to the Review Team (Great Britain, Supplementary Benefits Commission, 1979). It repeated its persistent claim that, given current economic conditions and the continued growth in the unemployed and single-parent claimants, the scheme would break down unless reformed.

With regard to the discretionary payments, it favored the lump-sum approach it had suggested in the 1976 *Annual Report*. However, it was strongly of the opinion that discretionary payments could not be reduced unless the scale rates and a "sufficiently generous" lump-sum payment, made at regular intervals, were made adequate, all rights of appeal were preserved, and there remained residual discretion for local offices to help out families that still could not get along.

THE 1976 REFORM AND SUBSEQUENT REFORMS

Given the current economic crisis in Great Britain, it was not surprising that the government, in a White Paper, adopted the Review Team's no-cost approach. Its position was simply stated: "Additional resources are not now available [Great Britain, Department of Health and Social Security, 1979, p. 2]." The recommended changes would not bring any increases in expenditure or staff costs. According to the government, all claimants would benefit from stronger legal entitlements, published rules, and a simpler scheme. Substantively, some would lose by the change, and others gain. In benefits, there would be some movement toward closing the gap between the long- and short-term rates, and the qualifying period for the long-term rate would be reduced from two years to one. The number of scale rates for children would be reduced. Rules covering people leaving school, housing costs, treatment of resources, and the differential treatment between men and women would be changed. Concerning discretion, the proposed legislation and accompanying White Paper were very brief: Discretion for ENPs would be tightened through regulations that would spell out what was covered in the scale rates, the additional items for which ENPs could be used, and under what circumstances. Except for natural disasters, there would be no ENPs for nonrecipients of Supplementary Benefits, and the allowance for laundry expenses would be raised.

The White Paper was subsequently incorporated into legislation.[18] The Supplementary Benefits Commission was abolished. The DHSS is responsible for policy decisions and the issuance of entitlement rules. The advisory function of the SBC was turned over to a new Social Security Advisory Committee, which would give advice on a broad range of income maintenance programs.

Contrary to government expectation, the statute and accompanying regulations are far from simple. As might be expected, the complexity of the regulations reflects the complexity of the task. As to discretionary payments to meet emergencies and individual needs, the government rejected the idea of a single, automatic lump sum and residual discretion for unforeseen exceptional circumstances. Instead, the government tried to cut down sharply the discretion for "single payments" (the new name for ENPs) and "additional requirements" (formerly ECAs). The regulations list approximately 16 categories of items for which single payments can be made (e.g., maternity, funeral, essential household and furniture), covering most of the standard items formerly paid for through discretionary grants. The regulations also specify what "additional requirements" can cover (e.g., heating, special diets, transportation to hospital, etc.). The approach is to list the specific items, specify the conditions, and then give the allowable costs. For example, clothing costs will not be covered if the loss is due to "normal wear and tear" or the "normal course of events" (children outgrowing their clothes), but will be covered for loss or theft or pregnancy or sudden and significant changes in weight, and so forth. The single-payment regulations attempt to eliminate repeat requests and items the government feels are nonessential, for example, education-related expenses (uniforms, lunches), transportation, automobile-related expenses, holidays, court appearances, etc. If there is still a need, but one not covered by a listed item, or the conditions have not been met, then there is a provision for "dire emergency"—a single payment if such a payment "is the only means by which serious damage or serious risk to the

[18]Supplementary Benefits Act 1976, as amended by Social Security Act 1980.

health or safety of any member (of the household) may be prevented [New Supplementary Benefit Regulations, 1980, p. 23]."

All in all, the regulations governing discretionary payments are detailed and complex. They do represent a considerable effort to tighten up discretion, but there are still plenty of vague "reasonable" words that will allow discretion to creep back in. And as economic conditions fail to improve, or worsen, pressures to do so will increase.

For the present, the government's position amounts to an evasion of responsibility; the government is attempting to delegate the tough issues in welfare policy and to wash its hands of the consequences. This has already been happening to some extent. In various parts of the country, SBC offices have been more insistent that SB claimants first seek help at the various local authority offices, with predictable results, namely that, overall, help given by local government agencies is uneven. Claimants who are supposed to be part of a national welfare system are subject to a great deal of local variation and discretion, and there are numerous instances of hardship caused either by outright denials or because claimants are caught between conflicting jurisdictions. The empirical evidence concerning local authority programs is not encouraging for clients.[19]

The government claims that its approach is the only approach consistent with enhancing a system of entitlements and reducing discretion, but by delegating this aspect of claimant needs to the local authorities, the government will push a substantial number of claimants into another highly discretionary system, and it is likely that more claimants will be subject to more discretionary authority than if the SBC continued to handle discretionary payments.

This analysis does not necessarily lead to the conclusion that the government is wrong in seeking to routinize its system. The government argues, with a good deal of force, that because no government in Great Britain has fulfilled the Beveridge principle of an adequate insurance system with Supplementary Benefits providing only a small safety net, SB has been forced into a mass role, and that role can only be adequately performed by a standardized system. Nevertheless, the result is that the government is proposing a dual system of income maintenance for the British, and therefore it is abandoning another basic principle of the *Beveridge Report*, namely, that there be a national system for all welfare recipients. Instead, there will be the basic income maintenance program handled by the national system, but individual

[19]See Lister (1977b). For an earlier account of local authority discretion in granting money for "exceptional circumstances," see Handler (1973).

need will be handled by a local system. This might be a rational jurisdictional division, but not as presently proposed. If individual needs are to be dealt with at the local level, it is the responsibility of the government to make sure that the local systems maintain certain standards of performance.

THE LESSON OF THE BRITISH EXPERIENCE

The British experience provides some major insights into the problems of meeting individual needs in a large income maintenance program. The principal lesson is the dynamic nature of the problem. Try as they might, the British have not been able to contain the discretionary elements of their scheme. Routinization is an attempt to freeze the world, but the world does not stand still.

It was vain for the Review Team to hope that out of the present reform effort, history would not repeat itself. Rather, it is the sign of a responsive, human program that history will repeat itself. The task is not to create a rigid, uncompromising system that keeps the lid on the problem, but rather to recognize that change has to and should occur, and to plan for the orderly incorporation of that change. One of the jobs that a properly functioning discretionary payments program can do is to flag weaknesses in the existing income support system. Then either the basic system can be changed to meet the emergent need, or changes in other parts of the social welfare system can be sought.

Out of the experience of Great Britain and the United States, one can identify certain underlying themes or problems with a discretionary payments system. From the client's perspective, a clear goal has to be improving access to the system. For a variety of reasons, it is unfair to rely wholly on a client-initiated system. Clients may lack the requisite information—or the ability to make effective use of the information. Agencies, again for a variety of reasons, impose a rationing system, through the denial of information or other bureaucratic means, such as delay, an appointments system, or inconvenient location of offices, to satisfy the agencies' needs rather than the clients'. Another problem is the moral attitudes in the administration of discretionary grants. Even in Britain, where there has been approval of a universal welfare system and more public discussion of the issues, there is still resentment on the part of the staff of those who cannot get along on the basic welfare grant and those who, in the view of the staff, could try harder to find a job.

Although Britain and the United States come from different historical experiences, there now appears something of a convergence of problems and attempted solutions. General economic conditions have forced cutbacks in basic grants, increasing the pressures on the emergency programs. Both countries are trying to hold the line by eliminating certain categories (e.g., the double payments), increasing specificity, and generally trying to tighten administration. Finally, in both countries the problems of meeting emergencies and special needs are being delegated outside of the system. In the United States, applicants are increasingly sent to private charity; in Great Britain, there is pressure to force clients to use local authority and other agency funds.

CHAPTER 10

Striking the Balance

THE SYSTEM WE HAVE

The trend during the 1970s in the United States was toward standardization and simplification of income maintenance programs. Ideologically, the goal is to achieve horizontal equity; administratively, to reduce error, fraud, and administrative costs. But welfare policy, at least in this country, never speaks with a single voice, and countering this broad trend toward consolidation are the strong traditions of state and local variation, discretion, and the need for welfare programs to meet individual needs.

Our data indicate that virtually every income maintenance program reflects these conflicting pressures, in varying degrees. The balance of pressures differs from state to state, and even within states. The Aid to Families with Dependent Children (AFDC) program demonstrates the variation. Some states follow closely the model of a "pure" consolidated grant, covering "ordinary" needs, with little or no provision for emergency needs and special circumstances; other states, even though they have formally adopted the consolidated grant, appear to have changed little, in that the law still allows considerable variation. Most states, however, fall between these two positions.

Formally, use of the consolidated grant for welfare programs has swept the country: Supplementary Security Income (SSI) has replaced the various programs for adults, and 46 states have consolidated grants for AFDC. Yet, many states, while adopting the consolidated grant for SSI and AFDC, have also retained several "special circumstances" or "special needs" components that can be used to modify the consolidated grant in individual cases. Although it is difficult to precisely assess how significant these special provisions are, given the limits of the data, our view is that these additions are small and do little to alter the essential nature of the consolidated grant.

In addition to AFDC-related programs covering special circumstances or special needs, most of the states report having a variety of emergency assistance and special needs programs that are not attached directly to a basic grant. The variety and range reflect the looseness of concepts and definitions. The definitions of what is or is not an emergency need or a special need are, for the most part, arbitrary, and the actual programs seldom fit neat categories. Although some are simple enough—such as those that provide aid after natural disasters—others are programs that one would not ordinarily think of as providing emergency assistance or special needs—for example, aid given through Title XX social services and General Assistance. These programs can and are being used for emergencies and special needs, and several states list them as such.

Overall, there are state emergency assistance and special needs programs that in theory may cover broad types of situations and categories of clients, such as AFDC–Emergency Assistance, state emergency programs, and SSI–Special Needs. There are also state programs that are specific to certain kinds of situations, the most prominent being fuel assistance, but also including Expedited Food Stamps. Title XX is a state program that gives services, not money. There are also local programs, principally General Assistance. In some communities GA operates like an emergency assistance or special needs program: people apply for grants for particular needs. In other localities, GA is administered as a flat sum per month, which has the appearance of a mini consolidated grant, though the state or local government considers it an emergency program.

No one state claims to have all of the existing emergency assistance or special needs programs, but looking at the states as a whole, we find an impressive number of programs. These, however, are programs on the books. Within the limitations of the data, our general finding is that these programs are, in fact, small, variable, and discretionary in administration. Like weeds searching for cracks in a straight and unyielding concrete road, these programs struggle for existence against the dominant ideology of routinization and reduction of cost, error, and fraud. Overall the many fragmentary provisions for emergency assistance and special needs give little aid to clients, leave large gaps in coverage, and possess great heterogeneity. The budgets are extremely small when compared to the amounts states spend on their regular income maintenance programs. Thus AFDC–EA, one of the most important specialized programs, exists in less than half of the states, and the average expenditure for AFDC–EA in those states is only 1.5% of the average AFDC expenditure. Minnesota, one of the most generous states, spends about 3% of its welfare budget on specialized aid. Not many weeds are poking through.

Further, in the melange of specialized programs, varying groups of clients and types of needs are covered in different jurisdictions. By contrast the consolidated grant in almost all of the states represents a conscious policy choice to move in the direction of uniformity. Although there are differences in eligibility based on income levels, and programs like General Assistance, AFDC–Unemployed Parent may or may not exist, in general there is great similarity in types of coverage and rules. While some items or types of clients are more commonly the focus of programs, we find no such common policy with emergency assistance and special needs. No one program exists in even a majority of the states, and the states vary in terms of number of programs, type of programs, and what they choose to label emergency assistance and special needs programs. In contrast to the consolidated grant, which was intentionally adopted, these programs seem either to have been left over from an earlier time or to have been enacted as a result of special pressures to meet specific needs. A common need that many cover is fuel, but such odd provisions as grants for the deaf and for blind children are probably the work of special-interest lobbies.

The lack of planning, the struggle to remain in existence, and the reactive nature of these programs are reflected in the third major characteristic: discretionary administration. As administered at the state level there is a strong concern over costs, client eligibility, and types of needs, and only limited concern over the specifics of administration. At the local level, one finds both strict general rules and broad discretion. Most of the programs, regardless of the extent of theoretical coverage, in practice specialize in certain types of emergencies or needs. Discretionary specialization may reflect state rules, or specialization may occur locally within broader state guidelines (as in Oneida County, New York, where theoretically broad coverage is restricted to cover natural disasters). Although the decision to specialize is itself discretionary, specialization tends to reduce the discretion of the caseworker simply because there are fewer options.

Rules vary for almost every other aspect of the programs. Some provide fixed amounts for particular items; other items are paid "as needed." Sometimes there are rules regarding repeat requests, sometimes not. Eligibility and verification also vary, although our general impression is that rules here are less restrictive than they are for AFDC. Apparently administrators are more worried about eligibility errors in the major programs, which cost far more than these small emergency assistance and special needs programs.

One administrative practice, however, is quite general. Despite varying state rules, a high proportion of grants (over 80%) are in the form of vendor or voucher payments. (Of course, all assistance through Title XX is in services, not cash.) Students of welfare are familiar with the cash versus in-kind approaches, and this characteristic of emergency assistance and special needs programs speaks volumes concerning attitudes and policies. Vendor, voucher, and in-kind payments maximize control over clients and situations. There is little client autonomy in deciding how the money will be spent. One of the major reforms of the original Social Security Act passed in 1935 was to insist that public assistance be in cash, to increase client dignity and control by allowing welfare recipients to make their own household and budgetary choices. Vendor, voucher, and in-kind payments represent the opposite—restricting client choice and controlling their decisions. Payments of this sort reflect "older" attitudes of suspicion and stigma. Programs for emergency assistance and special needs are old-style welfare: Clients have to request it, there are no entitlements, decisions are discretionary, payments are small, and control is maximized. The form of payment reflects county concerns about moral worth, error, fraud, and abuse.

Because the programs are so discretionary, they are perfect vehicles for the expression of general attitudes and values related to welfare. State and county perceptions that clients are undeserving result in limited programs of specialized assistance. The size of the specialized effort varies depending on the commitment to individualization, standardization, restrictiveness, or organizational maintenance. Community pressure also plays a role. The two most significant factors may be how generous a state is toward welfare in general, and whether officials in states that are not generous perceive a need to meet the most severe problems resulting from inadequate levels of public assistance.

The styles of administration of specialized programs also bear on the relationship between the public and private sources of emergency aid. Although public programs vary in their requirements that applicants exhaust other sources of aid, including private charity, before obtaining assistance, nonpublic sources are becoming increasingly important throughout the country. Their importance is growing because of increasing hard times for welfare recipients. Income maintenance budgets have fallen far behind inflation; in several of the areas that we studied there have been dramatic rises in the cost of basic necessities (housing costs as well as heating); and there are major gaps in the coverage of the emergency public programs, which, as noted, are tiny to begin with.

The growing reliance on private charity exacerbates the worst features of programs that deal with emergency assistance and special needs: the miserliness of the relief, its variability, and the discretion in its dispensation. Private charities, understandably, resent the new role being thrust upon them—picking up the pieces of inadequate public programs. They never have regarded themselves as primary sources of cash assistance and they, too, face severe budgetary problems. Private programs are no doubt even more variable than public programs, and their rationing devices are probably even more discretionary. They are under no obligation to publicize their services, and their clients have no rights or entitlements. Furthermore they can make demands in exchange for benefits. Without apology, the mission of private charity can be, and often is, to change the behavior and the attitudes of the poor.

All of the problems of emergency assistance and special needs programs are intensified by the lack of systematic outreach. Our data show that little organized outreach effort is made, and that basically it is up to the individual caseworkers to decide how much information is given to applicants and recipients. The British have always been afraid to publicize their specialized programs for fear of stimulating too many requests (Handler, 1973). Traditional American special needs programs also remained relatively unknown (Handler and Hollingsworth, 1971). Given the grudging nature of present policy and the fear of rising demands and costs, it seems unlikely that the new programs are looking for business. Lack of outreach is, of course, a very serious matter. Programs that depend on client initiative will tend to favor the more articulate and knowledgeable rather than those most in need. The passive, the weak, the frightened, and the ignorant are most likely to suffer under the present system. If programs for emergency assistance and special needs are to meet needs more effectively, there must be systematic outreach.

Social scientists, politicians, and public administrators may agree on the advantages of the consolidated grant for the reasons that have already been discussed, but in real life emergencies and special needs lie outside that grant. These needs increase as income maintenance grants fall behind the rising costs of basic necessities. Money spent on high rent leads to food shortages at the end of the month. There is no margin of safety for accidents, theft, illness, or the loss of a job. The poor are facing increasingly hard times, but public aid programs, including emergency assistance and special needs, are responding in increasingly less generous ways. One of the ironies of the current situation has been the appearance of "sunshine funds" within public departments of welfare. The street-level workers, those in touch with recipients' lives, chip in themselves to give $5 or $10 to clients in desperate need. When public workers, not overpaid themselves, reach into their worn pockets to relieve suffering, times are indeed difficult.

ACHIEVING ADEQUATE COVERAGE OF SPECIAL NEEDS AND EMERGENCIES

What should the role of the specialized program be in public welfare? According to this study, the specialized programs currently both reflect and react to income maintenance policies and practices. Emergency assistance programs are particularly important in taking up the slack when the basic income maintenance grant does not meet all of the basic expenses that clients face. In many states, emergency assistance is intentionally used as an alternative to the basic AFDC or SSI or GA grant programs, providing temporary aid to clients who might not otherwise be served.

This current function of emergency assistance programs should not be taken to imply that emergency assistance programs successfully compensate for an inadequate basic income maintenance program. Our research quite strongly suggests that the basic grant, particularly in AFDC and General Assistance programs, is generally quite low. In each of our case studies, workers and client advocates told us that many clients are suffering from inadequate support in general and that public and private emergency programs can only alleviate temporarily the most severe, and even life-threatening problems. No matter how the emergency program is structured, there is clearly a growing need for large expansions in basic income maintenance grants.

Nevertheless, we believe that our research indicates the need for a stable and consistent emergency and special needs network in every state and locality. The growing inadequacy of basic grants certainly is one reason for the emergency assistance and special needs system. In many sites, the programs face pressures to meet problems caused by the failure of the basic grant to meet continuing costs of food, shelter, or fuel. Without special programs, it is unclear how clients can get by—and evidence from San Diego indicates that when emergency assistance is cut back, some families, unable to find the means to keep going, are forced to break up.

While inadequate basic grants make emergency and special needs assistance particularly important, programs are essential even when the grant is sufficient to meet the predictable, daily expenses of most clients. Although in flat-grant systems, individuals with similar incomes and family structures receive the same amount of aid, needs are not always equivalent. Emergency and special needs programs are an important way of taking individual differences into account without completely reversing the trend toward standardization and error reduction.

Another rationale for emergency assistance and special needs aid stems from the inevitability of emergencies, even if the basic grant is flexible. Individuals with limited incomes have no reserves to deal with crises. Often the financial need generated by an emergency is so great that only a public program will suffice to cover it. Furniture wears out, washing machines break down, and sudden, unanticipated expenses arise periodically. Emergencies will always be with us, and to meet them, special programs are a necessity.

What type of program will best fill the roles discussed above? We believe that most existing programs, particularly those intended for AFDC and General Assistance clients, are too specialized in the circumstances they cover. It is important to establish a network that meets the broad range of needs clients may experience. Particularly notable, and particularly unlikely to be covered sufficiently, are problems clients face in meeting basic needs. Currently natural disasters and other acts that are considered to be less "morally hazardous" are covered more often, although some programs do not include these circumstances and we would prefer that they did. Finally, it is important to include special services, particularly medically related services or costs arising from special diets and the like.

We also favor universal coverage. Currently, certain groups of people, particularly migrants and transients, poor individuals who do not receive basic grants, General Assistance clients, and poor families in which both parents are present, are often denied aid. These very same groups are likely to be turned away by private programs, as well. Real needs of certain groups of clients are thus left unmet in many states and counties.

Part of the problem in public programs stems from the categorical nature of the basic programs to which emergency programs are attached. SSI–Special Needs programs, AFDC–Special Needs or AFDC–Emergency Assistance, and some local General Assistance programs are limited to actual or potential clients for the basic grant to which the emergency program is attached. As a result, the coverage of emergency assistance programs is uneven.

Then what public program should be used as the base to which specialized aid is attached? As long as the public welfare system relies on categories of aid, it seems inevitable that one single program cannot be developed. Perhaps specialized aid should be available to both SSI and AFDC clients, and even to recipients of food stamps. It is more difficult to ensure that General Assistance clients are eligible and aware of specialized programs, but perhaps the use of the Food Stamp program as a base would be partly useful in this respect. In any event, wherever programs are located, outreach efforts will have to be undertaken if the most needy are to be helped.

We also feel that the current policy of refusing repeated requests should be altered. Clients should be able to obtain emergency assistance as long as emergencies actually exist. We found that in the AFDC–EA program, in particular, the once-a-year rule is a major barrier to appropriate service. It forces clients to store up difficulties until they are overwhelming. Such a regulation may be counterproductive in the long run.

We lack sufficient information to present a detailed plan for administrative rules and procedures, such as verification requirements, the use of cash, voucher, or vendor payments, and so forth. At the aggregate level, our analysis reveals that most of these regulations are of only limited importance in affecting the size of the programs—although they may be important in dictating which clients are served and which are not. Except for our findings that mandates requiring publicity in writing tend to increase the caseload, and rules requiring that clients exhaust private resources first apparently decrease the caseload, we have no solid criteria for choosing one pattern of administration over another, although our bias is toward relatively lenient rules and procedures.

Even if we could specify a set of rules and procedures, the comparison between county and state programs indicates that compliance to the mandates would not necessarily be achieved. Many local procedures and rules are virtually invisible to those at higher levels. Furthermore, important street-level procedures cannot easily be controlled by rules.

More than this, we believe that it is nearly impossible to draw up a single set of detailed rules that would be useful in practice, even if compliance could be achieved. Rules remove flexibility from the system. Specifying rules can cause caseworkers to deny aid to those who are needy and to dispense aid to those who are not. Rules can also be dysfunctional, forcing workers to spend more time on office routines than on helping clients. Perhaps the tendency of state administrators to be more concerned over costs and caseloads than over individual decisions, and the tendency of local officials to alter rules slightly, make sense, given the difficulties of establishing useful, specific rules.

One implication of the difficulty of making useful specific rules at a high level, along with the tendency of workers to modify rules that are not useful, is that emergency programs will tend to be discretionary. As a result, it seems inevitable that the use of emergency and special needs assistance will vary to some degree as a function of the prejudices of local officials and even of local workers. Although rules on eligibility, circumstances covered, and repeated assistance dictate the budget of the assistance programs to a large degree, local areas will still vary. Assistance seems to be tied to very basic moral questions, such as how deserving certain groups of clients are, and how much one should worry about fraud and error. Unfortunately these basic beliefs will continue to be important in the allocation of funds.

Discretion may be unavoidable in the administration of specialized programs, but whether or not a state adopts a program should not be a matter of discretion. We believe that the more the program is made mandatory, the more likely it is that there will be some uniformity from state to state. Otherwise, as our analysis indicated, basic income maintenance issues involving error and fraud, equity and standardization, individualization, and so forth, greatly affect the emergency and special needs effort across states. Nevertheless, the specific rules adopted by states will probably continue to vary with their public welfare commitments. Indeed, we recognize that in nearly all states, concerns over administrative costs, error, fraud, and public criticism tend to limit the overall commitment of officials to the programs.

Emergency assistance and special needs programs, then, must be described as two-edged swords. They are humane programs, a necessary part of any public welfare system. However, because they must be discretionary, they create problems. Agencies and workers can misuse specialized programs, either by not giving aid to those who need it most, or by using these programs to keep costs of the basic grant programs low. Agencies may also set up unnecessarily harsh conditions that control the lives of recipients needlessly. Once the programs are adopted, problems, questions, and complaints from the community and from workers are inevitable, although the limited size of even the most generous programs is such that these complaints may not present a particularly acute hazard.

What is the appropriate jurisdiction of the programs? Here our evidence is sparse. We know that locally funded programs are smaller than programs funded by the state or federal government, but it is unclear if this is due to a dislike of these programs at the local level, or, as seems more likely, the fact that less money is available at the local level. Clearly, federal and state support is necessary to ensure local participation in emergency and special needs programs, but once this support is guaranteed, we cannot judge whether local, state, or federal administration is more appropriate. Our data imply that locally administered programs may lead to the coverage of more groups of clients, but it may also lead to the use of more conditions and rules of eligibility.

Ideally, the programs should be federally funded in part, matched in a manner equivalent to that of the basic grant. If the federal match for an emergency program is higher than the match for the basic grant, there will be a strong tendency to rely on the emergency program as an alternative to the basic grant, perhaps in the long run leading to programs refusing to serve some eligible clients in the basic program. If the match is too low, states may refuse to establish emergency programs, as indicated by our finding that states with a higher AFDC match adopt specialized programs less often.

A very important policy question is, How much will an adequate program cost? But in all honesty, we cannot come up with a complete estimate. We know that costs of the largest AFDC–EA programs are about 3% of the basic grants, and this is our best guess. The problem with attempting to estimate costs is that, at present, only a very small sample of states have cost data. Estimations based on local responses are even more problematic. The control of costs seems to largely involve rules restricting types of clients, circumstances covered, and repeated aid.

Once a network of programs is available, many modifications will probably be needed in time. It may be helpful to follow British attempts to categorize emergencies, and use a combination of administrative devices to control the programs. Currently, however, the emphasis should be on providing comprehensive programs. Refined suggestions should be delayed until more adequate basic benefits are provided.

BALANCING STANDARDIZATION AND INDIVIDUALIZATION

Even though the clear trend in public welfare is toward standardization, most public welfare systems have some combination of standardization and individualization. The basic grants—AFDC, SSI, and Food Stamps—are generally flat, but there are some emergency and special needs programs that respond to individualized needs and problems. To adequately meet individual needs while maintaining program integrity, the trick is to separate out those parts that can be standardized from those parts that must be individualized—separating the administration of the basic grant from the administration of emergency and special needs programs. This is not unlike the traditional suggestions in the literature concerning complex organizations calling for the establishment in business organizations of separate administrative units to deal with the more routine and less routine functions.

The individualized side, emergency assistance and special needs programs, must in itself be partly bound by rules (although some may say that the fact that it dispenses aid to only some individuals makes it inherently individualizing) and partly discretionary. Even though we have argued that some discretion is inevitable, in theory one can envision a specialized grant that is almost as uniform as the regular income maintenance grants. State rules can determine exactly who is eligible, what conditions must be met, how aid should be dispensed, how much each emergency need should cost, and so forth. If this were always the case, each state would have an individualized program that was in itself quite rigid. The British are trying to go this route. But it is more common for states to set general rules that control costs and minimize political problems, and to allow specific decisions to be made by local offices and workers. In this manner borderline situations can be dealt with. A rigid specialized system would simply create the need for a third set of programs, one flexible enough to cover all of the unanticipated problems.

In judging the adequacy of the current system, the question of whether most existing programs are "predominantly" discretionary or standardized is a difficult one that may actually be almost meaningless. The answer depends upon the type of issue to which one is referring. Total costs in existing specialized programs are usually controlled from the top—either by state officials, top county administrators, or legislatures. General rules concerning who is eligible and how aid is granted are also usually set at these levels. But in most cases line workers seem to be free to make decisions concerning which specific clients should be granted aid—and should be encouraged to apply—within broad guidelines. Inequities and abuse are always possible in this discretionary system. Separation of the standardized income maintenance grant from the nonstandardized specialized programs confines the problems of discretion to the small peripheral programs. This general trend in the United States makes sense.

Even so, one can object to the extent to which most communities in the United States individualize their programs. In England, prior to the Thatcher government, the specialized programs were allowed to expand as new needs surfaced. Although it may not have been intentional policy, British administrators could use the growth of emergency and special needs grants as a measure of the adequacy of the regular grants. When specialized expenditures got too high, the basic grant could be increased and smaller specialized programs established. If these become too costly, the cycle could again be repeated. In the United States, the specialized grants are kept so small they cannot serve as a gauge of the adequacy of the basic programs.

Thus, the extent to which a separate, discretionary program exists has implications for the entire welfare system. Without the possibility for a barometer, adequate information and pressure concerning problems in the adequacy of the larger, basic grant system do not arise. Given the usually limited levels of generosity in the United States, this may be the situation preferred by officials—the lack of a specialized program in which needs become readily apparent may reduce the pressure to increase the size of the flat grant. In other words, adequate emergency and special needs programs can do more than just meet short-term problems. They can contribute to the formation of a more appropriate structure wtihin the standardized part of the system.

Standardization and individualization are always in flux, and a good test of how humane a welfare system is might very well be the extent to which it can simultaneously deal with the two demands. In the United States, the limited programs for emergencies and special needs indicate that we have a long way to go.

References

Atkinson, A. B. 1970. *Poverty in Britain and the reform of social security*. Cambridge, Mass.: Cambridge University Press.

Atkinson, A. B. 1975. *The economics of inequality*. London: Oxford University Press.

Bell, W. 1965. *Aid to Dependent Children*. New York: Columbia University Press.

Bendick, M., Levine, A., and Campbell, T. 1977. The anatomy of AFDC errors. Research Paper No. 5902-01, The Urban Institute, Washington, D.C.

Beveridge, W. M. (Lord). 1942. *Social insurance and allied services* (the *Beveridge Report*), Report of the Inter-departmental Committee on Social Insurance and Allied Services consisting of opinions and recommendations only. New York: Macmillan (published by arrangement with His Majesty's Stationery Office).

Bradshaw, J. 1978. The Supplementary Benefits review. *Social Work Today*, 9, 7–10.

Bull, D. 1975. Supplementary Benefits: Rationing against the "undeserving poor." *Royal Society of Health Journal*, 95 (August), 201–205.

Bull, D., ed. 1976. *Dear David Donnison*. Birmingham, England: British Association of Social Workers.

Bull, D. 1977. Free speech. 1976 fashion. *Social Work Today*, 8 (30), 7–10.

Bull, D. 1978. Diminishing discretion. *Social Work Today*, 9 (45), 10–11.

Bull, D. 1980. Open government and the review of Supplementary Benefits. In M. Brown and S. Baldwin (eds.), *The yearbook of social policy in Britain, 1978*. London: Routledge and Kegan Paul.

Bull, D. n.d. Exceptional needs payments: A guide for advocates (with special reference to clothing, bedding, and household equipment), University of Bristol, School of Social Work Administration. Mimeo.

Campbell, T., and Bendick, M. 1977. *A public assistance data book*. Washington, D.C.: The Urban Institute.

Characteristics of State Plans for AFDC. See U.S. Department of Health, Education, and Welfare, 1978.

Child Poverty Action Group. *See* Lister, 1975, 1979; Merseyside Child Poverty Action Group, n.d.

Citizens' Study Commission on Poor Relief. 1977. *Report of the Citizens' Study Commission on poor relief, findings and recommendations*, 129 East Market Street, Room 700, Indianapolis, Ind. 46204.

Congressional Research Service of the Library of Congress. 1977. *Administration of the AFDC program*. Washington, D.C.: U.S. Government Printing Office.

Council of State Governments. 1976. *Book of states, 1976–1977*. Lexington, Kentucky: Council of State Governments.

Dahler, C., and Savage, L. 1975. General assistance in Michigan: Profile of program recipient characteristics. *Studies in Welfare Policy*, 5. Lansing, Mich.: Michigan Department of Social Services.

Donnison, D. 1977. Against discretion. *New Society, 41*, 534–536.

Etzioni, A. 1975. *A comparative analysis of complex organizations* (revised edition). New York: The Free Press.

Fimister, G. 1978. Dear Claimant. *New Society, 46*, 37.

Friedman, M. 1962. *Capitalism and freedom*. Chicago: University of Chicago Press.

Galm, S. 1977. Welfare—An administrative nightmare: The administration of the AFDC program. In Congressional Research Service of the Library of Congress, *Administration of the AFDC program, a report to the Committee on Government Operations*. Washington, D.C.: U.S. Government Printing Office.

Gellhorn, W. 1967. Poverty and legality: The law's slow awakening. *William and Mary Law Review, 9*, 285–301.

Gordon, L. K. 1975. Bureaucratic competence and success in dealing with public bureaucracies. *Social Problems, 23* (2), 197–208.

Great Britain, Department of Health and Social Security. 1978. Social assistance: A review of the Supplementary Benefits scheme in Great Britain. Report of the Special Review Team, London. Mimeo.

Great Britain, Department of Health and Social Security. 1979. *Reform of the Supplementary Benefits scheme*. Cmnd. 7773. London: Her Majesty's Stationery Office.

Great Britain, Supplementary Benefits Commission. 1975. *Annual report*. London: Her Majesty's Stationery Office.

Great Britain, Supplementary Benefits Commission. 1976. *Annual report*. London: Her Majesty's Stationery Office.

Great Britain, Supplementary Benefits Commission. 1977a. *Annual report*. London: Her Majesty's Stationery Office.

Great Britain, Supplementary Benefits Commission. 1977b. The commission's inspectorate report of an enquiry into the use of discretion. Memorandum 974. Mimeo, December.

Great Britain, Supplementary Benefits Commission. 1978. *Annual report*. London: Her Majesty's Stationery Office.

Great Britain, Supplementary Benefits Commission. 1979. Response of the Supplementary Benefits Commission to "Social assistance: A review of the Supplementary Benefits scheme in Great Britain." Department of Health and Social Security, SBA Paper No. 9. London: Her Majesty's Stationery Office.

Great Britain, Supplementary Benefits Commission. n.d. Review of Supplementary Benefits, discretionary power to reduce or withhold benefits. File no. RSB (77) 36. Mimeo.

Gross, E. 1968. Universities as organizations: A research approach. *American Sociological Review, 33* (4), 518–544.

Hall, R. 1977. *Organizations: Structure and processes*, second edition. Englewood Cliffs, N.J.: Prentice-Hall.

Handler, J. F. 1972. *Reforming the poor: Welfare policy, federalism and morality*. New York: Basic Books.

Handler, J. F. 1973. *The coercive social worker: British lessons for American social services*. Chicago: Rand McNally.

Handler, J. F. 1980. 'Proportional' vs. 'creative' justice—discretionary benefits in income-maintenance programs: The British Supplementary Benefits scheme. Institute for Research on Poverty Discussion Paper no. 603–80, Madison, Wis.

Handler, J. F., and Hollingsworth, E. J. 1971. *The "deserving poor": A study of welfare administration*. New York: Academic Press.

Hill, M. 1975. Policies towards the unemployed. *Social Work Today, 6* (13), 390–391.

Jordan, B. 1977. Against Donnison. *New Society, 42*, 69–70.

Jordan, B. 1978. Dear Claimant. *New Society, 45*, 355, 407, 458, 513, and 573.

Kershaw, D., and Fair, J. 1976. *The New Jersey income-maintenance experiment*, Volume I. New York: Academic Press.

Kincaid, J. C. 1975. *Poverty and equality in Britain: A study of social security and taxation*, revised edition. New York: Penguin.

Koppell, Murphy, and Craig. 1977. A study of GA programs. National Association of Counties Research Foundation, December.

Levin, J. 1978. Supplementary Benefit: A new legal structure? *Legal Action Bulletin*, September.

Lister, R. 1975. *Social security: The case of reform*. Child Poverty Action Group, Poverty Pamphlet 22. London: CPAG.

Lister, R. 1977a. Budgeting for families. *New Society, 42*, 467.

Lister, R. 1977b. The frontier problems that won't go away. *Social Work Today, 8* (31), 8–11.

Lister, R. 1979. *The no-cost no-benefit review*. Child Poverty Action Group, Poverty Pamphlet 39. London: CPAG.

Lister, R., and Carroll, H. 1976. For your client's benefit: Tipping the scales. *Social Work Today, 8* (9), 16.

McClements, L. 1978. *The economics of social security*. London: Heinemann.

MacDonald, M. 1977. *Food, stamps, and income maintenance*. New York: Academic Press.

McGovern, S. 1979. General relief. Revised working paper, Wisconsin Department of Health and Social Services, Madison.

Marshall, T. H. 1965. *Social policy*. London: Hutchinson.

Martin, P. 1979. Public assistance of an adequate minimum income in old age: The erratic partnership between social insurance and public assistance. *Cornell Law Review, 64*, 437–520.

Mays, J., et al. 1975. *Penelope Hall's social services of England and Wales*, revised edition. London: Routledge and Kegan Paul.

Mechanic, D. 1962. Sources of power and lower participants in complex organizations. *Administrative Science Quarterly, 7* (3), 349–364.

Merseyside Child Poverty Action Group. n.d. Cut off and cold: A survey of 130 families whose fuel was disconnected in the winter of 1975/76. Liverpool: Merseyside CPAG. Mimeo.

Mills, G. B. 1981. Quality control in welfare administration: An analysis of payment error in Aid to Families with Dependent Children. Ph.D. thesis, John F. Kennedy School of Government, Harvard University.

Mott, P. 1976. Meeting human needs: The social political history of Title XX. National Conference of Social Welfare, Columbus, Ohio. Mimeo.

Moynihan, D. P. 1973. *The politics of a guaranteed annual income*. New York: Random House.

New Supplementary Benefit regulations. 1980. *Journal of Social Welfare Law*, pp. 341–380.

Piliavin, I., Masters, S., and Corbett, T. 1979. Factors influencing errors in AFDC payments. In *Social Work Research and Abstracts, 15* (4), 3–17.

Piven, F. F., and Cloward, R. A. 1971. *Regulating the poor: The functions of public welfare*. New York: Pantheon.

Piven, F. F., and Cloward, R. A. 1977. *Poor people's movements: Why they succeed, how they fail*. New York: Pantheon.

A Public Assistance Data Book. 1977. Washington, D.C.: Urban Institute.

Public Assistance Recipients and Cash Payments by State and County. 1979. Washington, D.C.: U.S. Department of Health and Human Services.

Public Assistance Statistics. Monthly. Washington, D.C.: U.S. Department of Health and Human Services.

Robbins, P., Spiegleman, S., and West, R. 1980. *A guaranteed annual income: Evidence from a social experiment*. New York: Academic Press.

Scheff, T. J. 1961. Control over policy by attendants in a mental hospital. *Journal of Health and Human Behavior, 2*, 93–105.

School of Advanced Urban Studies. 1976. Discretionary payments in the Supplementary Benefits scheme. Paper no. 4, Review of Supplementary Benefits, Bristol. Seminar.

Segal, S., Baumohl, J., and Johnson, E. 1977. Falling through the cracks: Mental disorder and social margin in a young vagrant population. *Social Problems, 24* (3), 387–400.

Selznick, P. 1949. *TVA and the grassroots*. Berkeley: University of California Press.

Sheehan, S. 1976. *A welfare mother*. New York: Houghton, Mifflin.

Simon, H. A. 1964. On the concept of organizational goal. *Administrative Science Quarterly, 9* (1), 1–22.

Sinfield, A. 1977. Supplementary Benefits and the unemployed. Unpublished paper presented at the Fabian Seminar: Reform of Supplementary Benefits, October 22.

Smith, D. 1965. Front-line organization of the state mental hospital. *Administrative Science Quarterly, 10* (3), 381–399.

Sosin, M. 1982. Emergency and special needs programs: Administrative issues. *Administration in Social Work*, 6(4), 1–13.

Stack, C. 1979. *All our kin: Strategies for survival in a black community*. New York: Harper and Row.

Stapleton, W. V., and Teitlebaum, L. E. 1972. *In defense of youth: A study of the role of counsel in American juvenile courts*. New York: Russell Sage.

Statistical Abstract of the United States. 1979. Washington, D.C.: U.S. Government Printing Office.

Stevenson, O. 1973. *Claimant or client? A social worker's view of the Supplementary Benefits Commission*. London: Allen and Unwin.

Tunnard, J. 1976. For your client's benefit: Policy and practice at your local social security office. *Social Work Today, 7* (13), 362–363.

U.S. Congress, Joint Economic Committee. 1974. *Income security for Americans, recommendations of the public welfare study*. Washington, D.C.: U.S. Government Printing Office.

U.S. Department of Commerce. 1977. *The County and City Data Book, 1977.* Washington, D.C.: U.S. Government Printing Office.

U.S. Department of Health, Education, and Welfare. 1969. *OAA and AFDC: Cost standards for basic needs and percent of such standards met for specified types of cases, July 1969.* NCSS Report D-2 (7/69). Washington, D.C.: U.S. Government Printing Office.

U.S. Department of Health, Education, and Welfare. 1970. *OAA and AFDC: Standards for basic needs for specified types of assistance groups, July 1970.* NCSS Report D-2 (7/70). Washington, D.C.: U.S. Government Printing Office.

U.S. Department of Health, Education, and Welfare. 1972. *Public assistance programs: Standards for basic needs, July 1971.* HEW Publication no. (SRS) 72-03200, NCSS Report D-2 (7/71). Washington, D.C.: U.S. Government Printing Office.

U.S. Department of Health, Education, and Welfare. 1973. *Public assistance programs: Standards for basic needs, July 1972.* HEW Publication no. (SRS) 73-03200, NCSS Report D-2 (7/72). Washington, D.C.: U.S. Government Printing Office.

U.S. Department of Health, Education, and Welfare. 1974. *Public assistance programs: Standards for basic needs, July 1973.* HEW Publication no. (SRS) 74-03200, NCSS Report D-2 (7/73). Washington, D.C.: U.S. Government Printing Office.

U.S. Department of Health, Education, and Welfare. 1975. *Aid to Families with Dependent Children: Standards for basic needs, July 1974.* HEW Publication no. (SRS) 75-03200, NCSS Report D-2 (7/74). Washington, D.C.: U.S. Government Printing Office.

U.S. Department of Health, Education, and Welfare. 1976. *Aid to Families with Dependent Children: Standards for basic needs, state maximums and other methods of limiting money payments, July 1975.* HEW Publication no. (SRS) 76-03200, NCSS Report D-2 (1/75). Washington, D.C.: U.S. Government Printing Office.

U.S. Department of Health, Education, and Welfare. 1977. *Aid to Families with Dependent Children: Standards for basic needs, July 1976.* HEW Publication no. (SRS) 77-03200, NCSS Report D-2 (7/76). Washington, D.C.: U.S. Government Printing Office.

U.S. Department of Health, Education, and Welfare. 1978. *Characteristics of state plans for AFDC under the Social Security Act Title III-A.* HEW Publication no. (SSA) 78-21235. Washington, D.C.: U.S. Government Printing Office.

U.S. Department of Health, Education, and Welfare. 1979. *AFDC standards for basic needs, July 1978.* HEW Publication no. (SSA) 79-11924, ORS Report D-2 (7/78). Washington, D.C.: U.S. Government Printing Office.

U.S. Department of Health and Human Services. 1980. *AFDC standards for basic needs, July 1979.* SSA Publication no. 13-11924, ORS Report D-2 (7/79). Washington, D.C.: U.S. Government Printing Office.

U.S. Department of Health and Human Services. 1981. *AFDC standards for basic needs, July 1980.* SSA Publication no. 13-11924, ORS Report D-2 (7/80). Washington, D.C.: U.S. Government Printing Office.

Urban Systems Research and Engineering, Inc. 1978. *Characteristics of General Assistance recipients in twenty states.* Cambridge, Mass.: Urban Systems Research and Engineering, Inc., 36 Boylston Street.

Yuchtman, E., and Seashore, S. E. 1967. A system resource approach to organizational effectiveness. *American Sociological Review, 32* (6), 891–902.

Zald, M. 1970. *The political economy of the YMCA.* Chicago: University of Chicago Press.

Index

A

Abuse of programs and community pressure, 100, *see also* Error and fraud
Access, *see* Outreach
Additional Requirements, *see* Exceptional Circumstances Additions
Adequacy of specialized programs, 176–182
  vs. coverage, 30
Administration, *see also* Organizational maintenance
  case workers and higher-level officials, 147–167 *passim*
  cost and caseloads, 137–138
  patterns of, 137
  problems related to, 169–170
  public welfare policies, 138–145
  relationship between states and counties, 167
  variation as result of program size, 137
  welfare officials' views of, 172, 174–176
Administrative efficiency, 45
Administrative strategies, *see* Balance; Compensation; Consistency; Costs, control of; Delegation of authority; Denial; Discretion; Flat grant
Administrators, *see* Welfare officials
Adult protective services, 75–76
Advocacy programs
  Lutheran Social Services, 200, 204
  Salvation Army, 201
  Senior Citizens, 209
  Volunteer Information Code, 199
AFDC, *see* Aid to Families with Dependent Children
AFDC-EA, *see* Aid to Families with Dependent Children–Emergency Assistance
AFDC-Special Needs, *see* Aid to Families with Dependent Children–Special Needs
AFDC-UP, *see* Aid to Families with Dependent Children–Unemployed Parent
Agriculture, Department of, 36
Aid to Families with Dependent Children
  adequacy of coverage, 177–178

as base for specialized programs, 244
in Beaumont, Texas, 182
compared to other programs, 62–71, 103–106, 140–141, 160
as consolidated grant, 23–33
decline in benefit levels of, 10–11
differences among states of, 237–238
funding problems of, 183
history of, 7, 24
influence on specialized programs of, 100–101, 140–141
quality control review of, 132
Aid to Families with Dependent Children–Emergency Assistance
in Boulder, Colorado, 166–167
certification procedure of, 64–65
compared to AFDC, 62, 103
coverage of, 66–71
and double payments, 69
eligibility criteria for, 62, 65
error and fraud in, 67, 68, 143–144
and external maintenance, 107, 109
factors related to higher costs and caseloads in, 140–141
factors related to size, 107, 108, 111, 112, 115, 141–145, 239
history of, 11
legal decision concerning, 62n2, 93
in Minneapolis, Minn., 68–71, 166
in Minnesota, 157
in New Jersey, 128
in Oklahoma, 157
once-a-year rule, 244
in Oregon, 158
outreach, 65
size of grant, 64, 66
and SSI-Special Needs, 35
state and county programs compared, 157–159
by state, 60–61
in Trenton, N.J., 66, 128, 166, 172, 183–184, 188–189
types of payments, 65–66
types of programs, 116
in Utica, N.Y., 67–68, 166
in West Virginia, 63
in Wyoming, 62
Aid to Families with Dependent Children–Special Needs
costs and caseload figures, 30
coverage of, 26, 29–30
forms of payments, 129
eligibility for, 31
in Oneida County, New York, 31, 33
protective payee, 130
variation among counties, 28
variation among states, 27–28
Aid to Families with Dependent Children–Unemployed Parent, 65, 124–125, 135
adequacy of coverage, 177–178
costs and caseloads, 133–134
forms of payments, 130
receiving GA in Boulder, Colorado, 87
and AFDC-EA eligibility, 65
and SSI eligibility, 33
Attitude
of welfare officials, 45–52
of politicians, 52–57

B

Balance, of individualized treatment and standardization, 12–13, 97–100, 247–248
Battered women, 75
Beaumont Association for Senior Citizens (BASC), 209–210, 213, 214
Beaumont, Texas
AFDC in, 182
elderly in, 91
funding in, 182
General Assistance in, 182
housing problems in, 187
private agencies in, 208–212
SSI in, 182
Title XX in, 182
Beveridge Report, 216, 221, 233
Bonus value of food stamps, 37
Boulder, Colorado
AFDC-EA in, 166–167
EA eligibility in, 152
Expedited Food Stamps in, 196
fuel assistance in, 77–78
funding in, 181–182
General Assistance in, 86–88
housing problems in, 187
private agencies in, 197–199
response to increased demands in, 184–185
Title XX in, 90

C

California, *see also* San Diego, California
elderly in, 91–92
loan program in, 34
SSI-Special Needs program in, 34
CAP, *see* Community Action Program
Carter administration, 38n8–39
Caseloads, effect on rules and factors determining, 132–138
Caseworkers, as viewed by officials, 170–173
Cash payments, 128–130, 154
Catholic School Services (CSS), in Utica, New York, 207–208
Catholic Welfare Bureau, in Trenton, New Jersey, 205–206
Certification for specialized programs, 65, 83
in Boulder, Colorado, 86
Charity, *see* Private charity; *individual public programs*
Child abuse
programs related to, 74, 75
and Title XX, 75
Child Poverty Action Group, 226, 230–231
Chore services, coverage of, 29–30, 126–127, 154–155
Church agencies, *see* Catholic School Services; Catholic Welfare Bureau; Lutheran Social Services; Salvation Army
Circumstances covered by specialized programs, 119, 125–128, 178–183
Citizen Advocacy program, in Boulder, Colorado, 198
Coalition of Emergency Services Agencies (CESA), in San Diego, Calif., 199–200
Colorado, elderly in, 93, *see also* Boulder, Colorado
Columbia Center, in Boulder, Colorado, 198
Communication, 134, 136
between state and county levels, 156–157, 172, 173
Community Action Program (CAP), 77–79, 83
Community groups, relation to AFDC-EA size, 144–145
Community pressure, 100, 110–112
measurement of, 102
Community resources
action taken in absence of, 194
availability of, 192–195
Community Services Administration (CSA), 76
Compensation
principle of, 98, 99–100, 109, 115
as strategy, 15–17
Comprehensive Employment and Training Act (CETA), 75
Computer Reporting Network (CRN), in Wisconsin, 80
Computer, use of, 45
Conditions for receiving aid at county level, 155–156
protective payee, 130, 131
work requirements, 130
Consistency
principle of, 98, 104, 106–107, 115, 118
as strategy, 15
Consolidated grants, *see also* Flat grant
adoption of, 23–24, 26
items included in, 25
Costs, control of, *see also* Size, overview of
and AFDC-UP, 133–134
effects of rules on, 132–137
factors determining, 133–138, 161–164
Counties
acceptance rate, 163, 164
administration and program size, 159–164
case studies, described, 20
communication with states, 156–157, 172, 173
conditions for receipt of aid in, 155–156
costs of programs in, 161–164
EA specialization in, 152–153, 154
external maintenance in, 160
in-kind aid in, 154
outreach in, 149–150
protective payees in, 155–156
relations with states, 16, 50–52, 147–167 *passim*
rules in, 150–162
strategies of in operating specialized programs, 16
variation in, 28
vendor payments in, 154–155
vouchers in, 154

welfare officials' goals in, 50
work requirements of, 156
County officials, effect on specialized programs, 102
County Supplemental Assistance (CSA), in San Diego, California, 88–89
County surveys, described, 20–22
Crisis House in San Diego County, California, 202
Crisis Intervention Program in San Diego County, California, 77, 202–203

D

Day care
as special need, 73
as Title XX service, 74
coverage of, 29–30, 126–127, 154–155
Deinstitutionalization, 75, 76, 268
Delegation of authority
as administrative strategy, 13–15
between county and state administration, 131, 132
in Great Britain, 233
to private agencies, 213
to private charities in Wisconsin, 193
in states, 13–14
Denial, as administrative strategy, 13, 192–193
Department of Health and Social Security in Great Britain, 229–231, *see also* Great Britain, welfare system of
Department of Public Welfare, in San Diego County, California, 203–204
Department of Social Services, in Boulder, Colorado, 197
Deserving vs. undeserving poor, 95
Destitute, defined for Expedited Food Stamps, 37
Discretion, 13–14
concern over in Boulder, Colorado, 87
in conflict with basic income maintenance programs, 117
county use of, 158–159
dangers of, 245–246
effect on communication, 134–136
as goal of welfare officials, 50, 57
in Great Britain, 222, 225, 227–230, 232–234
vs. legal right, 6
measurement of, 46
need for, 1–2
in specialized programs, 239–240
states' use of, 13–15, 34
Domestic violence, 188–189
programs related to, 198
Double payments, 9, 14, 29–30, 180, 189–190
and AFDC-EA, 69
in Great Britain, 225, 230, 235
in Minneapolis, Minnesota, 69

E

Echo House, Boulder, Colorado, 198
Education needs, coverage of, 29–30, 126–127, 154–155
Efficiency, measurement of, 46
Elderly
attitude toward welfare of, 209–210
in Beaumont, Texas, 91
in California, 91–92
overview of programs for, 94
programs for, 94, 209
special consideration for, 95
as underserved group, 87
Eligibility, 134
for country programs, 151–152
for Food Stamps, 37
for General Assistance in Beaumont, Texas, 90
for specialized programs, 122–125
for SSI, 33
Eligibility rules, defined, 119
Eligibility technicians, 7
in Boulder, Colorado, 86
Emergency assistance, *see also* Specialized programs; Aid to Families with Dependent Children–Emergency Assistance
and community pressure, 110–112
factors affecting size, 15–16, 110–111, 141–142
factors determining need for, 23
need for, 8–10
problems in defining, 72–73
states' provision of, 59–62
Emergency assistance and special needs, *see also* Specialized programs

defined, 9–10, 26
reasons for programs, 23
Emergency Assistance for Families (EAF), in Utica, New York, 67–68
Emergency Assistance to Adults in Utica, New York, 92
Emergency Family Assistance (EFA), in Boulder, Colorado, 198
Emergency–General Assistance, in Minneapolis, Minnesota, 84–86
Employment needs, coverage of, 29–30, 126–127, 154–155
Energy Assistance Payments program (EAP), 76–77
in Wisconsin, 79–80
Energy Crisis Assistance (ECA), in New York, 78
England, *see* Great Britain
Equity, *see also* Horizontal equity of individualized treatment, 3, 5–6
measurement of, 101
and size of AFDC program, 107, 108
and size of AFDC-EA program, 141–142
Error
and community pressure, 100
press and public concern over, 110–111
and political groups, 52, 53, 55, 57
and size of AFDC-EA program, 143–144
Error control, 45
Error and fraud
concern over, 16–17, 55, 57
treatment of, 148
Error rates, 132
of AFDC, selected states, 4n3
"Essential spouse" payments in Boulder, Colorado, 93
Evictions, 44
Exceptional Circumstances Additions (ECA), 222–225, 230, 232
Exceptional Needs Payments (ENP), 223–225, 230, 232
Expedited Food Stamps
in Boulder, Colorado, 196
eligibility for, 36–37
External maintenance
and AFDC-EA size, 107, 109
at county level, 160
measurement of, 101
relation to cost at county level, 163
relation to specialized programs, 106–107

F

Family Assistance Plan (FAP), 5
Family and Community Services Program in Trenton, New Jersey, 205
Federal financial match, 104–105, 140–141, 246
Financial Crisis Unit, in Minneapolis, Minnesota, 69
Flat grant
advantages of, 98–99
decision to use, 15
defined, 243
and emergency assistance caseload, 107, 108
"flatness" of, 21–22
and horizontal equity, 12
inadequacies of, 99–100
SSI as, 23, 33
Focus, in San Diego County, Calif., 203
Food bank, in Utica, N.Y., 207
"Food shelves," 70
Food shortage, coverage of, 29–30, 126–127, 154–155, *see also* Expedited Food Stamps
Food Stamp Act
of 1964, 36
of 1977, 36
Food Stamp program, 178, *see also* Expedited Food Stamps
history, 7, 35–37
as possible base for specialized programs, 244
reforms in, 36, 37
Fraud, *see also* Error and fraud
and community pressure, 100
dangers of, 13
and political groups, 52, 53, 55, 57
press and public concern over, 110–111
and size of AFDC-EA program, 143–144
Friedman, Milton, 7
Friends, as last resort of poor, 193–199
Fuel assistance program
in Boulder, Colorado, 77–78
characteristics of, 77
Energy Assistance Payment (EAP), 76–77
history of, 76
in New York, 78
success of, 185–186
in Trenton, New Jersey, 79
in Wisconsin, 79–80

Funding, *see also* Federal financial match
certainty of, 180–181
lack of, as major problem, 190
sufficiency of, 180–183
Funding of specialized programs
in Beaumont, Texas, 182
in Boulder, Colorado, 181–182
in Trenton, New Jersey, 181
in Utica, New York, 182

G

General Assistance programs (GA)
adequacy of coverage, 178
administrative rules of, 84
in Boulder, Colorado, 86–88
certification procedure, 83
compared to Emergency Assistance, 81, 94
eligibility for, 42
as emergency program, 44, 80–91
future of, 94–95
history of, 38–39
items covered by, 81, 83
and legal rights, 42
in Minnesota, 84–86
in New Jersey, 43
overview of, 94
payments, 83
in San Diego, California, 88–89
standardization of, 39–40
in Wisconsin, 40–43
Goals of welfare officials, 45–52, 106–110, 148
God, acts of, 30
Grandfather clauses, 34
Great Britain
Family Allowance Act, 216
National Assistance, 216–218, *see also* Great Britain, Supplementary Benefits program
National Assistance Board, 216
National Insurance–Industrial Injuries Act, 216
National Insurance, 216–218
population shifts, 217
Supplementary Benefits program, 218–225
and U.S. compared, 234–235, 248
welfare system of, 215–225
Griffiths, Martha, 5

H

Handicapped, as underserved group, 87
Health and Human Services, Department of, 76
Hennepin County, Minnesota, *see* Minneapolis, Minnesota
"Home care" in Boulder, Colorado, 93
Home relief, in Utica, New York, 67–68
"Homelessness" in Trenton, New Jersey, 66
Horizontal equity, 4, 5–6, 7, 45, 98–99
as dominant ideology, 12
factors opposing, 237
in Great Britain, 220–224, 228
measurement of, 46
Housing and Urban Development, Department of (HUD), 187
Housing problems, 185–188

I

Individualized treatment, *see also* Discretion
and AFDC-EA size, 107, 109, 115, 142–143
balance with standardization, 12–13, 97–100
importance at county level, 148
in public welfare, history of, 3–4, 8
Inequity, *see also* Horizontal equity
concern over in Boulder, Colorado, 87
In-kind payments, 128–129, 154
Interest groups
and AFDC-EA size, 111, 112, 144–145
measurement of influence, 102
Internal maintenance, 101, 106, 107
Internal welfare organization, 48

J

Jefferson County, Texas, *see* Beaumont, Texas

K

Kennedy, John, F., 36

L

Landlords, credit furnished by, 186n, 193

Legal rights
in the 1960s, 6, 7
and welfare administration, 42
Line workers, *see* Caseworkers
Loan program, in California, 34
Local officials, views of political influence on welfare, 56–57
Local policies, relation to state policies, 147–167 *passim*
Lost benefit checks, coverage of, 29–30, 126–127, 154–155
Lutheran Social Services (LSS), in San Diego, California, 200

M

Mandley v. *Quern*, 93
Maryland, SSI-Special Needs program in, 34
Meals-on-wheels, in San Diego, California, 200
Medicaid, 76
Mercer County, New Jersey, *see* Trenton, New Jersey
Minneapolis, Minnesota
AFDC-EA in, 68–71, 166
General Assistance in, 84–86
housing in, 187
protective payees in, 70–71
vendor payments in, 70
Minnesota, *see also* Minneapolis, Minnesota
AFDC-EA in, 154
as case study, 18
General Assistance in, 84
size of specialized aid in, 239
Monitoring and control devices, 45
defined, 119
Monitoring specialized programs, 13–14
Moral hazard, 13, 14, 30, 94, 126–127, 189, 243
Moral judgments reflected in welfare policy, 3
Mothers' Pensions, 24, *see also* Aid to Families with Dependent Children

N

Natural disasters, coverage of, 29–30, 126–127, 154–155
Negative Income Tax (NIT), 4–5
New Jersey, General Assistance program in, 43, *see also* Trenton, New Jersey
New York, *see also* Utica, New York
AFDC grant coverage in, 25–26n1
AFDC–Special Needs program in, 27
Nixon, Richard M., 36

O

Oklahoma, AFDC-EA in, 157
Older Americans Act program, 76
in Wisconsin, 193
Oneida County, *see* Utica, N.Y.
Oregon, AFDC—EA in, 158
Organizational maintenance, 48
Outreach, 65, 71–72, 120–122, 149–150
at county level, 149–150
lack of, 32, 87, 120–121, 241
lack of need for by Salvation Army, 202
need for, 87, 244
relation to costs and caseloads, 135–136

P

Payment, forms of, 128–129, 154–155
Policy recommendations, 242–246
Political groups, effect on AFDC-EA, 111–112
Political influence
and emergency assistance programs, 52–57
measurement of, 102
Political risks of programs, 13
Politicians, attitudes of, 52–57
Poor
deserving, 3, 30, 118, 126, 138, 143
deserving vs. undeserving, 118, 143, 195, 213–214, 240
means of coping when no programs available, 193–194
undeserving, 3, 118, 126, 127, 138, 143, 162
working, 183
Press, concern over error and fraud, 110–111
Private agencies, *see also* Beaumont Association for Senior Citizens, Crisis House, Lutheran Social Services, Salvation Army
persons served by, 195–196

pressures on, 196–197
and public agencies, 196–197, 203–209, 212–213 *passim*
Private charity
as alternative to public programs, 68
availability of, 192–195
in Boulder, Colorado, 197–199
coverage, 212
growing reliance on, 241
missions of, 212–214, 241
need to apply to in order to get state assistance, 122
and public programs, 241
in San Diego, California, 199–204
in Trenton, New Jersey, 204–206
variability of, 212
Private resources, exhaustion of, 135
Proposition 13, 88–89, 94, 181, 182
Protective payee, 130, 131, 134, 155–156
in AFDC-EA, 65–66, 70
at county level, 155–156
in Minneapolis, Minnesota, 70–71
Public, concern over error and fraud, 110–111
Public groups, influence on size of EA program, 110–111
Public information, *see* External maintenance
Public opinion, in Beaumont, Texas, 209

Q

Quality Control Review, 131–132

R

Red Cross, in Boulder, Colorado, 198
Rehabilitative services, need for, 189, 208
Relatives, as a last resort of poor, 193–194
Repayment agreements, 84, 87, 130
Repeat requests, 88, 130, 131, 133, 134, 136, 244
policies of private agencies toward, 200, 202, 205, 211, 212
Rescue Mission, in San Diego, California, 201
Resource exhaustion, 122
county rules requiring, 150–151
Resources and verification rules, defined, 119
Restrictive orientation, 162–163
Restrictiveness, 170–171, 183
of AFDC–Special Needs programs, 31
as goal of officials, 46–47
of programs, 109
Rhode Island, coverage of AFDC grant in, 25–26n1
Rules
for AFDC-EA, 67
development of in states, 14–15
effect on costs and caseloads, 132–137
eligibility in counties, 151–152
eligibility in states, 124–125
monitoring of, 131–132
need for, 1
outreach in counties, 149–150
outreach in states, 119–120
problems caused by, 245
relation to behavior, 120
variation in counties and states, 148
verification in counties, 150–151
Rules and procedures, 244–245
adequacy of, 170–176

S

Salvation Army
in Beaumont, Texas, 209
extensiveness of, 194–195
mission of, 214
policy of, 214
in San Diego County, California, 200–202
San Diego, California
AFDC–Special Needs program in, 32
funding in, 182
General Assistance in, 88–89
private agencies in, 199–204
and Proposition 13, 13, 88–89
relationship of county AFDC program to state, 32
responses to increased demand in, 185
Title XX in, 74–75
San Diego County, California, *see* San Diego, California
Scale rates, 218, 220–221, 227–228
Single men, restrictive welfare policies toward, 201–202
Single payments, *see* Exceptional Needs Payments

Size of specialized program
  factors determining, 15–16, 54–55, 63–64, 137
  overview of, 23–45 *passim*, 59–95
Social Security Act of 1935, 2, 240
Social services, as part of War on Poverty, 6
Social theory and the welfare system, 99
Some Other Place (SOP), in Beaumont, Texas, 210–212, 213–214
Special Circumstances Payment (SCP), in California, 92
Special condition, occurrence of, 131
Special needs, *see* Emergency assistance and special needs; Specialized programs
Special needs programs, *see also* Aid to Families with Dependent Children–Special Needs; Specialized programs
  need for, 8–10
Special requirements
  in counties, 154–156
  defined, 119
  of specialized programs, 128–131
Special Review team of DHSS, in Great Britain, 229–231
Special Supplemental Payments program, in Minneapolis, Minnesota, 69
Specialization
  in counties, 152–153, 154
  in specialized programs, 126–128
Specialized aid, character of, 16–17
Specialized programs
  adequacy of coverage, 176–183
  breadth of, 152–154
  changes recommended in, 243–244
  circumstances covered by, 178–183
  control and monitoring of, 131–132
  costs of, 246
  county administration of, 147–167 *passim*
  division of power between states and counties, 247
  eligibility requirements for, 122–124
  factors that influence provision of, 100–102
  factors determining size of, 15–16
  and flat grant, 98–99
  items covered by, 125–128
  jurisdictions for, 246
  measurement of, 102–103
  monitoring of, 131–132
  need for, 242–248
  outreach, 120–122
  range of, 59–62
  relation to AFDC, 103–106
  requirements for, 122–124, 128–131
  rules for, defined, 119–120
  state administration of, 117–144 *passim*
  variation in, 97–100, 238–240
Standardization
  in balance with individualized treatment, 12–13, 97–100, 247–248
  effects on specialized programs, 107, 108, 115–116, 141–142
  as goal of welfare officials, 46–47, 50, 57
  growth of, 2–3, 7–8
  in Great Britain, 233
  of Food Stamp program, 36, 37
  measurement of, 10, 46
  need for, 12
  trend toward, 45, 247
Standardized grants, *see* Flat grants; Consolidated grants
States
  communication with counties, 172, 173
  comparison of AFDC to AFDC-EA, expenditures, 62–64
  vs. counties, 16, 50–52, 147–167 *passim*
  discretion used by, 117–118
  EA program size compared to counties, 164–167
  emergency assistance programs, provided by, 59–62
  and Expedited Food Stamp programs, 37
  monitoring of individualized programs, 138
  nonparticipation in SSI–Special Needs programs, 35
  reasons for EA program variation among, 97–100
  role of in shaping specialized programs, 117–145
  rules for specialized programs, defined, 119–120
  three basic types regarding AFDC-EA, 116
  and uniformity of emergency assistance coverage, 93–94

variation in AFDC–Special Needs coverage, 27–28
variation in consolidated grant coverage, 25
variation of SSI–Special Needs program, 34
welfare officials' goals, 48–50
State Emergency Assistance programs, 71–72
State surveys, described, 18–20
State welfare officials
and outreach, 122
views of political influence on welfare, 52–57
Strategies
of state bureaucracies, 13–14
of welfare administrators, 13–16
Sunshine funds, 196–197, 206, 214, 242
Supervision, of specialized programs, 13
Supplemental Security Income (SSI), 7
adequacy of coverage, 177–178
as base for specialized programs, 244
in Beaumont, Texas, 182
differences among states, 238
eligibility requirements for, 33
funding problems of, 183
in Minneapolis, Minnesota, 178
objectives of, 33
size of, 34
states' discretion in administration, 34
in Wisconsin, 193
Supplemental Security Income–Special Needs, 34–35
Supplementary Benefits Commission (SBC), in Great Britain, 221–227
Supplementary Benefits Program, *see* Great Britain, Supplemental Benefits program

T

Texas, *see also* Beaumont, Texas
General Assistance in, 89–90
Title XX, 61, 72–76
in Beaumont, Texas, 182
in Boulder, Colorado, 93
description of, 72, 73
and domestic violence, 188, 189
as emergency assistance, 73, 76
in San Diego, California, 74, 75
in Trenton, New Jersey, 75
in Utica, New York, 75–76
in Wisconsin, 74, 193
Training programs, 74–75
Travelers' Aid in San Diego, California, 201
Trenton, New Jersey
AFDC-EA in, 66–67, 128, 166, 172, 183–184
domestic violence in, 188–189
fuel assistance in, 79
funding in, 181
General Assistance in, 43–45
housing problems in, 187
Expedited Food Stamps in, 38
private agencies in, 204–206
responses to increased demands in, 183–184
Title XX in, 75
weatherization programs in, 79

U

Unborn child needs, coverage of, 29–30, 126–127, 154–155
Undeserving poor, 3, 118, 126, 127, 138, 143, 162
United Way, in Boulder, Colorado, 198, 199
Universal coverage, need for, 243–244
Utica, New York
AFDC-EA in, 67–68, 166
AFDC-Special Needs in, 31, 33
domestic violence in, 189
elderly in, 92
Expedited Food Stamps in, 37–38
fuel assistance in, 78
funding in, 182
adult protective services in, 76
housing problems in, 187–188
private agencies in, 207–208
responses to increased demands in, 185
Title XX in, 75–76
vendor and voucher payments in, 92
weatherization programs in, 78
Utility bills, coverage of, 29–30, 126–127, 154–155
Utility cutoffs, 77
moratorium on, 186

V

Vendor payments, 77, 128–129, 134, 136, *see also* Vendor and voucher payments
  at county level, 154–155
  in Boulder, Colorado, 88
  in Minneapolis, Minnesota, 70, 86
  in Oneida County, New York, 92
Vendor and voucher payments, 128–131, 154
  in AFDC-EA, 65–66, 67, 70
  counties' use of, 16
  in General Assistance, 84, 86, 87, 88
  private agencies' use of, 201, 205, 208, 211
  in specialized programs, 240
Vendors, negotiations with, 172–173
Verification
  AFDC-EA, 64–65
  in counties, 150–151
  for EA, 123–124
Volunteer Information Center (VIC), in Boulder, Colorado, 199
Vouchers, *see* Vendor payments; Vendor and voucher payments

W

War on Poverty, 6
Weatherization, 78–79
Welfare administration strategies, 13–16
Welfare officials
  assessment of caseworkers, 170–172
  communication between state and county officials, 131
  and discretion, 50, 57, 117–118
  effect of on EA program size, 110–112
  goals of, 46, 52
  perceptions of about administration, 172, 174–176
  ranking of goals by, 48–52
  responses of to increased demand, 183–185
  and standardization, 50–57
  state vs. county officials' goals, 50–52
  views of about adequacy of EA coverage, 176–180
Welfare rights organizations, 6
West Virginia, AFDC-EA in, 63
Winterization programs, 76–80
Winter needs, coverage of, 29–30, 126–127, 154–155
Wisconsin
  as case study, 18
  denial of need for additional resources in, 192–193
  Fuel Assistance program in, 79–80
  General Relief and legal rights, 42
  General Relief program (General Assistance), 40–43
  Title XX in, 74
Work requirements, 130, 156
  for General Assistance, 41–42
Workers, *see* Caseworkers
Working conditions in welfare agencies, 3–4
Wyoming, AFDC-EA in, 62

Institute for Research on Poverty
Monograph Series

Published

Joel F. Handler and Michael Sosin, *Last Resorts: Emergency Assistance and Special Needs Programs in Public Welfare.* 1983

Irwin Garfinkel, Editor, *Income-Tested Transfer Programs: The Case For and Against.* 1982

Richard V. Burkhauser and Karen C. Holden, Editors, *A Challenge to Social Security: The Changing Roles of Women and Men in American Society.* 1982

Jeffrey G. Williamson and Peter H. Lindert, *American Inequality: A Macroeconomic History.* 1980

Robert H. Haveman and Kevin Hollenbeck, Editors, *Microeconomic Simulation Models for Public Policy Analysis, Volume 1: Distributional Impacts, Volume 2: Sectoral, Regional, and General Equilibrium Models.* 1980

Peter K. Eisinger, *The Politics of Displacement: Racial and Ethnic Transition in Three American Cities.* 1980

Erik Olin Wright, *Class Structure and Income Determination.* 1979

Joel F. Handler, *Social Movements and the Legal System: A Theory of Law Reform and Social Change.* 1979

Duane E. Leigh, *An Analysis of the Determinants of Occupational Upgrading.* 1978

Stanley H. Masters and Irwin Garfinkel, *Estimating the Labor Supply Effects of Income Maintenance Alternatives.* 1978

Irwin Garfinkel and Robert H. Haveman, with the assistance of David Betson, *Earnings Capacity, Poverty, and Inequality.* 1977

Harold W. Watts and Albert Rees, Editors, *The New Jersey Income-Maintenance Experiment, Volume III: Expenditures, Health, and Social Behavior; and the Quality of the Evidence.* 1977

Murray Edelman, *Political Language: Words That Succeed and Policies That Fail.* 1977

Marilyn Moon and Eugene Smolensky, Editors, *Improving Measures of Economic Well-Being.* 1977

Harold W. Watts and Albert Rees, Editors, *The New Jersey Income-Maintenance Experiment, Volume II: Labor-Supply Responses.* 1977

Marilyn Moon, *The Measurement of Economic Welfare: Its Application to the Aged Poor.* 1977

Morgan Reynolds and Eugene Smolensky, *Public Expenditures, Taxes, and the Distribution of Income: The United States, 1950, 1961, 1970.* 1977

Fredrick L. Golladay and Robert H. Haveman, with the assistance of Kevin Hollenbeck, *The Economic Impacts of Tax–Transfer Policy: Regional and Distributional Effects.* 1977

David Kershaw and Jerilyn Fair, *The New Jersey Income-Maintenance Experiment, Volume I: Operations, Surveys, and Administration.* 1976

Peter K. Eisinger, *Patterns of Interracial Politics: Conflict and Cooperation in the City.* 1976

Irene Lurie, Editor, *Integrating Income Maintenance Programs.* 1975

Stanley H. Masters, *Black–White Income Differentials: Empirical Studies and Policy Implications.* 1975

Larry L. Orr, *Income, Employment, and Urban Residential Location.* 1975

Joel F. Handler, *The Coercive Social Worker: British Lessons for American Social Services.* 1973

Glen G. Cain and Harold W. Watts, Editors, *Income Maintenance and Labor Supply: Econometric Studies.* 1973

Charles E. Metcalf, *An Econometric Model of Income Distribution.* 1972

Larry L. Orr, Robinson G. Hollister, and Myron J. Lefcowitz, Editors, with the assistance of Karen Hester, *Income Maintenance: Interdisciplinary Approaches to Research.* 1971

Robert J. Lampman, *Ends and Means of Reducing Income Poverty.* 1971

Joel F. Handler and Ellen Jane Hollingsworth, *"The Deserving Poor": A Study of Welfare Administration.* 1971

Murray Edelman, *Politics as Symbolic Action: Mass Arousal and Quiescence.* 1971

Frederick Williams, Editor, *Language and Poverty: Perspectives on a Theme.* 1970

Vernon L. Allen, Editor, *Psychological Factors in Poverty.* 1970